Britishness, Identity and Citizenship

BRITISH IDENTITIES SINCE 1707
Vol. 2

Series Editors:

Professor Paul Ward
School of Music, Humanities and Media,
University of Huddersfield

Professor Richard Finlay
Department of History, University of Strathclyde

PETER LANG
Oxford · Bern · Berlin · Bruxelles · Frankfurt am Main · New York · Wien

Catherine McGlynn, Andrew Mycock
and James W. McAuley (eds)

Britishness, Identity and Citizenship

The View From Abroad

PETER LANG

Oxford · Bern · Berlin · Bruxelles · Frankfurt am Main · New York · Wien

Bibliographic information published by Die Deutsche Nationalbibliothek
Die Deutsche Nationalbibliothek lists this publication in the Deutsche Nationalbibliografie;
detailed bibliographic data is available on the Internet at http://dnb.d-nb.de.

A catalogue record for this book is available from the British Library.

Library of Congress Cataloging-in-Publication Data:

Britishness, identity and citizenship : the view from abroad / Catherine
McGlynn, Andrew Mycock and James W. McAuley (eds.).
    p. cm.
  Papers from an inter-disciplinary conference, Britishness: identity
and citizenship: the view from abroad, held in June 2008 at the
University of Huddersfield.
  Includes bibliographical references and index.
  ISBN 978-3-0343-0226-5 (alk. paper)
    1. National characteristics, British--History--Congresses. 2. Group
identity--Great Britain--History--Congresses. 3. British--Ethnic
identity--Congresses. 4. Great Britain--Colonies--History--Congresses.
5. Great Britain--Civilization--Congresses. I. McGlynn, Catherine,
1973- II. Mycock, Andrew. III. McAuley, James W.
  DA118.B726 2011
  941--dc23

                            2011022254

ISSN 1664-0284
ISBN 978-3-0343-0226-5

© Peter Lang AG, International Academic Publishers, Bern 2011
Hochfeldstrasse 32, CH-3012 Bern, Switzerland
info@peterlang.com, www.peterlang.com, www.peterlang.net

Printed in Germany

Contents

CATHERINE MCGLYNN, ANDREW MYCOCK AND
JAMES W. MCAULEY

Introduction – Britishness, Identity and Citizenship: The View from Abroad[1]

Recent years have witnessed an increase in the profile of debates about national identity and citizenship (two separate but often conflated concepts) in the UK. A palpable sense of a crisis of Britishness can be discerned within this debate, which has been conducted in academic, media and political circles. The former British Prime Minister Gordon Brown clearly hoped that one of the key achievements of his time in office would be the successful re-shaping of British identity to underpin a strongly articulated sense of belonging based on nationally-located values such as fair play, tolerance and liberty, which he saw as a 'golden thread' running through British history.[2] These values together with enduring British institutions such as Westminster, the BBC and the NHS would form the basis of an inclusive civic citizenship that could accommodate an increasingly diverse population.

In the end this project was not the hallmark of Brown's tenure, as the sharp recession engendered by the international banking crisis became the focal point of political discourse and action. However, while the economy may now dominate British political debate, the fashioning of a 'national' narrative that can bind citizens together is still a much sought-after, if

1   As organisers of the conference *Britishness, Identity and Citizenship: The View From Abroad*, we were grateful to receive financial and administrative support from our institution the University of Huddersfield which played host to the conference in June 2008. We would also like to acknowledge the support of the British Academy through the provision of conference grant BCG-48407.
2   See, for example, Brown's speech to the Fabian Society on 14 January 2006 or his article, 'The golden thread that runs through our history', *The Guardian* (8 July 2004).

inherently contentious, goal. At first sight it would appear that Brown's successor Prime Minister David Cameron's understanding of Britishness and UK citizenship is informed by a similar set of institutions and values. But Cameron prioritises a more organic and emotional sense of national identity that seeks to prioritise 'forgotten' institutions such as the monarchy and the armed forces combined with, as we note in our own contribution to this volume, an innate faith in the potential for school history to 'teach the nation' – though he appears less sure which nation that is.[3]

One of the most notable aspects of this debate has for us been the astonishing amount of introspection on display. On the surface, discussions about defining the legal and cultural bonds between citizens in the twenty-first century United Kingdom are inherently enmeshed within international forces, as globalization has through the increased movement of information, capital and people, challenged the sovereignty of states and offered ways of creating and sustaining community memberships that stretch mentally and physically beyond borders. In addition, one of the most divisive issues for commentators has been how to acknowledge and interpret an imperial past. However, the resonance of the legacy of empire and the ongoing significance of constitutional and emotional ties is overlooked for the most part, meaning that even migrants from the Commonwealth are seen as outsiders requiring tutoring in the values of Britishness before they can successfully attain citizenship.[4]

This myopic focus on what Kumar terms the 'inner Empire' of Great Britain has, in our opinion, truncated contemporary understandings of Britishness as an identity.[5] To act as if Britishness has been shorn of any transnational dynamic beyond that of the potential for social, economic and cultural forces to penetrate the UK from outside is to remove many potentially rich layers of connection that could create an understanding

3   D. Cameron, 'Proud to be British', *ConservativeHome* (10 July 2009) http://conservativehome.blogs.com/platform/2009/07/david-cameron-proud-to-be-british.html, accessed 6 August 2010.

4   A. Mycock, 'British citizenship and the legacy of empires', *Parliamentary Affairs* 63 (2) (2010), 339–55.

5   K. Kumar, *The Making of English National Identity* (Cambridge: Cambridge University Press 2003).

of British community far beyond the limited formalities of legal citizenship. The interconnected relationships between national, multi-national and transnational constructions of citizenship and national identity ensure that debates about national and imperial Britishness cannot be confined within sovereign nation-state parameters. Moreover, the intersections between the post-imperial and the post-colonial mean that established and new conversations about Britishness must be recognised if we are to understand how old and new voices connect.

This was the guiding conviction that prompted the organisation of an inter-disciplinary conference, *Britishness: Identity and Citizenship: the View from Abroad*. The conference, held in June 2008 at the University of Huddersfield, brought together a range of international scholars who presented work that revealed the dynamism of contemporary and historical experiences of Britishness through popular cultural transmission, education, and travel and migration. The chapters in this volume have all been drawn from the conference and together they act as a challenge to the increasingly inward-looking popular, political and academic debate about identity and citizenship in the UK, asking commentators to acknowledge that the transnational nature of Britishness transcends a simple home/abroad dichotomy.

The View from Abroad

In some ways the work in this volume could suggest that Britishness appears as a more easily pinned-down phenomenon when viewed from abroad. Whether that view is a positive one, such as the admiration historically displayed with an element of deference in other educational systems for literature, the political system, military prowess and supposedly innately British and values, or the less laudable figures of the drunken British stag or the aloof and superior colonial administrator, a defined picture of the British and a sense of assured self-confidence about the virtues of Britishness is projected. This perception is noticeably of an Anglo-Britishness. For example, the historical enmity the French media detected in what was seen as Prime Minister Tony Blair's capitulation to a long-standing Euroscepticism has been presented as an element of the 'forging' of Britishness in the eighteenth century.[6] However, this was built on a much older antagonism between the English and the French and the contemporary Eurosceptic position is deeply imbued with an Anglo-British identity.[7] In addition, the canon of literature exported as the hallmark of British civilization and its physical geography (From Wordsworth's Lake District to Shakespeare's Stratford) overlaps with the borders of England and Englishness, cementing the conflation of Englishness and Britishness.

It could be easy to assume, in such a light, that the projection of Britishness abroad both during the era of empire and in the modern world has obscured the problems of promoting cohesion within a multi-national state, problems that have become increasingly apparent when the concept is discussed domestically.[8] In fact, many of the contributions to this volume show how these problems are replicated in many ways in settings outside the UK, reflecting the struggle experienced by other core ethnic groups (such as the Russians) in a time of imperial disintegration.[9] This replication can be detected both amongst those coming to Britain and those leaving it.

For many of those travelling outwards, it is apparent that their sense of Britishness did not – and does not – replace strong ethnic affiliations, even if like William Knox they consciously saw themselves as representing and furthering the interests of the empire. However, for the English the legacy of denying an institutional framework for their identity has played out in a similar manner across the former empire as it does within an increasingly constitutionally devolved UK. The work here on migration to Australia shows how the English Diaspora can struggle to define itself once legal and

---

6   L. Colley, *Britons: Forging the Nation, 1707–1837* (New Haven and London: Yale University Press 1992).

7   C. Gifford, 'The UK and the European Union: Dimensions of British Sovereignty and the Problem of Eurosceptic Britishness', *Parliamentary Affairs*, 63 (2) (2010), 321–38.

8   For an excellent discussion of the multi-national nature of the UK state please see C. Bryant, *The Nations of Britain* (Oxford: Oxford University Press: 2005).

9   V. Tolz, *Russia: Inventing the Nation* (London: Arnold, 2001).

cultural ties to Britishness diminish in importance in post-independence Commonwealth states and how the long subsuming of Englishness within Britishness has eroded both a civic institutional and an ethno-cultural basis for a twenty-first century Englishness. The experience of those travelling to the UK further illuminates the tension between civic Britishness and the hidden ethnic base of Englishness from another perspective. For example, the experiences of the educated Indian middle class show how those who envisaged a sense of fraternity through the shared connection of literature and culture also had to struggle with the exclusion and derogation they experienced when they came to visit the origin of this community of which they saw themselves as full members.

In light of this it could be argued that the global ties established through migration, imperialism and cultural profile do not actually have much to offer to debates about defining an accommodating contemporary Britishness within the UK. If the transnational dynamics merely replicate the complications and tensions of the debate at home, what need is there for British citizens and policy-making elites to turn their gaze outwards? In addition, the broad popularity enjoyed currently by historians such as Niall Ferguson who attempt to present the imperial past as largely positive, not just for the UK but for the former empire (if not the entire world) suggests how deep-seated the resistance to learning about Britishness from those whose connection is not based on birth and citizenship could be.[10] The strong unease stoked when modern politicians are called upon to apologise for past actions rests on anxiety about 'a broader decline in national self-belief and standards of behaviour, highlighting the seemingly limitless potential for British national history to be debunked', suggesting that this kind of confrontation with the legacy of Britishness abroad can only lead to negative consequences.[11]

---

10   N. Ferguson, *Empire: How Britain Made the Modern World* (London: Allen Lane and Penguin, 2003).

11   A. Mycock, 'Sorry Seems to be an Easier Word: Brown and the Politics of Apology', *Open Democracy* (30 November 2009) http://www.opendemocracy.net/ourkingdom/ andy-mycock/sorry-seems-to-be-easier-word-brown-and-politics-of-apology accessed 20 August 2010.

It is also worth asking what value taking this transnational perspective would be to those with connections to Britishness abroad, especially in former colonies. Over the course of the twentieth century it was the case that the formal connections with the metropolis were severed in large part by immigration and nationality legislation passed at Westminster. However, states across the former empire were not passive recipients of such actions. They too were re-defining themselves and seemingly leaving Britishness behind, either through their own formulations of citizenship and right of entry or through cultural and educational exploration of their own developing national identity, marking a clean break from any sense of deference and cultural cringe. If these states are so positive about moving forward to a post-colonial sense of community and place in the world it would seem logical to ask what value their citizens would find in exploring the legacy of British connections, especially when more recent waves of immigration mean that for many residents and citizens there would be no personal element to that connection.

The Value of Transnational Dynamics

Whilst acknowledging that times have changed, we still contend that exploring these broader bonds is an exercise that does have much to reveal about 'national' stories as they are re-interpreted for modern communities. In fact, it is precisely the way in which many of these contributions reveal that identifications with and understandings of Britishness do not mean that states make a choice between sticking with anachronistic imperial affiliations or removing these links entirely that tells us why these connections still have meaning and relevance. For example, in looking beyond the caricatured visual Britishness of Gibraltar, Levey presents us here with a 'far more complex community with a unique identity which has been forged, not only as the result of British and Spanish external influences, but also in spite of them'. British identity remains an important element of how

Gibraltarians see themselves but despite first appearances the British connection is not an atrophying agent that prevents development and change. The contributions on citizenship and civic education in this volume also show that whilst rejecting what in recent decades began to look like paying undue obeisance to Britain was a logical way of asserting a new post-colonial sense of communal pride, airbrushing historical connections removed important contextual understanding of the development of constitutional and cultural practices. In addition, it will never be less than vital to shine a light on the appalling treatment of peoples and the promotion of ethnic hierarchies and division in the imperial era, but to assign the blame to 'the Brits' and present these problems as an ages old story of historical injustice will not solve the current and keenly felt inequalities between groups in the modern day. A nuanced and rigorous exploration and understanding of Britishness in historical and contemporary settings does not have to be a revisionist apologia or a forcefully and artificially placed full stop on an era, rather it can promote a deeper awareness of the ethno-cultural basis of norms and practices which could aid many states in their anxieties over the promotion of social cohesion.

For the debate in the UK the potential consequences of acknowledging the transnational dynamics also means embracing difficult historical realities and examining their ongoing legacy. However, there are a number of obvious advantages to overcoming the current tunnel vision when it comes to exploring Britishness as a sense of belonging and community. Firstly, these contributions remind us that those travelling literally or figuratively under the Union Flag have often held and valued a number of identities and that rather than looking at sub-state nationalism or increasing cultural plurality within the UK as centrifugal forces, this multi-layered understanding of allegiance and connection should be acknowledged as something that has long been a feature for those who understand themselves to be shaped in some form by a connection to Britishness. Secondly, and again without having to retreat to a rose-tinted view of the past, the way in which British high and popular culture has engendered a sense of shared experience suggests that there remains a strong potential to foster horizontal bonds on such a basis if input and contribution from others to defining and understanding what Britishness is can supersede the current emphasis on elite formulation and top-down instruction. Finally, in finding a way to acknowledge the enduring strength of constitutional ties, most notably the monarchy, the debate within the UK can start to deal with elements of Britishness that, if they are discussed at all, are dismissed out of hand as anachronistic. Bringing these broader transnational dynamics into debates about national identity will allow all of us to make use of the past in a positive but realistic way.

The volume is divided into four main sections, all comprising discussions of identity and citizenship in historical and contemporary settings. The ways in which the contributors explore the representation and interpretation of Britishness abroad supports our contention that from the imperial era onwards the construction of Britishness has not been a unidirectional journey from a metropolis to the periphery. Rather, understandings of the concept are contained in a number of culturally and politically dynamic relationships which affect both the development of identity and citizenship in the UK and elsewhere. Embracing this knowledge offers the potential to synthesise historical and contemporary debates about both identity and citizenship and offer a way out of what has become an introspective and un-necessarily narrow discussion.

The Empire: Constructions of Britishness

CHARLES V. REED

1 Respectable Subjects of the Queen: The Royal Tour of 1901 and Imperial Citizenship in South Africa

Historian Vivian Bickford-Smith has recently characterized Britishness as South Africa's 'forgotten nationalism,' lost in a historiography that pays far more attention to African and Afrikaner nationalisms than to Britishness.[1] It has been remembered, we might suggest, in a flurry of recent scholarship on the subject. Historians of the 'British world,' for instance, have understood Britishness as a kind of trans-nationalism, born out of the diaspora of British ideas, institutions, and people throughout the world. At the same time, scholars of Britishness have been apt to stress that it was not some pre-packaged set of ideas or identities, but the product of complex historical discourses and processes mediated and remade by local perceptions and encounters. This chapter explores the reception of the 1901 royal tour to South Africa by the independent African press, the editors of which imagined the British Empire to be their political and cultural universes.

Scholars, however, have rarely presented Western-educated people of colour in such a light. Post-colonial and other area studies scholars have treated the historical actors presented here in skilful and sophisticated ways but struggle perhaps too diligently to excise them from the spectre of collaboration, to really see them as sly subverters of the colonial order or to understand 'mimicry' as a form of anti-colonial resistance.[2] On the

1   V. Bickford-Smith, 'Writing About Englishness: South Africa's Forgotten Nationalism', in G. MacPhee and P. Poddar, eds, *Empire and After: Englishness in Postcolonial Perspective* (Oxford: Berghahn Books, 2007), 57–72.

2   L. de Kock, *Civilizing Barbarians: Missionary Narrative and African Textual Response in Nineteenth-century South Africa* (Johannesburg: University of Witwatersrand Press, 1996); H. Bhabha, *The Location of Culture* (New York: Routledge, 1995).

other hand, scholars of British history and British imperial history fail to see them as relevant to their political discourses. With these historical traditions in mind, Saul Dubow has proposed a revised understanding of Britishness, as a global cultural space open to borrowing, appropriation, and redefinition, arguing for the usefulness of:

> a concept of Britishness that dispenses, as far as is possible, with connotations of racial or ethnic ancestry and which decouples the idea of Britishness from a British state or the 'ethnological unity' of Greater Britain hankered after by J. R. Seeley. It does so by challenging the unstated assumption that the British Empire refers to territories and peoples which were somehow *owned* or collectively possessed by the United Kingdom and proposes instead a more capacious category capable of including elective, hyphenated forms of belonging... Britishness, in this sense, is better seen as a field of cultural, political, and symbolic attachments which includes the rights, claims, and aspirations of subject-citizens as well as citizen-subjects – 'non-Britons' as well as 'neo-Britons' in today's parlance.[3]

This chapter aims to explore the responses of pro-empire, 'respectable' people of colour in the British Cape Colony – specifically, a comparatively small group of cosmopolitan newspaper writers who claimed British rights and imperial citizenship derived from their loyalty to the empire and the monarchy. It may be easy, with the benefit of hindsight, for us to condemn these historical actors as out of touch with the zeitgeist of history, but they did not have the luxury of knowing what was to come. The newspaper editors of this analysis were advocates of a non-racial respectable status and identity, who saw themselves as imperial citizens and as the more authentic heirs of British constitutionalism.

The royal tours offer a fascinating lens through which to write a global history of loyalism and Britishness in the British Empire. These respectable people of colour in the Cape Colony shared a basic worldview with a global class of respectable subjects across the British Empire, all of whom commented on and responded to the royal tours in comparable, if different languages of loyalty. This global history of Britishness and imperial citizenship serves to provincialize the British Isles in rather profound ways, to

---

3   S. Dubow, 'How British Was the British World? The Case of South Africa,' *Journal of Imperial and Commonwealth History* 37 (March 2007), 2–3.

demonstrate that many people of colour could and did embrace an imperial identity despite the racial determinism, violence, and dispossession that came to dominate the colonial experience during the nineteenth century. Like so many other products of trans-cultural contact, they were *bricoleurs*, using the cultural building blocks of a larger world to make sense of their lives. During the royal tour of 1901, they appealed to the liberal-humanitarian rhetoric of empire, which cloaked the more brutal reality that often lay beneath the surface, to demand their rights as imperial citizens and loyal subjects of the Queen. The history of British imperial citizenship is relevant and important not only to the history of Britain and its colonies but also to the narratives of world and transnational histories. The work of Marilyn Lake and Henry Reynolds traces the development of a 'global colour line' and the transnational counter-discourses that emerged to challenge the dominance of the white, the male, the European.[4] They reconceptualize the Eurocentric narrative of human rights, from the Declaration of the Rights of Man and the Citizen to the 1948 Universal Declaration of Human Rights. While European constructions of human rights often 'rested on and reinforced imperial distinctions between so-called civilized and uncivilized peoples,' men and women of colour across the colonized world constructed alternative discourses of rights that transcended national and racial communities. While the historical actors of this chapter imagined a non-racial political and cultural community that was uniquely imperial and framed their rights in the language of British traditions, they undoubtedly participated in a larger struggle against a 'global colour bar,' the results of which could not have been predicted at the time.

During the nineteenth century, Britishness and respectability became increasingly associated with 'white skins, English tongues, and bourgeois values.'[5] The Western-educated native came to represent, among other caricatures, 'the Dangerous Native,' 'a misadjusted, urbanized, male agitator,

---

4   M. Lake and H. Reynolds, *Drawing the Global Colour Line: White Men's Countries and the International Challenge of Racial Equality* (Cambridge: Cambridge University Press, 2008).

5   V. Bickford-Smith, *Ethnic Pride and Racial Prejudice in Victorian Cape Town* (Cambridge: Cambridge University Press, 1995), 39.

his lips dripping with wild and imperfectly understood rhetoric about rights'.[6] Simultaneously, men and women of colour throughout the British Empire, who had not been born in or (in most cases) had never seen the British Isles and who had no *ethnic* claim to 'being' British, imagined themselves to be British people. While definitions of citizenship in the late nineteenth and early twentieth century British world were increasingly defined along ethnic and racial lines, there also persisted more open-ended and universalist discourses of imperial citizenship. They centred, in particular, on a mythologized image of Victoria the Good, the maternal, justice-giving queen. While the African intellectuals of this chapter were fundamentally social conservatives, interested in protecting and enhancing their own power and status, they also demanded a radical transformation of imperial culture by demanding, as respectable subjects of the queen, the rights and responsibilities of imperial citizenship.

The Independent Press in South Africa

John Tengo Jabavu, editor of *Imvo Zabantsundu*, Francis Z. S. Peregrino, of the *South African Spectator*, and Alan Kirkland Soga, editor of *Izwi Labantu*, differed in their political allegiances and in their opinions on the war, but all celebrated and promoted the importance of formal politics within the bounds of the British constitution. In South Africa, independent African newspapers were the products and by-products of missionary schools. In fact, the editors of *Imvo Zabantsundu*, the *South African Spectator*, and *Izwi Labantu* were all Christian mission students; two were the sons of prominent African clergymen. They were excluded from service in colonial or local governments yet actively participated in the local and imperial politics of South Africa.[7] As missionary students, they expressed a

---

6   M. O. West, *The Rise of an African Middle Class* (Bloomington: Indiana University Press, 2002), 14.

7   R. Ross, *Status and Respectability in the Cape Colony, 1750–1870: A Tragedy of Manners* (New York: Cambridge University Press, 1999), 174.

brand of sub-imperialism centred on a civilizing mission for those socially beneath them. Through education, they argued, all people of colour might achieve civilization and citizenship and they looked toward hereditary and colonial-appointed chiefs with scorn, as atavisms in a modern age. During the royal tour, they all appealed to *British* constitutionalism and justice, investing their status as African *respectables* in promoting the vote, education, and empire loyalism.

This brand of respectable politics became acutely pronounced, and challenged, during the South African War (1899–1902), an imperial war fought between the British Empire, including thousands of African and Coloured subjects, and the Afrikaner republics. The propaganda of the war was cast in language that contrasted British liberty with Afrikaner tyranny. The Prime Minister Lord Salisbury appealed to the mythology of the Great Queen when he told the House of Lords in October 1899 that:

> the moment has arrived for deciding whether the future of South Africa is to be a growing and increasing Dutch supremacy or a safe, perfectly established supremacy of the English Queen.... With regard to the future there must be no doubt that the Sovereign of England is paramount; there must be no doubt that the white races will be put upon an equality, and that due precaution will be taken for the philanthropic and kindly and improving treatment of those countless indigenous races of whose destiny, I fear, we have been too forgetful.[8]

People of colour overwhelming recognized this difference and served the imperial war effort in great numbers, through 'irregular armed service, scouting, spying and intelligence, supplying crop, livestock, and other goods, and in providing remount, transport riding, and other labour for logistical services'.[9] While local *respectables* challenged the practices of British rule, they broadly attested to the centrality of the British constitution and their great patron the Great Queen as bulwarks against colonial and Afrikaner abuse: 'for them, Britain and its Empire stood for justice, fairness and equality before the law, which meant above all non-racialism in the sense of

---

8   *HL Deb 17 October 1899 vol. 77 cc 21–2.*
9   B. Nasson, *The South African War, 1899–1902* (Oxford: Oxford University Press, 1999).

"equal rights for all civilized men".[10] The royal tour of 1901 was designed to reinforce this propaganda and to thank colonial subjects across the world for their service to the empire. The year 1901 also marked the first negotiations aimed at ending the war. When the Boer general Louis Botha tried to negotiate the non-racial franchise out of the war settlement, he posed a threat not only to the franchise, but to respectable status itself, serving to crystallize the difference between British liberty and Afrikaner tyranny. The Cape's non-racial franchise was one of the most prized possessions of African *respectables*. It was remarkably democratic for the nineteenth century: the 1853 constitution required property worth £25 or a salary of £50 in order to vote.[11] The non-racial franchise was slowly eroded through a series of registration and voting acts (1887, 1892, 1894), which purged many African and Coloured voters from the voting rolls.[12] Yet, even after 1892, nearly half the voters in the colony were people of colour.[13]

Imvo Zabantsundu (*Native* or *Black Opinion*) of King William's Town was the first newspaper published independently by a person of colour in South Africa. It was a weekly newspaper published in English and Xhosa by a twenty-five year old Methodist lay preacher named John Tengo Jabavu starting in 1884, with around 10,0000 readers in the Cape, Natal, Basutoland, and the Afrikaner republics.[14] Jabavu's family identified themselves as Mfengu ('Fingo') people, but he was educated at the Methodist mission station at Healdtown and took up a teaching post at Somerset East. He was an avid student and teacher of languages, including English, Latin, and Greek, and wrote for the liberal settler newspaper *Cape Argus* under a nom-de-plume.[15]

10   C. Saunders, 'African Attitudes Toward Britain and Its Empire,' in D. Lowry, ed., *The South African War Reappraised* (New York: St Martin's Press, 2000), 141–3.
11   Ross, *Status and Respectability*, 174; Stanley Trapido, 'The Origins of the Cape Franchise Qualifications of 1853,' *Journal of African History* 5 (Winter 1964), 37.
12   Ross, *Status and Respectability*, 174.
13   Ibid.
14   L. Switzer, 'The Beginnings of African Protest Journalism,' in L. Switzer, ed., *South Africa's Alternative Press: Voices of Protest and Resistance, 1880–1960* (Cambridge: Cambridge University Press, 2009), 60.
15   D. D. T. Jabavu, *The Life of John Tengo Jabavu, Editor of Imvo Zabantsundu, 1884–1921* (Lovedale: Lovedale Institution Press, 1922), 11–12.

Between 1881 and 1884, he had edited *Isigidimi Sama Xosa* (*Xhosa Messenger*) for the Scottish missionaries at Lovedale but was ousted for openly criticizing the Cape government one too many times.[16] Jabavu became an important and active figure in Cape politics, campaigning for white politicians and advocating a brand of non-racial, respectable liberal politics. He was allied with a group of progressive Cape politicians, which included John X. Merriman, James-Rose Innes, Saul Solomon, and J. W. Sauer, and was a sought-after electioneer in districts where African votes affected election outcomes. His political allies also provided the funding for the newspaper, which was printed on the presses of the *Cape Mercury*.[17]

Framing South African politics as a struggle between British liberty and Afrikaner tyranny and republicanism, he was, until 1898, a staunch and vocal opponent of the Afrikaner Bond, the Cape political party that represented the interests of Dutch-speaking South Africans, and worked tirelessly to organize an English-speaking progressive coalition in order to defeat it.[18] In 1897, his dream of a broad-church English party emerged in the form of the Progressive Party, led by Cecil Rhodes, with whom he briefly allied; political disagreements with the Progressives and the alliance of his friends John X. Merriman and J. W. Sauer with the Bond, however, pushed him toward a shift of allegiance.[19] In March 1898, Jan Hofmeyer, the Bond leader, proclaimed that he was not and never had been hostile to African political rights, beginning his campaign to vie for African voters.[20] Jabavu declared Hofmeyer the new standard-bearer for 'true British principle' in South African politics, in opposition to Cecil Rhodes' 'equal

---

16   L. and D. Switzer. *The Black Press in South Africa and Lesotho: A Descriptive Bibliographic Guide to African, Coloured, and Indian newspapers, Newsletters, and Magazines 1836–1976* (G. K. Hall, 1979), 4; C. Higgs, *The Ghost of Equality: The Public Lives of D. D. T. Jabavu of South Africa, 1885–1959* (Cape Town and Johannesburg David Philip, 1997), 11.

17   Switzer, 'The Beginnings', 60–1.

18   Trapido, 'White Conflict and Non-White Participation', PhD Thesis University of London, 1970, 290, 304.

19   Trapido, 'White Conflict', 309; De Kock, 336–77.

20   Trapido, 'White Conflict', 331.

rights for white men only'.[21] His allegiance to the Bond, combined with his pacifism during the South African War would make him a lightening rod of political controversy, to the point that his voice, *Imvo Zabantsundu*, was silenced in August 1901 by the military government of the Cape.

Francis Z. S. Peregrino, editor of the Cape Town English-language newspaper *The South African Spectator*, came to South Africa only in 1900 because, he said, 'at the outbreak of war... [he] turned his thoughts to South Africa and anticipating that when peace had been proclaimed and the whole country is under the British flag, progress and prosperity are bound to follow, [and] he made up his mind to come here to devote his pen and brain to the service of the native people'.[22] He had been born in Accra in Gold Coast to a family involved with local Wesleyan missionaries (his uncle was an African missionary in the Wesleyan Church).[23] He was educated in England and lived there until c. 1890, when he moved to the United States.[24] He demonstrated particular interest in the African Methodist Episcopal (AME) Church, an evangelical missionary organization founded by African Americans in Philadelphia, and pan-Africanist ideology. He often deferred to his colleagues at *Izwi Labantu* on local matters he considered controversial, but always stressed the need for cooperation among people of colour. Despite only coming to South Africa a year before the royal tour, he was chosen by a committee of other respectable men of colour to present the 'native address' to the Duke and Duchess of Cornwall. Having widely travelled the British world, Peregrino articulated his belief in British citizenship through education, the ballot box, and empire loyalism.

Within fifteen months of the paper's founding in 1897, Alan Kirkland Soga became editor of *Izwi Labantu* (*Voice of the People*), founded by Walter Benson Rubusana and published in Xhosa and English from East London.

---

21   *Imvo Zabantsundu* (31 March, 1898), cited in De Kock, *Civilizing Barbarians* 336–77.
22   *South African Spectator* (7 September 1901).
23   Ibid.
24   Ibid.

Soga's mother was Scottish, and he was educated in Scotland.[25] His father Tiyo Soga, an important advisor to the Xhosa chief Sandile, was trained at the University of Edinburgh and became the first African Presbyterian minister.[26] Alan Soga was apparently a clerk in Tembuland as late as 1897 when he resigned, according to the *Cape Argus*, because he could not:

> consistently with the position he occupied in the service, render the Natives the assistance which is desirable in the present crisis... He charges that his action, which has been taken on his own initiative, will act as an incentive to Native and Coloured friends to vote solidly for the British party and the maintenance of that supremacy which is necessary for their welfare in the future.[27]

Izwi Labantu was founded, in a very real sense, to counter the dominance of Jabavu and his paper, which was by then seen by many of his opponents as an organ of the Afrikaner Bond.[28] Soga apparently had distaste for Jabavu, as a Mfengu, but this ethnic rivalry was a minor sub-plot to a far more vibrant political one. While subsidized by the arch-imperialist Cecil Rhodes and his Progressive Party, Soga's paper maintained a stridently independent editorial perspective.[29] He loudly supported the British cause in the war against his nemesis Jabavu, who also claimed to be pro-British, and could hardly contain his satisfaction when *Imvo* was banned.

The cosmopolitan publishers of independent African newspapers were bi- or multi-lingual men, who were well-versed in the political discourses of the larger British world, and beyond. *The South African Spectator* boasted on its masthead to be 'positively cosmopolitan. We know a man and not colour: principles, and not creed'.[30] Jabavu, for instance, was a founder of Imbumba Yama Nyama (South African Aborigines Association) and was in contact with the Aborigines' Protection Society in Britain, which included Charles Dilke and Thomas Fowell Buxton among its members,

25   G. M. Fredrickson, *Black Liberation: A Comparative History of Black Ideologies in the United States and South Africa* (Oxford: Oxford University Press, 1995), 41.
26   S. Trapido, 'White Conflict', 333.
27   *Cape Argus*, July 23 1898, cited in Stanley Trapido, 'White Conflict', 333.
28   Switzer, 'Beginnings', 65.
29   Ibid.
30   *South African Spectator* (August 23 1902).

and frequently wrote letters to their newspaper *The Aborigines' Friend*.[31] He was a leader of a 'Native Combination' in 1885 that agreed, unsuccessfully, to form a branch of the Empire League, and considered himself a proud 'Gladstonian Liberal'.[32] He petitioned and corresponded with government officials in Britain, mailing copies of *Imvo* to British MPs.[33] Yet, as Peregrino's life story demonstrates, South African culture was not only shaped by Britain and the British Empire but by the United States pan-Africanism, and other transnational currents.

These men did not desire to be white, or to be ethnically British, but imagined themselves to be, in a very real sense, British people. These African intellectuals were creating and participating in an imperial political culture that was often communicated in both the vernacular (Xhosa or Tswana, for instance) and the lingua franca of empire (English). Their message was accessible to the imperial, to colonial administrators and sympathetic parties in Britain and the empire, and to the local, to literate and non-literate people in their local communities. During the royal tours, they negotiated, contested, and re-made the national, or transnational, 'imagined community' of empire in print.

Colonial officials were deeply concerned by the politicization of Africans in the empire. While their politics of the independent African press were often radical, particularly in challenging the dominant racial discourses of imperial culture, they always framed their notions of citizenship in loyalty to the monarchy and the British Empire. Importantly, the South African Native National Congress, founded in 1912, seen as one of the foremost anti-colonial and nationalist political organizations of the twentieth century, swore allegiance to the British monarch. Colonial officials, however, conflated politicization with disloyalty. Officials also worried that the dissemination of news and information from the newspapers, through the gossip of the local bazaar or 'the Native school master who read it to them,' would inevitably lead to the politicization of non-literate people of colour.[34]

---

31   Higgs, *The Ghost of Equality*, 12; *Imvo Zabantsundu* (April 30 1901), 3; Trapido, 'White Conflict', 290, 297.

32   Trapido, 'White Conflict', 291–2.

33   Ibid. 290, 297.

34   H. S. Caldecott to Gordon Sprigg, February 11, 1896, Rhodes Papers, vol. 6.2, No. 96, cited in Trapido, 'White Conflict', 321.

Respectable Subjects, Imperial Citizens

The non-racial politics of the South African newspapermen – Jabavu, Soga, and Peregrino – demonstrate that this modern racial order was not a foregone conclusion. While they and their progressive settler allies were characterized by what might be described as imperialist tendencies, to transform others in their own image, the notions of citizenship they articulated cannot be conflated with the more racialist and exclusionary politics of imperial culture. They invested their notion of imperial citizenship in the politics of respectability and in the medium of an independent print culture. They imagined a future in the empire, where all respectable citizen-subjects of the queen shared the same rights and privileges.

The most prized possession of their respectability – the 'liberal' Cape franchise – came under attack during the late nineteenth century. In this context, these *respectables* understood the South African War to be a defining moment in the future social and political order of southern Africa. They feared, rightfully so, that the post-war settlement would solidify white dominance, a union of British and Boer, over the non-white populations of southern Africa. And, the Cape franchise was one of the earliest and most controversial impasses during the negotiations to end the war. Jabavu foresaw, appealing to the language of *The Aborigine's Friend*, that *white* settlers would 'come together... over the body of "the nigger"'.[35] Jabavu, Soga, and Peregrino sought to avert this fate and to make a new future for South Africa by claiming their rights as British subjects. Alan Soga fiercely disagreed with John Tengo Jabavu's pacifism, and their fierce political rivalry only developed further over the course of the war. While they disagreed with each other over the politics of the war, they all interpreted its meaning through the lens of an imperial citizenship.

The Duke and Duchess of Cornwall – the future King George V and Queen Mary – visited South Africa in the summer of 1901, months after the death of George's grandmother, Victoria. The tour itself was a by-product of the South African War, designed by Joseph Chamberlain the Colonial Secretary to convey thanks for imperial service in the war and to bolster

35   *Imvo Zabantsundu* (30 April 1901).

loyalty during troubled times for the empire. The death of the Great Queen and the on-going conflict profoundly informed the responses by people of colour to the royal tour. They had firmly stood by the empire in a time of war and appealed, as loyal subjects of the Great Queen and their new king, and future subjects of the Duke of Cornwall, for a post-war South Africa where all people shared the rights and responsibilities of imperial citizens.

In Victoria's death, these African intellectuals sought to redeem the promise of her rule by promoting a social order that did not deny any of her loyal subjects their rights. *Imvo Zabantsundu* expressed grief over the loss of this queen 'so precious to all of her subjects because of her transcendent virtues, and not less to her Native subjects in South Africa'.[36] Jabavu celebrated the Victorian era as an age of improvement, of 'increasing comfort and well-being for the masses,' liberty 'advancing in all directions,' new and improved technology, the advance of education and Christianity, and less crime.[37] Of course, her reign was also an era of violence, dispossession, and even disenfranchisement for people of colour in South Africa and the empire. But, Victoria the 'Mother, wife, and Queen' as a symbol represented progress toward justice and equality for *all* of her subjects, an unfulfilled promise.[38] *The Spectator* predicted, as a consequence of her death, 'the dawn of a new era, one of understanding and perfect concord between the races.'[39]

In face of intense criticism, most notably from Soga, the 'pro-Boer' Jabavu sought to prove his loyalty to the empire through expressions of grief. In a letter to *Imvo Zabantsundu*, 'N. S. B.' complimented Jabavu's impeccable loyalism and his deep, heartfelt articulation of grief (the author also noted that the paper's black border of mourning was much more pronounced than that of other King William's Town journals).[40] The South African War was a rather dark period in Jabavu's political career, and his need to express loyalty was particularly acute. The political discourses

36   *Imvo Zabantsundu* (28 January 1901).
37   *Imvo Zabantsunu* (28 January 1901; 18 March, 1901).
38   *Imvo Zabantsundu* (28 January 1901).
39   *South African Spectator* (23 February 1901).
40   *Imvo Zabantsundu* (11 February 1901).

over his loyalty in the days following Queen Victoria's death, particularly his very public disagreements with Soga, reflect on the complexities of 'native politics'.

Jabavu's 'support' for the Afrikaner Bond was framed without a discourse of British politics. While Soga identified him as a traitor, the real danger Jabavu represented to the wartime British government of the Cape was in demanding the rights of citizenship and in rejecting the jingoism of the war, arguing that, from the perspective of the colonized, there was *very* little difference between British and Boer settlers. Despite the intense criticism, *Imvo* claimed itself to be the most authentic voice of *British* political culture in South Africa and participated in a larger imperial political discourse about loyalty, jingoism, and the war.

Both Soga and Peregrino strongly supported the British war effort. The pacifism and pro-Boerism of *Imvo* was unacceptable to Soga, who belittled Jabavu's politics as treason in a time of war. He condemned those who, like Jabavu, dared to conflate Briton with Boer. Both of the pro-war papers (*Izwi Labantu* and *The South African Spectator*) advertised Boer atrocities and promoted African service to the empire. In this context, Peregrino confidently asserted that:

> the loyalty of the coloured people during these troublons [sic] times has been spontaneous and unquestionable. From all parts of the Colony they appeal to be allowed to bear their share in the responsibilities, and to participate in the sacrifices necessary to the firm, and permanent establishment of His Majesty's beneficent rule under which the coloured people, are afforded full protection.[41]

As an advocate of the war, Soga was also a militant supporter of men such as Cecil Rhodes and Alfred Milner, the brand of arch-imperialist who represent the empire's most xenophobic and expansionist tendencies. Few histories of the British Empire account for such complexities – of pro-empire, pro-Boer, even pro-imperialist people of colour. They did not support British rule as the better of two evils, but as an investment in a just and more equitable future that lived up to the promises of Britishness.

---

41   *South African Spectator* (4 February 1901).

On the eve of the royal visit, Jabavu's *Imvo Zabantsundu* was suppressed by the military government of the Cape. Colonial officials kept a careful eye on independent African newspapers, and Jabavu's pacifism and 'pro-Boer' politics were deemed too dangerous for the royal visit and the war effort. Soga was elated by the silencing of Jabavu, even if they shared an enormous amount in common despite their differences. *Izwi* celebrated its rival's demise with the headline, 'IMVO R. I.P':

> NEMESIS – which publishes arrogant and tyrannical abuse of prosperity, has found out our native contemporary at last.... Frankly, we have consistently opposed the pro-Boer policy of 'Imvo,' and its unfriendly attitude towards those friends of progress and good Government, who made it possible for that paper to establish itself... We feel deeply the humiliation cast upon the native press, just entering on the threshold of life. ... What an opportunity for our enemies to seize upon! ... The magnanimity of the British race is wonderful. Perhaps the moral lessons to be gained by this serious blow, will not be altogether lost, but will work out for the good to the future of the native press that has to be.[42]

Soga, in haste to judge an old rival, unfairly concluded that Jabavu was disloyal, the same error that was often made by settlers and colonial officials about the African press as a whole. They confused independent political opinions with disloyalty.

In the context of this political crisis, the royal tour represented an important opportunity for the South African intelligentsia to mourn the loss of the Great Queen, to celebrate their new king, and to demonstrate loyalty to *their* empire. Peregrino looked forward to the 'spontaneous outbursts of loyalty' that would remind the king's subjects why they were fighting and inform the rebels as to the futility of their exercise.[43] These men were particularly heartened by the inclusion of notable *respectables* in the tour. *Imvo Zabantsundu* celebrated that loyal Africans would be recognized important members of the imperial community.[44] Despite this inclusion, the independent press came to question imperial dedication to

---

42 *Izwi Labantu* (27 August 1901).
43 *South African Spectator* (24 August 1901).
44 *Imvo Zabantsundu* (21 June 1901).

the king's loyal subjects of colour, in part because they were marginalized in royal ceremonies in favour of hereditary elites.

Peregrino, who had only arrived in South Africa a year earlier from the United States, was chosen by the community to deliver a 'native address' to the Duke and Duchess of Cornwall. He denied rumours that the Colonial Office had screened his address or that a 'white man' had presented it to the duke.[45] The address was overwhelmingly directed not at the duke's father, Edward VII, but to the memory of his grandmother, Victoria the Good, under whom 'the shackles of slavery were struck off our feet'.[46] Moved by the duke's response, Peregrino noted that he 'dwelt not on any distinctions of race and colour' and was 'deeply touched by the display of loyalty'.[47] Whether or not the duke was acting out a scripted performance, in a part that he had played dozens of times, is irrelevant. South African elites such as Peregrino invested, and found, in him the promise of imperial citizenship.

While encouraged by this encounter, all three men were concerned that the stagecraft of colonial officials would suppress demonstrations of spontaneous loyalty by common people and misrepresent the character of South Africa's native population.[48] Specifically, they were concerned that the people of South Africa would be represented by 'chiefs and headmen,' rather than 'the most enlightened of our people'.[49] To Soga, this exclusion would deny the duke and duchess a 'fair opportunity of gauging the true state of civilization and improvement arrived at by the natives'.[50] Much of their scorn was directed at 'tribal' rituals and war dances, and the hereditary elites who performed in them.

They argued that these rituals misrepresented the progress of South Africa during the reign of Queen Victoria and focused the duke's attention and a corrupt and dependent aristocracy. *The Spectator*, for instance,

45   *South African Spectator* (24 August 1901).
46   *South African Spectator* (24 August 1901).
47   *South African Spectator* (24 August 1901).
48   *Imvo Zabantsundu* (21 June 1901).
49   *Imvo Zabantsundu* (21 June 1901).
50   *Izwi Labantu* (27 August 1901).

mocked plans for the performance of a Zulu war dance as 'buffoonery,' a cultural relic of an uncivilized past'.[51] *Izwi Labantu* shared the 'amazement and feelings of disgust at the perpetuation of customs that are condemned by all civilized natives' and suggested that natives ought to sing the national anthem instead.[52] They argued that the genuine loyalty of both the lower classes and of the enlightened, respectable classes was being suppressed by the colonial officials.[53] It was the African intelligentsia, who 'fully realise[d] the trend of British policy, and the advantage that loyalty offers'.[54]

In the aftermath of the tour, Soga and Peregrino pressed for a war settlement that considered the service and loyalty of South Africa's non-white population. To use John Darwin's explanatory frame in a somewhat subversive way by applying it to 'the colonized', the intelligentsia of the independent South African press were articulating a brand of 'Britannic nationalism', of imperial citizenship and identity, even so far as to advocate imperial federation![55] Loyalty to the monarchy was framed in a vision of British rights and respectable status. The editors of these papers were not only claiming Britishness but also arguing that their understanding of it was more authentic, closer to its *true* ideals, as clearly articulated in their debates over the terms of peace. In April 1901, *The Spectator* had argued that the settlement must be ended on 'amicable' terms but that:

> it would be contrary to all precedent and altogether at variance *with British traditions* to surrender the rights and endanger the safety of the loyal native and coloured citizen even to that end. We believe that in view of all the circumstances precedent to the assumption of hostilities, that an unconditional surrender would have been in order, but failing that, we believe that the conclusion of peace on any basis other than that of equal rights to all His Majesty's *civilized subjects*, would be a retrogression.[56]

---

51   *South African Spectator* (13 July 1901).
52   *Izwi Labantu* (2 July 1901).
53   *Imvo Zabantsundu* (21 June 1901).
54   *Izwi Labantu* (20 August 1901).
55   J. Darwin, 'A Third British Empire? The Dominion Idea in Imperial Politics', in J. M. Brown and W. R. Louis, eds, *The Oxford History of the British Empire*, vol. IV *The Twentieth Century* (Oxford: Oxford University Press, 1999), 64,-87; *Imvo Zabantsundu* (9 April 1901).
56   *South African Spectator* (20 April 1901).

When the *Imvo Zabantsundu* returned to the presses in October 1902, over a year after being proscribed, Jabavu began not with a defence of his politics but with an ode to Queen Victoria and the profound progress accomplished during her reign.[57] He went on to imagine a post-war South African politics where 'Dutch, British, and Natives have a right to be' and all 'should be accorded the common rights of *citizenship*,' of shared 'prosperity' and 'responsibility'.[58] This imperial political culture survived its betrayal during the South African War intact.

The alternative print culture of South Africa expanded rapidly in the decade following the war. No fewer than nine new African, Coloured, and Indian newspapers began publication between 1901 and 1910.[59] Jabavu and Soga remained fierce political rivals. When Soga helped found the Native Press Organization (NPA), Jabavu refused to participate.[60] They participated in separate political organizations and organized separate protests.[61] In April 1901 *Izwi Labantu* closed.[62] *Imvo Zabantsundu* survived, with the editorship succeeded by Jabavu's son Alexander in 1921, but Jabavu's consistently erratic politics and the emergence of a new generation of political leaders limited his influence. Peregrino continued to publish *The South African Spectator* until 1908, but he has left little in terms of a historical record.

The fate of African loyalism in the empire and its limits in the aftermath of the South African War are exemplified in the life of Sol Plaatje (1876–1932), a co-founder of the South African Native National Congress. The Tswana-speaking Plaatje was educated at the Berlin Missionary Society's station near Boshof in the Orange Free State, where his father was a deacon, but was by and large an auto-didactic, teaching himself English,

57 *Imvo Zabantsundu* (8 October 1902).
58 *Imvo Zabantsundu* (8 October 1902).
59 Switzer, *South Africa's Alternative Press*, 4–5.
60 Switzer, 'The Beginnings', 67.
61 Ibid. 68–9.
62 Ibid.

Dutch, German, and 'at least' five African languages.[63] During the Siege of
Mafeking (1899–1901), Plaatje served the British war effort by gathering
and communicating intelligence from African informants and wrote about
his experience in his *Mafeking Diary*, first published in 1973.[64] He edited
two newspapers, *Koranta ea Becoana*, or *Bechuana Gazette* (1902–10),
and *Tsala ea Becoana*, or *Friend of the Tswana* (1910–12), both of which
were published in English and Tswana. Like the other historical actors of
this chapter, he emphasized the importance of cleanliness and sobriety, a
respectability of action and disposition essential to citizenship. As a political activist for African rights, he advocated for a non-racial citizenship and
appealed directly to imperial responsibility to South Africans as the legacy
of Queen Victoria.

The end of the South African War brought about a transformation
of South African politics that would effectively shut out non-whites and
inspire a nationalist politics. The Treaty of Vereeniging (1902) brought the
whole of South Africa effectively under British rule, with promises of local
rule under the British Crown for the former Boer republics. The issue of
African voting rights was temporarily avoided, and the pre-war franchises
remained largely intact. The Union of South Africa (1910) created a federal state that abandoned the enfranchisement of non-whites in the name
of '[white] unity and reconciliation'.[65] Despite this imperial betrayal, the
loyalist South African Native National Congress, co-founded by Plaatje,
John Dube, and others in 1912 as a response to the political and social order
of the union, continued to agitate the British government – the monarchy,
in particular – to redeem the promises of imperial citizenship.

Plaatje's impassioned opposition to the Natives' Land Act of 1913,
which sought to dispossess and segregate the 'native' population of southern Africa, took him to the imperial metropole as a representative of the

---

63   B. Willan, *Sol Plaatje: South African Nationalist, 1876–1932* (London: Heinemann,
      1984), 15–20.
64   S. Plaatje, *Mafeking Diary* (Northern Ilinois University Press, 1990 reprint).
65   L. M. Thompson, *The Oxford History of South Africa*, ed. M. Wilson and L. M.
      Thompson, vol. II: South *Africa, 1870–1966* (New York: Oxford University Press,
      1971), 358.

SANNC and inspired his greatest work, *Life in South Africa Before and Since the European War and the Boer Rebellion* (1916). He arrived in Britain on the eve of the First World War, in 1914. During the war, the SANNC would pledge to 'hang up their grievances' and support the imperial war effort.[66] Plaatje framed his plea for imperial intervention against the Natives' Land Act in the familiar language of imperial loyalty. His case was helped by the recent rebellion of Boer settlers against South Africa's support of the British war effort, and he employed this incident to contrast Boer tyranny and republicanism with African loyalty.[67] The promises of imperial citizenship would go unfulfilled. Britain failed to effectively intervene, largely because imperial policy had moved toward self-government for the white colonies of settlement. As South Africa drifted out of the British orbit of influence, so went the promises of imperial justice. In 1909, Jabavu wrote, 'That cow of Great Britain has now gone dry'.[68]

Conclusion

These *respectables* claimed British political traditions and claimed Britishness in an effort to transform the very *un*-British practices of colonial rule. As Leon de Kock argues, they demonstrated 'evidence of *desired identification* with the colonizing culture as an *act of* affirmation, a kind of publicly declared "struggle" that does not oppose the terms of a colonial culture but insists on a *more pure* version of its originating legitimation'.[69] They imagined their political, cultural, and social universe as an imperial and transnational one. Educated in missionary and other British schools, these

---

66   Willan, *Sol Plaatje*, 197.
67   Ibid. 187.
68   *Imvo Zabantsundu* (August 31, 1901).
69   L. de Kock, 'Sitting for the Civilization Test: The Making(s) of a Civil Imaginary in Colonial South Africa', *Poetics Today* 22 (2001), 392.

elites were nurtured by the British to be the intermediaries of empire. In embracing an imperial culture, however, the 'native' intelligentsia of South Africa, and other locales across the British Empire, articulated a vision of imperial citizenship that challenged the conceptual space between the theory and reality of British rule.

Imperial citizenship represents a vibrant cultural and political tradition of the nineteenth- and early twentieth-century British world. Its failure as a discourse was as much about British inaction to live up to the promises of the liberal Empire as violent and illiberal action. As a transitional period, the late nineteenth-century empire was a dynamic and interconnected political space where a modern, global politics of respectability and imperial citizenship was made. In this context, the nationalist political movements of the twentieth century have their origins in the intellectual milieu of imperial politics. The cosmopolitan and modern authors, intellectuals, and activists of this chapter are relevant and important to the history of Britain and Britishness, even if their claims to Britishness and citizenship fell on deaf ears.

ANTOINE MIOCHE

2   Britishness: The Imperial Vision of William Knox (1732–1810)

In the roughly two decades that followed the outbreak of the Seven Years War (1756–63), architects of empire on either side of the Atlantic envisaged a variety of structures for Great Britain's increasingly expansive transoceanic society. It is possible, through their pamphlets and memoranda, to recapture discourse about empire and nation at a time when the definition of both was in flux, when attempts at the definition of the one impinged on beliefs regarding the true foundations of the other, and when their mutual reconciliation was the object of much agonised ingenuity. William Knox was one such architect.

Knox was born in Ulster to an Anglo-Irish family which claimed descent from the famous reformer John Knox. From the age of twenty-five until his death, he either played a direct role, or manifested an active interest, in the affairs of Britain's empire, taking in his native Ireland and the whole of British America, including the Caribbean. His steadfast adherence to mercantilist views, with which interest in his imperial thinking has tended to concern itself almost exclusively, and his support for war on the American insurgents as late as 1781 – placing him, unrepentant, on the losing side, both politically and intellectually – have drawn on him more than a fair amount of historiographical opprobrium.[1] But, for all his conservatism,

---

1   See for instance K. Knorr, *British Colonial Theories 1570–1850* (Toronto: Toronto University Press, 1944) for an exclusive focus on Knox's support for mercantilist views ; and J. M. Bumsted's review of L. J. Bellot, *William Knox*, in *Reviews in American History* 6 (2) (June 1978), 196–202, for the opinion that Knox's imperial views lacked consistency and that Knox, far from deserving credit as an imperial theorist, was merely a self-serving, double-dealing official of little consequence.

Knox did not lack intelligence or vision. He developed throughout his life an understanding of the Empire as a complex political, social and economic unit, evolving over the years from a virtually exclusive stress on parliamentary sovereignty to a richer picture of a still Anglo-centric, yet variegated, world-wide British community.

This chapter proposes to examine Knox's colonial and imperial career and writings, with a view to throwing light on the manner in which Britishness might be comprehended and shaped, at individual level, by an accumulation of experiences in a multiplicity of locations, and on the strains which, in turn, the Empire placed on Britishness.

His life and Career in Brief

Knox served from 1756 to 1761 as Provost Marshal and member of the provincial council of Georgia.[2] While he was there, he began the acquisition of a large estate near Savannah, which eventually comprised some 8400 acres and 122 black slaves, until it was lost in the upheaval of American rebellion and independence. On his return to England in 1761, he worked in London as the agent of the colony, as well as of East Florida between 1763 and 1765.

In those same years, Knox also began to show a strong concern for the welfare of his native country. By his own account, this manifested itself as early as 1761, when, after his return from America, he laid (unspecified) proposals for the alleviation of Irish ills 'before a respectable body of Irish

---

2   Unless otherwise specified, this section draws on the following: M. M. Spector, *The American Department of the British Government 1768–1782* (New York: Columbia University Press, 1940), 75, 102–3, 105, 112, 137; J. M. Sosin, *Agents and Merchants: British Colonial Policy and the Origins of the American Revolution, 1763–1775* (Lincoln: University of Nebraska Press, 1965), 10; J. P. Greene, 'William Knox's Explanation for the American Revolution', *The William and Mary Quarterly*, 3rd ser. 30 (2) (April 1973), 293–306; and L. J. Bellot, *William Knox: The Life and Thought of an Eighteenth-Century Imperialist* (Austin & London: University of Texas Press, 1977), 174–6, 202, 210–12.

noblemen and gentlemen, who called themselves the Donnegall Society, whose avowed purpose was to promote the interests of their country'.[3] In 1763, he evinced the same preoccupation when, during the negotiations that concluded the Seven Years War, he sought to persuade the Earl of Halifax, then Lord Lieutenant of Ireland, of the benefits to be derived from a reduction of Spanish duties upon Irish linens so as to bring them into line with those Spain imposed on the equivalent French article. In both cases, his efforts were to no avail.[4] But it is significant that Knox's imperial vision, even at this early stage, should have been shaped not simply by his comparatively short stay in an inchoate British overseas settlement, but also by his Irish perspective, set within both an international and a global British framework.

During those early years, it was nevertheless as an expert on the colonies that Knox became seriously involved in imperial affairs. In October 1763, the Royal Proclamation, which sought to contain the American seaboard colonies' westward expansion after the conclusion of the peace and the removal of the French threat in North America, seems to have drawn in part on 'hints' he had prepared with the former governor of Georgia, his fellow Irishman and mentor, Thomas Ellis.[5] Two years later, Knox assumed for the first time the role of an anonymous pamphleteer in defence of Lord Grenville's imperial policies by writing *The Claim of the Colonies to an Exemption from Taxation* (1765), an unabashed apology for the Stamp Act which cost him his post as agent for Georgia. There followed *The Present State of the Nation* (1768), which advocated colonial representation at Westminster as part of a raft of measures focusing on trade, and earned him a scathing response from Edmund Burke; and *The Controversy between Great Britain*

---

3   W. Knox, *Extra-Official State Papers addressed to the Right Hon. Lord Rawdon, and the other members of the Two Houses of Parliament, associated for the preservation of the constitution and promoting the prosperity of the British Empire* (London, 1789), Vol. I, Part II, 1–2.

4   Ibid.

5   W. Knox 'Hints Respecting the Settlement of our American Provinces', in T. C. Barrow, 'A Project for Imperial Reform: "Hints Respecting the Settlement of our American Provinces", 1763', *The William and Mary Quarterly*, 3rd ser. 24 (1) (January 1967), 108–26.

and her Colonies Reviewed (1769), a brilliant debunking of the case made by American colonists against parliamentary authority.

On the strength of this record, Knox was chosen in 1770 to be one of two under-secretaries in the newly created American Department in Whitehall. Under the successive administrations of Lords Hillsborough, Dartmouth and Germain, he played a significant role as an architect of American policy until 1782, when the Department was disbanded. He was a key influence on the Quebec Act of 1774, in the defence of which he also authored a vigorously penned pamphlet, and acted regularly as an adviser on the conduct of military operations, as well as on the logistical management of the war.

The confidence which was reposed in him by his political masters by the late 1770s was such that, in circumstances of patriot agitation in Ireland against a backdrop of war in America, Knox was not only allowed, but positively encouraged, to conduct the bulk of the correspondence with Irish officials regarding a contemplated relaxation of Irish trade restrictions, a move that clearly encroached on the sphere of the rival Southern Department, traditionally in charge of domestic and Irish policy. It may even be the case that Knox's uncompromising views on the rebellious colonies owed something to the belief, encouraged by Lord North's cordial reception of his objectives for Ireland, which was that once America had been disposed of, the Irish trade restrictions would be removed.[6] Knox was also instrumental in 1780 in defusing Irish patriot resistance to Westminster's legislative supremacy.

The American Revolution terminated Knox's career as an official. For the next twenty-seven years he carried on a vain struggle to secure adequate compensation for the confiscation of his American property, which he valued at some £16,000. He died in 1810, having served as provincial agent for Prince Edward Island from 1801 until 1807, as well as for the Loyalist colony of New Brunswick, which he had helped bring into existence in 1784 and where he received a grant of land in gratitude for his services to the colony, until 1808.

6   Ibid.

The American Crisis:
A Defence of Parliamentary Sovereignty

It was not just birth, ambition, or the geostrategic and commercial interests of a selfish metropole that dictated Knox's outlook. Principle was at stake too. To him, the test and badge of Britishness was the sovereignty of the Westminster parliament.

In *The Claim of the Colonies*, as also later in *The Controversy between Great Britain and her Colonies Reviewed*, Knox considered and rebutted the arguments made by the Americans for alternative modes of association between Britain and the continental colonies. The common law, he explained, was rather a protection against abuses of the prerogative than the basis for exemption from the authority of Westminster. Similarly, charter rights could not meaningfully be invoked, unless the crown were authorized to grant an exemption to any subject of Great Britain from the jurisdiction of parliament, and thus to dispense with acts of parliament or with the common law altogether. Parliament, for its part, had legislated for the colonies 'since the first settlement of America by British subjects' and would need to continue to do so for as long as the twenty-eight or twenty-nine colonies of America, comprising the West Indian islands, failed to agree among themselves upon the proportion to be raised by each as their contribution to the public charge.[7]

---

7   W. Knox, *The Claim of the Colonies to an Exemption from Internal Taxes Imposed by Authority of Parliament, Examined: In a Letter from a Gentleman in London, to his Friend in America* (London, 1765), 3–4 (on the common law), 8 (on charter rights), 9–10 (on precedents for parliamentary regulation of trade), and 17–19 (on the lack of a serious alternative to parliamentary levies). Also W. Knox, *The Controversy between Great Britain and her Colonies Reviewed; the Several Pleas of the Colonies in Support of their Right to all the Liberties and Privileges of British Subjects, and to Exemption from the Legislative Authority of Parliament, Stated and Considered; and the Nature of their Connection with, and Dependence on, Great Britain, Shewn upon the Evidence of Historical Facts and Authentic Records* (London, 1769), 101–5 (on charter rights).

Knox wished to emphasize the unifying and freedom-enhancing role of the alliance of crown and parliament throughout the Empire. Was not the parliament of Great Britain, he asked of the colonies, 'the sure stay of all their liberties, and the protector of all their rights and possessions', rather than the crown alone? Did not denial of parliamentary sovereignty amount to a contention 'that there is no supreme power in the state'? And 'if the authority of the legislative be not in one instance equally supreme over the Colonies as it is over the people of England, then are not the Colonists of the same community with the people of England'.[8] 'The laws of *God* or of *Nature*, or the *common rights* of mankind' were not enough to confer on them a status which they were otherwise renouncing.[9] Put differently, if the Americans were allowed to have their way, there would be an end to freedom under constitutional monarchy and a dissolution of the bonds of transatlantic British, but also of colonial American, society as each member of the Empire became a prey to its neighbour.[10]

It was, then, the fact of a shared constitution which gave substance to Britishness within the Empire. It clearly implied subordination, but the nature of this subordination was such that the colonies were nonetheless in a position to force the metropole to consider adjustments. Knox thus felt compelled to spell out the essentials that must be safeguarded. First, he pronounced, consent to taxation under the British constitution was not popular consent, because representation was not of the people, but of the land and corporations. This was a capital difference between the American and the metropolitan conception of representation, and one which was to lead Knox to accord great importance to land and the aristocratic element of government. However, secondly, the subjects of Great Britain were not 'bound by laws, nor [was] their money taken from them without their own consent given by their representatives. *The King, Lords, and Commons are*

---

8   Knox, *The Controversy*, 34–43, 50–1. Quotations at 50.

9   Ibid. 18.

10   See also W. Knox, *The Justice and Policy of the Late Act of Parliament for Making more Effectual Provision for the Government of the Province of Quebec, asserted and proved; and the conduct of administration respecting that province, stated and vindicated* (London, 1774), 5–6.

their representatives; for to them it is that they have *delegated* their individual rights over their lives, liberties, and property'. What was required was a balance between all three elements of the representation. Neither the royal nor the democratic component must be allowed to disrupt this balance, which hinged ultimately on the aristocratic, land-owning class. As appears from Knox's other writings, the argument was applicable to both America and Ireland, where the democratic element, in his view, was over powerful. Thirdly, quoting Locke back at the Americans, Knox argued that 'every man that hath any *possessions or enjoyment of any part of the dominions of any government, doth thereby give his tacit consent, and is as far forth obliged to obedience to the laws of that government during such enjoyment, as anyone under it*'. This was consonant with the notion that only land provided a stake in the country and with the implicit belief that land-ownership made for loyalty to government, if not for subservience to particular policies. Lastly, Knox declared that it would be absurd to suppose that a minority could refuse to pay a tax agreed to by a majority.[11]

Knox's plea, in the last analysis, was for London not to relinquish control of Britishness by letting the colonies affect the constitutional fabric beyond what the pragmatism of government might reasonably require. 'Nothing', he was later to write, 'could argue greater folly and wickedness, in any government, than the suffering the people of the ancient dominions to be destroyed, for the sake of raising a new Empire, and new subjects, in another part of the world'.[12] But, provided these essentials were safeguarded, Britishness dictated that imperial governance should be reformed so as to encompass the colonies clearly within a single, if flexible, political-constitutional order.[13]

---

11   W. Knox *The Controversy*, 59–90. Emphasis in the original text.
12   W. Knox, *The Interest of the Merchants and Manufacturers of Great Britain, in the Present Contest with the Colonies, Stated and Considered* (London, 1774), 5. See also *Extra-Official State Papers*, Vol. II, 12.
13   *Extra-Official State Papers*, Vol. II, 29.

The American Crisis:
Knox's Critique of Imperial Governance

To begin with, Knox explained in *The Claim of the Colonies*, it would have
been proper to mitigate the assertion and exercise of parliamentary sovereignty by caution and a capacity for empathy with fellow subjects across
the Atlantic. Thus, although he referred his reader to the pamphlet published anonymously by Thomas Whateley, Grenville's lieutenant, entitled
The Regulations Lately Made Concerning the Colonies, for comprehensive
exposition of the case for virtual representation, a claim that the colonists
were represented in the same way as were British non-voters and urban
centres which returned no MPs to Parliament, he was also careful to signal
his disagreement on one point. The difference in the circumstances of the
colonists, he insisted, did not 'in the least affect the right of parliament,
or impeach its jurisdiction'. But it did offer 'strong reasons why the parliament, in the article of taxation, should be more tender in the exercise of its
jurisdiction over the subjects in the colonies, than over the non-electors in
Britain'. It was that 'the non-electors in Great Britain' were unlikely to be
taxed immoderately or unnecessarily by members of parliament who were
also the proprietors of land within the kingdom of Great Britain, because,
if the latter did so, they would, as land-owners, hurt their own interests.
By contrast, it might seem tempting to lighten the metropole's tax burden
by shifting it onto the colonies. It was important to observe, in this regard,
that any tax affecting non-voters in Great Britain would also affect electors,
and that the latter would thus act as the guardians of non-voters' interests.
Protection of this sort was denied the Americans.[14]

Three years later, in *The Present State of the Nation*, Knox sought again
to stress the need for moderation and balance, when he warned that 'the
friends of liberty and the constitution should be careful not to vest the
whole authority of the community in the House of Commons, by deem-

---

14   Knox, *Claim of the Colonies*, 16–17, 28–9. T. Whateley, *The Regulations Lately Made
     Concerning the Colonies and the Taxes Imposed upon Them, Considered* (London,
     1765), 100–14.

ing that house *alone* the representative of the people', for there would be a risk in 'the king and peers' being 'independent of the community'. And he advocated colonial representation at Westminster, not, as he was careful to emphasize, so that the House of Commons should thereby be entitled to tax the Americas, or 'make other laws to affect the lives or liberties of the subjects in the colonies', but so that, in view of 'the prodigious extent of the British dominions in America, the rapid increase of the people there, and the great value of their trade', 'more attention should be paid to their concerns, by the supreme legislature'.[15]

In the colonies, likewise, London was, in Knox's view, to blame for allowing poor constitutional arrangements to undermine its authority. Significantly, these appeared poor to Knox in proportion as they upset the balance of power there also. As early as 1763, he had cast the faulty imperial relationship in terms that emphasized excessive demands on both sides. 'The House of Commons', he wrote, 'has resolved in the Case of Jamaica that the Colonys [*sic*] have no Constitution, but that the mode of Government in each of them depends upon the good pleasure of the King, as expressed in his Commission, and Instructions to his Governor'.[16] On the other side, the colonists had sought to enjoy 'a greater measure of Liberty' than that enjoyed by the people of England – a tendency, Knox argued, encouraged by the existence of royal colonies alongside charter or proprietary colonies, which served as benchmarks of colonial freedom. The result had been a battle of wills in which colonial governors had been led to grant fatal concessions, which were injurious to the royal prerogative, not only through their sheer accumulation over time, but also through their being claimed at a later stage by other colonies than the initial beneficiary.[17]

---

15   W. Knox, *The Present State of the Nation: Particularly with respect to its trade, finances, &c. &c. addressed to the King and both Houses of Parliament* (London, 1768), 39–40.
16   This was a reference to the passing of resolutions by the House of Commons in May 1757, in which Jamaican claims to legislative autonomy were met by a firm reassertion of the crown's right to withhold assent to colonial bills that might affect the prerogative or imperial trade. The resolutions drew attention to the fact that the governor was for this reason instructed to see that a clause should be inserted in colonial legislation, which suspended execution until the crown's pleasure should be known.
17   Knox, 'Hints', 117.

In addition, confusion had resulted in abuse on both sides. Since the commission and the instructions alike failed to declare whether the governor's council was to be regarded as a branch of the colonial legislature or merely as the governor's privy council, contests had been rife over powers of legislation. And as governors misused the power of suspension of council members, and colonial assemblies resisted what they saw as encroachments by the councils, royal power had become at once a source of ill-treatment and an object of derision.[18] The metropole and its officers in the colonies, in other words, had shown themselves at once presumptuous and weak.

Knox later expanded on this argument in his 'Considerations on the great Question, what is to be done with America?', which seem to have been written for ministers sometime between the appointment of the Carlisle Peace Commission in the spring of 1778 and mid-1779. What had begun, a dozen years or so before, as a diagnosis, seemed to be confirmed by experience. When one considered besides that, in the absence of any declaration by the crown of the laws of England, passed before the colonies existed, which were to be of force overseas, colonial assemblies had assumed 'the authority of deciding which of those Acts should be of force and which not, and by an Act of their own declared Acts of Parliament binding or useless as they judged proper', it was hardly likely, Knox now concluded, that the colonists 'should readily acquiesce in the claim of absolute uncontrollable Jurisdiction all at once set up by Parliament, and that, not for the benefit of the Colonies, but for burthening them'. Rather, it was to be expected that 'they should embrace the alternative of renouncing all Connection with Great Britain in preference to a submission which left them neither Rights nor Property'.[19]

In short, the problem of Empire was that it failed to guarantee the colonists a degree of security comparable to that provided for Britons at home by the constitution. The Empire was divided against itself. It was not British throughout.

---

18   Ibid.119–20. See also Knox, *Extra-Official State Papers*, Vol. II, 21.
19   Greene, 'William Knox's Explanation', 300–5. Spector (*The American Department*, 148) believed the 'Considerations' to have been prepared between 1776 and 1778, and probably in the latter year.

Ireland

Knox was aware that little could be done to correct this until an opening presented itself for implementing a full programme of reform. Only a major crisis would make change on the necessary scale possible – an outlook which may also explain in part why Knox was so intent, and for so long, on pursuing the war in America. So, meanwhile, his imperial thinking turned to Ireland.

It is worth noting that his thoughts on the two imperial regions seem to have matured together. On the one hand, he detected in Ireland some at least of the defects that he had observed in the constitution of the Empire in America, and on the other, he found in Ireland a testing ground for the development and the implementation of his imperial vision. Did he not suggest, in his *Considerations on the State of Ireland*, composed in 1772, but only published six years later in order to quieten down patriot agitation, that he aimed to bring to the service of his 'parent country, and [of] the empire at large', 'the knowledge or influence' which his activities had enabled him to acquire?[20]

America had taught Knox that the most fundamental problem of Empire was size. 'His Majesties possessions in North America', he declared in 1763, 'are so many times more extensive than the Island of Great Britain, that if they were equally well inhabited, Great Britain could no longer maintain her dominion over them'. The easy availability in America of cheap and fertile land, which he would later perceive in political terms as a root cause of American egalitarianism, favoured demographic expansion in conditions of relative peace. It was necessary to check this through a policy of containment, for if the colonists moved further inland, they would be too far removed from the channels of British trade and would set up for themselves. They would thus ultimately become competitors, not only on their own markets, but on the whole American colonial market. If the metropolitan

---

20   W. Knox, *Considerations on the State of Ireland* (Dublin, 1778), v, vii, viii. The date of 1772 is given by Knox in *Extra-Official State Papers*, Vol. I, Part II, 4, Note (a).

and colonial economies were to remain instead complementary, under terms of exchange whereby the colonies raised bulky agricultural commodities and imported finished products, they must be confined to establishments on the sea coast and alongside river banks, from where trade might more easily be conducted and naval protection-cum-control exercised. This would also palliate the political risk that, if the colonies expanded westward, their dependence on Great Britain, too, would be jeopardized. To that end, firstly, Quebec was to be used to divide and rule British North America, so as to constitute there 'as much as possible a separate People, and without any great intercourse with the Old Colonys'. Secondly, the Indians were to be used as buffers to western expansion and a means of pressure on the seaboard colonies. This was to be achieved through their conversion to agriculture and land ownership, as well as to Protestantism. And thirdly, in order to ensure the stability of southern society as a complement to pressure against westward expansion by means of the Indians, black slaves should be made into Christians and British subjects fully 'within the purview of action by Parliament or the King's privy council'.[21]

---

21   Barrow, 'A project for Imperial Reform' 113–16. Knox was to return to the view of the Indians as a useful buffer in *Three Tracts Respecting the Conversion and Instruction of the Free Indians, and Negroe Slaves in the Colonies. Addressed to the Venerable Society for the Propagation of the Gospel in Foreign Parts* (London n.d [c.1768]), a series of short reports drawn up at the desire of Archbishop Secker, a member of the SPG (see William Knox, *A letter from W. K. Esq. to W. Wilberforce, Esq.* (London, 1790), 3). Indians, in law, were not British subjects, and Britain was for several years after 1763 unable to lay down a stable diplomatic framework for Anglo-Indian relations in North America. The Quebec Act of 1774 was in part intended to remedy this failure by making expansion beyond the boundary of a much extended Quebec subject to sanction by the crown, so that the Indians could be placed under the King's protection without being made subjects. See D. V. Jones, *License for Empire. Colonialism by Treaty in Early America* (Chicago and London: University of Chicago Press, 1982), 3, 7, 14, 58, as well as chapter 4, especially 75–92; and G. Evans Dowd, *War under Heaven: Pontiac, the Indian Nations, & the British Empire* (Baltimore & London: Johns Hopkins University Press, 2002), ch. 6, 174–212. As under-secretary in the American Department, Knox was to manage Indian affairs from 1776 (Bellot, 'William Knox' 152–4). As regards black slaves, Knox may well have had in mind the comparative quiescence of the Caribbean plantation colonies, where the presence of vast numbers of slaves set a limit to settlers' restlessness vis-à-vis London.

The relevance of this American lesson to Ireland was self-evident to Knox. If only she was given a proper stake in the Empire, the island could provide a counterweight to American expansion, as well as political support nearer home in the pursuit of this policy. As in the case of the American colonies, this could be achieved through a reworking of her constitution and an opening up of trade. Ireland, on the other side of the Atlantic Ocean, could be both another America for prosperity, and also another Quebec for strategic value. In his *Considerations on the State of Ireland*, Knox emphasized only the former. But, set within the broader context of his already abundant writings, the latter was also clearly intended.

Ireland's progress, wrote Knox, compared unfavourably with that of the North American colonies. 'In a little more than a century', the latter had overtaken the former in terms of shipping, trade, credit and the general welfare of the population, despite labouring 'under more restraints from English laws than Ireland did, with a soil much less fertile, and a climate neither so temperate or salutary'.[22] The change, Knox argued, was wholly owing to separation from, or rather incomplete alignment with, England, starting with legal discrimination in the medieval period, proceeding through religious divisions from the time of the Reformation, and culminating from the Restoration in the exclusion of Ireland from the benefits of English and colonial trade.[23]

Knox drew from this assessment of the discrepancy between Ireland and British America conclusions which had implications far beyond Irish politics in the years of patriot agitation. First, it was wrong to blame the English government for excluding the natives 'from the common rights of subjects, and even of men'. The real culprits, upon whom were 'to be charged all the misery, wretchedness, and destructions that have befallen us', were Irishmen, 'but more especially our Irish rulers'. Secondly, their chosen instrument, and thus the source of all evil, had been the Irish parliament. The Irish legislature had been used since the reign of Henry V to deprive the native Irish, and later the Catholics, of the benefits of English laws.[24]

---

22   Knox, *Considerations*, viii–ix.
23   Ibid. 9–21, 27–38, 55–6.
24   Ibid. 38–45.

Lastly, therefore, the alternatives now facing Irishmen if they wished to restore the union were legislative union or 'other means'.[25]

What these 'other means' were to have been, is suggested, again, by considering two proposals earlier made by Knox, probably bearing in mind the lessons for him of colonial America. The first of these was a rebalancing of the Irish constitution. One of Knox's first suggestions regarding Ireland, after he had entered into a political career, had been for a reform of the Irish parliament. Because the King's representative only resided in the country while parliament was sitting, the executive branch of government was, he claimed, in effect committed 'to the leaders in the House of Commons'. This imbalance was 'the source of all the mal-administration in that kingdom'. Short of constant residence, changes should therefore tend to 'the exaltation of the Peers', and 'the protection of the lower people' by means of a limit to the duration of parliaments (Irish MPs were at the time elected for life) in order to 'compel their representatives to pay attention to their interests'. Knox advised a septennial bill on the English model.[26] Of particular relevance here to the interplay of Empire and Britishness is the fact that Knox was actuated, in making this recommendation, by his frustration with Irish divisions and what he saw as the resulting parochialism of Irish politics. With some constitutional adjustments, local politics might be framed within, even harnessed to, an imperial perspective and agenda.

The second proposal which Knox had previously made to tighten the bonds between Ireland and Britain was almost exactly contemporary with the first. It was a liberalisation of Irish trade. In *The Present State of the Nation* (1768), Knox sought to provide Britain's political rulers with a detailed outline of an integrated, world-wide, financial and commercial system. He argued that, in return for bearing a fair share of expenses made in the interest of the whole Empire, the country's dependencies should be

---

25   Ibid. 59.
26   Knox, *Extra-Official State Papers*, Vol. I, Part II, App. I, 1–9, memorandum presented in 1767 to Lord Frederick Campbell when he was appointed Chief Secretary to Lord Townshend, Lord Lieutenant of Ireland.

able to expect specific benefits from their connection with Great Britain. For some of the American colonies, this was to include representation at Westminster. For Ireland, it was to be the removal of the restrictions on the export of coarse woollen manufactures which had been imposed in the latter years of the seventeenth century, and the opening up of Britain's colonial trade – 'not an entire and compleat union of the two kingdoms, but a community of interests'.[27] This he secured in large measure and by stages between 1776 and 1778, obtaining in the latter year a declaration by act of parliament that Irish ships were to be deemed British in all respects whatever. His declared hope was that 'a gentle and mutually agreeable commercial band [would] be added to the other ligaments which tye, and, I hope, will forever bind, the two islands together'.[28] And here, too, beyond his native island, he really looked to the Empire as a whole. His object was

> to increase the magnitude of the head to a nearer proportion with the vast body, by connecting Ireland with Great Britain in the trade with the Colonies, and taking her weight out of the scale of the dependencies, and throwing it into that of Great Britain, by giving her the same interest with Great Britain in continuing the Colonies dependent upon her...[29]

It is important to note in contrast that by 1792, Knox had clearly opted for legislative union, although this need not preclude intra-imperial trade liberalisation designed to foster the growth of the colonies in the interest of the metropole and its dependencies.[30] In *A Letter to the People of Ireland*,

---

27 Knox, *Present State*, 34. Richard Koebner comments that, in devising his *quid pro quo*, Knox is likely to have borrowed from an earlier plan by Malachy Postlethwayt (*Britain's Commercial Interest Explained and Improved*, London, 1757). See R. Koebner, *Empire* (Cambridge: Cambridge University Press, 1961), 179.

28 Spector, *The American Department*, 146; Knox, *Extra-Official State Papers*, Vol. I, Part I, 55 (quotation) and App. XV, 86–90; Part II, 4–9.

29 Knox, *Extra-Official State Papers*, Vol. II, 30.

30 On intra-imperial trade liberalisation, really mercantilism writ large, see *Extra-Official State Papers*, Part I, Vol. I, App. VII, 'Plans for improving the Correspondence between Great Britain, Ireland, and the several British Colonies in America, the West Indies, and the United States, and between each other', 21–49.

published in that year, he remonstrated with Irish Protestants that, rather than deny the right of the British Parliament to make laws for Ireland, they would buttress their claim to govern the Catholic majority 'by taking shelter again under that parental wing from which you so inconsiderately withdrew'.[31] This proposal is interesting in providing confirmation that Knox's idea was to create an Anglican bloc on the eastern side of the Atlantic, which would counterbalance the Dissident bloc that had been formed on its western side. The legislative union Knox advocated was thus not directed at Catholics. He wished, indeed, for such a measure to be accompanied by the lifting of restrictions on Irish Catholics.[32] Commercial and constitutional links were to prevail over, and against, religious animosities which had been one of the sources, not only of those divisions within Ireland (as previously across the Atlantic) that fostered a constricted vision of Britishness, but of the disunion between Ireland and Britain that now appeared so harmful equally to Britain, Ireland and the whole Empire.

Canada

By his own admission, Knox's perception of the divisiveness of the religious issue in Ireland had an impact on his estimation of Canada in a continental and an imperial context. That he was alert from an early date to the potential of formerly French Quebec as an instrument of colonial partition and containment is obvious from the hints he drafted at the time of the peace of Paris in 1763. But these make no explicit reference to Catholicism and, in those early stages of the British presence, rather evince understandable prudence in stating merely that it would be well for the new colony and the old ones to have as little as possible to do with one another. His interest in Quebec as a Catholic colony seems therefore to have been awakened by his mulling over Ireland in 1772. By 1774 and Knox's passionate defence of

31   Bellot, *William Knox*, 209. Irish legislative autonomy had been restored in 1782.
32   Ibid. 209.

the Quebec Act, there was an added symmetry in his thinking. Not only would Ireland, through its enlistment on the side of metropole and Empire, become another strategic asset, but Quebec, a Catholic outpost, was now seen as a latter-day Ireland – and one, importantly, in which the fact that the British connection was so recent made it possible to envisage, even test, radical measures. Catholics on either side of the Atlantic, provided they were admitted to the benefits of British liberty, would act as the vanguard of imperial defence. The tenor of the Act, which Knox and his fellow under-secretary had recommended late in 1773, shows as much.

The statute reversed the Royal Proclamation of 1763, which foresaw the introduction of elective assemblies, by vesting power firmly in the military governor and an appointive legislative council until the (mostly French) inhabitants were deemed ready for representative institutions. In addition, it recognised the right of Catholics in Quebec to the free exercise of their religion, subject to the king's supremacy over his imperial dominions. The Test Act requiring communion in the Church of England was waived in order to allow them to serve on the governor's executive and legislative councils. Finally, the Act guaranteed the extension of the colony south-wards to the Ohio River so as to include French-speaking settlements. All four innovations appeared to the Americans to the south of Quebec to partake of a policy of strengthening executive control at the expense of the freedom of Protestant subjects.

But, aside from its polemical tone, there also run through the pages of his pamphlet suggestions of Knox's hankering after a somewhat romanti-cized old feudal order, in which representative government was unknown and the populace was correspondingly loyal. Considering the French *Cana-diens* or *nouveaux sujets*, Knox warms to 'a hardy industrious race of men, equally skilled in the management of the plough, the fishing-net, and the musket', people who showed fondness for their home country and its reli-gion and who, when English laws were introduced by the Royal Proclama-tion of October 1763 and Roman Catholics were excluded from all public offices, petitioned meekly for 'the restoration of their former laws and customs'.[33] This old order was now giving way in the rest of British North

---

33   Knox, *Justice and Policy*, 7–8, 11–16.

America to a more fluid, commercial society, whose rebellious spirit was inspired by dissenting Protestantism and encouraged by the existence of democratically inclined representative assemblies.

The *Canadiens'* behaviour, Knox declared, mirrored that of Irish Catholics after the Glorious Revolution in being respectfully submissive to the crown, notwithstanding injustice. And it was the precedent of Ireland, Knox explained, which now justified the departure from the course foreshadowed in 1763.[34] Penal legislation directed against a population of not quite a million Irish Catholics, 'four-fifths of the whole', and debarring them, among other things, from the right to own, inherit or mortgage land, to bear arms, and to provide an education other than Protestant for their children, had been ineffective 'after the experience of almost a century' in shaking off either their faith or winning them over to English government. And so, if, notwithstanding the absence of a rebellious spirit,

> severity has so little served to attach these infatuated people to the *English* government and their fellow-subjects; what success may we hope for from the like methods in *Canada*, where the *Roman* catholic inhabitants are five hundred to one protestant, and those *Roman* Catholics ten years ago were subjects of France, and every man bearing arms against *England*; in possession too of a country situated three thousand miles from *Great-Britain*, and all access to it denied by nature to our fleets and armies for six months in every year[?]

Loyalty was the reward of a government which understood that religious toleration and the lifting of restrictions on property would fix Quebeckers' as well as Irishmen's affections in their native soil and in the enlightened authorities who made this possible. Minorca proved the point, which had been perfectly quiet ever since its cession by the treaty of Utrecht, notwithstanding two wars with Spain in the interim.[35] To have set up in Quebec an assembly from which Catholics were to be excluded, would have gone against this wise policy.[36]

---

34   Ibid. 19–26. Quotations at 23 and 26.
35   Ibid. 26–7.
36   Ibid. 32–3.

Knox, then, conceived of the relations between the metropole and its continental American colonies, and of the remedies of which they were capable, in more than strictly constitutional, or even administrative, terms. His vision encompassed both sides of the Atlantic and mobilized economics, politics and geostrategy. As the case of Quebec makes clear, by the mid-1770s at the latest, it also resorted to something we recognise as (perhaps rudimentary) sociology. Knox's advance down the path of sophistication is striking, and it is wholly owing to his inscription of Britishness on a transatlantic canvas. The process culminated during the war of American independence.

The American War: Knox's Call for Imperial Reform

Knox's remedy in 1763 to the sorry state of relations between the metropole and its continental American colonies was to have been the institution throughout the colonies of a single 'Mode of Government'. Parliament would revoke the charters, purchase the proprietaryships, and in this manner impose a uniform system, in which the hand of governors and their councils would be strengthened.[37] By the end of the decade, he also reasoned in terms of mutual guarantees. He thus intended in 1768 to include in *The Present State of the Nation* a plan which contemplated yielding the right of taxation by Parliament as long as the colonies contributed their quota to imperial defence, and only deleted it at Grenville's request. During a conference in 1770 at the American Department over the disturbed state of Massachusetts, he seems, in the same conciliatory spirit, to have opposed all remedial measures other than changes in the governor's council, causing a rift between Hillsborough and himself. Early in 1775, he was still prepared to do no more than resurrect his plan of 1768.[38] Of course, his Irish

---

37   Barrow, 'A Project for Imperial Reform', 118–19.
38   Spector, *The American Department*, 138–40.

and Canadian schemes must be fitted into this picture of moderation. Yet, the overall impression remains that what the Empire required was constitutional and commercial reform, and that the restive colonists were to be persuaded, by words, example or pressure, to amend their ways.

With the outbreak of war, however, Knox seems to have seized an opportunity to go further. It is hard to resist the impression that his analysis of Quebec led him to lay a great deal more emphasis on altering, no longer just the governance, but the social circumstances of colonial life that had produced first deadlock, and then conflict. In his apology for the Quebec Act he had ascribed the forbearance and loyalty of Catholics to the country's enviable combination of a centralised system of government, feudal tenure of the land, and the strong grip of the Roman Catholic Church on people's minds through religious seminaries. He now held that the root of constitutional imbalance in North America was to be found in the absence of a proper religious hierarchy and the easy availability of cheap land, which made for a wide diffusion of property and a relatively undifferentiated social system. Neither authority nor rank, as a result, could sway the public, which tended to strike out for themselves, both religiously and politically.[39] Altering colonial society, Knox hoped, would help recast the imperial relationship.

In his 'Considerations', he thus proposed widespread forfeiture and re-granting of the land under conditions prescribed by Parliament. In future, landholders were, on pain of confiscation, to subscribe a declaration of the supremacy of the king and parliament over the colonies. The purpose of this scheme was not merely to ensure loyalty, but also, by restraining land ownership, to promote the emergence of a colonial, land-holding aristocracy with a vested interest in the regime and social control over a large tenant class.

---

39   'Every Man', he wrote, 'being thus allowed to be his own Pope, he becomes disposed
      to wish to be his own King, and so great a latitude in the choice of a religious system
      naturally begets republican and independent ideas in politics' (See Greene, *William
      Knox's Explanation*, 303).

Similarly, the establishment of the Church of England in the colonies, by instituting a religious hierarchy, would help offset the spread of republicanism. Knox foresaw a system whereby clergymen would be appointed by the governor, paid by warrant from the crown out of a general fund raised through provincial taxation, and expected to take the same oath of allegiance as that required of landholders.[40]

Even more illuminating, perhaps, Knox conceived a policy of territorial partition, based on the substitution of eight provinces for the original thirteen colonies. Although he remained vague on the boundaries of these new units, Knox clearly thought that larger political entities would provide greater opportunities for gradation in rank, and thus combat the democratic egalitarianism which had done so much to undermine colonial government. There was in addition to be a return to the policy of containment of westward expansion through a restoration of the west to the Indians by Act of Parliament, complemented by representation of the colonies at Westminster.[41] About the same time, Knox also seems to have laid before Lord Germain a plan for dividing 'the eastern side of the Continent into three great Governments, a northern, a middle, and a southern one, and [putting] each upon the same footing with Ireland'.[42]

That Ireland, as seen through his own imperial prism, provided Knox with a model of loyalty and conformity to a metropolitan model of constitutional and social balance, is also clear from another project. In 1778, taking up an idea first vented three years earlier by Sir Francis Bernard, former governor of Massachusetts, Knox proposed to erect in Maine a Loyalist colony by the name of New Ireland. Modelled on that of East Florida, whose agent Knox had been, the constitution of the new province would consist at the outset of a governor and an appointive legislative council, but no assembly. Members of the legislative council were to hold their seats for life. Executive

---

40 Ibid. 151 For a similar plan regarding Nova Scotia while he was under-secretary, see copy of a letter of Knox to Pitt, 7 August 1787, in *Extra-Official State Papers*, Vol. I, Part I, App. V, 13–18.
41 Ibid. 149, 151.
42 See Knox, *Extra-Official State Papers*, Vol. I, 26–8. The date of this proposal is not clear.

councillors, complete with colonial aristocratic titles, were to compose a majority in the legislative council. Land grants were to be provided for all Loyalists who took an oath of allegiance to the king and parliament. The Church of England was to be the established church of the new colony. The plan could not be implemented, although ministers and the king himself had expressed support and steps were taken to establish the colony by early in 1781.[43] The idea of establishing a Loyalist colony persisted, however, and was eventually implemented to a different purpose when New Brunswick was carved out of Nova Scotia in 1784.[44] And in Nova Scotia itself, Knox again recommended the regulation of imperial trade, the establishment of the Church of England, and a policy of land grants.[45]

Conclusion

History has not been kind to Knox. He was without doubt inclined at critical times to rely too much, in charting his political course, on what he believed was the correct legal position. To that extent, he may reasonably be accused in retrospect of a lack of political judgement as well as a penchant for juristic righteousness. But his blind spots seem consistently to have been the result, not simply of his having to advise his political masters, but even more of his dedication, arguably as an Irishman of Anglo-Scottish descent, to Britishness as an imperial bond of brotherhood.

43   Spector, *The American Department.*, 144–6; Knox, *Extra-Official State Papers*, Vol. II, 60–1; Ibid. App. XX, 82; Note from Germain to Knox dated 7 August 1780 (showing support of Lord Germain for the New Ireland project), and App. XXI, 83, Note from Germain to Knox dated 11 August 1780 (showing the king's support).
44   See M. Gilroy, 'The Partition of Nova Scotia', *Canadian Historical Review* 14 (4) (December 1933), 375–91.
45   Knox, *Extra-Official State Papers*, Vol. II, App. XIV, 'New Establishments of the American Loyalists', 47–54. App. XV, 54–6, untitled, contemplated accommodating southern Loyalists in the Bahamas.

This, Knox made clear, was strongly underpinned by adhesion to the tenets of a balanced constitution and society. In parliament, as well as in society at large, the landed aristocracy could, indeed must, protect the legitimate interests of the people as well as the indispensable authority of the crown. Knox's stance, it has been well said, was 'neither arbitrary, nor authoritarian'.[46] Britishness was capable of, indeed required, modulation in the common interest of the metropole and the colonies. The subordination of the colonies to the will of Westminster and the interests of an Anglo-centric empire entailed an obligation in the sovereign imperial parliament to recognise their specificities and promote their welfare. Only when it seemed to Knox that colonial impatience threatened the essential order and unity of the Empire did he abandon a course of persuasion.

Remarkably, Knox's imperial perspective owed a great deal to a very personal combination of private and public ties to various parts of the transatlantic community which he sought to define, bolster and perpetuate. There was his emotional tie to his native Ireland, but also a realisation that the causes of Ireland and of the Empire as a whole might be served by the same policies. There were his offices and properties in America, to be sure, but also a perception of the deficiencies of colonial government there, which shaped a global understanding of the place which each part of the Empire might occupy in the global British community. There was an element of geostrategic cynicism, when Ireland, Quebec and, perhaps less overtly, Britain's West Indian islands emerged as counterweights to the so-called Thirteen Colonies. However, there was room also for religious toleration and liberalized trade in the interest of strengthening imperial ties.

Always one region helped shape Knox's understanding of the situation in another, and suggested to him the manner in which it might best be fitted into the Empire in the interest of the one and the other. The continental colonies of the late 1750s and early 1760s held lessons for Ireland, which in turn threw light on Quebec, and ultimately on what was needed to reform continental America and preserve the whole Empire. This learning process, this habit of comparing, while keeping the essentials of the metropolitan constitution in mind, were put in the service of a vision of Britishness as a shared, though inflected, identity.

46   Bellot, *William Knox*, 215.

ANGELA MCCARTHY

3 Scottishness and Britishness among New Zealand's Scots Since 1840[1]

Within Scottish historiography there is an overarching assumption of concentric loyalties for Scots in which 'a powerful sense of being Scottish has
gone hand-in-hand with a powerful sense of being British for centuries'.[2]
Not all, however, are convinced by such a broad claim. Richard Finlay, for
instance, has suggested that for eighteenth-century Scots, national and
regional identities were untouched by notions of Britishness.[3] Indeed,
the issue of dual allegiances is problematic on at least two fronts. Firstly,
the evidence for such an assumption is generally confined to the elites or
the public arena. What the ordinary Scot thought and felt, at a public
and private level, has yet to be assessed. Secondly, assessment based solely
on homeland perceptions by insiders and outsiders runs the risk of contamination. As David Fitzpatrick has indicated in his arresting study of
the Irish in Australia, monitoring the mentality of those outside Ireland
avoids 'much of the imbalance and distortion of home-bound assessments'.[4]
To establish a more considered view of identities, then, we should embrace
perspectives beyond the point of origin.

1   This paper is based on research that was funded by the British Academy (SG-40172)
     and the Faculty of Arts and Social Sciences, University of Hull. Much of the research
     was undertaken during my appointment as the 2005 J. D. Stout Fellow in New Zealand
     Studies at Victoria University of Wellington and I am grateful to the Stout Research
     Centre for awarding me this fellowship.
2   T. C. Smout, 'Perspectives on the Scottish Identity', *Scottish Affairs* 6 (1994), 112.
3   R. J. Finlay, 'Caledonia or North Britain? Scottish Identity in the Eighteenth Century',
     in D. Broun, R. J. Finlay, and M. Lynch, eds, *Image and Identity: The Making and
     Re-making of Scotland Through the Ages* (Edinburgh: John Donald, 1998), 151.
4   D. Fitzpatrick, '"That beloved country, that no place else resembles": Connotations
     of Irishness in Irish-Australian Letters, 1841–1915', *Irish Historical Studies* 27 (108)
     (1991), 326.

Even this approach, however, is prone to difficulties. In the New Zealand context, for instance, scholars have tended to merge the country's assorted ethnic elements under a broad 'Pakeha' (non-Maori) label while Scots have often been subsumed as British. In part, these categorisations are also a repercussion of an emphasis on elites. They are also a consequence of scholars adopting a modern-day bicultural vision of New Zealand's past societies which, as one scholar warns, 'systematically denies the complexity of the nineteenth and early twentieth century Pakeha culture'.[5] The complexity of this culture is, however, increasingly being illuminated and this chapter, in considering the representations of Scottishness and Britishness in New Zealand, is a modest contribution to that ongoing research agenda.

How, though, should ethnic identities be conceived? Many models have been developed citing key ingredients, with one useful formulation devised by Anthony D. Smith, containing six main aspects including a collective proper name; myth of common ancestry; shared historical memories; one or more elements of a common culture; association with specific homeland (attachments and associations rather than residence); and a sense of solidarity.[6] Such elements are certainly evident when exploring the Scots in New Zealand, but their applicability is generally dependent upon the type of source examined. Smith's model, for instance, appears to have largely been based on a public and associational definition of ethnic identity, rather than a private, individual one. Other conceptualisations of ethnic identities highlight the importance not simply of institutional attachment, but the personal sense of belonging held by individuals encompassing emotions, thoughts, and feelings. Furthermore, many approaches to ethnic identities typically focus on the representations of ethnic groups by others. To overcome such distortions, this chapter incorporates the representations of Scottishness and Britishness at individual and collective levels, as expressed by outsiders *and* insiders. What do the public and private representations of

---

5   D. H. Akenson, *Half the World from Home: Perspectives on the Irish in New Zealand, 1860–1950* (Wellington: Victoria University Press), 196.
6   A. D. Smith, *National Identity* (London: Penguin, 1991), 21.

Scots reveal about their ethnic identities in New Zealand? How pervasive was a sense of being a Scot, a Brit, a Highlander, or a native of particular localities? Drawing on assorted sources encompassing shipboard journals, personal letters, ethnic presses, poetry, and lunatic asylum records, this chapter argues that it was the varied Scottish ethnic identities rather than an overarching Britishness which was the dominant identity articulated in connection with migrants from Scotland in New Zealand and that Britishness, when expressed, was limited to specific sources and situations.

Shipboard Journals

In his formulation of ethnicity, Don Handelman identifies the ethnic category as the broadest level of identification in which ethnic groups are perceived as different and defined by intermittent rather than regular contact.[7] For Scots, these broad labels encompassed being termed a 'Scot' or 'Scotch' as well as differences at a regional level such as their identities as 'Highlander', 'Lowlander', and 'Islander'. The assessment of these designations arose in two main ways: professing one's own sense of being Scottish or attesting to another's Scottishness. The differences discerned could be based on practices viewed as Scottish or apparent characteristics attributed to Scots. Such reports are particularly prolific in shipboard journals and personal letters where writers mentioned encounters with other Scots. According to Shetlander Thomas Pole Hughson during his voyage in 1879, 'the most of us scotchmen got into a circle and joining hands we sang auld lang sine. I may also add that they were a good many of us Scotties'.[8] Scots were also differentiated, and distinguished themselves, as distinct on board ship through their language, dress, eating habits, music, customs, and

7   D. Handelman, 'The Organization of Ethnicity', *Ethnic Groups*, 1 (1977), 189–94.
8   Shipboard journal of T. P. Hughson, 31 December 1879, 10, Alexander Turnbull Library [ATL], MS-Papers-4182.

religious practices.[9] The latter, in particular, was often expressed in contrast with the Episcopalian services conducted at sea. As William Runciman explained in 1881, 'The first Lords Day the Captain had no services but one of the passengers, a r. Gregory held the English Service himself, in the 3rd. Cabin with what passengers were there but it was a very formal and uninteresting affair to any of us scotch folks. At night Mr. Whytock held his meeting and it was enjoyed by all of us'.[10] While further comparative work is required, it appears that Scots, in their personal testimonies, were more likely than their Irish or English counterparts to articulate an overarching national identity. It also appears, at least from the New Zealand evidence, that John MacKenzie's claim that an 'overall conception of Scotland had been created by the later nineteenth century' can be re-dated to an earlier time period.[11]

Official Immigration Reports

Official reports similarly referred broadly to the 'Scots' or 'Scotch', and equated these categories with assorted national characteristics. Interestingly, despite being official accounts, many of the emigration agents were Scottish including the Reverend Peter Barclay who claimed, 'It is well known the Scotch people are cautious, and do not readily take in a new thing'.[12]

---

9   This mirrors the findings of Scots at sea bound for Australia. See M. Prentis, 'Haggis on the High Seas: Shipboard Experiences of Scottish Emigrants to Australia, 1821–1897', *Australian Historical Studies* 36 (124) (2004), 294–311.

10   Shipboard journal of William Runciman, 1881, 5, ATL, MS-Papers-1414.

11   This summation is based on A. McCarthy, *Representations of Scottishness and Irishness in New Zealand Since 1840* (Manchester: Manchester University Press, in press); J. M. MacKenzie, 'Empire and National Identities: The Case of Scotland', *Transactions of the Royal Historical Society*, 6th series, vol. 8 (1998), 225.

12   Enclosure 3 in No. 1, *Appendices to the Journals of the House of Representatives [AJHR]*, 1872, D-No.1C, 6.

This alleged equation of Scots with prudence was also levied by agents in Scotland acting for competing destinations.[13] While such summations may be accurate, an emphasis on Scottish caution is likely to be prevalent in official emigration reports as an explanation as to why agents sometimes failed to attract participation in various schemes of emigration.

Coexisting with an overarching identity of being Scots or Scotch was acknowledgment of varied Scottish geographical identities. Once again, official accounts equated various regions with specific stereotyped attributes. The most frequently discussed divisions related to Highlanders, Lowlanders, and Islanders. Immigration officials in 1872, for instance, alleged that 'The Highlanders are well known to be good labourers and farm servants: the Islanders excel as fishermen, sailors, and crofters'.[14] Less readily explored in historiographical studies are divisions along east and west axes such as Barclay's claim that 'On the West Coast the people are intensely clannish, and, as a rule fond of their church'.[15] The divide between west and east was also categorized in the following way: 'Things are entirely different in almost every respect in the West Highlands and Islands from what they are in Aberdeenshire. There is a different race, a different language, and labour on an entirely different footing'.[16]

Indeed, one group that received sustained comment, in part because of attempts to attract a group settlement to New Zealand, were Shetlanders: 'It must be remembered that a Shetlander, unless he has been out of his native islands, has never seen a tree, scarcely a plough, that he is very ignorant'. Yet, paradoxically, it was observed, 'The charge of ignorance cannot be laid against the Shetlanders, nor of unwillingness to go from home, since as sailors they visit every part of the world'. They were also considered 'very

13   'The Scotch are proverbially cautious', wrote W. G. Stuart, the sub-agent for Canada. See M. Harper, 'Enticing the Emigrant: Canadian Agents in Ireland and Scotland, c. 1870–c.1920', *Scottish Historical Review* 83 (1) (2004), 46.

14   Enclosure 2 in No. 42, *AJHR*, 1872, D-No.1, 49.

15   Revd. P. Barclay to Dr Featherston, Enclosure 3 in No. 1, *AJHR*, 1872, D-No. 1.

16   Revd. P. Barclay to Dr Featherston, 10 January 1873, Enclosure 3 in No. 36, *AJHR*, 1873, D-2, 38.

clever and docile and apt to learn'.[17] Furthermore, Shetlanders were also regarded as 'Scandinavian Scotch, without much of the Celtic element, and that they speak English and not Gaelic'.[18] More local connections were also fundamental in defining Scots but were more often discussed at the level of an ethnic network rather than an ethnic category. These overarching classifications reflect the long history of viewing Scots as a people apart and again fail to demonstrate a pervading sense of Britishness.[19]

Personal Letters

Within the wider historiography, scholars have testified to the importance of informal and formal ethnic networks for the Scots.[20] The more informal character of such social networks equates to the second part of Handelman's formulation in which such connections are characterised by regular interaction possessing an ethnic flavour.[21] Unfortunately, major studies of the Scots in New Zealand, as well as elsewhere, have not yet included sustained analysis of migrant letters, a particularly illuminating source which has demonstrated the extent and character of Irish social networks in New Zealand.[22] Indeed, only a few extant published chapters utilise the

17   Revd. C. S. Ogg to A. F. Halcombe, 24 January 1873, Enclosure 1 in No. 49, *AJHR*, 1873, D-1, 43.
18   Enclosure 3 in No.4, *AJHR*, 1871, D-No.1A, 8. For Shetlanders in New Zealand see S. and G. Butterworth, *Chips off the Auld Rock: Shetlanders in New Zealand* (Wellington: Shetland Society of Wellington, 1997).
19   M. G. H. Pittock, *Celtic Identity and the British Image* (Manchester and New York: Manchester University Press, 1999).
20   See, for instance, A. McCarthy, ed., *A Global Clan: Scottish Migrant Networks and Identities since the Eighteenth Century* (London: Tauris Academic Studies, 2006), and the articles in *Immigrants and Minorities* 23 (2) and (3) (2005).
21   Handelman, 'The Organization of Ethnicity', 195.
22   A. McCarthy, *Irish Migrants in New Zealand, 1840–1937: 'The Desired Haven'* (Woodbridge: Boydell Press, 2005). Letters have, however, been used in conjunction

personal correspondence of Scottish migrants in New Zealand.[23] Nor do we yet have analyses of the probates of Scottish migrants, a source that has been fruitfully mined in connection with the Irish.[24] It is therefore difficult to ascertain to what extent Scots frequently mentioned acquaintances or other contacts in relation to specific places at home and how their personal networks facilitated access to marriage partners, lodging, and work. Were they as clannish as some contemporary commentators believed or were networks other than ethnic ones more important?

Some insights are available from a cursory consultation of the personal testimonies of Scots which demonstrate the importance of providing lodging, work, and fellowship for their fellow ethnics. In this way, broad county identifiers were often highlighted. According to Ebenezer Hay of Canterbury in 1858, 'I have Two men David McMillin from Ayrshire at 60£ Per anun David McGregor from Pairthshire 45£ a year and in Barbras place Ann Boag from Pairthshire 35£ a year'.[25] More intimate linkages prompted Alexander Campbell's testimony in 1863 from Matakana, north of Auckland, of a 'little reunion of Saltcoats friends and we had many a talk

---

with oral sources to examine alternative aspects of Scottish migration in New Zealand. See, for instance, A. McCarthy, 'Personal Letters, Oral Testimony, and Scottish Migration to New Zealand in the 1950s: The Case of Lorna Carter', *Immigrants and Minorities* 23 (1) (2005), 59–79; and A. McCarthy, '"For Spirit and Adventure": Personal Accounts of Scottish Migration to New Zealand, 1921–1961', in T. Brooking and J. Coleman, eds, *The Heather and the Fern: Scottish Migration and New Zealand Settlement* (Dunedin: University of Otago Press, 2003), 117–32.

23   T. Brooking, 'Weaving the Tartan into the Flax: Networks, Identities, and Scottish Migration to Nineteenth-Century Otago, New Zealand', in McCarthy, ed., *A Global Clan*, 183–202; T. Bueltmann, '"Where the Measureless Ocean Between us will Roar" Scottish Emigration to New Zealand, Personal Correspondence and Epistolary Practices, c.1850–1920', *Immigrants and Minorities* 26 (3) (2008), 242–65; McCarthy, 'Personal Letters, Oral Testimony, and Scottish Migration' and '"For Spirit and Adventure"'.

24   See, for example, L Fraser, *To Tara Via Holyhead: Irish Catholic Immigrants in Nineteenth-Century Christchurch* (Auckland: Auckland University Press, 1997).

25   Ebenezer Hay (Annandale, Pigeon Bay) to family (Scotland), 24 July 1858, Canterbury Museum, ARC 1990.8.

over old times about Saltcoats'.[26] Initial fledgling acquaintances based on ethnicity rather than existing kith and kin connections could also evolve into useful alliances including the assistance provided to Andrew Roy by the Grays who hailed originally from Uddingston near Glasgow: 'I have only one in the country that I know well that is the man Mr Gray & Mrs Gray that came out with me. They were very kind when I was in Invercargill last. They told me when I came back again not to go to a boarding house but come to their house and make it my home when in town which was very kind'.[27] As evident from these examples, 'neither the practice of ethnic culture nor participation in ethnic organizations was essential to being and feeling ethnic'.[28] Rather, an ethnic affinity was helpful in overcoming the myriad obstacles associated with relocation abroad.

Comments from those outside the Scottish ethnic group certainly convey recognition of a strong networking element to Scottish migration and settlement throughout New Zealand. According to Irishman John Birmingham in Otago in 1870, 'Well wages is coming down very fast for their [*sic*] is a constant flow of Immigration to New Zeland all poor Miserable Scotch coming out to their Scotch friends so that no Irish need apply'.[29] Rather less scornfully, an Irish Catholic nun reported from Auckland in 1872 on the influence of Rothesay-born Thomas Bannatyne Gillies: 'this is a very Protestant place, the present superintend is Scotch. He has got out a muster of his country men & women so Scotland stands very high in Auckland'.[30]

---

26   Alexander Campbell (Matakana) to James Campbell (Saltcoats), 23 March 1863, Auckland Museum Library, MS 50, 96–7.

27   Andrew Roy (Maorie Point, Shotover, Otago) to his parents (Glendevon), 10 Jan 1864, Otago Settlers Museum, DC-0683.

28   H. J. Gans, 'Symbolic Ethnicity: The Future of Ethnic groups and Cultures in America', *Ethnic and Racial Studies* 2 (1) (1979), 14.

29   John Birmingham (Otago) to his parents Patrick and Mary Birmingham (Kildare), 22 November 1870, National Library of Ireland, Ms 17801. I am grateful to David Fitzpatrick for providing me with a transcript of this letter.

30   Sister Mary Cecilia to Mother M. Catherine, 17 January 1872, Auckland Catholic Diocese Archives, CRO 6–2/1.

While these fleeting examples demonstrate the existence and operation of ethnic networks, we still require further investigation into the extent of such contacts. We also require research into those Scots who may have desired ethnic or other networks but found none. Even those with family in the colony suffered in this respect. A young man recently arrived in the 1890s from Stirlingshire was admitted to the lunatic asylum at Dunedin which his half-cousin attributed to 'Melancoly. Being strange in a foreign country. Not knowing where to find a friend'.[31] Another sibling of a migrant from Greenock also admitted to the asylum reported, 'I may mention that after my sister's arrival in the colony she lived with me for about ten months – and she became insane but recovered in about three months. I lived in a very solitary place at that time and I thought the solitude coupled with the life on board ship might be the cause'.[32] Ongoing analysis of lunatic asylum records, in conjunction with other sources, offers potentially enlightening information relating to robust and absent ethnic ties.

Ethnic Associations

Turning now to the third element of Handelman's typology, the ethnic association is conceived of as members pursuing group goals in an agreed location.[33] Recent musings on these ethnic associations suggest that 'the collective identities of arrivals were heightened not only by contrast to those of the native population but also by contrast to those of other newcomers'.[34] Evident from most examples is that such ethnic societies, irrespective

---

31   Seacliff Hospital – Medical Casebook (1894–5), Archives New Zealand Dunedin Regional Office, DAHI/D264/19956/46, case 2801.
32   Dunedin Lunatic Asylum and Seacliff Hospital – Medical Casebook (1863–c.1920), Archives New Zealand Dunedin Regional Office, DAHI/D265/19556/1, folio 644.
33   Handelman, 'The Organization of Ethnicity', 196–7.
34   J. C. Moya, 'Immigrants and Associations: A Global and Historical Perspective', *Journal of Ethnic and Migration Studies* 31 (5) (2005), 839.

of whether they took national, regional, or local Scottish identifiers, also connected to the local areas in which migrants settled. As such we find the Gisborne Scottish and Caledonian Society, expressions of the old and new lands linked. What objectives, though, characterised Scottish associational culture in New Zealand? Throughout the length and breadth of New Zealand, cultural endeavours characterised Scottish associations. To the far south, the Caledonian Society of Otago, established in 1862, focused on benevolence, education, literature, customs, and accomplishments.[35] Such aims continued into the twentieth century as evident through investigation of other district associations like the Gisborne Scottish and Caledonian Society who aimed to: foster national sentiment; promote good fellowship among the Scottish community; encourage the study of Scottish music, literature, and dancing; and endeavour to give information to newly arrived Scots.[36] As for the Dannevirke Highland Society, its monthly socials 'are of a most social character and thoroughly Scotch, and are the means of keeping up the old Scotch element amongst Scotch residents and their families'.[37] Meanwhile, the Wellington Scots Club, which formed in 1926, met monthly and 'The programmes submitted are all of Scots character. The dances are the real thing, and, as membership is confined to those of Scots birth and descent (and this is insisted upon), the Club is "Scots" in every sense of the word'.[38] Even those Scottish associations formed later in the twentieth century took a cultural slant such as the Pahiatua and District Scottish Society. Incorporated in 1958 the Society sought the following: cultivation and knowledge of the records and traditions of the history of

35   Caledonian Society of Otago, 56th Annual Report, 15 November 1918, Hocken Collections, MS-1045/6.
36   'Constitution and Rules' (1925), Gisborne Scottish and Caledonian Society Incorporated, Archives New Zealand Auckland Regional Office, BANF/5706/Box 6/1925/4.
37   The New Zealand Scot, 2 (3) (20 January 1914), 19. Copies of the Scottish ethnic press are lodged at ATL, Serials Collection, Per NZ SCO, The Auckland War Memorial Museum Library, and Hocken Collections.
38   The N. Z. Scotsman 1 (8) (15 October 1927).

Scotland; the promotion of Scottish music, literature, and songs; and the encouragement of Scottish dancing and wearing of the Highland dress.[39]

Scottish language societies adopted similar aims although there was a greater focus on the regional dimension. This was especially the case with the linkage of the Gaelic language with Highlanders. The Gaelic Society of New Zealand, for instance, sought with its formation in 1881 'to foster and perpetuate the Gaelic Language, to encourage the cultivation of Gaelic literature and music, to establish branch societies throughout the colony of New Zealand, to generally take cognisance of all matters which may be considered of special interest to Highlanders'.[40] Wellington's Gaelic Society echoed these aims, providing lectures on Highland themes such as traits in the Highland character, Highland poets, and Highland regiments. Such was its focus on its Highland character that a query in 1949 concerning widening its membership criteria beyond Highlanders and those of Highland descent was answered, 'the club would be in danger of losing its identity'.[41]

A critical aim of these societies was to nourish the Gaelic language among the younger generation. As the Caledonian Society of Otago observed in the early 1900s, 'There were many Highlanders who could speak the language freely, but the young people had no opportunity of learning it'.[42] The President of Wellington's Gaelic Society also emphasised in 1930 'the importance of instructing the children in the language and traditions of their fathers'.[43] The Scots language, meanwhile, was important in other societies including Clan Mackay which established a Jessie

---

39   'Rules of the Society', 1, Pahiatua and Districts Scottish Society, Inc, Archives New Zealand Wellington Regional Office, CO-W/2/12/598.

40   E. Entwistle, *History of the Gaelic Society of New Zealand, 1881–1981* (Dunedin, 1981), 13.

41   20 May 1949, Comunn Gaidhealach Wellington Minute Books, ATL, MSX-3055–3061/4.

42   Caledonian Society's Social, c.1904, 140, Caledonian Society Minute Book, Hocken Collections, MS-1045/8.

43   Minutes, 10 May 1930, 8, Comunn Gaidhealach Wellington Minute Books, ATL, MSX-3055–3061/1.

Mackay cup in order to perpetuate Jessie's memory as a writer of poetry in Scots. This generated some concern as to the correct pronunciation of words in her poems. In response to those who adopted the Scots form of words written in English, the committee decided that there should be strict adherence to the author's version.[44] By 1948, 'Owing to the incapacity of the judges in the matter of the Scots dialect, her best poems had been avoided in recent years'.[45]

While clan associations also echoed elements of other Scottish ethnic associations, they differed by having a strong leaning towards genealogical aspects. This is evident from the proposed constitution of the Shetland Society which in 1995 sought fellowship with people interested in Shetland in order to foster interest in the traditions and activities of the Shetland past, and promote interest in family history and ancestry.[46]

The Ethnic Press

In Handelman's formulation the final manifestation of ethnicity is that of the ethnic community in which an 'ethnic identity is attributed generally to all persons who reside within the territory'.[47] Scholarly focus on geographical boundaries has resulted in studies of Scottish ethnic communities in New Zealand and elsewhere.[48] More recent conceptualisations of community, however, perceive it along the lines of Benedict Anderson's 'imagined

44   Minutes, 3 September 1947, 137, Clan MacKay Society of New Zealand Minute Book, Hocken Collections, Misc-MS-1433.
45   Minutes, 12 February 1948, 143, in Ibid.
46   Shetland Society, Hocken Collections, 97–095-1.
47   Handelman, 'The Organization of Ethnicity', 198.
48   See, for instance, M. Molloy, *Those Who Speak to the Heart: The Nova Scotian Scots of Waipu, 1854–1920* (Palmerston North: Dunmore Press, 1991); Marianne McLean, *The People of Glengarry: Highlanders in Transition, 1745–1820* (Montreal and Kingston: McGill-Queen's University Press, 1991).

community' which stretches beyond territorial borders, fixed or fluid.[49] In other words, 'Locality is no longer the only or even the primary vehicle for sustaining community'.[50] Such communities are generally founded on shared cultural outlooks and values rather than physical proximity. Key in this formulation is that neither participation in nor continuity of such communities is guaranteed.[51] An ethnic community also differs from an ethnic association by being a vehicle for contemplating cultural difference rather than being an institutional practice.[52] The Scottish ethnic press is an important source in this regard.

The first issue of *The New Zealand Scot* appeared in November 1912. According to its banner the periodical aimed "To unify and inspire Scotch patriotism in New Zealand, and to voice the doings of Scottish, Highland, Gaelic and Caledonian Societies throughout the Dominion'. In later incarnations, the periodical was manifested as *The Scottish New Zealander* (1925–6) and finally as *The N. Z. Scotsman* (1927–33). Indeed, in its various forms the periodical was a crucial vehicle for disseminating news and historical memories, supplying monthly reports from Scottish societies around the country, and reproducing photographs from a number of associational gatherings. In many respects the periodical mirrored the aims of *The South African Scot* which first appeared in 1905 and both contained similar contents including articles on famous Scots, obituaries, news and gossip.[53] In what ways, though, did these Scottish periodicals in New Zealand express cultural difference and consciousness?

49 B. Anderson, *Imagined Communities: Reflections on the Origin and Spread of Nationalism* (London: Verso, 1983).

50 P. Kennedy and V. Roudometof, 'Transnationalism in a Global Age', in P. Kennedy and V. Roudometof, eds, *Communities Across Borders: New Immigrants and Transnational Cultures* (London and New York: Routledge, 2002), 13.

51 Ibid. 8.

52 V. Amit citing G. Baumann in 'Reconceptualizing Community', in V. Amit, ed., *Realizing Community: Concepts, Social Relationships, and Sentiments* (London and New York: Routledge, 2002), 5.

53 J. M. MacKenzie with N. R. Dalziel, *The Scots in South Africa: Ethnicity, Identity, Gender and Race, 1772–1914* (Manchester: Manchester University Press, 2007), 249.

It is impossible to convey the full extent of Scottishness articulated in the journals though the most obvious manifestation was through symbolic applications. In this regard, tartan, pipes, and heather featured regularly, in articles and in photographs. As one statement from 1928 put it, 'There are three things which every Scot holds sacred, and for which his soul longs when he is exiled in distant lands – the bagpipes, the heather, and the tartan'; of these the 'cloth of the clans remains the dearest of all'. The periodicals also engaged with characteristics that were levied at Scots including the suggestion of Scottish parsimoniousness: 'the reason why the Scot laughs at any joke concerning Scot meanness – *he knows it is only a joke!*'[54] The periodical was furthermore replete with other items such as book reviews, recipes, and jokes, all of which had a Scottish focus. A particularly humorous example of the latter concerned the joke about an Englishman who proudly claimed he was born English, reared English, and would die English. The Scots retort was 'Hae ye nae ambition?'[55]

A further important element of the ethnic press which sets it apart from the manifestations of Scottishness evident in other sources, but which exemplifies a broad Scottish identity, is the engagement with and depiction of Scottish history. In part this was to ensure continuing identification with Scotland among the multigenerational descent group. As one report in 1928 put it, 'We must see to it that our children are embued with the spirit of Scotland; with a love of Scots history, of Scots song and story, of Scots literature and tradition, and of the Scots vernacular.'[56] To achieve this it was felt that the best method was to connect history with individuals; 'the history of the king is the history of the nation.'[57] Indeed, despite some articles on the Clearances, most features focused on individuals including Mary Queen of Scots, Flora Macdonald, William Wallace, David Livingstone, and Robert Burns. The problem with the dissemination of Scotland's history and other subjects in the periodicals, however,

---

54   *The N. Z. Scotsman*, 1 (2) (7 April 1927), 54.
55   *The N. Z. Scotsman*, 4 (45) (15 December 1930), 267.
56   *The N. Z. Scotsman*, 2 (14) (15 April 1928), 56.
57   *The Scottish New Zealander*, 4 (7) (26 July 1926), 1.

concerned its accuracy. As one report put it, the speeches of leading Scots in New Zealand about 'Scots history and Scots literature was wonderful and weird'. To demonstrate their point the critic noted that the St Andrew's Cross had been called the 'blue cross of Scotland' and the Rampant Lion the National flag of Scotland. Such incidents, it was heatedly claimed, 'are a reproach to Scotsmen and an insult to Scotland'.[58]

A further element which fits a broader interpretation of Handelman's ethnic community focus was the transnational dimension of the periodicals. This was demonstrated by reports on the activities of Scottish associations and individuals around the world. Such reports included the activities of Scots in London and the visit to Scotland of Scottish-American clans.[59]

Britishness

By contrast with varied expressions of Scottishness found in diverse sources, a sense of Britishness was only occasionally conveyed. When it did feature, it tended to appear in the ethnic press and in the records of Scottish societies, and generally only in relation to war, royalty, or discussions of the British Empire. As the Taranaki Provincial Scottish Society claimed in 1913, the 'British Empire stood where it was to-day – the greatest power on earth – because Scotchmen had done a great part of the building'.[60] The paradox of this, however, was observed in a letter from 1913 sent to Lloyd George from Scots in New Zealand relating to England's planned land policy in Scotland: 'the wonder is, that thousands of Scottish descendants are not filled with implacable hatred to the British Crown and Constitution'.[61]

58   *The N. Z. Scotsman*, 3 (33) (15 November 1929), 664.
59   *The N. Z. Scotsman*, 1 (1) (7 March 1927), 12, and 2:19 (15 September 1928), 208.
60   *The New Zealand Scot*, 1 (4) (20 February 1913), 19.
61   *The New Zealand Scot*, 1 (12) (20 October 1913), 3.

War and royalty were also the prime generators of manifestations of Britishness in the poetry of Scots in New Zealand. At Khartoum, for instance, 'Britain's mighty dead are praised'.[62] Meanwhile, the return of troops from Soudar prompted Andrew Kinross to prophesise 'British friends will welcome us with cheers'.[63] Royalty also prompted declarations of Britishness. As Hugh Smith queried in his poem on Queen Elizabeth, 'Where is the Scot that would not die for thee /O'er all the earth? In every clime or scene'. Smith asserted, 'And none of all the bravest, best and free/ Could be more loyal than the Scot to thee'.[64] There were also occasional references to Britain as the place of birth of Scots. According to Hugh Smith, ''Tis British blood that fires us'.[65] William Hogg, meanwhile, declared: 'Let us all rejoice that Britain/Is the land that gave us birth'.[66] Britain's links to New Zealand were also emphasised with Kinross considering the colony 'Britain's glorious land'.[67] John Liddell Kelly, meanwhile, mused 'So from the grand old British tree we sprang'[68] while John Barr declared, 'There's not a snugger bit of land/Beneath the British crown'.[69]

The sense of Britishness conveyed in the poetry of Scots in New Zealand, however, pales in comparison to the strong sense of Scottishness that is expressed. This Scottish identity encompassed the landscape, patriotism, historical figures and events, and also included cultural markers particularly

62   A. Kinross, 'On General Gordon', in *My Life and Lays* (Invercargill, John Ward, 1899), 80.

63   A. Kinross, 'On the Return of the Troops From the Soudar', in *My Life and Lays*, 80.

64   'Queen Elizabeth', in B. Sinclair, ed., *The Poetical Works of Hugh Smith (The Bard of Inangahua)* (Papanui: Hugh Smith Jnr, n.d.), 252.

65   'Our Motto', in Sinclair, ed., *The Poetical Works of Hugh Smith*, 274.

66   W. Hogg, 'No III Britain's March. A Song', in *Lays and Rhymes Descriptive, Legendary, Historical, Local and Lyrical* (Nelson: R Lucas and Sons, 1875), 313.

67   A. Kinross, 'The Old Land and the New', in *My Life and Lays*, 79.

68   J. L. Kelly, 'Prologue to "Britannia and her Daughters" – Britons and British', in *Heather and Fern: Songs of Scotland and Maoriland* (Wellington: New Zealand Times Co, 1902), 124.

69   J. Barr, 'Otago Goes Ahead, My Boys', in *Poems and Songs, Descriptive and Satirical* (Edinburgh: John Greig & Son, 1861), 212.

in relation to the Highlands such as dress, language, bagpipes, and dance.[70] Where the poetry of New Zealand's Scots differs in comparison to other sources is the greater sense of nostalgia and patriotism for Scotland. In part, the nostalgia and patriotism expressed by Scottish poets was tied to the exploits of Scottish heroes and significant historical events, with William Wallace, the most frequently referenced Scottish historical figure.[71] Yet although contained in the ethnic press and creative literature of Scots, such individuals and events are absent in personal correspondence. Nevertheless, ddespite the occasional sense of being British in some sources, such expressions fail to suggest a powerful concentric loyalty.

Conclusion

Throughout the nineteenth and twentieth centuries, then, Scots in New Zealand possessed a strong sense of their Scottish ethnic identities. This finding challenges the narrow notions of New Zealand society as one in which Scottish, Irish, English and Welsh were seen as a collective unity, lumped together under overarching 'British' or 'Pakeha' labels. Instead, Scots saw themselves and were seen by others as different and apart. There is little in the documentation consulted that reflects a sense of Britishness. While Britishness may have been a broad identity proclaimed in politics and public life this can be seen as superficial. At a fundamentally personal level Scots saw themselves and were seen by others as resolutely Scottish. As John M. MacKenzie has argued, Empire did not create an overarching national identity but 'enabled the sub-nationalisms of the United Kingdom

---

70   Based on consultation of the following poets: John Barr, John Blair, Alan Clyde, Dugald Ferguson, Robert Francis, William Hogg, John Kelly, Andrew Kinross, Angus Cameron Robertson, Hugh Smith, and William Stenhouse.

71   Robert the Bruce and Robert Burns also received frequent mention. See, for example, the works of Andrew Kinross, John Barr, Angus Cameron Robertson, Robert Francis, Hugh Smith, and William Hogg.

to survive and flourish'.[72] Or, as Richard Finlay has put it, 'Britishness, if anything, was conditioned more by pragmatic reasons, rather than notions of national sentiment. Indeed, the clannishness of Scots in the Empire tends to suggest that their Scottishness was of paramount importance'.[73]

What factors, though, led to the positive assertion of cultural Scottishness in New Zealand? A number of explanations can be offered. First, Scots arrived in New Zealand with a sense of Scottishness influenced by their experiences at home. That Scots saw themselves and were seen by others as different is evident in the numerous shipboard journals maintained during the transition to their new world. Scottishness, therefore, did not simply emerge after settlement although its character could be shaped by the colonial environment. Second, the admission of other ethnics in some societies with a Scottish tone (for example, Burns Clubs and Caledonian societies) and participation by other ethnicities in what were demonstrably Scottish festivals (such as Caledonian sports days) further facilitated a positive dimension. Third, Scots responded with humour and banter rather than annoyance or rage to acts that may have been regarded as discriminatory such as the stereotype of Scottish parsimoniousness and the teasing those Scots wearing kilts endured. Fourth, there was a deliberate attempt in New Zealand to ensure that rivalries from home were not transported abroad. As politician John Sheehan stated, 'one of the grandest lessons which the colonies are teaching to the mother country is that contained in the forbearance and tolerance shown by the English, Irish and Scottish colonists towards each other, and in the forgetfulness of national and religious prejudice'.[74] Or, as the Scottish-born poet Andrew Kinross echoed in similar tones: 'Let English, Scotch, and Irish join upon New Zealand's strand/And show that over all the earth there is no freer land'.[75]

72   MacKenzie, 'Empire and National Identities', 230.
73   Finlay, 'Caledonia or North Britain?', 150.
74   J. Sheehan, 4 September 1872, *NZPD*, 13, 109.
75   A. Kinross, 'A Freeman's Lay', in *My Life and Lays*, 75.

DAVID LEVEY

4 National Identity and Allegiance in Gibraltar[1]

It is a culture shock to cross the border from the Andalusian town of La Línea de la Concepción to suddenly find an enclave on the Iberian Peninsula which appears to be as British as Britain, if not more so. There are Bobbies, red telephone boxes, Union Jacks, pictures of the Queen, the English press, British pubs offering pints of ale and fish and chips. There are road names such as 'Winston Churchill Avenue' and monuments to Britain's glorious military past. However, there is considerably more to Gibraltar than meets the eye. It is all too easy to fall into the trap of drawing simplistic conclusions based on first impressions and to make judgements based on stereotypes and hearsay. Once you see through and behind the façade, one discovers a far more complex community with a unique identity which has been forged, not only as the result of British and Spanish external influences, but also in spite of them.

The history of 'British' Gibraltar goes back more than three centuries to 1704 when Anglo-Dutch forces, supporting the Hapsburg claim to the vacant Spanish throne, occupied the strategic town. It was declared a 'free port' the following year and the first British governor was appointed in 1707. A decade later it was annexed to the Crown of Great Britain by the terms of the treaty of Utrecht (1713) which brought the War of the Spanish Succession (1701–13) to an end. Article X of this treaty still forms the legal basis for the British presence in Gibraltar.[2]

1   The findings presented in this work are part of an ongoing research Project 'Contacto de lenguas y variedades lingüísticas alrededor del estrecho de Gibraltar (PA105-HUM-01168) funded by La Junta de Andalucía.
2   The English version of the Treaty of the Treaty of Utrecht Article X (13 July 1713) states:

Although there has been a British military presence on the Rock for 300 years, the armed forces have generally kept themselves to themselves, forming a class apart. The civilian population in the early years after the British occupation was not primarily Anglo-Saxon, as many assume. Nor, for that matter, was there a notable Spanish presence, as most of the former inhabitants left with the defeated army. Initially, the new population was made up primarily of Genoese and Sephardic Jews who were drawn to the Rock because of its free port status and the trading opportunities it offered. Portuguese, Maltese and Indians would subsequently add further international colour, and in recent years Moroccans, amongst others, have added to the rich local multicultural tapestry. Peter Caruana, Gibraltar's Chief Minister, describes Gibraltar as:

> A people formed institutionally by traits derived from the British influence, but it is also a people of Mediterranean extract; for example, my family came from Malta and other families came from Italy, Portugal, Morocco and, of course, from Spain. Over the centuries, these families have formed a people with their own identity.[3]

Gibraltarian First, British Second... and Spanish Never

Gibraltarians have traditionally expressed a strong national allegiance towards Britain, and as often happens in colonial environments, they have earned the reputation of being 'more British than the British'. However, in

---

The Catholic King does hereby, for himself, his heirs and successors, cede to the Crown of Great Britain the complete and entire propriety of the town and castle of Gibraltar, together with the port, fortifications, and forts thereunto belonging; and he gives up the said propriety to be held and enjoyed absolutely with all manner of right forever, without any exception or impediment whatsoever.

3   Interview with Peter Caruana, in F. Oda-Ángel, *Gibraltar: la herencia oblicua. Aproximación sociológica al contencioso* (Cádiz: Diputación de Cádiz, 1998), 135. The original Spanish text was translated by the author of this article.

recent years, as Gibraltar's relationship with the UK changes, the Union Jack, although still evident, appears to have been eclipsed by Gibraltar's own red and white banner. Nevertheless, in times of crisis when Gibraltar's sovereignty is under threat, demonstrations and declarations of British patriotism become visible and vociferous.

While the strength of allegiance may vary from individual to individual, and change from generation to generation, the one sentiment that has always unified the whole population is a rejection of any suggestion that they are Spanish. To be mistaken for a Spaniard is as offensive to a Gibraltarian as it is for a Scotsman to be classified as English or a Dutchman to be called a German. The vast majority of Gibraltarians, or 'Yanitos' as they are known, vehemently defend their independence from Spain and their right to self-determination.

Two referendums have been held on the question of sovereignty. In the first, held in 1967, the vast majority of the population turned out to express their opinion. The result left little room for doubt. 12,138 voted 'voluntarily to retain their link with Britain', while only 44 expressed a desire 'to pass under Spanish sovereignty in accordance with the terms proposed by the Spanish Government to Her Majesty's Government on 18 May 1966'. The referendum of 10 September 1967 was a key date in the history of the Rock and is commemorated every year with street celebrations.

Thirty five years later, as Britain and Spain discussed the possibility of sharing sovereignty, the Government of Gibraltar called a second referendum in November 2002 to let the UK Government know the population's point of view. Once again, the turnout was large, and once again the outcome was a loud and resounding 'no' to Spain, with 98.5 per cent voting against the proposal of joint sovereignty.

Given the strength of sentiment, it might appear incongruous to hear the locals chatting away in dialectal Spanish, not dissimilar to that spoken on the other side of the border. It is not unusual for 'Yanitos' to follow the Spanish football results closely, watch Spanish TV and discuss Spanish popular culture. They will also eat local Andalusian food. But, as far as the Gibraltarians are concerned, sharing their neighbours' language, and enjoying their culture and customs does not make them Spanish or necessarily any less British:

The privilege of the Gibraltarian is to live two cultures, two worlds: the Anglo-Saxon culture and the Spanish culture. We like the good things of both countries. So we live two cultures and enjoy the best of each. We reject the worst of one and the worst of the other. But we choose what we want. That's the privilege of the Gibraltarian.[4]

English is the only official language and is the language of government and the press. Gibraltar follows the British education system and all lessons, with the exception of foreign language classes, are given in English. However, largely due to geographical proximity and historical community ties, Spanish is frequently used by the local population in their daily lives. This is particularly so amongst the older generations, although in recent years a significant shift towards English language use amongst younger speakers has been noted.[5] Language choice in Gibraltar is often subject to context and register. Spanish and 'Yanito' tend to be more widespread in familiar everyday environments, while English is more favoured in more formal ones.[6]

While a small minority may see language choice as a declaration of allegiance, most Gibraltarians tend to have a relaxed attitude towards language use, viewing it in pragmatic terms as a means of communication without any political overtones. Feeling British yet speaking Spanish is not generally seen as a contradiction.

In a multilingual community such as Gibraltar where most speakers can communicate, to varying degrees, in two or more languages, language choice cannot be viewed in simple binary terms. Speakers will tend to accommodate and adapt their speech forms and language choice to suit the situation and the linguistic strengths or preferences of their interlocutors.[7]

4   Interview with Luis Montiel (ex District Officer of the TGWU), in Oda-Ángel, *Gibraltar: la herencia oblicua*, 45. The original Spanish text was translated by the author of this article.
5   See D. Levey, *Language Change and Variation in Gibraltar* (Amsterdam/Philadephia: John Benjamins, 2008).
6   Ibid. 81–2; C. Fernández Martín, *An Approach to Language Attitudes in Gibraltar* (Madrid: UMI-ProQuest Information and Learning, 2003).
7   Levey, *Language Change and Variation in Gibraltar*, 165.

While Gibraltarians can speak English and Spanish independently, there is also a local tendency to use both languages simultaneously. As well as referring to a born and bred Gibraltarian, the term 'Yanito' (or 'Llanito') is popularly used to describe this unique code-switching variant. It is a form of Spanglish which also incorporates lexical borrowings from the various immigrant languages (Italian, Arabic, Hebrew etc) which have left their cultural mark on the Rock.[8]

'Yanito' is essentially a spoken language variant. There is, however, a regular column called *Calentita*, published in the news magazine *Panorama*, which reflects this local tendency to switch between Spanish and English mid-sentence. The somewhat exaggerated caricature takes the form of a telephone conversation between two Gibraltarian housewives from different generations who discuss, in their inimitable way, the week's political and social events. The sketch, which first appeared in 1975, has become a local institution which tends to poke fun at the Spanish and the British, as well as local Gibraltarian politics and society.

The episode cited below appeared in November 1981 after the passing of the British Nationality Act which finally made provision for Gibraltarians to acquire British citizenship. Although 30 years have passed, the linguistic forms as well as the underlying attitudes implied beneath the irony are arguably still relevant:

- Carambola, we are 100% British now. Que te parece, Cloti dear?
- Bueno, yo siempre dije que we were more British than the British, and now we are only like them.
- Mujer, tu que quieres que Inglaterra se integra con nosotros? Oh well, I've already decided to speak less Spanish and more English, and my Charlie is now eating bacon and eggs for breakfast, steak and kidney pie for dinner and rhubarb and custard for postre.

---

8   Several works have discussed 'Yanito' and the linguistic situation in Gibraltar. These include: A. Kellermann, *A New, New English: Language, Politics and Identity in Gibraltar* (Heidelberg: Herstellung, 2001); D. Levey, 'Yanito' in K. Brown, ed., *Encyclopaedia of Language and Linguistics* 2nd edn. vol.3 (Oxford: Elsevier, 2006), 724–5; M. Moyer 'Bilingual conversation strategies in Gibraltar' in P. Auer, ed., *Codeswitching in Conversation, Language and Identity* (London: Routledge, 1998), 215–34.

– ... Bueno, you must excuse me porque tengo que ir al Mackintosh Hall a los English lessons. Quien lo iba decir que a mi edad fuera yo de clase, pero como no aprenda inglés no me dan el pasaporte. Cheerio Cynthia dear.

– Tally ho![9]

Loving Thy Neighbour

Ever since the treaty of Utrecht, Spain has fought incessantly for the return of the Rock. While strategies and methods vary, no Spanish government has ever, nor could ever, completely relinquish its claims. However, although local governments and the press on both sides of the border often fuel fires, cross-border relations, on the whole, are relatively good. From a sociological, cultural and linguistic point of view, 'Yanitos' and 'Andaluces' have much in common, and intermarriage between the two communities, which has been extensive since the eighteenth century, has served to reinforce these ties. A cursory look at the local names is testimony to this mixed cultural heritage (e.g. Shane Collado, James Corbacho, Jeremy Martínez, Kayleigh Olivero, Jessica Pizarro, Giles Ramírez).

---

9   'Yo me crei que era más British que los British', *The Calentita Collection* (Gibraltar: Panorama, 1996), 20. (Originally published in *Panorama*, 2 November 1981). A monolingual version of the dialogue is given below, but much of the underlying humour, which is based on the colloquial interplay of languages, is inevitably lost in translation.

– Crikey, we are 100% British now. What do you think about that, Cloti dear?

– Well, I always said that we were more British than the British, and now we are only like them.

– Woman, do you want England to integrate with us? Oh well, I've already decided to speak less Spanish and more English, and my Charlie is now eating bacon and eggs for breakfast, steak and kidney pie for dinner and rhubarb and custard for dessert.

– ... Well, you must excuse me as I have to go to the Mackintosh Hall for my English lessons. Who would have thought that at my age I would be going to class, but if I don't learn English I won't be given my passport. Cheerio Cynthia dear.

– Tally ho!

Gibraltarians have always seen the Spanish authorities as their enemies, not the Spanish people. Relations reached their lowest point in 1969 when Franco's regime closed the border, or 'verja' as it is locally known, between Spain and Gibraltar, thereby completely isolating the Rock and its people. It was an act of frustration; a decision which was to have long-lasting consequences, leaving scars which have yet to heal. The blockade lasted thirteen years. This sad episode, its consequences and the personal tragedies it brought with it was to mark a generation. Manuel Rodriguez's memoirs offer an idea of this suffering:

> The saddest sight was seeing people behind the wire fences on both sides of the land frontier yelling at the top of their voices across the wide dividing space to enquire about the state of relatives, as telephone communications had been cut by the Spaniards. Local housewives with Spanish relatives in the Campo area kept their radios tuned to the nearby Spanish stations for news of family members who were gravely ill. In critical cases the parties concerned would rush to Spain via Tangiers but unfortunately sometimes the patient was dead and buried by the time they arrived. The Spanish authorities would not allow access across the land frontier even on compassionate grounds.[10]

The decision to close the frontier was undoubtedly a gross error of judgement. Rather than forcing the local population into submission, this singular action served to consolidate and strengthen their national sentiment, and at the same time increased anti-Spanish feeling. By closing the frontier Spain shut itself out, and any possibility of regaining Gibraltar, no matter how remote, vanished completely. Franco had effectively shot himself in the foot, and it was his own people on the other side of the border who were the innocent victims.

> The blockade, or the Fifteenth Siege as it became known, did not have the desired effect. Gibraltar did not fall 'like ripe fruit' as Castiella, Franco's foreign secretary, had famously predicted. Aided by the British Government, Gibraltar not only survived but actually thrived, and it was the local Andalusians on the other side of the frontier who were arguably hardest hit by the blockade. Neighbouring towns such as La Linea and San Roque, which had grown and prospered from Gibraltar's status, soon fell into depression; Spanish workers, who used to cross the border daily, suddenly found themselves jobless, adding to the rising number of unemployed in the Campo area.[11]

10   M. Rodríguez, *I Remember* (Gibraltar: Gibraltar Books, 2001), 97–8.
11   Levey, *Language Change and Variation in Gibraltar*, 35–6.

Some of those who lived through the blockade find it difficult to forgive and forget, and feelings of disgust and mistrust are inevitably passed on to subsequent generations. The closing of the frontier was to mark a before and after in Gibraltar's relations with Spain.

> The closing of the border destroyed us and created hatred because they were taking away part of the culture we liked, also they were preventing us from sharing our lives with our friends and families from La Línea. This is not easily forgiven. Today Gibraltarian pensioners who meet to chat on Main Street won't forgive, they are intractable, they transmit this idea to their children and grandchildren. They say: don't trust them.[12]

Although the mistrust and hatred was aimed at the Spanish Government, Gibraltar's relationship with its Spanish neighbours inevitably altered. When the *verja* was finally opened to pedestrians on 15 December 1982 (it would not be opened to traffic until 1985), it was impossible to just pick up where they had left off and pretend nothing had happened.

> The people from La Linea have always been considered in Gibraltar as cousins, i.e. part of the family. But La Línea has declined, it's not what it was. Since the closing of the border it has not recovered. The Gibraltarian no longer feels comfortable in La Línea, he visits relatives there and returns quickly. This is the consequence of the isolation we suffered during the closure of the border and the weakening of the economic pillars which once attracted Gibraltarians to La Línea. It will be difficult for Gibraltarians to recover these close links with La Línea.[13]

The border re-opened more than a quarter of a century ago, but the years of blockade are still present in the collective memory. Some claim, however, that this chapter in Gibraltar's history has been artificially preserved and exploited. Francisco Oda-Ángel, the recently appointed Director of the Instituto Cervantes, argues that this period has been used by Gibraltar as a political tool to avoid facing any changes which might forge closer links with Spain. He accuses the local politicians of constantly blaming the clos-

---

12   Interview with Luis Montiel, Oda-Ángel, *Gibraltar: la herencia oblicua*, 167–8.
13   Ibid. 169.

ing of the border and Franco's regime for the social problems in Gibraltar today, thereby diverting the public attention away from the true causes.[14]

Reading the Gibraltarian press, one gets the somewhat distorted impression that the question of the Rock is a constant obsession on both sides of the frontier. The bones of contention are frequently rattled in the local newspapers and accusations fly. Some would say that this ceaseless bombardment is a deliberate strategy of constant polarisation to ensure Gibraltar's independence from Spain. Others might argue that creating polemical issues sells newspapers.

Although Gibraltar features regularly in the local Spanish press, at national level, there are long periods of silence when Gibraltar is hardly mentioned. Perhaps, on the fundamental issue of sovereignty there is little left to say. It is only when some event occurs or a new issue arises offering a new angle that embers are stoked once again.

The question of the British rights and responsibility in the Bay and Straits of Gibraltar is a thorny one, and Spain has argued that the Treaty of Utrecht does not cover 'territorial waters', nor for that matter, 'airspace'. The sinking of the *New Flame* in 2007 and the environmental consequences it caused has added further friction, with Spain blaming Gibraltar for negligence and for not having acted sooner.[15]

British military operations and the presence of British nuclear submarines, such as *HMS Tireless*, inflame Spanish indignation, leading to vociferous protests from Spanish politicians who claim it is a threat to its national security, as well as from Spanish environmental groups.[16]

---

14   F. Oda-Ángel, 'Gibraltar a un año de la Declaración de Córdoba: la recuperación de la confianza', Working Paper N° 45/2007 *Real Instituto Elcano* (2007), 18.

15   The *New Flame* was a Panamanian cargo ship carrying scrap metal which collided with an oil tanker near Gibraltar. After several unsuccessful salvage attempts, the vessel broke up in December 2007 resulting in oil spillage and contamination. The extent of the damage and the matter of responsibility are still being investigated.

16   On 12 May 2000, the nuclear submarine *HMS Tireless* underwent extensive repairs in Gibraltar. It was to remain there for a year, straining diplomatic relations. With unfortunate timing, to say the least, *HMS Tireless* returned in July 2004 just before the Gibraltar's 300 anniversary celebrations were due to begin. Since then, several other naval war vessels have used the base in Gibraltar.

Throughout Gibraltar's history, Britain has often shown a lack of sensitivity to Spanish feelings. Royal visits, for example, have been considered by Spaniards to be acts of provocation and have created diplomatic tension in the past.[17] However, after these periodical storms relative calm returns. The question of Gibraltar's sovereignty is arguably not high on the average Spaniard's priorities. Although few would actively support a 'British' Gibraltar, Spaniards no longer seem to be particularly concerned about regaining it for themselves. In a survey carried out by the Spanish daily *La Vanguardia* in 2002, when bilateral talks on the question of sovereignty were taking place, 60 per cent of the 45,163 people surveyed supported Gibraltar's independence.[18]

Whereas in previous times a Spanish Gibraltar was a matter of national pride, cries of 'Gibraltar español!' are rarely heard today, except with tongue in cheek when imitating or parodying the attitudes of Franco's Spain. Some would argue that, deep down, Gibraltar has never really been a concern for Spaniards.[19]

---

17 When Queen Elizabeth II visited Gibraltar in 1954, Spain withdrew its consul from the Rock. After the announcement of Prince Charles and Princess Diana's planned honeymoon stop-over on the Rock, King Juan Carlos I of Spain declined their invitation to the wedding. Princess Anne's visit to Gibraltar in 2004 to attend celebrations to mark 300 years of British rule was met with official protests. The Princess Royal returned again in March 2009 to open a medical centre. Her visit was seen as an affront to Spanish sensibilities, particularly as the medical centre which bears her name is situated on the disputed isthmus. Spain complained officially to Britain. With the next round of tripartite talks taking place in London later that year, it was seen as 'innoportune' and undiplomatic.

18 The results of this survey, reproduced in *Panorama* (23 May 2002) were the following: 7.81 per cent (3527) felt it should remain part of the UK; 29.6 per cent (13,375) felt it should be Spanish; 2.16 per cent (974) felt sovereignty should be shared; 60.04 per cent (27,116) felt it should be independent. Although the message appears clear, the fact that *La Vanguardia* is published in Catalonia, where there is a strong independence movement, is a factor.

19 This view is well expressed by Juan José Tellez, the former editor of *Europa Sur*. In an article entitled 'Gibraltar español', he argues that Spanish interest in Gibraltar was artificially revived and imposed on the people during Franco's regime. This article is reproduced in Oda-Ángel, *Gibraltar: la herencia oblicua*, 193.

A Marriage of Whose Convenience?

Particularly in recent years, Gibraltarians have kept one watchful eye on Spain and the other one on their old colonial masters. Through experience, they have learnt to be wary – a character trait or a survival instinct which has developed out of 300 years of instability and uncertainty.

In earlier times, Gibraltarians looked up to Britain with humble colonial admiration, and like unloved abandoned children, longed and pleaded for the approval and attention of their mother. The 1967 referendum was a demonstration of their devotion, with the population turning out en masse amidst Union Jacks and placards expressing their loyalty to the Queen. National sentiment aside, Gibraltar was understandably defending its own interests. Franco's Spain was clearly not an attractive option, politically or economically, and Gibraltarians wanted to preserve the democratic lifestyle they had become accustomed to at all cost.

By the second referendum in 2002, when the British Government appeared to be prepared to negotiate a deal with Spain, there was a subtle change in attitude. Gibraltar had grown in political maturity, and was not prepared to simply sit and wait as their future was decided for them. Rather than pleading for recognition, they actively demanded what they felt was rightfully theirs. After years of having to defend their position, they had learnt to argue and lobby their case skilfully, and knew how to use the British national rhetoric to their advantage when needed. The people demonstrated in the streets and coordinated 'Keep Gibraltar British' campaigns were launched, seeking the support of the British press, in an attempt to bring their plight to the attention of the public in the UK. In an article entitled 'A shameful betrayal of people desperate to stay British', which appeared in *The Daily Mail* on 19 March 2002, Stephen Glover wrote:

> Never was there a clearer example that being British is not primarily a matter of ethnic origin. It has much to do with the ties of history, common allegiances and shared values... the people of Gibraltar see themselves as British. That is nine-tenths and more of being British. But it is not a mere academic identification. In the last

war the people of Gibraltar stood by Britain when the Rock was crucial to our survival as a nation. What better proof can there be of their loyalty, of their being as British as you or me?[20]

In a patriotic speech given at the Draper's Hall in London on 21 October 2002, Gibraltar's chief minister appealed for the support of the British people, urging them to press the British government not to give in to Spanish 'bullying and cajolement'. Amidst the fears and concerns of possible concessions being made to Spain, Peter Caruana said that it was time for the UK to reciprocate Gibraltar's loyalty and friendship, arguing that both Gibraltar and UK histories and traditions were inseparable:

> We value our links with Britain. We value our constitutional links and we value our British sovereignty. We want those strengthened. Not weakened or diluted at the altar of modern day European political pragmatism... The people of Gibraltar will stand firm. Over the years we have learnt, perhaps in the face of adversity to punch above our weight and we intend to continue punching above our weight until our political rights as a people are fully respected by all concerned.[21]

It is has always been clear that Britain is important for Gibraltar. The real issue is whether Gibraltar is still important to Britain. Some believe that if Gibraltar remains British, it is not out of a sense of loyalty, but because it is in Britain's own military interests that the strategic base on the Rock be preserved. The question is whether the Rock still has sufficient military importance for Britain to justify the cost (both economic and diplomatic). Dominique Searle, the Editor of *The Gibraltar Chronicle*, is in no doubt. Not only does he feel that it still important, but he argues that Britain has now realized that in order to retain this strategic military foothold, a good working relationship with the civilian population based on give and take is essential:

---

20   S. Glover, 'A Shameful betrayal of people desperate to stay British', *The Daily Mail* (19 March 2002).
21   Reported in *The Gibraltar Chronicle* (23 October 2002).

Because of the question of joint sovereignty, Great Britain realized the importance of good relations with the local population, which was in danger... You can't have a military base against the will of the people... it is important for England that Gibraltar functions. One should not doubt the fact that for England military interests are long term. Perhaps there are things that they don't need but which they maintain to ensure the people's support.[22]

The old colonial attitude that Britain was doing Gibraltar a 'favour' is changing. The local population is starting to realize that they have bargaining power, and are beginning to question and stand up to the Ministry of Defence (MoD).

The reality is that when it has suited British interests Gibraltar has put up with sieges military, social and economic. We have endured the 'class system' of the past where local people lived packed in limited housing whilst the military enjoyed a vast estate and privileges. ... Whilst it is true that we have moved on considerably from the tensions of inequality that were palpable even 20 years ago, there is little doubt MoD, indeed the UK cannot take Gibraltar for granted.[23]

Juggling the Hot Potato

The controversial question of Gibraltar has always been an obstacle for fluid Anglo-Spanish relations, and Britain has always had to play a shrewd political game of offering carrots and olive branches, yet ceding nothing of real substance.

A cloud of unease hangs over the Rock when Spain and Britain meet periodically to discuss the question of Gibraltar. These bilateral talks were established by the Brussels Agreement, the very mention of which raises

22   Interview with Lalia González Santiago, Editor of *La Voz de Cádiz* (26 December 2004).
23   'MoD Must Assume its Responsibilities', editorial in *The Gibraltar Chronicle* (17 January 2007).

local tension, since Gibraltar is shut out and feels powerless to defend themselves against any 'secret' deals made behind closed doors. This 1984 bilateral accord resolved to apply the earlier 1980 Lisbon Agreement signed by the British and Spanish Governments which 'agreed to start negotiations aimed at overcoming all the differences between them on Gibraltar'.

However, in both agreements an important disclaimer has been inserted, which amounts to a 'get-out clause': 'The British Government will fully maintain its commitment to honour the wishes of the people of Gibraltar as set out in the preamble of the 1969 Constitution'. The 'preamble' to this constitution states that: 'Her Majesty's Government will never enter into arrangements under which the people of Gibraltar would pass under the sovereignty of another state against their freely and democratically expressed wishes'.[24]

That is the 'Catch 22' which, on paper at least, has always made any talk on the future of Gibraltar just talk. Both the Spanish and British Governments know full well that Gibraltar will never willingly accept Spanish sovereignty, or joint sovereignty for that matter. Accepting the premise that it is in Britain's interest, at present at least, to preserve Gibraltar, this 'get-out' clause, for reasons of diplomacy, works to the UK Government's diplomatic benefit, since it can always be claimed that its hands are tied.

Gibraltarians have no delusions of grandeur: 'we are justly proud of our identity as a nation; but in global terms we are the equivalent of a small country town or a very minute territory – not large enough or sufficiently politically autonomous to be regarded as a country in its own right'.[25] They and their Government know full well that they can not go it alone and, like it or not (and some certainly don't), they are dependent on Britain and its support: 'any country large or small, must operate in the real world. Indeed that is largely the reason why most Gibraltarians seek a preservation of the British status and shun independence'.[26]

---

24   The Gibraltar Constitution Order 1969 (Prerogative Order in Council 23 May 1969 Unnumbered).

25   'How the Constitution encourages the abuse of power', Vox (25 February 2008).

26   'At the Precipice of Opportunity', editorial in The Gibraltar Chronicle (18 March 2006).

In a recent development, however, Gibraltar has started a new chapter in its history in which a considerable degree of independence appears to have been gained, although the full implications are still far from clear. In a referendum held on 30 November 2006, 60 per cent of the population voted in favour of a new Constitution which effectively gives the people of Gibraltar the freedom to govern their own internal affairs, and in so doing, they have apparently cut some of their colonial ties with Britain.[27]

Whereas previous plebiscites in Gibraltar have attracted large turnouts, clear outcomes, and ensuing jubilation, *The Gibraltar Chronicle*, in an article entitled 'The Quiet Yes...',[28] described the mood after the referendum as 'sombre', reflecting the general uncertainty of what future implications this decision may have.

There is still considerable confusion as to Gibraltar's present status. Peter Caruana has stated that Gibraltar is no longer a 'colony'. The opposition is not so sure and questions whether, in real terms, there is any change in the situation. They have demanded clarification, arguing that the carefully chosen nebulous terms used by the UK and Gibraltar Governments, which refer to a 'modern and mature relationship' which is 'non-colonial in nature', are unhelpful and have no legal basis.

> If Gibraltar is no longer a colony, why is it that the British Government does not come out clean and clear and say so? ... If Gibraltar had ceased to be a colony, there should have been a feast to welcome our new status in the world. This has not happened. Our status before and after the new Constitution is the same. So there you are, if our status has remained the same, it must mean that our colonial status has remained colonial.[29]

---

27 According to the preamble to 'The Gibraltar Constitution Order 2006, 14 December 2006', the new Constitution 'gives the people of Gibraltar that degree of self-government which is compatible with British sovereignty of Gibraltar and with the fact that the United Kingdom remains fully responsible for Gibraltar's external relations'.

28 Editorial in *The Gibraltar Chronicle* (1 December 2006).

29 'What has happened for some to think that we are no longer a colony?', *Panorama* (30 April 2008).

A Government of Gibraltar press release issued on 18 April 2008 attempted to clarify the situation. Citing various official UK Government statements, the Gibraltarian Government maintains its position:

> The UK Government's stated position thus fully underpins the Gibraltar Government's position, namely, that while Gibraltar's international status remains that of a UK Overseas Territory and under British Sovereignty (as is indeed stated in the Despatch to the New Constitution), its relationship with the UK is no longer a colonial one and is necessarily thus effectively decolonised.[30]

However, the statement has done little to calm the waters and the political war of words and semantic hair-splitting and rhetoric continues. The Rock's status is still far from clear, and some argue that it will remain so until the UN General Assembly itself votes to remove Gibraltar from its list of non-self governing territories.

Trilateral Talks: A New Climate?

Given that the Gibraltarians are not for turning, previous Spanish governments, particularly right-wing ones, have always felt that the only hope of regaining Gibraltar is through bilateral talks. However, after years of impasse, José Luis Zapatero's Socialist Government (PSOE) has adopted a new approach. Although the Brussels Agreement is still in place, in what *The Gibraltar Chronicle* hailed as 'one of the most significant developments ever in the Rock's international affairs', a Trilateral Forum of Dialogue has now been established in which Gibraltar has a voice.[31]

The first fruit of these talks is the Córdoba Agreement of 18 September 2006, which is fundamentally a declaration of good intentions to solve some of the practical problems 'so as to benefit both Gibraltar and the Campo de Gibraltar, and thus contribute to the creation of a constructive atmos-

---

30 Government of Gibraltar Press Release (n°. 88/2008) 18 April 2008.
31 'Tripartite Open Agenda Talks are Official', *The Gibraltar Chronicle* (17 December 2004).

phere of mutual trust, respect and co-operation'.[32] The communiqué made it quite clear that question of sovereignty did not form part of the agenda. Besides reiterating the commitment to continue the process of dialogue and encouraging collaboration and co-operation between the two communities, the Córdoba Agreement reached consensus on five points. The first of these was a settlement over the 'issue of the pensions of former Spanish workers in Gibraltar... who suffered the consequences of decisions adopted in the 1960s'. The second resolved to make arrangements to 'facilitate the enhanced use of the Gibraltar Airport for civilian air traffic for the benefit of Gibraltar and the Campo de Gibraltar'. The third point was a declaration of commitment to solve and periodically review the problem of long queues at the border and ensure 'more fluid movement of people, vehicles and goods between Gibraltar and the surrounding area'. The fourth area of agreement concerned telecommunications, with a resolution 'to both address the current limitation on the quantity of telephone numbers in Gibraltar accessible from and through the Spanish network, and also enable roaming agreements between networks in Spain and Gibraltar for mobile telephones'. The final point of consensus concerned the proposal by the Spanish government to 'establish in Gibraltar an Instituto Cervantes' and agreement by the Gibraltarian government to provide 'suitable premises' and 'facilitate its early establishment'.

This last point, which at first sight appears innocuous, has become a polemical issue which has led some, particularly those in the Opposition, to question Spain's ulterior motives and to cast doubt on the so-called 'new climate' between Spain and Gibraltar.[33] In the words of Nick Cruz, the Progressive Democratic Party (PDP) spokesman, it's the 'same dog, different collar'.[34]

---

32   Communiqué of the first ministerial meeting of the Trilateral Forum of Dialogue on Gibraltar ('the Forum').

33   An article entitled 'Their Target Gibraltar?', published in *Vox* (25 February 2008), an anti-Government tabloid, argues that the establishment of the *Instituto Cervantes* has immense significance which 'has gone almost unnoticed by the political leaders of our Opposition parties' and that the Spain has surreptitiously established a foothold in Gibraltar.

34   *The Gibraltar Chronicle* (3 April 2008).

The Instituto Cervantes is a public institution which promotes Spanish language and culture throughout the world. Many locals query Spain's reasons for promoting its language and culture in a place where Spanish is already widely spoken.[35] Furthermore, the fact that, in the first instance, the proposed head of the new venture, Agustín Gervás, was not a university professor with an academic background, but a diplomat with years of experience in foreign affairs and diplomacy, makes some suspect that it forms part of a subtle long-term strategy; a ploy to plant a 'propaganda machine' inside Gibraltar to gently persuade the local population to return to the fold with carrots such as grants and study opportunities in Spain.

An article entitled 'Gibraltar empieza a ser español' [Gibraltar starts to become Spanish] published in the Spanish news magazine *Tiempo* pulls no punches. The journalist describes the setting up of el Instituto Cervantes in Gibraltar as 'Spain's own Trojan horse in the form of an innocent cultural entity', and stresses the potentially important role of the director once inside:

> His presence as a diplomat will allow him to expound in private Spain's position before any capricious notions of independence that the Gibraltarians may have. Besides, as the official representative of our country will have an important role in designing the political strategy adopted by Madrid towards the British colony.[36]

In the end it was not Gervás but Francisco Oda Ángel who assumed the directorship of the Instituto Cervantes in January 2010. It seems to be a shrewd appointment. As well as having an academic background (Doctor in Sociology and Lecturer in the Faculty of Social and Legal Sciences at the University Rey Juan Carlos), Oda Ángel gained important diplomatic

---

35   There is evidence to suggest that as the use of English increases on the Rock, Spanish language competence has declined in recent years at its expense (see Levey, *Language Change and Variation in Gibralta* 63–4 & 98). Although Gibraltarians can communicate, to varying degrees of fluency, in both languages, one of the unfortunate casualties of years of political dispute is that Gibraltar's bilingual potential has never been fully realized at local Government level. However, while declining standards and lost opportunities may be lamented in certain local circles, the re-introduction of the Spanish language from Madrid, with all its political connotations, is another matter.

36   A. Rodriguez, 'Gibraltar empieza a ser español', *Tiempo* (14 December 2007).

experience as the former Head of Department of the *Escuela Diplomatica* in Madrid. In addition, as the former Director of the *Instituto Transfronterizo*, he has important local knowledge and press connections.

That Spain will be provided with an official institutional base on Gibraltarian soil is controversial. For the first time in more than half a century, when in protest to Queen Elizabeth II's official visit to Gibraltar in 1954 Franco closed the Spanish consulate in Gibraltar, the Spanish flag will fly on the Rock of Gibraltar. The symbolism is not lost on anyone. Yet, even if the worst political fears prove true, and Spain is indeed embarking on a plan to lure Gibraltarians back through exposure to the Spanish language and culture and the attractions it has to offer, what of it? Gibraltarians have always been exposed to the Spanish language and culture and have profited from the experience; Gibraltarians have always had contact with Spaniards and have enjoyed and benefited from their company... and Gibraltarians have always chosen to preserve their independence from their neighbours and all that goes with it. There is no real reason to suppose that things will change in the foreseeable future.

Conclusion

Throughout its history Gibraltar has lived in a constant state of vigilance, always on the lookout for signs of possible Spanish assaults. In the past these took the form of naval incursions which had to be repelled. While such attacks are no longer really feared today, the local population remains on guard. In a recent online poll carried out in January 2010, 84 per cent of Gibraltarians felt that 'Spain were still intent in recovering Gibraltar's sovereignty'.[37]

---

37   The opinion poll appeared on the website of the Gibraltarian tabloid *Panorama*, attracting 369 participants. The results, published on 18 January 2010 revealed that eighty-four per cent believed that Spain was 'Still intent to recover sovereignty'; eleven per cent said 'No' and four per cent said 'Don't Know'.

When new rounds of talks with Spain are announced, a certain nervousness is felt by many Gibraltarians. While efforts to overcome the practical problems affecting day-to-day living on both sides of the border are welcome, Gibraltarians are suspicious of ulterior motives or hidden agendas. Good neighbourly relations are fine as long as each returns to his own home at the end of the day.

Gibraltar's critics would argue that a cloud of paranoia partially covers the Rock, and that fears and mistrust are whipped up by a hostile anti-Spanish popular press. It is true that some scaremongering takes place in certain sectors of the media, but some would argue that this defensive stance is necessary to ensure survival. With so much at stake, Gibraltar can not afford to be caught unawares.

In recent years, Gibraltar has felt under threat from more than one flank. After the events of 2001 and 2002 when Spain and the UK held talks over possible joint sovereignty behind close doors, Gibraltar has become wary of British intentions. Although new UK Governments offer assurances that nothing will be ceded without the people's consent, Gibraltarians feel they cannot afford to be complacent. They have learnt to trust no one. Like the dog which has been mistreated in the past, while not biting the hand that feeds them, Gibraltarians are guarded.

Over the last decade, Gibraltar's relationship with the UK has undergone a subtle yet noticeable shift. It must be difficult to feel truly British if you feel that Britain may forsake you. Most of those who live on the Rock feel Gibraltarian first and British second – this has arguably always been the case, but now these feelings are more overt. There is a pride in being Gibraltarian and red and white flags are clearly visible on the Rock.[38] By contrast the Union Jacks appear to have become less manifest.

---

38   This sense of national pride was demonstrated recently when Kaine Aldorino, representing Gibraltar, won the Miss World beauty Pageant in December 2009. Reported crowds of 15,000 people were there to welcome the conquering heroine home, with the streets bathed in red and white. According to the usually restrained *Gibraltar Chronicle* (18 December 2009) 'There were unprecedented scenes of jubilation of enormous magnitude, with an entire population wanting to join in the once in a lifetime celebration, wanting to be a part of history – not just local but world history'.

With a new Constitution and a new-found political maturity Gibraltar is ridding itself of the last vestiges of their colonial mentality. As it gains a greater degree of independence, it is inevitably drifting somewhat from the mother ship, but without losing sight of her completely.

ELLEKE BOEHMER AND SUMITA MUKHERJEE

5   Re-making Britishness: Indian Contributions to Oxford University, c. 1860–1930[1]

For a century and more there have been few more recognizable icons of Britishness than Oxford or Oxford University – that is, Britishness as signifying British tradition resting on the twin struts of High Church Anglicanism and Royalist loyalty, as well as a certain understanding of educational privilege and intellectual debate backed by social aspiration. As embedded in the work of Matthew Arnold, Walter Pater, Thomas Hardy, Max Beerbohm, Evelyn Waugh, and others, images of the dreaming spires (as also of course the punting courses of the Cam) have signified a range of British national virtues: cultural 'sweetness and light', the value placed on book learning and knowledge, and the structures of class privilege that have safeguarded these other values.

Yet from around 1870 Oxford University – like Britain more generally, or cities such as London and Bristol, as well as Cambridge University – was host to growing numbers of Indian students, as well as visiting scholars, political reformers, speakers and seers, who significantly inflected and incrementally remade the British values with which the University had conventionally been associated. With this, the image of Oxford as symbol of a homogenously defined Britishness, too, came under pressure. From 1889–92, for instance, the woman lawyer Cornelia Sorabji, of Bombay Parsee origin, studied for the BCL, till then debarred to women,

1   This paper comes out of research from the AHRC-funded project 'Making Britain: South Asian Visions of Home and Abroad, 1870–1950' (AH/E009859/1). The authors would like to thank their colleagues on the project for their support, as well as the archivists of the Bodleian Library, Rhodes House Library, and St John's College, Oxford.

at Somerville College, Oxford. Symptomatically, in her memoir *India Call-ing* (1935), she describes her growing friendship while a student with the then Master of Balliol, Benjamin Jowett, in terms that suggest a gradual integration of her 'foreignness' with his social capacity for finding 'common ground'. Her wide-ranging conversations with Jowett, she writes, led to her 'getting England into my bones'. This is an extraordinary metaphor for an Indian writing at this time; one that suggests an accessibility, a certain porosity or sponginess to the settled, racially defined idea of Englishness, and so of Britishness more broadly. In a fascinatingly contradictory and yet far-sighted way, Sorabji allows for an eclectic makeup of British identity, even while in the same paragraph asserting the power of 'Breed' over 'Feed' (nature over nurture).[2] In respect of the separate yet related case of Indi-ans at Cambridge, Ranjit Sinhji, the Jam Saheb of Nawanagar (a princely state), attended the University as a student from 1889, and by 1895 was playing cricket for England against Australia. This example is interesting, too, for an understanding of a diversified Britishness, as this will have been one of the first times that an Indian, and indeed a non-white, cricketer participated at a national level, representing and embodying England, at this most English and still colonial of sports.[3]

This chapter will analyze and explore aspects of these processes of redefining Britishness through a radical infiltration of (here) Oxford on the part of visiting Indians in late nineteenth- century and early twentieth-century Britain. It will reflect on how this process laid the ground for the formation of new multi-layered constructs of the nation and of British cultural identities later in the 1900s, with that period's major waves of immigration from the Indian sub-continent. Our approach extends in the specific direction of Oxford, and of Indian presences, texts and cultural artefacts within the University, the valuable work of Catherine Hall on how empire – concepts of 'new colonial selves' and a displaced metropolis

2   C. Sorabji, *India Calling* (London: Trent, 2003), 21–2.
3   See for reference, C. L. R. James, *Beyond a Boundary* (London: Hutchinson, 1963).

– lay at the heart of nineteenth-century understandings of Britishness.[4] We will therefore challenge the idea, prevalent in studies of postcolonial migration and transnationalism to date, that a largely homogeneous British culture, and perceptions of that culture, only began to diversify after the Second World War. While it is true that this diasporic population became increasingly numerous and influential from the time of the end of empire, South Asians in Britain were in fact engaging with and challenging canonical culture well before this time, as in the case study offered here of Indians at Oxford.

The Early Production of India in Oxford

To set the scene, Oxford University in the second half of the nineteenth century, especially under the Vice-Chancellorship of Benjamin Jowett (from 1883), with his vision of the University as a place of secular training for Britain's administrative elites, became devoted not only to the education but the production, the 'civilization', of British colonial officers and other civil servants through a process of rigorous study of 'the Greats' (the Classics). Within this process, of all the territories of the Empire it was India that commanded particular attention. Indeed, in the period 1892–1914, Oxford produced more Indian Civil Service (ICS) officers than any other university.[5] *Oxford Magazine* in the period was consistently preoccupied with the entry of 'Oxford men' into the ICS. In respect of Indian students themselves – from 1871, when the regulation that students of the University be members of the Church of England was relaxed, Indians began to come to Oxford in ever growing numbers, many to study

---

4   C. Hall, *Civilising Subjects: Metropole and Colony in the English Imagination 1830–1867* (Cambridge: Polity, 2002).
5   R. Symonds, *Oxford and Empire: The Last Lost Cause?* (New York: St Martin's Press, 1986), 11, 306.

for the same ICS examinations, which had been opened to Indians from 1859. Forty-nine Indian students attended Oxford between 1871 and 1893, with 32 present in 1907.[6] Throughout the period, the majority of Indians at Oxford intended to enter the ICS and thus serve the British Empire in some or other capacity.

In 1883, the same year as Jowett became Vice-Chancellor, Professor Monier Monier-Williams was instrumental in the founding of the Indian Institute to provide a place of study for Indian Civil Service probationers as well as for Indian students at Oxford. All British and Indian candidates for the ICS had to take a probationary year after passing their Civil Service exams, during which they learned Indian languages, history and aspects of administration. For Monier-Williams it was especially important that Oxford take upon itself the role of representing and transferring western knowledge to the east: the Institute, he believed, would play a part in so doing by training the probationers properly. In 1875, he first put the idea to Congregation to found an institute to provide a place of study for these students, which would combine a library, reading room and museum. He then travelled to India on three occasions to secure moral and financial support for the Institute in formation, particularly from the Indian Princes who also donated items for the museum and library.

The Institute was opened by the Vice-Chancellor, Benjamin Jowett, on 14 October 1884, and rapidly became an influential zone of Indian scholarship, conversation and cultural exchange within the University, playing host to a wide range of visiting students and academics, the first of whom was the radical nationalist Shyamaji Krishnavarma (1857–1930), who worked as Monier-Williams's assistant from 1879 to 1883. Though the Institute library long since moved away (though to a nearby location), the Institute building itself with its distinctive gold-coloured elephant-and-howdah weather vane, and its foundation stone in Devanagri script, remains a reminder of how a small piece of India was, as it were, embedded within Oxford at this early date. The characteristic image on the weather vane is still set evocatively in amongst the dreaming spires.

6   Ibid.

In respect of the formation of ideas of Britishness at the time, what these developments surrounding the Indian Institute meant, was that Indian students and their British counterparts, many of them would-be civil servants of the Empire, were participating within the same space, or within overlapping domains of contact, in a wide-ranging discussion about the make-up of a 'Greater Britain' across the globe. Greater Britain, as a federal system linking Anglo-Saxon people, propagated in the work of Oxbridge historians like J. R. Seeley and J. A. Froude, was conceived by Liberals as a finely balanced political system, in which the lack of political representation for imperial citizens in one area, such as in India, was perceived to reduce the quality of freedom for all Greater Britain subjects.[7] A number of politically involved Indian students and activists at this time, including the young lawyer Gandhi in South Africa, drew on related ideas of 'impartial' admission to 'office in our service' in Queen Victoria's 1858 Proclamation, as a way of affirming freer and more equal interaction between her English and Indian subjects, and also the unfettered entitlement of Indians to imperial citizenship (despite the restrictions in practice on such entitlement).[8]

A picture thus emerges of active and sometimes heated exchange and interaction between India and Oxford, concerning or at least abutting upon ideas of Britishness, of which traces and leavings can still be found in the University's libraries and archives. Where Oxford had long looked to India for philosophical insight and historical knowledge, as part of the imperial project, though not exclusively so, and where India from around the middle of the nineteenth century in its turn approached Oxford in pursuit of higher learning, knowledge of the west, professional qualifications, career advancement, and so on, the marks of these conversational crossings were then embedded within the University's self-representations and documentary records. It is to these marks and traces that we will now turn – traces that record a gradual remaking of what is understood by Oxford as a British University, by Oxford's place in Britain, and by its role as a maker of ideas of Britishness in relation to the Empire and to India.

---

7   E. Boehmer, ed., *Empire Writing: An Anthology of Colonial Literature 1870–1920* (Oxford: Oxford University Press, 1998), 72–9, 212, 493–4.

8   E. Boehmer, *Empire, the Nation and the Postcolonial: Resistance in Interaction* (Oxford: Oxford University Press, 2002), 20.

Traces of India within Oxford in the Nineteenth Century Fin de Siècle

Traces of the early Indian presence in Oxford – the presence of Indian students first and foremost, but also of Indian concepts, knowledge, texts, forms of awareness – may be found in documents that reside at the very heart of the University, in the Bodleian library. Even in their inadvertency, their contingency (those qualities novelist Amitav Ghosh emphasizes as inherent to such faint historical markings), these traces evocatively suggest how Oxford, a bedrock of British values, was relatively early on striated at its core by its contact with India.[9] This section looks closely at two of these documents scored with a history of India-British contact, in order to suggest that they can be read as metonymical of the reshaping of British-ness by migrant presences and exchanges.

The eloquence of migrant markings emerges in clear ways from one of the earliest samples of Indian contact tracery in the University record, Professor of Comparative Philology Friedrich Max-Müller's homemade book of letters from Indian friends and contacts in India.[10] Collected and kept together by him in the 1880s, the 'text', such as it is, is marked throughout by that 'vast and sincere regard' for Hinduism that the professor evidently shared with his Indian correspondents. This is palpable both in what the letters say to the respected professor, and in his own marginal instructions to himself, mainly in pencil, to keep certain letters, presumably so that they might be sewn up and preserved for posterity, as they have been, in book form. Though Max-Müller himself never visited India, yet, as these letters show, he was always concerned that Oxford absorb Indian knowledge; that it be open to India in all senses. He himself would frequently consult with Indian contacts and informants on matters of Hindu belief, ritual and interpretation.

9   A. Ghosh, *In an Antique Land* (Delhi: Seagull, 1992).
10   F. Max-Müller, Correspondence book, MS. Eng. d. 2352.

The letters in the book are in divers hands, both from Indians who had physically met the great Oxford Sankritist, and those who had never travelled to Britain, nor had plans to, yet who sought contact because of his reputation as a scholar of ancient India. The letters request his professional approval for life choices taken, send gifts or favours, or seek his advice on questions of philological or religious interpretation – which questions, significantly, had been picked up from his publications, and from reports in the Indian press. Word was evidently getting through from Oxford to India, as from India to Oxford, word that there was a certain epistemological openness to India present in Oxford in the form of Professor Max-Müller and his circle. The bundle thus captures in a tangible way, in its conjoined, woven-together form, how in Oxford, or through the channel of Oxford, Indian and British scholars and students, as well as professors and seers, might be bound into relationships of cultural interchange. It evokes how they held political, cultural and religious ideas, energies and interests in common, interests which then drew them into intercontinental conversations, the leavings of which, in the form of this book of letters, have sedimented onto a shelf in the Bodleian archive.

Max-Müller, also translator of the *Rg Veda* (which was published by Oxford University Press), held various positions in the University from 1851. Despite the huge disappointment of losing out in the election of Boden Professor of Sanskrit to his rival Monier-Williams, referred to above, Max-Müller continued to pursue his studies in Sanskrit and the Vedas at Oxford, as Professor of Comparative Philosophy at All Souls, and was widely known and respected in India, something to which the book of letters testifies. Indeed, if anything, the loss of the election and what it suggested of the prejudice of the University's Congregation, and hence of the British establishment, drove this German-born liberal Lutheran the more in the direction of India and his Indian interlocutors, while also drawing India more closely into his own scholarly purview.

Right across his career, Max-Müller cultivated friendships with Indian scholars through correspondence and invited many Indian visitors to the University. In particular, he became close to Keshub Chunder Sen, who had been the proselytizer for the nineteenth-century Hindu reform organization the Brahmo Samaj from the time he joined the organization in

1857. As an organization, the monotheistic Brahmo Samaj, too, interested Max-Müller – he saw it as a natural sect of Christianity. Several of Max-Müller's correspondents, in addition to K. C. Sen, were involved in the Brahmo Samaj, but, like him, Sen in particular was animated by an interest in finding points of synthesis between the different religions of the world. Indeed, the interest in spiritual communion that he shares with the Professor fosters an active interpersonal communion that runs like a current through Sen's three letters in the book. In Max-Müller's private view at the time, Sen's emphasis on love as the fundamental spiritual culture in which everyone could participate might go so far as leading him to convert to Christianity.

Significantly, none of the letters in Max-Müller's letters book are concerned with empire as such, or with colonial or anti-colonial issues, though they *are* motivated by ideas of communion between India and Britain, and, importantly, by notions of the oneness underlying all religious approaches, such as had been actively promoted by the Brahmo Samaj. The underlying belief expressed by virtually every one of the letter-writers is that Max-Müller is a friend to India and a sympathizer with Hinduism to the extent that he virtually embodies an ideal of spiritual oneness. The correspondent V. S. Mitra in a letter of 1887, for example, speaks of Max-Müller's 'genial sympathy with the natives of this land in every matter connected with their welfare'.[11]

The heterogeneous appearance and makeup of Max-Müller's letters book, bound together in rough chronological order, staggered and sewn in a higgledy-piggledy way, can be seen as symptomatic of the truncated, contingent connectivity in which the circle of interlocutors is engaged, though also of their binding interest in common, fostered within the Sanskritist's Oxford domain, despite the friends' disparate locations and concerns. The rough-edged aspect thus in no way detracts from the overriding emphasis across many of the letters on the 'Union of East and West' (something that again points to Max-Müller's rationale in putting the selection together). The structure of belief that brought the letter writers into conjunction in

11   Letter 7, MS Eng. d. 2352.

the first place was clearly the idea of an underlying religious unity, a one-ness of spirit, a sense of an 'all-ruling Providence', as Debendranath Tagore expresses it here, to which they all variously subscribed. It was this that drew their often passing, even one-off exchanges into some sort of meaningful constellation. The East-West 'Union' had of course in part been fostered by Max-Müller's own work in translation, and, conversely, the belief in under-lying oneness was a starting premise at the time for the kind of comparative work between religions as that which was carried out by Max-Müller. And, subsequently, once this oneness was established as a starting condition, the further contacts and exchanges that are recorded and acted upon in these pages might be developed. As a letter from the prominent Brahmo figure Debendranath Tagore, Rabindranath's father, has it:

> By the publication of the Rg Veda and the Upanishads you [Max-Müller] have brought within easy reach of European Scholars the thoughts and aspirations of our ancient Ritchis, hitherto hidden in inaccessible manuscripts, and it is to be hoped that the dissemination of the knowledge of our ancient literature will help to cement the bonds of union between the two people who, brought up under a common roof, parted from each other and scattered over distant quarters of the globe, [are] again to be brought together under the mysterious decress of an all-ruling providence.[12]

The sense of communion or oneness between Max-Müller and India, and, by extension, Oxford and India, was experienced in a very real, physical way within the University and the city, as all eminent Indian men of letters, as well as seers and gurus, when they visited Oxford in the later decades of the nineteenth century, made sure to visit him. South Parks Road and Banbury Road were well known to be thoroughfares for Indians plying back and forth to enjoy his legendary hospitality, and the family home in Norham Gardens was a fixed destination on the map of any Indian visit-ing Oxford, as a letter from Keshub Chunder Sen in the bundle of letters emphasizes. Here, in these spaces, the crossings and interchanges that his letters note down, or hanker for, were retraced and writ large. Cornelia Sorabji dropped by in the 1880s; Vivekananda visited in 1896; and Sen

---

12 Letter 27, MS Eng. d. 2352, p. 3.

recalled crossing paths with Max-Müller on several occasions. Indeed, had the professor still been alive when Rabindranath Tagore visited Oxford in 1913, the poet too would certainly have been a guest in Norham Gardens. As it was he had to be content with having lunch at the home of Poet Laureate Robert Bridges where, as Shahid Suhrawaddy rather typically described it, East and West physically met; the eastern grace of Tagore was confronted with the 'unexotic' British Poet Laureate Bridges.[13]

As for Max-Müller and his special interlocutor K. C. Sen, the first time the two men met was in 1870, in London, in the company of the Dean of Westminster and Prince Leopold, son of Queen Victoria. Sen at the time had travelled to England to deliver sermons at various Unitarian churches, and carried an invitation to speak at Manchester College. In due course, not very long after the London meeting, he came to Oxford to stay with the Max-Müller family, and engaged in a debate about salvation with Dr Pusey of the Oxford Movement. In their correspondence, Sen and Max-Müller, discussing controversies within the Brahmo Samaj, hark back to these happy times. In a letter of 2 May 1881, referring obliquely to the controversy unleashed by the marriage of his daughter at the age of thirteen, yet expressing also his great appreciation for the friendship of the All Souls Professor, Sen suggestively writes:

> In writing to me you need not conceal your real feelings. Discriminating criticism cannot pain me. Even the reprimands of a true friend are acceptable and must prove beneficial. I have read your letters with the deepest interest, and I only wish I could sit with you under one of those shady trees in Oxford which I saw during my short visit, and talk over the many important subjects referred to therein, for hours together. My heart is full.

Read collectively, as an epistolary accumulation, the letters show that the binding recognition of East-West bonds worked its changes on all parties concerned: it drew them if not into a palpable spirit of friendship, then into a theoretical sense of closeness, at the least.

---

13   S. Suhrawardy, 'Tagore at Oxford', *Calcutta Municipal Quarterly: Tagore Memorial Special Supplement* (13 Sept 1941).

A palpable spirit of friendship, built onto further tracings of cultural exchange between India and Britain, with Oxford as its site, may also be found in another volume in the Bodleian Library, this time in the form of a published text, a book of poems by four hands. Here once again, in the juxtaposition or indeed interleaving of the poems, in particular those by the St Paul's School friends Laurence Binyon and Manmohan Ghose, we see dramatized on the page the active collaboration between India and Britain that Oxford played host to, and, at certain times, and in discrete pockets, encouraged.

The volume concerned is *Primavera*, a collection of the work of four student poets (Arthur C. Cripps and Stephen Phillips, as well as Ghose and Binyon), all noticeably inspired by the aestheticism of Brasenose tutor, Walter Pater.[14] The polysyllabic strands of typical 1890s decorative devices that run through and across the poems, made as they are by English and Indian hands, lightly suggest that the decadent poetry that emerged out of the 1890s, and defined turn-of-the-century art, bore also an Indian stamp, and emerged even if in small part out of Oxford-India contact and collaboration. Indeed, as the interleaving of the poems by the different student poets on the page suggests, *Primavera*, named in recognition of the 'freshness' of Botticelli's atmospheric painting (highly valued by Pater), grew like a plant out of the trans-cultural interchange between the poet Ghose and the later art historian and translator Binyon, an interchange that had begun when they were both at school in London.[15]

Though their University days represented alienated and alienating times for both of them, especially for Ghose (Binyon's college Trinity did not accept Indians on religious grounds), the two young poets clearly found in their friendship a mutual 'capacity to be intoxicated by poetry', which was also extended into their anti-materialist criticism of imperial exploitation, and their interest in alternative religious understandings of

---

14   L. Binyon *et al*, *Primavera* (Oxford: B. H. Blackwell, 1890).
15   W. Pater, *The Renaissance: Studies in Art and Poetry* (1873; Oxford: Oxford UP, 1986), 40.

the natural world.[16] Each found in the other an impassioned soul, which
might find expression both in friendship and in poetry, the more so when
the poetry of the Oxford College quad became a coded expression of the
intense one-to-one friendship that was lived out in and around its pathways. In *Primavera*, an interesting call-and-response pattern runs across
and interconnects the poems by these two friends in particular. They are
seen to hold certain concerns in common, a straining for 'life' and 'youth',
which is repeatedly overshadowed and threatened by a world-weary pes-
simism that such visions of joy and promise can ever be realized; the sense
that it might ultimately be best to foster these as visions only.[17]

In the following section on Indian students' lived involvement with
Oxford, these brotherly or horizontal forms of Indian-British relationship,
which fundamentally ran against the grain of empire's hierarchies, are more
closely examined in their day-to-day rather than textual form.

Ghetto or Contact Zone: Indian Students' Contributions to Oxford University Life

As the number of Indians in Oxford grew, the charge was frequently made
(a charge that was often levelled against visible migrant communities), that
they only socialized with themselves, and formed cultural ghettos separate
and removed from a mainstream and homogeneous British society. The
Majlis Society was cited as a case in point.

Founded in 1896, the Majlis was a student debating society for Indians
at Oxford. It met every Sunday evening for political debates, modelled on
those in the Oxford Union, often considering the nature of India's position

16   L. Gandhi, *Affective Communities: Anticolonial Thought, Fin-de-Siecle Radicalism
      and the Politics of Friendship* (Durham and London: Duke University Press, 2006),
      162–71.
17   See, in particular, *Primavera*, 5–9 ('Youth' by Binyon; III by Ghose).

within Empire. The group brought Indians from different regional and cultural backgrounds together and allowed them to see, perhaps for the first time, that India could be constituted as a 'nation'.[18] In time, members were inspired by the Majlis's proto-political nationalist organization to join and lead nationalist parties in India that would eventually challenge the supremacy of the British Empire. When the number of Indians at Oxford in the first half of the twentieth century peaked in 1922 with 149 students enrolled, nearly all these Indians joined the Majlis, even those entering into the ICS.

Yet, although the University was often a breeding ground for political dissent and resistance, as the particular instance of radical debate in the Majlis, and the accompanying reputation of its inwardness, corroborates, at the same time many Indian students were also involved with societies that represented British cultural life in a more mainstream way. For British undergraduates, interaction in these societies was deeply influential for developing a masculine, adult identity and the friendships and networks that were grounded through student societies became the bedrock of professional networks in British government and finance. The Indian students who immersed themselves in these societies, were thus gaining a foothold in central contact zones of British public life at the heart of the University.

The college environment, too, created important networks between fellow students, tutors and alumni, and the alumni office retained ties with Old Boys by maintaining college registers detailing the careers of former students. In this respect, too, Indians were involved in areas far outside the closed domains of their specific groups and societies. The pages of the College Registers revealingly situate Indian names alongside their British counterparts: they are seen to participate in the matriculation ceremony together, take tutorials together and to become members of the same college societies, in another instance of Indian-British contact tracery. As Judith Brown in *Windows into the Past* has explored in relation to Balliol College, it is possible to build up an institutional history through the lives

---

18 S. Mukherjee, *Nationalism, Education and Migrant Identities: The England-Returned* (London: Routledge, 2010).

of the individuals within in it.[19] Here, St John's College can be used as a case study to identify some of the Indian students who for a time became of this distinctive British establishment. Indeed, the difficulty in quantifying these students testifies to the success of their infiltration into the key British institution of the Oxford College.

One method of identifying the Indian students in the University record is by recognizing or even decoding Indian surnames. This method, however, can become victim to the worst kind of Orientalism, categorizing certain surnames as 'Eastern' or 'foreign-sounding'. Islamic names such as Ali or Khan could denote students from the Indian sub-continent or from the Middle East, and further, names such as Ram or Pal/l could arguably have European heritage. The college register gives details of where the students were educated before joining St John's and so one can note those who were schooled in India; yet this criterion also creates problems. Many sons and daughters of British officials serving in India were born and educated in India, but would one classify them as Indian? As this shows, when Britishness is interrogated in relation to India, it is paramount that one also evaluates Indianness in relation to Britain. If place of birth is less important than racial or ethnic background in categorizing identity, how does one incorporate the offspring of mixed parentage? And, as an imperial Britishness becomes more inclusive, does a colonized Indianness become more exclusive? It is these kinds of questions that are raised by a reading of Indian presences in the Oxford College record.

A number of Indian students became members of the St John's Debating Society, including Har Dayal (1905), Indrajhit Kalabhai (1897), Jaipal Singh (1922) and Ishwar Chanda Nanda (1924). Indians from various colleges including St John's also became members of the Oxford Union. Established in 1823, the Oxford Union attracted a number of high-profile speakers and bred a number of international politicians. Many of the debates related to Indian issues, including a debate during the First World War about the deployment of Indian troops. Many South Asian students tried (with

19   J. M. Brown, *Windows into the Past: Life Histories and the Historian of South Asia* (Notre Dame: Notre Dame Press, 2009).

varying degrees of success) to become a part of the Union Society commit-tees, all of which were decided by election. For example, M. C. Chagla was elected to the Library Committee in 1921. In Michaelmas 1923, Solomon Bandaranaike was elected secretary of the Union, and treasurer in Trinity 1924. He stood for the presidency of the Union, but was defeated, and some believed that many old life-members turned out for this election specifi-cally to defeat Bandaranaike – who was later to become Prime Minister of Sri Lanka. Humayun Kabir was elected to the Library Committee in 1929, was elected secretary in 1930 and then librarian in 1931. He was also unsuccessful in standing for president.

The first Indian president of the Oxford Union was D. F. Karaka from Bombay. He was president in the Hilary Term of 1934, having been sec-retary and librarian previously. As secretary of the Union in 1933, Karaka was present at the controversial debate: 'That this House will under no circumstances fight for its King and Country'. The motion was carried by 275 votes to 153, sparking national outcry and leading to a denouncement by Winston Churchill. Despite Karaka's achievement of being elected to lead a British institution steeped in tradition and influence, he was aware that the colour bar continued to exist and that 'whiteness' remained a defin-ing characteristic of Britishness at this time. In the final debate under his presidency, Karaka launched a scathing attack upon the colour bar with particular reference to the Oxford Carlton Club, where class and race were intimately intertwined.

Jaipal Singh, who was elected secretary in 1924 and then president in 1925 of the St John's Debating Society, was also a member of the Essay Society. As a member of the Debating Society, Singh spoke on motions ranging from a discussion of the merits of the public school system, the consumption of literature and the future of the British Empire. Additional-ly, as a member of the Essay Society, Singh attended meetings where essays on Matthew Arnold, the press, the devil, and Rabindranath Tagore were discussed. Once again, this individual's textual profile in the College record outlines the ways in which East and West were meeting through various forms of exchange in Oxford, and how Indian students were imbib-ing and shaping Britishness through their involvement in student societies. In the case of M. Gopal Singh's essay reading on Tagore, ideas about India were being discussed in the heart of the Oxford College, and, although many of the perceptions of India relied upon stereotypes, this dialogue was essential for developing transnational identities and bringing Britain and India to closer cultural and political understanding. As the St John's Minute Book records:

> After the paper, the usual discussion followed, during which conversation strayed in a pleasant way from Kipling's works to the art of peasant homes, from Indian craft-work and ivories to Indian jugglers, from jungle-snakes with two mouths, one at each end, to Kashmir shawls and sculpture; and Mr Gopal Singh took the opportunity of giving the Society a most able survey of Indian thought and customs.[20]

If student societies represented fertile ground for forging key friendships and networks within the imperial hub of Oxford, sporting societies were particularly significant for solidifying imperial masculinities, in the same way as was the Scout Movement for young boys.[21] Jaipal Singh was a member of the St John's College football XI in 1925–6, and the college hockey XI throughout his time at the college. Furthermore, he represented the University Hockey XI in Varsity matches from 1924–6. Singh started the Oxford Hermits – a sports society for 'Asiatics' in Oxford which mainly played hockey. Having obtained a 4th in PPE, Singh then took the ICS exams, and was a probationary student at St John's. As Singh wore the appropriate sports outfits, and participated fully in these sporting activities, it can be assumed that his presence will have challenged British ideas of racial difference that assumed the femininity and cultural difference of non-martial race Indians (Singh was the son of a farmer from Bihar in Eastern India). At the same time his inclusion in these sports clubs also put ideas of a homogenous British masculine identity under pressure.[22]

Singh was later involved in Indian students' hockey tours of Europe and the formation of the India Hockey Federation. In 1928, he captained the India Hockey Team at the Amsterdam Olympics. The team won all

---

20   St John's College Oxford Essay Society Minute Book, Vol. V. 1919–34.
21   J. M. Mackenzie, ed., *Imperialism and Popular Culture* (Manchester: Manchester University Press, 1986).
22   M. Sinha, *Colonial Masculinity: The 'Manly Englishman' and the 'Effeminate Bengali' in the late nineteenth century* (Manchester: Manchester University Press, 1995).

their games without conceding a goal, and was awarded the gold medal. Through the Darlington MP, Lord Pake Pense, Singh was introduced to Viscount Bearstead, Chairman of Shell Transport and Trading Company, who arranged for a job for Singh with the Burnham-Shell Oil Storage and Distributing Company of India. He was the first Indian to be appointed to a covenanted mercantile assistant in Royal Dutch Shell group, effectively promoted by his trend-breaking sporting prowess. After a probationary period in London, he was sent to Calcutta and then pursued a political career in Bihar campaigning for Adibasi (tribal) rights.

Where Singh thus went on to represent India in hockey, other Indians represented England at other sports. As well as the Prince Ranjitsinhji or Ranji, mentioned above, another Prince, the Nawab of Pataudi Iftikhar Ali Khan, is the only Test cricketer to have played for both England and India. He joined Balliol College in 1927 and won hockey and cricketing blues for the University. In a famous incident playing in the 1931 match against Cambridge, A. Ratcliffe of Cambridge set a new record for the University Match with 201 runs. Pataudi declared that he would beat that record and did exactly that in the next innings, scoring 238 not out; a record which stood until 2005. This feat, and his bravado in setting out to beat the record, were seen as a key indication of his manliness in this 'great and historic innings', cementing his place in the British record books.[23] Pataudi made the England squad for the infamous Bodyline series tour of Australia in 1932–3. On his Ashes and Test debut, he scored a century, but was dropped after the second test. He only played three tests for England, with a recall in one of the Ashes tests in 1934. Pataudi returned to India and had a chance to captain India in 1936, but withdrew from the series against England. In 1946, he did captain India against England, though he was already 36 years old. As with Singh, this University man's sporting prowess placed under scrutiny the stereotyped image not only of the effeminate Indian, but also of the anti-social or withdrawn Indian student, that British students brought with them to Oxford.

23   'Cricket: The University Match, Nawab of Pataudi's New Record', *The Times* (8 July 1931).

Conclusion

What then do these various layerings of involvement between Indians and British individuals within Oxford, say about formations of Britishness at the time? Our examples suggest, we submit, that far from these migrant presences being transitory, moving through this iconic British space without trace, Indian travellers to the University left behind cultural, visual and textual marks of their involvement and exchange that would eventually help to reshape the at-one-time culturally homogeneous Oxford environment in influential ways. Their input contributed to mapping the city as multi-cultural and even 'cosmopolitan', a development that would of course continue and ramify across the twentieth century.[24] Through their networks, friendships, associations and groupings they changed the University landscape both for other Indians and for the British, creating channels of connection which could be re-accessed, re-used and adapted by those who came after them – as the turn of the millennium Oxford novels by Indian novelists Amit Chaudhuri (1993) and Neel Mukherjee are sharply aware (2010).[25] They challenged how domestic British space and the national space of the sports ground were viewed; they inflected ideas of who belonged where; of Britain as at once 'foreign' space, yet 'home'.

24   Jonathan Schneer, *London 1900: The Imperial Metropolis* (London: Yale University Press, 1999).
25   Amit Chaudhuri, *Afternoon Raag* (London: Picador, 1993); Neel Mukherjee, *A Life Apart* (London: Constable & Robinson, 2010).

Representing Britishness: Culture and Identity

MEENAKSHI SHARMA

6 The Empire of English and Its Legacy: A Citizenship of the Mind

No attempt at defining or understanding English/British identity and culture can really be considered complete if it is limited to the viewpoint of the residents of the British Isles. Representations by 'others' and from outside the framework of the national culture have not been given much attention in existing debates around English/British identity and culture. The view from outside, and especially of those who were part of the British empire as colonial subjects, provides an important perspective to these definitions. In *Englishness: Politics and Culture, 1880–1920*, Robert Colls and Philip Dodd admit that an account of 'what the Empire or a part of it, thought of the English' would have made their treatment of the idea of Englishness more complete.[1] The centuries of imperial expansion had great significance in the cultural self-constitution and self-representation for the British; in Robert Young's words, 'colonialism, in the British example, was not simply a marginal activity on the edges of English civilisation, but fundamental in its own cultural self-representation'.[2] Dodd regards the 'ability to represent both itself to others and those others to themselves' as characteristic of 'the dominant version of Englishness' that was authorized during the emergence of the idea towards the end of the nineteenth century and in the early years of the twentieth century.[3] At the same time, colonialism and imperialism brought other peoples around the world into

---

1   R. Colls and P. Dodd, *Englishness: Politics and Culture, 1880–1920* (London: Croom Helm, 1986), Preface.
2   R. Young, *White Mythologies: Writing History and the West* (London: Routledge 1991), 174.
3   Colls and Dodd, *Englishness*, 2.

contact with English education and culture, and consequently created ideas and images of Englishness in their minds that came to be represented in various art forms. Without being tempered with these images from the outside perspective, the idea of English culture cannot be considered complete; just as Joseph Needham writes of the importance of the outsider's perspective on Europe as a whole: 'it is indispensable to view Europe from the outside, to view the history of Europe, the failures of Europe as well as its successes, through the eyes of that vast part of humanity which is formed by the peoples of Asia and Africa.'[4] In the case of England and India, specifically, Gerald Manley Hopkins poses the questions:

> How far can the civilization England offers be attractive and valuable and be offered and insisted on as an attraction and a thing of value to India for instance? Of course those who live in our civilization and belong to it praise it: it is not hard, as Socrates said, among the Athenians to praise the Athenians, but how will it be represented by critics bent on making the worst of it?[5]

As this chapter demonstrates, as a result of English education, educated Indians came to regard England and English culture not as 'critics bent on making the worst of it' but rather as Anglophiles who internalized textual images to form an idealized construction of England and a sense of identification with Englishness. Given the complexity of Indian society and of the colonial encounter, the responses to this imagined England as represented in Indian writing in English, are not simple or uniform. Yet, there is a dominant strain in this writing of English educated Indians of internalization of literary images of England and idealization of Englishness. This, in turn, leads to a strong sense of identification with Englishness that is at odds with the political reality of citizenship. While the experience of Anglo-Indians (in the old sense of the English in India rather than mixed breeds) is dismissed as 'un-English' by Indians who pride themselves on knowing 'true' Englishness, direct experience of England provides both recognition

---

4   Needham cited in A. Abdul-Malek, 'Orientalism in Crisis', *Diogenes* 44 (1963), 103.

5   Manley Hopkins cited in J. Meyers, *Fiction and the Colonial Experience* (Ipswich: Boydell Press, 1973), 6.

of things familiarized through texts, and shock when the mental images and sense of belonging and identification are rudely shaken.

This chapter examines the construction of England from afar – based largely on texts – and the consequent sense of identification with English-ness, by piecing together ideas and images from Indian Writing in English dealing with idealized constructions of England and first-hand encounters with it. Although in the texts examined here, the terms 'Englishness' and 'Britishness' were often used interchangeably, it is 'Englishness' that domi-nates the cultural aspirations and identifications though an internalisation of representations in English literature. Some writers were careful to dis-tinguish the two, reserving 'British'/'Britishness' for use in the context of imperial history and a sense of political identity and reference to political and legal institutions of state rather than to a cultural nationalism. This per-ception of the colonial Indians was not an aberration; as Langlands points out, 'at both national and imperial levels Britishness has always been defined more in terms of a common allegiance to the crown, rather than by any ethno-cultural homogeneity'.[6] With the focus of the chapter on cultural identification and internalization of cultural ideals, and the more frequent use of the term in the texts in question, 'Englishness' is used in preference to the term 'Britishness'. However, a tight distinction is not being argued, and hence at places, Englishness is used to cover the sense of Britishness without diverting from the thesis to make the distinction explicit.

Colonising the Mind: English Literary Education

The encounter of India and Britain was the encounter of an ancient cul-ture that had been shaped by countless forces through millennia, and of an empire that had recently risen out of naval might and enterprise. From the

6   R. Langlands, 'Britishness or Englishness: The Historical Problem of National Identity in Britain', *Nations and Nationalism* 5 (1) (1999), 63.

Eurocentric view, the new lands 'discovered' and colonized were sources of power for economic, political and military growth. Even humanist causes such as social upliftment and education were not untouched by the motive of power; such investments benefited the colonial powers by rendering the colonized willing and more malleable subjects. The insidious colonization of the mind through a slow and subtle indoctrination into the ethnocentric ideals of the ruling race was an achievement of English education and the English language. Throughout the empire these were used as powerful tools for the colonization of the mind and cultural co-option. One of the most successful cases of the transplantation of the English language was India where the adaptability that had ensured the longevity of this ancient seat of civilization gave it good soil for taking root. Although the successful transplant of the English language and the emphasis on literary education served its primary purpose excellently – producing an army of natives with the necessary skills for manning the lower rungs of the government machinery – it also created, not unintentionally, generations of Indians who had deeply imbibed the language, and through it, cultural ideals that became the new benchmark for 'civilisation'. Gauri Viswanathan has underlined how English education in British India was employed as a tool for acquiring 'cultural domination... by consent'.[7] Ashis Nandy has also stressed the role of 'cultural co-optation' as crucial in colonialism with many Indians seeing 'their salvation in becoming more like the British'.[8] However, while this class of culturally co-opted Indians went on to be the strongest supporters of the continuation of British rule, there were also unforeseen and troubling offshoots of this acculturation. The class did not remain a mere aid to the consolidation and administrative ease of the empire, but as a result of the formative influence of English education and exposure to western ideas, began to not only admire and imitate the English but also to raise politically and socially troubling questions of identity and citizenship

7   G. Viswanathan, 'Currying Favour: The Politics of British Educational and Cultural Policy in India, 1813–1854', Social Text 19/20 (1988), 85.
8   A. Nandy, The Intimate Enemy: Loss and Recovery of Self under Colonialism (Delhi: Oxford University Press, 1983), 7.

resulting from the gulf between the idealized plane where a strong sense of identification with Englishness could flourish and the political plane where identity and citizenship were determined by race and categories of ruler and ruled.

The idealized constructions of England/Britain, Europe, and the West generally, absorbed from literary and historical texts by the privileged minority who had exposure to English ideas through their education, became a lasting legacy of British imperialism. All discourse in the English language added up to ideas about England, with the terms 'England' and the 'West' becoming synonymous or interchangeable. Whether seen metonymically as the 'other' and all that was foreign, or as the generalized image crystallized from English texts, 'Englishness' came to stand for a conflation of Englishness, Britishness, and (Anglophone) Western-ness. The dominant version of identity in the colonial times was an English one wherein there was an 'unconscious conflation' of Britain and England on the part of the English, and Indians unconsciously came to absorb this conflation.[9] Robin Cohen too argues that the British diaspora of the colonial times looked to a Britain 'dominated by *English* aspirations'. 'By signalling their putative association with the English, upper part of the class structure back home' they further contributed to the conflation of Britishness with Englishness.[10]

As a result of the social insularity of the Anglo-Indians in India, especially during the Raj, the educated Indians' construction of England was based largely on literary texts, with very limited actual contact with English people. So strong was the hold of these idealized images of English life and culture that when the sample of English life encountered in the colonial set-up did not match up, it was discounted as an aberration from the ideal absorbed from literary texts. In fact, Indians who absorbed these literary images could claim to be more in tune with 'true' Englishness than the colonial English people they saw around them. This was not

---

9   Langlands 'Britishness or Englishness', 53.
10   R. Cohen, 'Fuzzy Frontiers of Identity: The British Case' *Social Identities* 1 (1) (1995), 45, emphasis added.

merely fortuitous; Viswanathan points to the strategic use of 'the body of knowledge represented by English literary texts' to efface 'the often sordid history of colonialist expropriation, material exploitation, and class and race oppression'.[11] For the colonized, the English literary text functioned as a 'surrogate Englishman in his highest and most perfect state'.[12] Such a calculated exposure to positive representations of Englishness was designed to deeply inculcate the superiority of English culture and create a corresponding desire for imitation. In this it met with much success, yet a troubling offshoot was that the educated Indians began to perceive the discrepancies between 'true Englishness' and the colonialist variant and consequently to feel 'more English than the English'! The resentment of the colonialists to the English-educated class was based on the perception that it produced in the colonized, a sense of equality with the ruling class, incongruent with the colonial situation with precise boundaries and categories. Nirad Chaudhuri's view that 'the acquisition of English by us was [perceived by the Anglo-Indians] like the possession of the English franchise' and hence deeply resented crystallizes the link between acquiring the English language, and through it, the ideas and sensibility of the English, and a strong sense of identification with Englishness.[13] Amidst the high-minded liberal rhetoric of Macaulay and Trevelyan, thought was not given to the anachronism that could result from producing such citizenship of the mind through education when the political and social reality was that of a people under foreign domination.

This legacy of empire also has consequences for the travellers and migrations from formerly colonized people to Britain – the 'striking back' of the empire as it were. The move is seen as much as a 'return home' by the coloured ex-colonized as by those from the settler colonies. Paradoxically

---

11   Viswanathan, 'Currying Favour', 98.
12   Ibid. 103.
13   N. Chaudhuri, 'The English Language in India: Past, Present and Future', in A. Niven, ed., *The Commonwealth Writer Overseas: Themes of Exile and Expatriation* (Brussels: Didier, 1976), 91. Nirad Chaudhuri, the most famous Indian Anglophile, who felt himself to be an Englishman except by birth, settled in Oxford at the age of 73 and lived the life of an Englishman till his death nearly 30 years later.

enough, the 'striking back' was motivated primarily by a sense of belonging rather than a reprisal. Actual encounters with the culture, the people, and the landscape produced responses ranging from recognition and identification to shock at the contrast between the text-derived images and hard reality, especially in terms of challenge to their sense of identification by race and citizenship. The troubling encounter of this 'homecoming' was hardly settled as benignly as in the exceptional case of Nirad Chaudhuri, complicated as it inevitably was, by the stress caused by the sense of belonging at an idealized plane and the reality of the political and social plane where British identity remained quite firmly a racial construction. These ideas can be illustrated with reference to autobiographical and fictional texts by Indian writers.

Autobiographical Accounts

Chaudhuri famously dedicated his *Autobiography of an Unknown Indian* (1951) to 'the memory of the British Empire in India, which conferred subjecthood upon us but withheld citizenship; to which yet every one of us threw out the challenge "*Civis Britannicus sum*" [I am a British citizen] because all that was good and living within us was made, shaped, and quickened by the same British rule'.[14] He offers an account of an England seen through the prism of text-based ideals in *A Passage to England* (1959). On his first visit to England when he was nearing sixty, Chaudhuri's predominant experience is that of 'recognition' as things already known through books take tangible form before his eyes. As he is at pains to stress, his familiarity with and mastery of English culture were based, not on the colonial community in India but were arrived at vicariously through literary texts and the English language. As he puts it in his essay, 'English Language in

---

14   N. Chaudhuri, *The Autobiography of an Unknown Indian* (London: MacMillan, 1951), n.p.

India,' the British community in India heartily disliked Indians who knew English and were to be given no credit for his acquisition of English or admiration for English culture which were based solely on his reading.[15] English education and literary texts successfully displace the image of the colonialist English people on the spot as the source of ideas about 'authentic' Englishness.

The literary idea of England is so powerful in Chaudhuri's mind that direct experience of England does not displace or even dent it. In the words of the contemporary novelist, Amit Chaudhuri, Nirad Chaudhuri's comparison of the 'authorized version' of the England he already knew with the makeshift version that was physically presented to his eyes is the outcome of a 'predilection for attributing a veracity, or priority, to text or word over 'actual' landscape or location (that) seems to be a habit of the colonial mind'.[16] Nirad Chuadhuri writes in a letter home from England that 'England has *not* become more real to me than it was' and he claims that 'in no case was the idea of England I had gained from books contradicted by anything I saw, it was on the contrary completed'.[17] Not only does he dismiss the samples of Englishness in India as 'inauthentic' (or aberrations of an ideal) on the strength of his textually-derived understanding of 'true' Englishness, he also dismisses 'real' England as less 'true'. He writes, with typical aplomb, 'my earlier, and *as I believe truer*, ideas of England were all acquired from literature, history, and geography'.[18] He trusts these 'truer' ideas and his familiarity with English literature as the best possible guide to the English scene. His claim that 'the only ties felt in the heart that we can have with England are those created by things of the mind' is substantiated by his strong feelings for England based completely on things of the mind – things to which even direct, first-hand sensory experience can

---

15   Chaudhuri, 'The English Language', 92.
16   A. Chaudhuri, 'POLES OF RECOVERY: From Dutt to Chaudhuri', *Interventions* 4 (1) (2002), 99.
17   N.Chaudhuri, *A Passage to England* (London: MacMillan, 1959), 14–15. Emphasis added.
18   Ibid. 4. Emphasis added.

add nothing.[19] His adulation for English poetry as 'the most wonderful thing in the world' is clearly at the base of his strong feelings for England itself. While Rupert Brooke felt that if he died in a distant land some part of that foreign soil would become forever England, Chaudhuri feels that if he 'died in England what would become forever England would be a little foreign flesh, and with that faith there was happiness in perishing in an English glade, with the robin and the wren twittering overhead'.[20] His desire came true with his death at the age of 101 in Oxford, after spending the last nearly thirty years of his life in England.

Even earlier than Chaudhuri, we find in Rakhal Das Haldar a mid-nineteenth century educated Indian whose Western education led to unquestioning indoctrination into imperialist ideology, loyalty to British rule, and admiration of England. These responses are clearly evident in his *English Diary*, an account of a visit to England in 1861–2 (published post-humously in 1903). The editor notes that 'the good qualities of the English people always appealed to him, but when he left the shores of England in July 1862, after a residence of about fourteen months his admiration for the people and their country was greater than ever before'[21] On setting foot on British ground at New Haven he describes it as near the land-ing point of William the Conqueror. But rather than fancying himself as another William the Conqueror, he experiences a sense of homecoming: 'I felt the same kind of joy I could have felt on reaching back the shores of Bengal. How was it that I felt as if I had come home?'[22] The literary image of England is sustained as his stay is marked by interaction with 'the most distinguished literary men of the day, such as Max-Müller, Goldstucker, H. C. Robinson, Dr Martineau and Sir Charles Trevelyan'.[23] What he sees of England goes to bolster, almost without exception, his text-derived idealized image. This early text prefigures later accounts that show how

---

19   Ibid. 16.
20   Ibid. 114.
21   R. D. Haldar, *The English Diary of an Indian Student 1861–62: Being the Scribbling Diary of the Late Rakhal Das Haldar* (Dacca: Ashutosh Library, 1903), xvi.
22   Ibid. 21.
23   Ibid. i.

literary images guide the traveller's perception and even itinerary in England. For instance, Haldar goes to: 'Three Mile Cross to see the house of Mary Russell Mitford, the authoress of "Our Village," etc. Long ago I had read about her and her residence in that delightful little volume, "Pen and Ink Sketches of Authors".'[24] He describes how once, passing within three miles of Stoke Poges, he felt 'it would have been a piece of unpardonable folly to have missed the opportunity of visiting it... I had read Gray's Elegy with tears in my eyes, and my feelings may be easily imagined when I entered the churchyard where the immortal Elegy was composed'. He made sure to stand under 'the identical "shady yew tree," and to see other objects alluded to in the exquisite Elegy' and brought back with him some ivy leaves from 'the ivy-mantled tower'. As they drove back from Stoke Poges he 'looked longingly on the picturesque church-steeple and regretted that the tolling of the curfew and the parting day were wanting to complete the picture given in the Elegy. The human mind is satisfied with nothing short of perfection'.[25] He refers to Stratford-upon-Avon as a 'holy' place and 'proud of being (apparently) the first Bengali who has paid a visit to this poetical shrine', he writes his name in a visitor's book at Shakespeare's house as 'a pilgrim from the far Ind'.[26] He describes his 'first experience of a genuine English home' as 'simply paradise'.[27] Describing a walk in the countryside, Haldar writes:

> [We] passed through hills, dales, woods, meadows, and purling streams, the glories of England – all that inspired her favoured sons and daughters. What wonder that Englishmen in India should long for 'home', such an exquisitely beautiful and sweet home as this? Howse made a very just remark that the secret of the greatness of England was the readiness with which Englishmen could abandon this paradise of existence for the toil and hardships of the battle-field when their country's interest was at stake. Yes, this is true heroism![28]

24   Ibid. 71.
25   Ibid. 76.
26   Ibid. 84 and 82.
27   Ibid. 22–3.
28   Ibid. 73.

The sense of identification with Englishmen is so great for this 'citizen of the mind' that like them, he too experiences the acute pain of parting from 'this paradise on earth' that feels like home to him.[29]

About a century later, Sadhan Kumar Ghosh in *My English Journey* (1961), similarly records his experience of England as only validating the ideas derived from literary texts. The London of his dreams is a patchwork of literary ideas and images: "'I love walking in London,' said Mrs. Dalloway. So did I'.[30] Walking the streets of central London, he is aware that 'Lamb must have trudged these streets over and over again'.[31] He describes London as a city which had 'haunted' his imagination and dreams and which, 'the modern megalopolises notwithstanding, is still the centre of civilization'.[32] The strong literary idea of London causes 'a vicarious nostalgia' for a 'vanished' London – 'a compost of my dreams and others' memories'.[33] Ghosh adds, 'London I had always envisaged – despite Margery Sharp, Norman Collins, and, of course, Virginia Woolf – as a late-Victorian or Edwardian city. But the London I had dreamt of as a child was a compost of a lot of fog ('the London Particular'), women selling violets in Leicester Square, Fannies by gaslight, the hansom cab, and the muffin man'.[34]

The vivid text-derived image of London leads to some disappointment with the actual London: 'I should... have thought better of London, if it still had the *London Mercury*, the *New Age* and the Poetry Bookshop'. Similarly, he writes that at Oxford, 'I felt a longing, almost a heartache, for the Oxford of long ago, the Oxford I could never have seen but which I knew better than my own home town'.[35] The literary basis of this intimate familiarity is clear in a passage such as the following:

29 Ibid. 94.
30 S. K. Ghosh, *My English Journey* (Calcultta: Writers Workshop, 1961), 133.
31 Ibid. 139.
32 Ibid. 9.
33 Ibid. 141–2.
34 Ibid. 132.
35 Ibid. 20 and 35.

When I visited Oxford, the sight of Cumnor cowslips brought back Arnold's memory, but in the grassy harvest of the Eynsham water meadows the fritillaries were blowing no longer. It saddened me to think that the scholar-gipsy would be a stranger and a sojourner in an Oxford where the car is heard oftener than the cuckoo... the bridle-track from Appleton down which the troops of hunters came in *Thyrsis* has a brash, industrial look.[36]

Ghosh's entire account offers a self-congratulatory *literary* view of England. The 'English Journey' of the title is really an English *literary* journey. Although it is an account of a first visit to England by Ghosh late in life (as in the case of Chaudhuri), it is filled with 'recognition' rather than discovery. The England he experiences is already 'known' and loved, albeit textually. C. M. Bowra, in his Foreword to the book, refers to Ghosh's use of 'his knowledge of English literature to enable him to see the many elements of our life in a clear perspective... for him all that really matters in English life can be found, sooner or later, in English literature.'[37] Swinnerton's introduction to the book notes Ghosh's exceptional familiarity with English literature 'not only as a scholar, but as an enthusiast whose literary loves were formed and whose interest in 'England's green and pleasant land' was as keen as comprehensive reading in Shakespeare, Johnson, Wordsworth, and more modern authors could make him'. Like Haldar, Ghosh uses the image of a pilgrim and calls the book 'the end of a pilgrimage... [which] began as a journey of the mind when the glory of English literature was first revealed to me.'[38]

The undisguised idealization of England is not a stray paragraph or sentiment – rather, it represents the dominant tone and sentiment of the whole book. Although Ghosh calls his experience of England an entry into 'a new world', it is not really a new world for him as it resonates with vivid images acquired from literature. The weeping willows along the Avon 'bring Desdemona's song to mind', the deer at Charlecote House make him wonder if one of them has any connection to 'the one Shakespeare is supposed – according to familiar legend – to have pinched', and the

36   Ibid. 21.
37   Ibid. 2.
38   Ibid. 4.

'misty mornings and the starlit silences' are keys for 'reach[ing] the inner Wordsworth'.[39] The textual expectation which marks Ghosh's approach to England is explicitly acknowledged in the case of All Souls, for which 'perhaps A. L. Rowse, the historian, had set my expectations too high', and of 'nostalgia' for Oxford which was 'created by Lamb... and perpetuated by Arnold, Newman and Andrew Lang'.[40] His sources of familiarity with Cambridge are clear when he lists Christopher Isherwood's *Lions and Shadows*, Gwen Raverat's *Period Piece*, M. R. James's *Eton and Kings*, and E. M. Forster's *G. Lowes Dickinson* as 'books which arouse a vicarious nostalgia for Cambridge throughout the world'.[41]

As in Chaudhuri's *Passage to England* we find in Ghosh's account that the internalisation of the ideal offered through literary education is so great that when 'reality' proves discordant, it is displaced in order to keep the ideal intact. These writers even criticize contemporary England for falling short of the ideals of true Englishness as they have imbibed these from English literature, and feel completely qualified to teach the English how to be English. When Ghosh finds something to criticize in English culture, he lays the blame not on 'Englishness' *per se* but on 'certain social changes in England' and on 'the hazards of metropolitan life and a telly-snack bar culture' as in the case of his perception of the 'general apathy' towards elderly citizens.[42] Similarly, his disapproval of hunting in England is distinctly limited to present-day England: 'In the England of to-day Schweitzer, St Francis of Assisi and the Ancient Mariner would be de trop, sadly out of things'.[43] He is pained at the 'passing of familiar things' – a familiarity, we must remind ourselves, based solely on texts. In contemporary England, he is distressed to find that 'no-one in England... bother[s] about first impressions or second thoughts on dewdrops on nasturtiums, or the tiny, stammering song of the yellowhammer in hedger-rows full of honeysuckle and the almondlike tang of the meadowsweet'.[44]

39   Ibid. 47–53.
40   Ibid. 27 and 36.
41   Ibid. 37.
42   Ibid. 109–10.
43   Ibid. 118.
44   Ibid. 105.

In many such instances we find the more-English-than-the-English Indian disappointed by the Englishness of the English. He feels that only he can identify with a 'quintessential' England while 'no one in England' can do so; the implication being that such appreciation was part of true Englishness which present-day English people have allowed to disappear. The hankering after a 'true' England which is distinct from the power and position of the political entity is reflected in his quotation from E. M. Forster about the disappearance of the 'stray elm, puddles full of ranunculus, or mole hills covered with thyme; and they, not the grandeur, are England'.[45] A startling appropriation of Englishness by an Indian is to be seen in such instances of the internalisation of literary ideals and identification with 'true' Englishness.[46]

Fictional Accounts

While autobiographical accounts represent the Anglicisation and the consequent idealisation of England and identification with Englishness as a result of English education and internalisation of literary images in a sympathetic, even self-congratulatory manner, in fictional accounts the figure of the anglicized Indian is represented sympathetically in some texts and in others used to send up the class. Instances of the latter tendency represent the disdain in which the brown Englishmen who aped the foreign culture and looked down upon Indianness (and often sided politically with British rule), were often held by the majority of Indians. A wonderful example of a fictional character who 'knows' and admires England thorough English

45   Ibid. 106.
46   Elsewhere I have worked on the subversive potential of such apparently flattering imitation and appropriation of language and narrative/descriptive power. See M. Sharma, *Postcolonial Indian Writing in English: Between Co-option and Resistance* (Jaipur: Rawat, 2003).

literary texts is Banerrji, in G V Desani's *Hatterr* (1948). The simplistic reduction of Banerrji's text-derived ideas into an ossified image of England is wonderfully satirized in his advice to Hatterr to go 'to the Western hemisphere. England is the place for you':

> You will progress there. ... The climate is non-tropical, and the weather extremely bracing. ... You have nothing to fear in England. I respectfully disagree with Henry the Fifth, Act IV, when it states, Have you a ruffian that will swear, drink, dance? Be happy, England will give him office, honour, might! On the contrary, I wholeheartedly agree with the view expressed by the bastard, King John, Scene VII, Come the three corners of the world in arms, and we shall shock them. Nought shall make us rue, if England to itself do rest but true. England *is* true.[47]

Banerrji claims that 'Shakespeare, literature, Shelley's heart, flowers and other beauties is what I live for'.[48] He speaks in a pastiche of literary quotations and paraphrases. His love for literature extends to everything English:

> I... love England. And Englishmen, women and children. I often wish I could change my maiden name 'Nath' to 'Noel'. I have recently formed several English connexions myself, and I like dogs too. If you require a proof of my sincerity, I am a member of the English Tail Waggers', although I had the clear nationalist choice to join the Kennel Club of India.[49]

The 'love' of England, English men, women, and children is taken to a ridiculous extreme to satirize the anglophile's dog-like adulation of Englishness. The willing subjection of the colonized Indian becomes crystallized in this image of the fawning dog.

Another fictional character – the eponymous 'Chacha' in Ved Mehta's *Delinquent Chacha* (1967) – serves to sometimes touchingly and sometimes satirically, ridicule the pathetic and ridiculous position of anglicized and anglophilic Indians. Chacha is presented as an Indian who, through a text-based familiarity, identifies so completely with Englishness that he

47   G. V. Desani, *All About Mr. Hatterr: A Gesture* (London: Aldor, 1948), 125.
48   Ibid. 221.
49   Ibid. 197.

vehemently argues in an English court that 'at heart I am an Englishman, and *ipso facto*... not a foreigner in any sense of the word. It is in India that I am an alien. I am acquainted not only with the distinction between E-s-q and C. M. G. but with K. B. E., O. B. E., K. C. S. I., O. M., K. O. S. B., K. G., O.St J'.[50] This identification makes him completely acquiescent in, and unquestioningly receptive to, the colonizers' self-aggrandising accounts of themselves and the representations of those they colonized as inferior. Despite having lived under the inequities of British rule in India, and having witnessed the trauma of partition, Chacha simple-mindedly echoes the colonialist interpretations of history and culture. In his mind, British rule was a privilege – because it gave him 'the advantage of a chivalrous association with the British'.[51] He lives by the unshakeable motto that all that is good is English, and dreams of not only reaching England one day, studying at 'Ox-Ford', and even being honoured by the Queen, but also of restoring British rule to India as the panacea for all her ills.[52] Through the comic characterisation of Chacha and his unquestioning acceptance of the equation of 'gentlemanliness' with 'Englishness', Mehta exposes the insidious effect of colonising the mind through English literary education.

In Anita Desai's novel *Bye-Bye, Blackbird* (1971) the English-educated Indians – Dev and Adit – are presented more sympathetically and provide a vivid picture of England as seen through the eyes of those who have internalized literary images and come to feel a sense of belonging and identification from afar. In Dev, we meet the new immigrant coming to England with a mental baggage of literature-acquired concepts about England, its institutions and people. An education at St Xavier's School in Calcutta run by black-frocked Jesuits has, he thinks, 'well prepared' him to enter this world 'by fifteen years of reading the books that had been his meat and drink, the English books that had formed at least one half of his conscious existence'.[53] In the National Gallery he delights in 'seeing the

50   V. Mehta, *Delinquent Chacha* (London: Collins, 1967), 94.
51   Ibid. 47–8.
52   Ibid. 53.
53   A. Desai, *Bye Bye Blackbird* (Delhi: Hind Pocket Books, 1971), 11.

originals of what he has so far only seen reproductions. He is not so much discovering... as recognising them'.[54] When Adit points out Rotten Row to him, he scornfully replies: 'Of course I know. You don't have to tell me... I have always known them... ever since I could read'.[55] Both Adit and Dev, 'brought up as they were on dog-eared copies of Palgrave's *Golden Treasury*' can relate to an England they know and idealize through their reading.[56] In the English countryside Dev finds 'the England her poets had celebrated so well that he, a foreigner, found every little wildflower, every mood and aspect of it eerily familiar'.[57] Sitting in a London coffee bar 'London's history shrank and crept closer to him, cosily, familiarly, with Dr Johnson and Boswell tripping down the road to their coffee bar next door and Dryden having a session of his own across the road'.[58] The beauty of the English countryside affects him so greatly that he claims that he can appreciate England better than the English themselves.[59] However, despite all the familiarity with the English scene and love of England's countryside, he cannot easily relate to the people he sees and they, in turn, treat him as an alien. When he is treated insolently by a shopkeeper and called 'wog' on the street, the disillusionment coming on the heels of his strong sense of identification and love for England through its literature, is crushing: 'You rush out shouting, "look this is what Milton wrote about! Look, here's Tennyson's poem in real life! Isn't it fine? Isn't it splendid?" and out comes a man with red hair, flings his duster in your face and says "It's not for you buster"'.[60] The brown Englishmen forget that despite all their internalisation of Englishness, they are always marked as alien by race and skin colour as well as by the history of colonial relations.

In Kamala Markandaya's *The Nowhere Man* (1972), we are faced with the contrast between the English people's perception of the travellers/

54   Ibid. 68.
55   Ibid. 73.
56   Ibid. 78.
57   Ibid. 195.
58   Ibid. 116.
59   Ibid. 195.
60   Ibid. 185–6.

immigrants as aliens in England and the sense of idealisation and internalisation of Englishness felt by the latter.[61] The narrative deals with an
Indian family settled in England, and the small and big blows to their
sense of belonging and identification with Englishness. These blows come
not only to the older couple who, although of a generation that grew up
on English literary texts and internalized the images of the land and its
culture, stick out like sore thumbs because of external markers, but also to
their sons who grow up in England and one of whom enlists and dies in
the war and the other who marries an English girl and distances himself
from his parents. Srinivas, the father, the 'nowhere man' of the title, real-
izes the falsity of the ideal of England with which he has long deluded
himself when he is intimidated by a couple of English policemen on his
own street. The 'nowhereness' and foreignness of the coloured emigrant
gets written on his flesh, as it were, when he contracts leprosy. The gradual
patchy whiteness of the pigmentation as it steals across his brown skin as the
most visible marker of the disease becomes a telling image of the confused
status of the brown/white, English/Indian/nowhere man. The novel ends
with Srinivas' naïve and idealistic love for England and his identification
with the English proving tragically illusory when he is burnt alive in his
home in a racist attack.

Conclusion

These images from autobiographical and fictional works of Indians in English reveal idealized constructions of England and Englishness based on
an English education and chiefly on English literary sources. The resultant
sense of identification with a culture assimilated through texts emerges often
as so strong that it is hardly dented by the discrepancies that emerge from
a direct encounter. But as some accounts show, the sense of identification

---

61   K. Markanadaya, *Nowhere Man* (London: Allen Lane, 1972).

receives traumatic – even fatal – blows when it comes face-to-face with the reality of being a coloured colonized or ex-colonized in England. In these instances the citizenship of the mind clashes horribly with the reality of history, politics, and race and reveals that although these hybrid Indian/ English identities are the outcome of changes initiated by colonialism, they have no place in the definitions of Englishness and of British citizenship. Although the colonial experience wrought immense transformations in the world view and identity formation of generations of postcolonial people, the self-definitions of the English have not sufficiently expanded to incorporate these 'others' who identify with Englishness on the strength of ties of the mind rather than race or birth or citizenship.

FRANCOISE UGOCHUKWU

7 From Nwana to Adichie: Britishness goes Full Circle in Nigerian Literature

According to Ayandele:

> The intrusion of the White man into Nigerian society in the nineteenth century was a new experience for people beyond the coast. Caught by surprise and mystified that there were peoples with pigmentation different from that of Africans, many Nigerian communities initially doubted the White man's humanity and had deep-rooted distrust for him. ... By the end of the nineteenth century, Nigerian communities were to realize that the wearer of white skin, whom they at first pitied and looked upon with contempt, was a superman who was bent on becoming their ruler.[1]

Since those early years of British contact with Nigeria, Nigerian literature has been reflecting on the changing persona of the British in the country through its frequent inclusion and handling of British characters. In doing so, it had to take into account the multiple faces presented by the British explorers, missionaries, traders and administrators who pursued different aims and objectives, in a country equally characterized by a huge variety of cultures and local traditions. It painted them both individually and as a group, revealing their initial prejudices, but also their gradual acculturation and understanding of local cultures through their interaction with Nigerians, as they trod through unchartered territories and got gradually attached to the country they once considered as a possession. This representation of the British will be considered here from the Igbo point of view, based on novels written in Igbo, Pidgin and English between 1933

---

1   E. A. Ayandele, 'External Relations with Europeans in the Nineteenth Century: Explorers, Missionaries and Traders' in I. Obaro, ed., *Groundwork of Nigerian History* (Ibadan: Heinemann, 1999), 367–8.

and 2006. This study will track changes in Nigerian writers' perception of Britishness, from the prejudiced or accommodating colonial administrators and district officers of *Omenuko* to the city girl's husband of *People in the City*; from the young female teachers of Emecheta's school to the arrogant university professors sketched by Ike and the lonely journalist that dominates Adichie's second novel. Focusing on the last of these novels, this chapter will then reveal a significant shift in the presentation of British attitudes and interests, with the central character of Richard Churchill, the young journalist from Shropshire, standing out as very different from his compatriots. He desired to see the country, and his move away from the partying of Lagos to the University of Nigeria in Nsukka gradually leads to his transformation as he falls in love, learns Igbo and chooses to stay in Igboland through the war years. He ends up writing an essay to denounce the British stand on the civil war – *The World Was Silent When we Died*, embedded in the novel. This latest write-up, while echoing Achebe's district officer's monograph on *The Pacification of the Primitive Tribes of the Lower Niger*, stands in sharp contrast with it, as its author now takes sides with the embattled Biafrans.[2]

Colonial Figures

The first foreigners who settled in Igboland in the late 1850s were missionaries. The Church Missionary Society (CMS) settled in Onitsha in 1857. Its British evangelical missionaries were later joined by French Catholic missionaries from the Holy Ghost Fathers in 1885. The Eastern province became part of the British Empire on 5 June 1885 but on the ground, the British presence only became effective in 1891. Yet *Omenuko* (1933), the first Igbo fiction, makes no mention of missionaries, portraying the colonial

---

2   Whereas the colonial essay is published, Richard's write-up will not progress beyond the first chapters – another difference between him and the colonial British.

administrators instead. Written by Pita Nwana, it starts towards the end of the nineteenth century and ends with the hero's return to his ancestral village at the end of October 1918; the last chapter mentions the great 1929 depression, dating the end of the story to 1930. The novel straddles two generations, giving readers a hint of the British progressive takeover of Igboland, with most of the narrative covering the years 1910–20. It is interesting to note that Nwana presents the British as far removed from village life, where they hardly intervene. This sense of distance has been discussed by a number of observers. Ayandele notes that 'not a single convert was made for a generation by the CMS Niger Mission' and that at the beginning of the twentieth century, 'knowledge of the interior East of the Niger remained rather sketchy'.[3] According to Basden, in 1900, 'foreign influence had not appreciably affected Onitsha. Very largely, the people and the country were as they had been for generations'.[4] Igboland continued its resistance to the colonial administration well beyond 1914 and the British relied on indirect rule to manage the affairs of the colony.

To legalize the power they exercised over their fellow countrymen, each of those recognized as chiefs by the colonial administration was given a certificate to that effect. This certificate was known as a 'Warrant' and the chiefs came to be popularly known as 'Warrant Chiefs'.[5] Having put into place this system of indirect rule through warrant chiefs, the British left the people to govern themselves and, whenever they met with delegations of village elders, showed prudent respect and appreciation for local customs. The novel is the life history of Omenuko, a local trader and the hero of a rags to riches tale – he works his way out of poverty into immense wealth; when tested by a mishap in which he loses all his goods in a river, he sells some of his load carriers and apprentices into slavery to buffer himself, and later flees to seek refuge in another village. There he gets into local politics, becomes a Warrant Chief and eventually redeems all the

3   Ayandele, 'External Relations', 373.
4   G. T. Basden, *Niger Igbos* (London: Frank Cass, 1986), 114.
5   A. Afigbo, 'The Eastern Provinces under Colonial Rule', in Obaro, *Groundwork*, 417.

people he sold. He then returns home and spreads his wealth around. The relationship between the colonial District Commissioner (DC) and the Warrant Chief is portrayed as cordial: they enjoy semi-informal chats and interact as equals.[6] Omenuko's leadership benefits immensely from the DC's good will: the man is instrumental to Omenuko's success, gives him his warrant and later supports his chieftaincy. Omenuko on his part uses the DC as an ally against his envious compatriots, courts his favour and manipulates him and the power behind him to his advantage.

Subsequent novels, several of them focused on the same colonial past, present a very different and more diverse picture of the British. In Chinua Achebe's *Things Fall Apart* (1958), set in the last years of the nineteenth century, the whites, represented here by both missionaries and administrators, have imposed their presence and taken the upper hand in Igbo village affairs, to the detriment of villagers. From his exile, Okonkwo first hears about the coming of the British. Rumour has it that they are 'strange', even 'mad', and they certainly have 'no sense'.[7] Why? Probably because reports about their behaviour seemed to indicate that these strangers were unpredictable and difficult to understand. The fact that missionaries, traders and administrators all came from the same Europe, yet sometimes behaved very differently, did not make matters easier. This impression of strangeness is mainly derived from day to day observation of these foreigners' behaviour. Villagers report the white man as saying 'that our customs are bad'; Rev. James Smith 'saw things in black and white. And black was evil'.[8] Most of these missionaries not only deliberately ignore tradition and customs, but go against them and encourage locals to do the same. They teach converts 'to get rid of all the customs that were not good and praying to idols'.[9]

---

6   In the hierarchical order of the colonial service, 'the Assistant District Commissioner (Officer) was the lowest in the hierarchy and the Governor the highest. In between were the District, Divisional and Provincial Commissioners' See Afigbo, 'The Eastern Provinces', 415.

7   C. Achebe, *Things Fall Apart* (London: Heinemann, 1958).

8   Ibid. 124 and 130.

9   B. I. N. Osuagwu and E. C. Nwana, *The Story of the Life of Pita Nwana, Author of Omenuko* (Umuahia, Abia State: Ark Publishers, 1999), 7.

They build their church in the evil forest, take on abandoned twins and challenge python-worship. After meeting the white evangelists, Nwosu goes fishing in the lake that was taboo and clears the evil forest.[10] Some of the colonial officers may appear more liberal than others: Achebe's DC asks his guards 'to treat the men with respect because they were the leaders of Umuofia', but he later puts the village elders in jail for destroying the church.[11] Using divide and rule tactics, the colonial master sows division in the midst of the African community: 'Now he has won our brothers and our clan can no longer act as one. He has put a knife on the things that held us together and we have fallen apart'.[12]

While *Omenuko* and *Things fall apart* focused on village affairs and presented the British as powerful, yet peripheral, later novels gradually penetrate expatriate circles and describe Europeans as prisoners of their walled compounds and homes partly furnished with imported items, enjoying English dishes they trained their stewards to cook, staying in big cities like Lagos or secure settlements and seldom exploring the interior. Usually sent by their Church or Government, the British perceive themselves as members of a select club. Always presented as part of a group, they stick together in spite of their class, educational and other differences, each one hoping to be like those men who 'have made the Briton the law-maker, the organizer, the engineer of this world'.[13] They spend their leisure time in their homes, throwing parties for other expatriates, or in select clubs such as the old regimental mess of Okperi, reserved to Europeans where they exchanged derogatory comments and negative views about the natives. They are portrayed as often arrogant, pompous, condescending and persuaded, like Prof James Brown,[14] that they belong to 'a higher culture' and that the 'natives' are just 'like children'.[15]

---

10   Ibid. 8.
11   Achebe, *Things Fall Apart*, 138.
12   Ibid. 124.
13   C. Achebe, *Arrow of God* (London: Heinemann 1964), 33.
14   C.Ike, *Naked Gods* (London, Collins 1970), 88.
15   Achebe, *Arrow of God*, 38.

Communication continues to be a major hindrance in the uneasy
relationship between the British and the Igbo. The British use interpret-
ers to talk to the natives; they either despise the Igbo language or find it
too difficult and refuse to learn more than a few phrases, contented with
speaking pidgin to communicate with their servants. After all, even Ugwu
considers English as 'a superior tongue, a luminous language... rolling
out with clipped precision'.[16] Achebe had already put in writing what the
locals, on their part, thought of those strangers who do 'not even speak
our tongue'.[17] This behaviour is encouraged and facilitated by the fact that
the British find themselves in a relationship often new to them, of master-
servant, priest-layman or teacher-pupil, enjoying an intellectual, financial
and social superiority they often did not enjoy in their home country.
The British on their part are often not faring better in their relationship
with their own superiors back home, with their reports ignored and their
advice 'constantly overruled by starry-eyed fellows at headquarters'. As
Winterbottom puts it, it is all 'words, words, words'.[18] Communication
difficulties mean that colonial officers and other Europeans end up being
first and foremost defined by their actions. Missionaries spread the gospel,
build schools, win converts, send evangelists to remote areas and often lose
their lives in the process. District Officers administer the region allocated
to them, settle disputes and organize forced labour, with the help of warrant
chiefs like Omenuko. They are all consequently appreciated for the material improvements they bring: hospitals, schools, roads and other ameni-
ties – a generosity that leads locals to believe that the strangers came from
the sky and that, according to Emecheta, 'going to the United Kingdom
must surely be like paying God a visit'.[19] Some of the Brits sketched in the
literature show some degree of interest and respect for the cultures they
have come to influence, even though this often condescending interest is
usually motivated by a desire to rule more effectively. The first DC presented by Achebe is 'a student of primitive customs' and prepares to write

---

16   C. Adichie, *Half of a Yellow Sun* (London: Fourth Estate, 2006), 22.
17   Achebe, *Things Fall Apart*, 124.
18   Achebe, *Arrow of God*, 56.
19   B.Emecheta, *Head above water: An Autobiography* (London, Heinemann 1986),
       24.

a book on Igbo culture. 'As he walked back to the court he thought about that book. Every day brought him some new material. The story of this man who had... hanged himself would make interesting reading. ... He had already chosen the title of the book, after much thought: *the pacification of the primitive tribes of the lower Niger*.'[20]

Arrow of God (1964) is set in the 1920s, when the number of Brits gone to Eastern Nigeria 'to answer the call' and represent their Government had increased.[21] In the novel, the British presence at their headquarters in Okperi numbers five. The five on Government hill are: Clarke, the ADC, fresh from Britain; Roberts, in charge of the police; Wade who supervises the prison and Wright from the Public Works Department. The first to be mentioned is Captain T. K. Winterbottom, 'a hardened coaster' with fifteen years of Nigeria and the local title of *Otiji Egbe*, breaker of guns, acquired after he ended a local war by confiscating all the guns.[22] 'Determined to do his duty', and proud of his country's achievements, Winterbottom 'would not now exchange the life for the comfort of Europe' in spite of finding Nigeria 'demoralizing'.[23] He reads DC Allen George's *Pacification of the primitive tribes of the lower Niger* mentioned at the end of *Things Fall Apart* and offers it to read to his new assistant Tony Clarke, who replaces another Brit who died of cerebral malaria. Clarke, the Cambridge-educated son of a bank clerk, has sympathies for Igbo customs. Women too had answered 'the call': Dr Savage 'the severe and unfeminine missionary doctor... locally known as Omesike, one who acts with power' is in charge of the local hospital.[24]

20   Achebe, *Things Fall Apart*, 147.
21   Achebe, *Arrow of God*, 32. Achebe, the son of an Anglican catechist, carefully chose this religious expression, taken from the Bible and Jesus' call of his disciples, to draw a parallel between those who left everything and followed Christ into the mission field, and those who left the comfort of Britain and their families to go and 'civilize' that corner of Africa, even though they were not sent as religious missionaries.
22   Achebe, *Arrow of God*, 29. These Igbo titles and salutations acquired by foreigners, such as *Omesilincha*, meaning 'the one who entirely finishes his work', given to the missionary Basden (see Basden, *Niger Igbos*, xxii) recognized their ability and achievement; they also established them as co-opted members of the Igbo society.
23   Achebe, *Arrow of God*, 32.
24   Ibid. 150.

No Longer at Ease (1960) completes the two earlier novels by covering the years immediately prior to Independence, with the British still recorded as a people who 'claimed to teach other nations how to live'.[25] William Green, the colonial administrator, aptly represents the colonial officers of those last days before Independence: he arrived with noble intentions but soon gets sidetracked by his prejudices and ignorance of the culture, and ends up considering Africans as corrupt and inferior. The novel is the fruit if Achebe's desire to 'revaluate [his] culture' in the face of that criticism.[26] The three novels, acknowledged by their author himself in 1962 as constituting 'only one, a kind of trilogy', at a time when he was still writing *Arrow of God*, thus bring readers up to Nigerian Independence.[27]

Ulasi's *Many Thing You no Understand* (1970), set in the 1930s, fills the chronological gap left by Achebe's trilogy and centres around a case of head-hunting following the local chief's death, with two British officers on the case, the younger one very concerned, the other one, with a longer experience of Nigeria, very reluctant. The novel opposes two very different ways of dealing with the locals: the young Assistant District Officer (ADO) MacIntosh, fixed on high moral grounds, is bent on showing a better way to the people; as for the DO Mason, with fifteen years of rural life in Nigeria and a diet of pepper soup, 'rice and stew and egusi soup [that] hasn't affected [him]', he prefers just letting people go on with their way of life and trying not to interfere, while studying them.[28] One interesting point highlighted in that novel is that knowing the other's language can change a situation – and the fact that the DC can speak pidgin does not help him understand Igbo. The whole novel is written in Pidgin English, setting the issue of language at the centre of the plot. Pidgin is presented there as a middle ground that gives the British the false impression they communicate and penetrate the Igbo mind. The man whose brother was beheaded in preparation for the chief's funeral went to report the murderers in writing to the DO – 'If Sylvester no speak ADO language he no for go

25   C. Achebe, *No Longer at Ease* (London: Heinemann, 1964), 57.

26   B. Lindfors, ed., *Conversations with Chinua Achebe* (Jackson: University Press of Mississippi, 1997) 45.

27   Ibid. 7.

28   A. Ulasi, *Many Thing You No Understand* (London: Michael Joseph 1970), 163.

to lodge complaint to ADO ear, he for come to us elders... But with church and school now, any young man who speak ADO language fit go to him'.[29] For Ulasi, white men are strong but they too are human and juju can affect them just the same. In the end, the ADO loses his sanity and the DO is lured into a deadly trap. The last words he will hear will be: 'many thing you no understand here, Mr DO... And I no think say you go fit understand them if you live here for one hundred year!'[30] In an interview in 1969, Achebe, in response to a question about his portrayal of Europeans who came to Igboland, sums up his thoughts and those of other writers on the colonial masters: 'I think they were very ignorant. And that's very bad, you know, when you are trying to civilize other people. But you don't really need to be black-hearted to do all kinds of wrong things. Those who have the best intentions sometimes commit the worst crimes'.[31]

Independence and the British Lingering Presence

Reflecting on the first years of Nigerian independence some thirty years later, Osaghae notes that, at the time, 'relations with Britain and the West were conducted in a manner that sometimes casts doubts on the country's independence'.[32] In the 1960s, there were still a good number of expatriates among secondary school teachers, as in Emecheta's Methodist Girls' High School: Miss Davies, the Welsh music teacher; Miss Osborne from Scotland; and Miss Humble, the young English teacher with her MA in English from Oxford. Emecheta recalls that Miss Humble loved her language to the exclusion of others and 'probably felt that [it] was too good for the likes of me to want to use as a means of expression'.[33] Only a few expatriate priests

29   Ibid. 118.
30   Ibid. 188–90.
31   Lindfors, *Conversations*, 30.
32   E. Osaghae, *Crippled Giant: Nigeria Since Independence* (London: Hurst, 1980), 51.
33   Emecheta, *Head Above Water*, 21.

were left in Igboland; primarily employed as part of the growing Nsukka academic community, they were expected to lend a hand in nearby parishes.[34] In Adichie's *Purple Hibiscus* (2004), Father Benedict insists on Latin only for the Mass, with clapping kept to a minimum. The white priests' attitude is still globally presented as misleading as their teaching transforms the father of the house into a cruel man, a criminal, wife-beater and child molester.[35]

People of the city (1954) was the first Nigerian novel in English to reflect on the growing, 'modern' Nigerian city life; published in Britain, it gained international acclaim. In opposition to the practice alluded in *Arrow of God* (1964), and in answer to that novel's question: 'How widespread was the practice of white men sleeping with native women?' it was equally the first to bring together (albeit briefly) an interracial couple.[36] Grunnings, a British engineer who left a wife and children in England marries Beatrice, a city girl, according to native law and customs. He seems to care about her, but never takes her with him on his vacations to Britain. Beatrice, on her part, considers that Grunnings 'can never be a real husband' and after giving him three children, decides to leave a life she finds boring, to go back to the city streets.[37] The publication of Achebe's first novel four years later eclipsed Ekwensi's contribution and put the focus back on traditional Igboland and colonial British figures, who still ruled by proxy.

Fifty years later, the creation of Richard Churchill, one of the main protagonists of Adichie's second novel, presents readers with a complete departure from earlier depictions of Europeans. Born in a Shropshire village, he lost both his parents aged nine, was raised by an aunt in London and does not have many happy childhood memories. He says of himself: 'I've always been a loner and I've always wanted to see Africa, so I took leave from my humble newspaper job and a generous loan from my aunt'.[38] Unlike his predecessors, he does not travel to Nigeria on a Government or Church mission but leaves on his own, running away from his orphaned past.

---

34   The University of Nigeria, Nsukka, known as UNN, opened in 1960 and briefly renamed 'University of Biafra', was the first independent Nigerian university.
35   C. Adichie, *Purple Hibiscus* (London: Fourth Estate, 2004).
36   Achebe, *Arrow of God*, 103.
37   C. Ekwensi, *People of the City* (London: Heineman, 1963) 32.
38   C. Adichie, *Half of a Yellow Sun* (London: Fourth Estate, 2006), 62.

New Brits for a New Country

Igbo culture rates behaviour as being far more important than looks, and this could explain why details of the Europeans' looks are rather sketchy and conventional in the novels studied: a face that has 'the colours of condensed milk and a cut-open soursop' with a 'British nose... pinched and narrow', a 'pale and thin' figure.[39] Richard Churchill cannot deny his 'stained-glass blue' eyes that betray his northern origin, but soon gets a tan and wants people back home 'to see him, the man he had become after his years here: to see that he was browner and happier'.[40] Like other Brits before him, he is initially perceived as strange by Nigerians – but for entirely different reasons: because he does not correspond to the stereotype of the typical European. 'He did not want to be shown around; he had managed well on his past trips abroad'.[41] He travels on his own, fulfils his dream of visiting the Igbo Ukwu archaeological site, reads and enquires about Igbo customs with the vague idea of a book about Nigeria in mind, and learns how to greet and how to behave in a gathering or when going on a condolence visit. Although he appears at first as just another colonial anthropologist, he will eventually prove to be genuinely interested in people and their culture, rather than on a purely scientific mission. This explains why he does not take any recordings or photos at Igbo-Ukwu, an attitude that leaves the locals asking: 'what kind of white man is that?'[42]

During his first few months in Lagos, Richard slides into a brief relationship with another Brit, Susan, a young lady slightly older than him who 'spoke with authority about Nigeria and Nigerians'. He moves in with her at her invitation and, while in Ikoyi, meets other whites, 'mostly English, ex-colonial administrators and business people from John Holt and Kingsway and GB Ollivant and Shell BP and United Africa Company. They were

---

39 Adichie, *Purple Hibiscus* (London: Fourth Estate 2004), 4 and Achebe, *Arrow of God*, 29.
40 Adichie, *Half of a Yellow Sun*, 154 and 137.
41 Ibid. 55.
42 Ibid. 72.

reddened from sun and alcohol' and 'discussed cricket, plantations they owned or planned to own, the perfect weather in Jos, business opportunities in Kaduna'.[43] He finds himself performing very poorly at those parties, where he feels out of place: 'This was expatriate life. All they did, as far as he was concerned, was have sex with one another's wives and husbands, illicit couplings that were more a way of passing heat-blanched time in the tropics than they were genuine expressions of passion'.[44] After moving to Nsukka on a research grant, he carries on with the same attitude, and frowns at the Enugu-based Brits 'still going off to play water polo and have cocktails at the Hotel Presidential' while soldiers fight at the door of Biafra's capital. At the time, Nsukka 'was full of people from USAID and the Peace Corps and the Michigan State University', yet he never sought to join them.[45] A rather shy and reserved person, he felt comfortable with the fact that Odenigbo and his fellow lecturers 'were casually accepting of him [and] did not pay him any particular attention'.[46]

Keen to learn the Igbo language, he seizes every occasion to practice, first with the stewards who did not care 'whether or not he got the tones right', then with people, any time and everywhere.[47] He feels greatly encouraged and honoured whenever people appreciate his efforts, as he takes it as a major sign of his integration. He tends to think poorly of himself and easily takes the position of a pupil, learning the language and the customs from people around him, even those below him on the social ladder. He enquires from his gardener about medicinal herbs to help with his nervous impotence, asks the steward Ugwu to take him to his hometown masquerade festival, goes there and asks many questions and interviews people. During the war, he will be faced with the fact that he can be used: unlike *Omenuko*'s DC, Richard perceives the manipulation attempt, because he understands the people and their language. Although his first reaction is to refuse to comply, he eventually understands the view shared by Biafran leaders and, because he really considers himself as a Biafran, eventually

43   Ibid. 53–5.
44   Ibid. 237.
45   Ibid. 182 and 76.
46   Ibid. 75.
47   Ibid. 113.

accepts to write for the Propaganda Directorate: as they explained, people 'will take what you write more seriously because you are white. Look, the truth is that this is not your war. This is not your cause. Your government will evacuate you in a minute if you ask them to. So... if you really want to contribute, this is the way that you can'.[48]

He has very basic needs and likes the sparsely furnished Nsukka guest-house – two arm-chairs, a single bed, and bare kitchen cupboards – where he 'felt instantly at home'. His steward boasts of a substantive experience of serving foreigners and only cooks foreign recipes. But Richard, who buys his groundnuts from hawkers and knows everything about haggling, considers that 'Nigerian food is quite all right' – he actually 'disliked the food of his childhood, the sharp-tasting kippers full of bones, the porridge with the appalling thick skin on top like a waterproof lining, the overcooked roast beef'.[49] We see him enjoying Odenigbo's pepper soup so much that a fellow lecturer concludes that 'this is proof that Richard was an African in his past life'.[50] Unlike Winterbottom, initially 'so depressed by the climate and the food', Richard never feels homesick, except for the day, in Port-Harcourt, where Kainene's humid garden reminds him 'of the crumbling house in England', 'the tall poplars and willows... and the fields'.[51] The fact that he associates these memories with those of his deceased parents is a clear indication that the land he evokes there only lives in his memory. His cousin Martin summarizes Richard's move in a letter: 'Is "going native" still used? I always knew you would!'[52]

Whenever Richard does something, it is in response to a request for help, and he enjoys acting as a bridge-builder – as when he serves as a guide to foreign journalists. He does not play politics, and is portrayed as a plain and simple-minded person. In particular, he never tries to influence people around him. His sole aim seems to be accepted as part of the population and each time he moves one step ahead towards this goal, he feels very happy. His progressive integration is signposted first by his leaving Britain for Lagos;

48 Ibid. 305.
49 Ibid. 72–3.
50 Ibid. 108.
51 Achebe, *Arrow of God*, 30 and Adichie, *Half of a Yellow Sun*, 77.
52 Adichie, *Half of a Yellow Sun*, 137.

then by his breaking away from Susan – a relationship she had initiated and led. Then there is his moving from Lagos to UNN and his later decision to identify with the Biafrans, leave Nsukka at the start of the war and join Kainene, the young Igbo lady with whom he fell in love while in Lagos. These successive decisions will be sealed at the end of the war by his rejoining the staff of the University as a researcher in the new Institute of African Studies – a decision he did not have to make, as Kainene never returned from an incursion across enemy lines in the last days of the war. This last decision, taken independently, ends Richard's quest: he has found his place.

It took the young Brit a whole novel to settle down – he did not seem to have anything to offer. The only real activity with which he is constantly associated is the writing of a book, for which he gets a scholarship and a lot of attention, does not come to anything in the end. He finally recognizes that 'the war isn't [his] story to tell' after all – a young houseboy will take over the writing of the book and change its title to that of 'Narrative of the Life of a Country'.[53] This apparent lack of material contribution shifts the focus to his character and the real purpose of his stay in the country. So why is he there? He is the catalyst that reveals the true character of people around him: his encounters with Major Madu, for example, reveal the Igbo officer as a rival whose ultimate aim is to take Richard out of the picture. Richard has a better insight into Nigerian politics, but 'the man made him feel inconsequential'.[54] More importantly, Richard's presence gives this novel on the Biafran war an international dimension. He is the only character able to compare the war with other killings he knew about – the previous massacres of Igbo people in the north, the bombings of German towns by the British at the end of World War II and the Rwandan massacres of the early 1960s. He represents a new generation of foreigners who, like the Count Von Rosen, come to a now independent country to learn and help, on an equal footing with the people.[55]

53   Ibid. 424–5.
54   Ibid. 136.
55   The Swedish pilot Carl Von Rosen, briefly mentioned in the novel, gained international fame when, after helping with relief planes to Biafra in August 1968, he decided to fight on their side and used his private plane to inflict several defeats on the Nigerian army.

Conclusion

Even though one could argue that Richard's fate was prepared by his personal history, the main factor that led to his personal transformation was his passion – his unreserved admiration for the culture that produced the roped pots of Igbo Ukwu, his love for a girl that stood out as different, and his empathy for a country he helped through the pangs of birth. In his own words, 'he would be Biafran in a way he could never have been Nigerian – he was here at the beginning, he had shared in the birth'.[56] Through his war experience, the British orphan discovers and embraces a new-found identity, whilst offering Nigerians he meets, the occasion to discover their own identity through their interaction with him:

> Through the evocation of the country's past history, the re-living of past struggles and shattering intercultural encounters, behind the multifaceted presentation of the British, Nigerian literature had been seeking to retrieve a lost identity. As Achebe put it in 1980. In fact it has been said that three or four hundred years ago we were taken out of our history and dumped into someone else's history. We lost the initiative – the historical initiative – and therefore for us it is a question of life and death that we recapture that initiative, and we situate ourselves again in the mainstream of our own thought and feeling and experience and perception. This is why it is very important that we understand who we are.[57]

With Richard Churchill, Adichie produced that last link in the chain – the one who gives its history back to Nigeria.

---

56   C. Adichie, *Half of a Yellow Sun*, 168.
57   Lindfors, *Conversations*, 58.

KARINE TOURNIER-SOL

8 Britishness and European Integration since 1997 in the French Press

In the context of European integration, for many years the French have characterized the notion of 'Britishness' as involving a certain reluctance towards any form of political integration. In the French press, this image has been in keeping with that of the 'awkward partner' identified by Stephen George.[1] From the other side of the Channel, the British are commonly seen as Eurosceptic, closer to the United States than to the continent, with a natural tendency to favour the famous 'special relationship' over their relations with the European Union. This perception owes much to the political climate of the Thatcher and Major years, which were characterized by increasingly strained relationships between the successive Conservative governments and their European partners.

In this context, the arrival in power of the Labour Prime Minister Tony Blair in May 1997 seemed to present a turning-point in the relations between Europe and the United Kingdom. As in many other member states, the French press paid much attention to the incoming British government's approach to Europe with one main question in mind, namely to what extent change would occur. Might Britishness one day be equated with Euro-enthusiasm?

As the longest period ever served by a Labour government in power has just come to an end, it seems worthwhile to look back at the Blair era and wonder about its impact on the perception of Britishness in Europe from the point of view of the French press. Of the entire ten-year period of Tony Blair's premiership, two stages can be identified, revolving around a decisive

1 S. George, *An Awkward Partner: Britain in the European Community* (Oxford: Oxford University Press, 1998).

turning-point which is, unsurprisingly enough, the war in Iraq. The first period can be described as a kind of honeymoon, although one not devoid of disappointments. The end of this first stage is particularly characterized by a growing impatience over the single currency. The second period starts with the war in Iraq in 2003, which definitely marked a turning-point in the French perception of Britishness in Europe. This radical change is reflected in the following years, when Britain's approach to European integration tends to be regarded with irritation by the French newspapers, bringing back the image of a country standing apart from its continental partners, in keeping with what can be described as a more traditional French vision of Britishness.

The Honeymoon: A Welcome Change

The new British Prime Minister was welcomed by the French press which mostly focused its attention on what the election meant in terms of its impact on European policy. In this respect, what is striking is that in the very first days after the general election, the key word in most of the press articles was caution. However, some of the papers were already quite optimistic, such as the leading quality daily newspaper *Le Monde*, which is at the centre of the political spectrum; in an article entitled 'Good News for Europe', it considered the election of Tony Blair as a 'happy event' which was definitely 'promising for Europe'.[2] Similarly, according to the leader of the economic daily newspaper *La Tribune*, 'the victory of Tony Blair [would] be a cause of rejoicing for convinced Europeans'.[3] Yet, interestingly enough, in both these articles, optimism was coupled with prudence. Though clearly supportive, both newspapers indeed carefully avoided to show overly enthusiasm at such an early stage. *Le Monde* thus read: 'Celebrating the good news should not obscure the great caution, even the

---

2   'Bonne Nouvelle pour l'Europe', *Le Monde* (3 May 1997).
3   P. Mundry, 'L'Europe avec Tony Blair', editorial, *La Tribune* (2 May 1997).

reluctance demonstrated by Mr Blair towards a more integrated union'. As for *La Tribune*, it mentioned the 'disappointing attitude' of Tony Blair over the European issue in his election campaign.

However, despite these hints of scepticism, for both these newspapers the arrival of Tony Blair was undoubtedly positive for Europe, especially compared with his predecessor in 10, Downing Street: 'In his mistrust of Europe, Mr Blair is more pragmatic than dogmatic, contrary to what the Conservatives had become'.[4] A strikingly recurring theme was indeed the stark contrast with the Major years which was stressed by all the French press. What was expected at this early stage was at least a change of tone if not of substance: 'In terms of substance, he will certainly be no less difficult. "UK first" shall remain his creed. In terms of style, he may be more open. All in all, this is not an insignificant advantage'.[5]

For literally all the French newspapers, the election of a new Labour government marked an opportunity to pass a very severe judgement on the European policy of its Conservative predecessor. They were unanimous in condemning what they considered as the 'systematic obstructionism' of the Major era – the term 'obstructionism' was used in nearly all the articles on the subject – which was held responsible for the deterioration of the atmosphere in Brussels.[6] According to *Le Monde*, 'a new atmosphere [was] to replace the ongoing guerrilla war waged by the Major government against everything coming from the continent'.[7]

Even for those newspapers which were less enthusiastic about Tony Blair's European approach, this change of government could only be for the better. Actually, it was clear that in the eyes of the press, nothing could be worse than the Major government. The left-wing quality daily newspaper *Libération* was hopeful that 'the new government [would] play the traditional game of searching for compromises acceptable for all, rather

---

4   'Bonne Nouvelle'.
5   P. Mundry, 'L'Europe avec Tony Blair', editorial, *La Tribune* (2 May 1997).
6   See for example, B. Bollaert, 'Europe: Examen Probatoire', *Le Figaro* (3 May 1997); 'Tony Blair très attendu sur sa politique Européenne', *Les Echos* (5 May 1997); 'Welcome Mister Cook', editorial, *Le Monde* (15 May 1997).
7   P. de Beer, 'Le nouveau gouvernement britannique se veut plus Européen', *Le Monde* (6 May 1997).

than the obstructionism, even "war", favoured by the Conservatives.'[8] War was indeed also a recurring image used by the French press in order to describe the relations between the United Kingdom and the European Union under John Major, which demonstrated how severely the French perception of Britishness had been damaged by the Conservative Prime Minister's European approach.

In fact, all the French press viewed the arrival of Tony Blair as a decisive turning-point in the relationship between Britain and its European partners. As the economic daily paper *Les Echos* put it, 'a page [was] being turned – that of the systematic obstructionism of the British'.[9] The French media's negative perception of Britishness in Europe had obviously been greatly influenced by the European policy of the Major years, characterized by a growing Euroscepticism within his party and government.

Yet, although all the French press acknowledged the break embodied by the election of Tony Blair, the majority of newspapers remained very cautious. They emphasized the moderate nature of the campaign led by Tony Blair on Europe, therefore not foreseeing any radical change of policy. *Le Figaro* bluntly declared: 'Nobody expects a revolution'.[10] *Le Monde* thought likewise, in an article entitled 'Brussels hopes for a return of the British in the European debate' but subtitled 'The fifteen do not however delude themselves'.[11] According to the journalist, the Blair government was very unlikely to show any 'boldness' on the European issue which was 'too sensitive across the Channel'. As for *Libération*, it considered that 'it would be a mistake to wait for Tony Blair to make radically different choices from those of his predecessor, after leading such a cautious campaign. On matters relating to sovereignty, ... Albion will remain Albion' – thus symbolising the enduring image of Britain as an awkward partner in Europe, reluctant to further integration which was perceived as a direct threat to its national sovereignty.[12]

---

8   P. Haski, 'L'Europe, dossier piégé mais prioritaire', *Libération* (2 May 1997).
9   'Tony Blair très attendu sur sa politique Européenne', *Les Echos* (5 May 1997).
10   B. Bollaert, 'Europe : Examen Probatoire', *Le Figaro* (3 May 1997).
11   P. Lemaître, 'Bruxelles espère un retour des Britanniques dans le débat Européen', *Le Monde* (3 May 1997).
12   P. Haski, 'L'Europe, dossier piégé mais prioritaire', *Libération* (2 May 1997).

In fact, most of the newspapers seemed to adopt a wait-and-see approach – apparently waiting for concrete signals and actions from the incoming Labour government. However, in stark contrast with the Major government, the omens were good. Tony Blair was 'seen in a favourable light' and there was 'hope' for an improvement in the relationships between the United Kingdom and Europe.[13] This definitely marked a significant change compared with the French perception of Britishness in Europe in the years prior to Blair's election.

The French press was quickly reassured, after the first contact between the incoming Labour government and Brussels which took place on 5 May 1997 – that is to say only four days after the arrival of Tony Blair in 10, Downing Street, which was in itself a positive signal sent to the other European heads of state. The new Minister for Europe, Doug Henderson, went to meet his European partners and told them that it was time for a new start between the United Kingdom and Europe. The change of tone was underlined in all the French newspapers as heralding the beginning of a 'new era'.[14] The new British government announced that it was ready to sign the social chapter of the Maastricht Treaty for which John Major had secured an opt-out. This move was welcomed by the press as a positive signal, 'a gesture of good will' in the words of *La Tribune*. Even *Libération*, which had been more cautious so far, acknowledged 'Tony Blair's small European gesture', as well as 'the new tone' of the Labour government which brought about a 'change of atmosphere in Brussels'.[15] In *La Tribune*, the atmosphere was described as 'constructive' – a word certainly not used in this context for several years.[16] *Les Echos* was even more optimistic, considering it as 'a promising turning-point' in an article entitled 'The British Labour government sees Europe as a chance and not as a threat anymore'.[17] Finally, the leader of *Le Monde* was enthusiastically entitled – in the original text

13   Haski, 'Bruxelles espère' and De Beer, 'Le nouveau gouvernement'.
14   T. Arnaud, 'Tony Blair pousse le Royaume-Uni dans l'Europe sociale', *La Tribune* (6 May 1997).
15   J. Docquiert, 'Le petit geste Européen de Tony Blair', *Libération* (6 May 1997).
16   Arnaud, 'Tony Blair pousse le Royaume-Uni'.
17   J. Docquiert, 'Les travaillistes britanniques voient une chance en l'Europe et non plus une menace', *Les Echos* (6 May 1997).

– 'Welcome Mister Cook'. It was delighted by 'the first European steps of the Blair government' which 'had not disappointed' its partners.[18]

Therefore it looked as if the new Labour government had the potential to change the French perception of Britishness in Europe, which had come to be associated with a fierce resistance to further integration and a general tendency to drag its feet in Europe. Whereas the United Kingdom had been seen lately as standing on the fringe of the European Union, the French newspapers appeared quite willing to change their own vision of Britain's attitude to Europe. It seems that it was now time for a fresh start for them, just as it was for the new Labour government.

Disillusion Sets In

The first subject to provoke disillusion for the French press was British participation in the single currency. From the end of September 1997, some newspapers took up the question which had been raised by the British press. There was speculation at the time about the date of entry that the government was expected to announce together with its agreement of principle. The uncertainty lasted for four weeks, during which time the French press largely commented on what *Les Echos* called in French the '*valse-hésitation*' of the Labour government – in other words, 'the British waverings' as the daily Catholic newspaper *La Croix* chose to entitle its article on the subject, adding: 'To be or not to be part of [the Euro], that is the question'. At this stage, the tone of most of the articles was one of understanding, rather than judgement and there was a sense of the French media trying to account for Blair's dithering.[19]

---

18   'Welcome Mister Cook'.
19   P. de Gasquet, 'La valse-hésitation des travaillistes sur l'Euro', *Les Echos* (7 October 1997); 'Balancements britanniques', *La Croix* (21 October 1997).

On 27 October 1997, Gordon Brown made a statement to the House of Commons, declaring that the new Labour government agreed to the principle of the single currency but that it would not be among the first countries adopting the Euro in 1999. This decision was received with disappointment by all the French press despite the fact that it had been expected for a few days. It is striking that the business newspapers were the most severe commentators, condemning the decision as much as the indecision which had preceded it – an indecision which was very damaging for the economic markets. For both *Les Echos* and *La Tribune*, the episode was 'the first *faux pas* of Tony Blair', the accusation being that 'By fostering confusion on the single currency, Tony Blair has just destroyed his reputation of the Midas of politics'.[20] The 'delay' announced by Gordon Brown 'amounted to a u-turn' for *Les Echos*, which, interestingly enough for a business paper, was not very receptive to the five economic tests set by the Chancellor of the Exchequer, considering that the Blair government was 'taking refuge behind the screen of [these] economic criteria', which looked more like a pretext to postpone Britain's adoption of the single currency.[21]

In most other newspapers, disappointment prevailed although some tried to remain positive and confident. In its leading article entitled 'The Euro Without Blair', *Le Monde* chose to underline not only the negative point in Gordon Brown's declaration but also its positive aspect, saying: 'There is some good news' – referring to the agreement in principle, through which 'Mr Blair puts an end to years of anti-European Conservative rhetoric'. This definitely marked a watershed. However, the article went on to add: 'There is some bad news', concluding: 'The style is Euro-enthusiastic; the substance is Euro-cautious'. *Le Monde* was not convinced either by the five economic tests, considering that Tony Blair '[was] hiding real domestic political concerns behind economic considerations'.[22]

---

20 T. Arnaud, 'Le premier faux pas de Tony Blair' (*La Tribune*, 21 October 1997); 'Le gouvernement britannique repousse l'idée d'une entrée rapide dans l'UEM', *Les Echos* (21 October 1997).

21 P. de Gasquet, Le gouvernement Blair veut se préparer à la monnaie unique pour 2002', *Les Echos* (28 October 1997).

22 'The Euro without Blair', editorial, *Le Monde* (29 October 1997).

Significantly, this event was interpreted by most of the French press as reflecting once more Britain's awkward relationship with Europe and its perpetual reluctance to further integration. This was interpreted as a sign of continuity of the typically British approach to the European Union, in stark contrast with the rhetorical break in Tony Blair's European discourse. *Le Monde* stressed the fact that this situation was not unprecedented: 'This is not the first time that the United Kingdom has missed the European boat. ... Once again, the price is likely to be heavy'.[23] This was an unmistakable reference to Britain's late entry into the Common Market in 1973. *La Croix* saw it as another sign of the United Kingdom's half-hearted commitment to European integration: 'Once more it reflects a permanent feature of the European construction: Britain has always had one foot in Europe and the other one elsewhere'.[24] For the left-wing weekly *Nouvel Observateur*, this decision was not surprising and corresponded to the traditional British line – in other words, this was Britishness: 'Tony Blair, traitor to his faith? Rather a hopeless pragmatist and an advocate, like his Conservative predecessors, of economic logic rather than political will'.[25] Once again stress was laid on continuity with past practice despite a rhetorical break.

However, despite this first sign of disenchantment, the honeymoon was not over yet in the eyes of the French press which was willing to give it the benefit of Blair's Britain the doubt. Most of the press still wanted to believe that it was a fresh start for the UK in Europe. At the start of the British presidency of the EU, in January 1998, the right-wing daily newspaper *Le Figaro* praised Tony Blair for his positive influence: 'Britain's attitude towards Europe has changed – and Tony Blair is the cause of this reversal'.[26] According to *Le Monde*, Tony Blair was on a mission: 'He wants to exorcize that European curse which has afflicted Britain since the war, often, admittedly, due to its own actions'.[27] The last part of the sentence

---

23   Ibid.
24   B. Frappat, 'L'Euro sans la livre', editorial, *La Croix* (28 October 1997).
25   J. G. Fredet, 'Euro: le "oui mais" des Anglais', *Le Nouvel Observateur* (30 October 1997).
26   J. Duplouich, 'Tony Blair: l'Euro pour les autres', *Le Figaro* (5 January 1998).
27   P. de Beer, 'Londres prend la présidence de l'Union à un moment crucial pour l'Europe', *Le Monde* (30 December 1997).

is typical of the French perception of Britishness in Europe according to which the United Kingdom deliberately stands on the fringe of Europe. Six months later, at the end of the British presidency, *Le Figaro* underlined what it considered as Tony Blair's main achievement: 'The British are less afraid of Europe – and that is quite something'.[28]

Therefore the beginning of the Blair era was characterized by a more positive French perception of Britishness in Europe. The impression conveyed by the French newspapers was that they really wanted it to change. In the following months, it appeared as a lasting trend, with, for instance, a leading article in *Le Monde* on 4 November 1998 which was entitled: 'Tony Blair, the European' and which considered that 'Blairism [was] in sharp contrast with Britain's attitude towards Europe under Margaret Thatcher and John Major'. According to the newspaper, which had been consistently supportive of Tony Blair since his arrival in Number 10 Downing Street, the Labour Prime Minister was at the centre of 'a major evolution of his country's European policy'.[29] Two months later, in January 1999, as the Euro was introduced in the rest of Europe, *Le Monde* addressed the British Prime Minister in the following words: 'Mr Blair, the Euro is waiting for you', adding: 'Europe and its young currency need you'.[30] Britishness, as traditionally perceived on the continent, was hinted at with gentle irony: 'It is well-known that you have the great habit of waiting for the European trains to depart before getting on them' – which was another allusion to Britain's late entry into the European Economic Community.

At this stage of Tony Blair's premiership, most of the French press still adopted a lenient attitude towards the United Kingdom on the issue of the single currency. They expected that the pro-European discourse of Tony Blair would soon be translated into actions, and that eventually he was going to take Britain into the Euro-zone. In spite of some early signs of disappointment, they wanted to remain positive and still hoped that Britishness would come to be equated with their vision of pro-Europeanism.

28   P. de Beer, 'L'Europe fait moins peur aux Anglais', *Le Figaro* (30 June 1998).
29   'Tony Blair, l'Européen', editorial, *Le Monde* (4 November 1998).
30   'M. Blair, l'Euro vous attend', editorial, *Le Monde* (5 January 1999).

Impatience over the Euro

However, as time went by, the impatience of the French press started to grow over the question of Britain's adoption of the single currency. As early as January 2000, the first signs began to show, with an article in *Le Figaro* which, while acknowledging Tony Blair's 'unquestionable personal commitment to the Union', regretted that 'regarding the single currency, he is stuck in a wait-and-see policy'.[31] Eighteen months later, *Le Monde* accused Tony Blair of 'eschewing the debate on the single currency', and using the five economic tests as a pretext hiding the real question: 'No one knows in detail what those famous criteria are, and everyone suspects that the main one is, in reality, highly political'.[32]

But the French newspapers were also very aware of the major reason for the Prime Minister's 'policy of excessive prudence', namely the force of British public opinion and the prevalence of Euroscepticism among the British people.[33] *Le Figaro* therefore justified Tony Blair's caution by acknowledging the 'fast-growing Europhobia in the United Kingdom', while *Le Monde* noted: 'given that the three-quarters of Her Majesty's subjects are against the Euro in principle, the strategy has consisted, for four years, in avoiding the question'.[34] In an unusually critical article, *Le Monde* had even bluntly considered that: 'The British are born Eurosceptics. ... There's no way round it. It seems that Albion will be forever tempted by "the open sea"'.[35] This was a direct reference to Winston Churchill's famous sentence to the General De Gaulle: 'each time we must choose between Europe and the open sea, we shall always choose the open sea'.[36]

---

31   J. Duplouich, 'Europhobie galopante au Royaume-Uni', *Le Figaro* (8 January 2000).

32   P. Claude, 'Tony Blair invite les conservateurs britanniques à ne pas "tourner le dos" à l'Europe', *Le Monde* (27 May 2001).

33   Duplouich, 'Europhobie galopante'.

34   Claude 'Tony Blair invite les conservateurs britanniques'.

35   L. Zecchini, 'Les Britanniques pratiquent l'"entrisme" communautaire pour mieux influencer l'Union', *Le Monde* (3 May 2000).

36   R. J. Lieber, *British Politics and European Unity: Parties, Elites and Pressure Groups* (Berkeley: University of California Press, 1970), 18.

The press was clearly growing disenchanted: Britishness still meant Euroscepticism, despite the pro-European discourse of Tony Blair, who had obviously not succeeded in convincing the British people so far. In April 2001, one of the articles of *La Croix* was entitled 'Britain on the fringe of Europe' – a title reminiscent of the years before Blair and typical of the traditional French perception of Britishness.[37] As the Labour Prime Minister finished his first term, the French newspapers reviewed his European policy and disappointment prevailed, although they acknowledged that some headway had been made on certain subjects – including defence and the social chapter. Yet, the British approach to Europe had not sufficiently changed according to them: 'All this is very disappointing for a Prime Minister from whom we expected so much, too much maybe'.[38]

Although this was certainly a first turning-point in the perception of Britishness and Europe in the French press, the major one was still to come.

The Turning Point: The Iraqi Crisis

The major turning-point of the Blair era was indeed caused less than two years later by the Iraqi crisis. First, preparation for the war in Iraq in the first months of 2003 had an indirect impact on the issue of Britain's adoption of the single currency, as according to *Le Monde*, the Prime Minister had changed priorities: 'preparation for the war in Iraq has replaced the Euro at the top of his agenda'.[39] Second, the conflict had revealed divisions within the EU member-states for which Tony Blair was largely held responsible by the French press, and which led a journalist from *Le Monde* to write: 'The

---

37 P. Martin-Genier, 'La Grande-Bretagne en marge de l'Europe', *La Croix* (19 April 2001).

38 Ibid.

39 J. P. Langellier, 'La crise irakienne a repoussé l'horizon d'un référendum britannique sur l'Euro', *Le Monde* (29 January 2003).

single currency has suffered from the anti-European atmosphere fostered by Tony Blair because of the conflict in Iraq'.[40]

Britishness as perceived by the French newspapers was now back to the way it had been seen for so long and could be summed up in one word: Atlanticism – which epitomized Britain's natural instinct in matters relating to foreign policy in the eyes of the French and was the major source of their grievance. *La Tribune* described Blair's awkward position, 'caught between his atlanticist commitment and his European ambitions'.[41] The British Prime Minister was guilty of having chosen the United States over Europe – once again. He had failed to act as 'a bridge' between both as he had originally intended to, and the special relationship with the United States had once more prevailed over the relations with the European Union. Hopes for a new British approach to Europe were therefore reduced to nothing, and Britishness in the eyes of the French was back to square one. The press was unanimous in condemning Tony Blair's Atlanticist preference. According to *La Tribune*, 'the Iraqi crisis will have once more emphasized the old traditional pattern' namely, the British and the USA on the one hand, and France and Germany on the other. *Le Figaro* took up the caricatures of Blair as 'George W. Bush's poodle', or as the 'governor of the 51st American state'.[42] In August 2003, *Libération* published a very critical article on the Prime Minister, entitled: 'Blair the European – the End of a Myth'.[43] The journalist condemned Tony Blair's failure to go forward on the single currency, and considered that 'the Iraqi episode [had] revealed the true nature of the European commitment of the British Prime Minister'. Finally, 'the American tropism' of Tony Blair was denounced as well as his 'unconditional pro-Americanism'.

40   J. P. Langellier, 'Les Britanniques ne sont "pas encore prêts" pour adopter la monnaie unique Européenne', *Le Monde* (10 June 2003).

41   P. Le Corre, 'Tony Blair pris entre son engagement atlantiste et ses ambitions Européennes', *La Tribune* (25 February 2003).

42   J. Duplouich, 'Tony Blair rejette l'Europe de Jacques Chirac', *Le Figaro* (29 April 2003).

43   P. Marlière, 'Blair l'Européen : la fin d'un mythe', *Libération* (28 August 2003).

Therefore the French press passed a very severe judgement on Tony Blair after the Iraqi crisis. Indeed, the Prime Minister had made the ultimate mistake in their eyes – favouring the special relationship with the United States over the relationship with Europe. This was to affect their judgement permanently. Most of the newspapers did not depart from their critical tone until the end of Blair's premiership.

The Referendum on the European Constitution

In April 2004, the issue of Britain in Europe was back in the columns of the French newspapers. Whereas Tony Blair had initially refused to submit the European constitution to a referendum, he finally went back on his decision. This move was unanimously presented by the French press as 'a volte-face'.[44] *Le Monde* questioned Blair's European credentials: 'Tony Blair, the European – really?'[45] It was interpreted as a sign of weakness, an 'opportunist choice' in a country where the majority of the public opinion and of the press was Eurosceptic: '[This] decision looks more like an admission of political weakness than to the act of courage of a Europhile'. Tony Blair had given in to the pressure of the Eurosceptic press. The expected and long-awaited referendum on the single currency was finally to be replaced by a consultation on the European constitution. This was also considered as quite revealing of Blair's new European approach. According to *Le Monde*, this battle was 'a poor and dangerous substitute for [the battle] on the Euro'.[46] This marked the comeback of the image of the 'perfidious Albion'

---

44   G. Dupuy, 'Blair : l'Europe vaut bien un référendum', editorial, *Libération* (21 April 2004); 'Blair fait volte-face sur la Constitution', *Le Figaro* (21 April 2004); 'Le pari de M. Blair', editorial, *Le Monde* (22 April 2004); J. P. Langellier, 'Tony Blair l'Européen, vraiment ?', *Le Monde* (30 April 2004).

45   Langellier, 'Tony Blair l'Européen'.

46   Ibid.

to symbolize Britishness in Europe. The initial enthusiasm for a British fresh start in Europe seemed long-forgotten for many French newspapers.

In the following months, the British Prime Minister's commitment to Europe was regularly questioned by various newspapers. After the European elections which had witnessed a heavy defeat for the Labour party and the surprise breakthrough of the United Kingdom Independence Party, the French press reproached Tony Blair for not speaking up about Europe: 'Europe is almost absent from his political discourse, and when it comes out, it is always in negative or defensive terms. ... The whole discourse of the Prime Minister, supposedly the most pro-European that the country has ever had, only denotes distrust of Europe'.[47]

One year later, as Tony Blair won his third victory as Prime Minister, *Le Monde* stressed the absence of the European issue from the general election campaign. After reviewing the two first terms of Blair in Number Ten Downing Street, the journalist expressed his disappointment: 'With hindsight, it seems that Tony Blair has failed in his pro-European commitment'.[48]

After the French and Dutch rejection of the European constitution in May and June 2005, Tony Blair decided not to go forward with the referendum. The French press did not miss this opportunity to underline that the double rejection of the Constitution had made the Prime Minister's life easier by enabling him to avoid 'the prospect of a near-certain defeat'.[49]

47 M. L. Cittanova, 'L'Europe, la grande absente de la politique de Tony Blair', *Les Echos* (18 June 2004).

48 J. P. Langellier, 'En Grande-Bretagne, le débat sur l'Europe est resté absent de la campagne pour les élections générales', *Le Monde* (6 May 2005).

49 A. Frachon, 'Europe, l'ironie du non', *Le Monde 2* (11 June 2005).

The Return of Franco-British Rivalry

In June 2005 a new episode occurred in the eventful relations between the United Kingdom and its European partners – and more particularly France. The old rivalry between the two countries resurfaced on the issue of the EU budget. The European council of Brussels where the member-states were supposed to finalize the budget for the years 2007–13 reached a dead end: Tony Blair refused to consider cutting the British rebate obtained by Margaret Thatcher in 1984 unless the European Union considered devoting less funding to the Common Agricultural policy (CAP) – a perspective rejected by the French President Jacques Chirac.

The French press held Blair responsible for the failure of the negotiations, *Le Monde* considering that 'The British Prime Minister, Tony Blair, [was] the first to blame for this fiasco' because of what the newspaper described as the 'stubborn refusal of Britain'.[50] The leading daily *Libération* which, as we have seen, had by then hardened its stance on Blair's European approach, bluntly depicted him as 'a man hanging on to his British cheque-book and to his selfishness'.[51] The journalist underlined the domestic dimension of Blair's European battle which appeared as 'a godsend for the Prime Minister' assuring him national applause at a time when his popularity was very low in the opinion polls. The left-wing weekly newspaper *Témoignage Chrétien* entitled its editorial 'Blair's Con' also condemning the Prime Minister's 'selfishness'.[52]

On 23 June 2005, only three days after the failure to reach an agreement at the European Council, Tony Blair made a speech to the European Parliament in which he delivered his vision of a modern Europe as an agenda for the British presidency of the European Union which was to begin on

---

50 T. Ferenzi, 'Tony Blair impose une remise à plat du projet Européen', *Le Monde* (19–20 June 2005).

51 A. Thoraval, 'Blair fait l'union des contraires britanniques', *Libération* (20 June 2005).

52 N. Bouttier, 'Les arnaques de Blair', *Témoignage Chrétien* (23 June 2005).

1 July 2005. The French press interpreted this speech as a direct attack on the French European approach – an attack on 'the old Europe' as opposed to 'the new Europe', according to the dichotomy initially underlined by the US Secretary of Defence Donald Rumsfeld in the run-up to the Iraq war – a new Europe of which Blair obviously wanted to take the leadership. For *Le Figaro*, 'War [was] declared'.[53] In an article entitled 'Mission: Impossible for Her Majesty's Prime Minister', the journalist wrote a parody of James Bond – with Tony Blair in the role of 007, against Dr No, in the form of Jacques Chirac. Without criticizing the substance of Blair's speech and vision for Europe, the author was doubtful of his ability to convince his European partners, because Britishness was still associated with Euroscepticism and reluctance: 'the sincerity of a British agent will always be questioned'. Obviously the Blair effect had reached its limits and the French perception of Britishness was back to the old clichés.

This analysis was taken up by *Les Echos* which admired Tony Blair's tactics although it considered that 'the past [did] not work in his favour'.[54] Similarly, after the beginning of the British presidency, *Le Figaro* wondered whether Tony Blair's wait-and-see policy on the single currency was an obstacle to his ambitions: 'Can they [the British] pretend to show the way for Europe today whereas they have stood timidly on the sidelines of monetary union?'[55] This emphasized the possible limits of Tony Blair's European credentials and aspirations.

Finally, an agreement on the budget was reached during the last days of the British presidency, whereby Britain agreed to the cutting of its rebate in exchange for a planned revision of the structure of the EU budget. A few weeks later, as Tony Blair made a speech in Oxford assessing the situation of the European Union following his country's presidency, *Le Figaro* reproached him for being too optimistic. In fact, the journalist questioned his credibility when talking about his achievements during those six months.

---

53   A. Bouilhet, Mission impossible pour le premier ministre de Sa Majesté', *Le Figaro* (24 June 2005).

54   M. L. Cittanova, 'L'Europe à l'heure Blairiste', *Les Echos* (30 June 2005).

55   C. Chatignoux, 'La Grande-Bretagne, grande absente de la zone Euro', *Le Figaro* (11 August 2005).

According to him, 'the promises [made in his speech to the European Parliament on 23 June 2005] were not followed up with actions'.[56] Once more, the British Prime Minister was accused of not having lived up to the expectations he had created. The criticism was then widened from the British presidency to the whole of Tony Blair's premiership:

> This ostentatious triumphalism poorly conceals a resounding failure. Despite all the fine words of its Prime Minister, the United Kingdom remains the most Eurosceptic of the entire Union. ... The fault lies with the unquestionable anti-European sectarianism – of the press, the Prime Minister asserts. Very well. But the 'Europhiles' underline that he did not manage – or did not want – to accompany his praiseworthy intentions by domestic initiatives, at the beginning of his premiership, in 1997, when he had every chance of convincing public opinion.[57]

Conclusion

As Tony Blair's premiership drew to a close, the French press assessed his contribution in terms of impact on Britishness in Europe. Unsurprisingly enough, the key-word proved to be disappointment, though some newspapers were more critical than others in their comment. This was not the case with *Le Monde* which had consistently been among the greatest supporters of Tony Blair throughout his premiership. The leading daily paper did not condemn the British Labour Prime Minister nor question his European credentials but regretted that he had failed to convey his pro-European beliefs to the British people who were still overwhelmingly Eurosceptic. In an analysis entitled 'A pro-European who has not been able to convince public opinion', the journalist stressed the reluctance of the British people: 'Mr Blair has not succeeded in 'selling' Europe to his fellow citizens, in

56   J. Duplouich, 'Tony Blair promet un avenir brillant à l'Europe', *Le Figaro* (3 February 2006).
57   Ibid.

giving it a better place in the heart of a people still resolutely insular'.[58] The image of the islander recurrent in the French perception of Britishness was used, once again, to account for Britain's awkward relationship with Europe and its reluctance to further integration.

According to the business newspaper *Les Echos*, the Prime Minister had failed to place Britain at the heart of Europe, as he had initially intended to. Yet he had managed to influence European integration: 'Britain has remained on the fringe of Europe but has succeeded in putting forward its ideas'.[59] There lay indeed one of the main paradoxes of Tony Blair's European policy: although he had certainly managed to bring the European Union closer to the British vision, the British people were still predominantly Eurosceptic. The newspaper also considered that the Prime Minister's stance on Europe had evolved: 'Whereas he was a convinced European when he entered Downing Street, Tony Blair has gradually lost his enthusiasm and eventually led a policy much more in line with the Eurosceptic British tradition'. In contrast with the initial change that Tony Blair had advocated, continuity had thus prevailed in terms of substance even if the style had proved different from the previous Conservative governments.

In fact, as regards Britishness, nothing had really changed. As *La Croix* put it, Tony Blair was 'European in the British way' – which was definitely different from the French way.[60] Both countries had different conceptions of what being European meant, resulting from their respective histories and experiences. This was maybe the source of the disappointment of the French press; they may have expected the impossible. Contrary to France, in Blair's Britain 'European interests and Atlanticism [were] one and the same'. It appeared clearly that for the French press, Atlanticism was one of the founding and distinctive elements of Britishness in the context of European integration. It may also be one of the major sources of misunderstanding between both countries' visions of European integration, and more generally of world politics. Because the fact is that in spite of

58   J. P. Langellier, 'Un pro-Européen qui n'a pas pu convaincre son opinion', *Le Monde* (21 April 2007).

59   Chatignoux, 'La Grande-Bretagne est restée'.

60   S. Maillard, 'Européen à la manière britannique', *La Croix* (23 June 2007).

everything that he may be – rightly or wrongly – blamed for by the French newspapers, Tony Blair remains the most pro-European Prime Minister to govern Britain since Edward Heath.

Interestingly enough, his successor in 10, Downing Street, Gordon Brown, was held responsible by the French newspapers for having kept Britain out of the single currency with the five economic tests that he had set up when he was still Chancellor of the Exchequer. During his three years at the head of the Labour government, he was seen by the French press at worst as a Eurosceptic, or at best, as a Prime Minister who was not the least interested in European integration. There is little evidence so far that his premiership has had any positive impact on the traditional French perception of Britishness in Europe.

Following the general election of May 2010, the coalition government formed by the Conservative party and the Liberal Democrats gathers two completely different –if not incompatible – visions of Britain's role towards European integration: the Conservatives' Euroscepticism coupled with the much more pro-European position of the Liberal Democrats. Such an improbable alliance seemed to reassure Britain's European partners who had initially feared the potentially negative impact of a Conservative victory on the relationship between the United Kingdom and the European Union. *Le Monde* thus mentioned the 'secret hope' harboured by the European heads of state in its article entitled: 'Europe counts on the Liberal Democrats to moderate the Conservatives' Euroscepticism.'[61] However, the coalition deal struck between the two political parties tends to suggest that such a scenario is very unlikely as the Conservatives are not ready to make concessions on Europe. Therefore, even if the coalition holds, it is hard to foresee any improvement regarding the French perception of Britishness in Europe under the premiership of David Cameron. On the contrary, given his European credentials so far, the new British Prime Minister is most likely to reinforce the image of Britain as an awkward and a reluctant European partner. He is undoubtedly far more Eurosceptic than both his Labour predecessors at Number Ten Downing Street.

---

61 P. Ricard, 'L'Europe compte sur les lib-dem pour modérer l'Euroscepticisme des conservateurs', *Le Monde* (13 May 2010).

Finally, what emerges clearly from this study is that the 'Frenchness' of the perspective overrides political differences between the newspapers, in that they tend to reflect the French desire to see Britishness in continental terms – therefore making disappointment inevitable. It seems that the French perception of Britishness also casts an interesting light on the French identity itself in the context of European integration – but that is a different story.

KATH WOODWARD, DAVID GOLDBLATT AND JAMES WYLLIE

9 British Fair Play: Sport across Diasporas at the BBC World Service[1]

Sport carries powerful links to identity, especially to national identities, which in the context of Britishness have frequently been expressed through the lens of empire. The BBC World Service (BBCWS), formerly known as the Empire Service, has played an important role in the contact zone of sports broadcasting, in which identifications are made and re-made. This chapter explores the construction of Britishness through sports broadcasting on the BBCWS, drawing upon material from the BBC Archive at Caversham, from the start of sports broadcasting at the BBC and the establishment of the Empire Service, in 1932, up to the late 1970s, in order to present an understanding of the legacy of Britishness in sport, especially as configured around ideas of impartiality and fair play. The BBCWS set up to broadcast to a British diaspora made strong claims to objectivity and impartiality which cohabit with the service's associations with colonialism.

Sport is a very significant, if sometimes elusive, aspect of BBCWS broadcasting. Sporting events have featured in schedules since the advent of the service, having already been a central aspect of the BBC output, but sport as a genre is more difficult to pin down in the literature on the BBC. This chapter draws out what is distinctive about sport on the BBCWS by exploring its development in the period up to the 1970s in order to explain

1 This research is part of the AHRC *Diasporas, Migration and Identities Programme* Project, *Tuning In: Contact Zones at the BBC World Service* (AH/ES58693/1). The project investigated the role of the BBCWS as an intra- and cross-diasporic contact zone and documented its activities of transnational cultural brokerage and diplomacy (http://www.open.ac.uk/socialsciences/diasporas/).

some of the histories and meanings of sport, through pivotal sporting moments, scheduling regimes and production minutes and communications.[2] We focus on particular sports and sporting events, in particular the Olympic Games and cricket, although the project included tennis, boxing, men's football world cups and rugby.[3] This focus has been chosen in order to create a picture of the way in which the presentation of sport was cast and its relationship to the service's wider mission of broadcasting of the British way of life and, especially how notions of fair play in sport feed into the wider constitution of British World Service impartiality and the versions of Britishness communicated by the BBCWS.

The notion of fair play which has become associated with the identifications with Britishness that are translated by a broadcasting service that has both strong links to impartiality and to empire and particularly to the reiteration of Britishness as a national identity is a major concern. The diasporic audience of sports broadcasting has been primarily an expatriate one, and thus the service could be construed as concerned with a reinstatement of British colonial values rather than opening up the possibilities for a more diffuse diasporic audience, but the objectivity and impartiality claimed by the service are also in play in sport, leading to some more diverse and less predictable outcomes in the story of sport on the BBCWS.

2   The first stage in this research has focused on textual and discourse analysis of data from the BBC Written Archive at Caversham Park, including the Empire Service, London Calling and General Files, which include programme records, schedules and production minutes. Radio Outside Broadcast Files included cricket Test Matches and series 1976–74 and the Olympic Games 1948–80. The ephemeral nature of the sporting event, albeit one that has resonance in the collective memory of the nation, may account for absences.

3   Football provides a particular case in which the BBC has no special privileges to cover the world cup, even when if it is held in the UK as was the case in 1966, when all memoranda were about hotel bookings and domestic arrangements, since nobody knew it was to be England's greatest ever moment. The BBC is just another provider, in awe of FIFA which distributes broadcasting rights.

Empire

In the discussion of setting up what was then called the Empire Service, the centrality of the ideological role of the service was explicitly identified as a primary objective. The language of empire was deployed and there is direct expression of an ideological purpose; the World Service was funded by the Foreign Office. For example, at the Imperial Conference of 1930, the service was supported in terms of its political powers of 'strengthening ties' between parts of the Empire'.[4] This view is reflected in a speech by John Reith, the BBC's first Director General, which was broadcast when the service opened. Broadcasting is identified as having come to involve, a 'connecting and coordinating link between the scattered parts of the British Empire'.[5] Empire and nation are re-instated through the routine coverage of cyclical events, which Scannell and Cardiff describe as:

> the noiseless manner in which the BBC became perhaps *the* central agent of national culture as its cyclical role; the cyclical production year in year out, of an orderly, regular progression of festivities, rituals and celebrations-major and minor, civic and sacred-that mark the unfolding of the broadcast year.[6]

Sport plays a big part in these 'noiseless' cycles, along with religion, which is another key element in the making of the nation. Sport marks out time for the listener, having 'developed its own calendar very quickly. The winter season had its weekly observances of football, rugby and steeple-chasing, climaxing in the Boat Race, the Grand National and the Cup Final. Summer brought in cricket and flat racing, the Test Matches, Derby Day, Royal Ascot and Wimbledon'.[7]

---

4   J. Reith 'Opening of the Empire Service' (19 December 1932) in 'Empire Service Policy 1932–3, E4/6.

5   Ibid.

6   P. Scannell and D. Cardiff, *A Social History of British Broadcasting 1922–1938* (Oxford: Basil Blackwell, 1991), 278. Emphasis in the original text.

7   Ibid. 279.

The BBC is 'noiseless' because the timetable is assumed and taken for granted as not only what *is* but what *should* be. Sport assumes the mantle of legitimacy which might also be sanctioned, by association with religion and the state as well as particularly gendered identities, especially masculinity.[8] These events are, of course, the ones that feature in the archive and in the general files and demonstrate the importance of particular sports as included in the making of the nation and also, by setting one agenda, indicate silences and absences. The coverage of sport is predominantly of men's sport at this point, coding the legacy of empire, as well as the reconfiguration of nation, as masculine and suggesting associations between particular versions of embodied heroic achievement in an alliance with patriarchy, as 'an exclusive respect for the genealogy of sons and fathers and the competition between brothers'.[9] Women, however, are not entirely absent; they can 'play the game' or at least some games.[10] Empire like nation, operates as an 'imagined community', too big to be grasped by individuals, as well as a material actuality.[11] Sport is very capable of creating a sense of what it means to be British through its powerful identifications, embodied heroic acts and competitions which resonate with conflict and combat as well as its more subtle injunctions. The routes of identification can be circuitous, however, and sport carries both positive and negative elements, for example in the extent to which it promotes or damages social inclusion.[12] At its most negative it might appear to present a pastiche of democratic processes of cohesion.[13] However, the dynamics of identification are rarely linear and, as we aim to demonstrate, there are inconsistencies and disruptions even

8   K. Woodward, *Boxing and Masculinity: The 'I' of the Tiger* (London: Routledge 2007); K. Woodward, *Embodied Sporting Practices, Regulating and Regulatory Bodies* (Basingstoke: Palgrave MacMillan, 2009).

9   L. Irigaray, *Sexes et Parentes* (Paris: Minuit, 1987), 202.

10   Woodward, *Embodied Sporting Practices*.

11   B. Anderson *Imagined Communities: Reflections on the Origins and Spread of Nationalism* (London: Verso, 1991).

12   J. Clifford, *Routes: Travel and Translation in the Late Twentieth Century* (Cambridge MA. and London: Harvard University Press, 1999); P. Gilroy *Post-Colonial Melancholia* (New York: Columbia University Press, 2004).

13   S. Žižek, 'Multiculturalism, or the Cultural Logic of Multinational Capitalism', *New Left Review* 225 (1997), 28–51.

when the voice is officially that of empire. The associations of sport with empire and nation demonstrate some of the mechanisms of assumption and the processes through which the discursive field becomes regulated and regulates itself in the re-production of a Foucauldian regime of truth.[14] Sport, at the outset was closely linked to empire and nation, but the experience of sport on the BBCWS is much more diverse and nuanced.

Sport on the BBCWS: An Overview of the Schedule

Sport is rarely classified as such in the literature of the BBCWS.[15] The classificatory systems deployed partially demonstrate the status of sport in the schedules; for example, certain sporting events are included unquestioningly in the schedule and, although the rationale is un-stated, the interconnections between dominant discourses remain unacknowledged. Sport is still associated with play and national identifications are assumed, but it does not occupy the overtly moral high ground of drama and discussion programmes, which attract more explicit ethical direction, as evidenced by the production minutes.

The coverage of sport at the BBCWS, during the period up to the 1970s, while retaining its corporate stance of objectivity, consistency of voice, attention to detail and thoroughness of preparation, was also fluid, flexible and responsive to changes in technology and audience, reflecting changing public tastes. Although the aim remained to offer something for everybody, the documents chart the rise and fall of particular sports and their popularity.

14 M. Foucault, *The History of Sexuality: Volume 1: An Introduction* (Harmondsworth: Penguin, 1981).
15 See for example, A. Briggs, *A History of Broadcasting in the United Kingdom, Volume II: The Golden Age of Wireless* (Oxford: Oxford University Press, 1995); G. Born, *Uncertain Visions: Birt, Dyke and the Reinvention of the BBC* (London: Vintage, 2005); Scannell and Cardiff, *A Social History of British Broadcasting.*

The BBC's 1966 report on the coverage of sport noted that the Overseas Service was alone amongst the various global external services (such as Voice of America, Deustche Welle and Radio Moscow) in providing regular coverage of sporting events, because it alone, could utilize the coverage of a major domestic sports broadcaster for both expertise and live transmissions.[16] By the mid 1960s, the domestic broadcasting of sport was spread across the BBC's three national networks; the Home Service, the Light Network and the Third Network, with the bulk of output on the Third. However, sport amounted to only just over 3 per cent of total broadcast hours of which three-quarters were live commentaries and the remainder predominantly results and round-up shows, though they were supplemented by the very occasional quiz or feature.[17] Of the live broadcasts, the core was provided by football and cricket commentaries. These are two sports with strongly inflected ethnicised, racialised, gendered and classed associations. Cricket had powerful links to empire.[18] On the other hand, British football represented a popular working class sport.[19]

The report notes that, by the mid 1960s, audiences were certainly down from the pre-television era. However Test Matches, League and FA Cup football, Wimbledon and the major horse races could still get ratings in the millions. The 1966 World Cup Finals had a domestic radio audience of over two and half million. For major events that were not covered on television, like the 1963 Cassius Clay-Henry Cooper fight, the audience could balloon; 21 million tuned in to hear the fight. Even at home the idea of a monolithic or single British sports culture was subtly challenged by the coverage of sport on BBC regional radio. On BBC Wales, for example, local events and sporting preferences reshaped the content of the network's programming.

16   BBC WAC E40/110/1 Sport General.
17   Ibid.
18   C. L. R. James, *Beyond a Boundary* (London: Stanley Paul, 1963); R. Guha, *A Corner of a Foreign Field: The Indian History of an English Game* (London: Picador, 2002).
19   R. Giulianotti, *Football: A Sociology of the Global Game* (Cambridge: Polity, 1999); R. Giulianotti and R. Robertson, 'Sport and Globalization: Transnational Dimensions', *British Journal of Sociology* 55 (4), 545–68.

The BBC's external services appear similar to the domestic services. In 1965 about 3 per cent of total output was sports coverage, predominantly live commentaries, supplemented by news and results services and the very occasional feature. The core of the network's sports programming was *Sports News* a fifteen minute results and news digest broadcast three times a day, plus one half-hour sports magazine programme a week. On the English-language overseas service, Saturday afternoon was given over to the third network's *Saturday Sport* show.

In scheduling terms, sports coverage was developed to meet listeners' demands. In promoting 'fair play' the BBC aimed to provide what listeners were seen to want. There was considerable variation across the sporting season and across the different language services, with sport constituting over an eighth of broadcasts to Australia and less than half a percentage point of air time on the German service. On the English language overseas service, sport actually made up 7.5 per cent of output, but in the summer, when cricket dominated the schedules, this could climb to over 10 per cent of air time. Two years later, an internal analysis by the BBC revealed that the audience for these English-language broadcasts was considerable. The African audience, especially in West Africa was the largest, followed by the Asian audience, though the report noted that there remained a significant contingent of British expatriate listeners.[20] Cricket's leading place in the schedules can be seen from the data for 1965 when live Cricket was aired for 133 hours, football for just thirty-two hours (although in 1966 this doubled with full coverage of the men's World Cup) and horse racing for twelve. Alongside these three mainstays of the scheduled External Service, coverage included the entire major World and Commonwealth boxing title bouts and live coverage form the leading tennis tournaments.

Across all of the language services, the report describes a unity of purpose and recognition of 'the season' in British sport:

> ... they all report major news and deal with sport in programmes reflecting the British way of life and events in this country. Accounts of major British sporting events such as Wimbledon, Henley or the Cup Final are featured in all the services; reports on

20   BBC WAC E40/110/1 Sport General.

international contests takes place in this country in which either the UK or teams from the target areas are broadcast regularly. When an international event of first class importance takes place in this country... the most recent example is the World Cup competition – this claims attention from all the External Services.[21]

One aspect of the British way of life which had spread and in which foreign audiences took a close interest was the pools, 'by taking advantage of the wide dissemination of British football pools coupons and relaying on our reputation for accuracy, the World Service gains many listeners for its service for football results'.[22]

Thus, even when attending to the core external service mission of representing the British 'way of life', in this case through sport, there was also considerable sensitivity to the diversity of the audiences actually being addressed. Acknowledgement of local audience needs meant that, at major sporting events where a local athlete was performing, coverage on the language services could soar as high as 25 per cent of a week's output. Over the previous decade, the Far Eastern Service had made a point of covering badminton and the Asian games, the Persian and Bulgarian Services had covered wrestling and winter sports were reported more assiduously on the Europe language services.

In the early 1960s the service had covered the East African Rally competitions; it was noted that this was at least in part designed to help give exposure to British car manufacturers in key African export markets. The External service would also provide ball-by-ball coverage of Test Matches in England for the visiting nations and even covered events not broadcast in the UK but of key importance elsewhere, for example the International Hockey Championship in Hamburg which was avidly listened to in Kenya, Pakistan and India. The External Service also continued to provide live coverage of major international sporting events, like the Olympics, for the many developing nations who had no independent coverage of their own.

In addition to taking live coverage, foreign radio stations had, for many years, been re-broadcasting External Service output. Here sport was central

21   Ibid.
22   Ibid.

to the network's success in promoting its cultural diplomacy. The fifteen minute *Sports-Round Up* broadcasting in the World Service three times a day was re-broadcast by twenty two different stations.[23] These twenty-two stations included countries as diverse as Kenya, Guyana, Malawi and New Zealand, while much of South Africa's radio sports coverage on a Saturday afternoon through the 1960s was provided by the BBC.

Further research into specific events and sports reinforces the evidence of the 1966 report that the cosmopolitan model of Britishness, the sensitivity to diverse audiences and their needs revealed within it were in evidence twenty years prior to its publication; trends that are evident in other sporting coverage.

The Olympics

We focus upon two sets of Olympic files, from the massive coverage of this sporting event in the archive for purposes of comparison and to demonstrate some of the transformations of Britishness that can be seen as occurring over this period. Such big moments make enormous demands on the organization of the system and demonstrate the massive scope of the service as well as the detailed work which went into providing coverage and the Olympics have the advantage of including clear classifications of the nation and a diverse range of sports, as well as explicitly, at this point, incorporating the amateur ideal.

Lord Aberdare, President of the British Olympic Committee used the External Service as an element of his campaign, broadcasting his appeal to the IOC to give London the Games in 1946. Aberdare was successful in his mission and alongside the Labour government of the day cast the Olympics in the same mould as the Festival of Britain as a pageant of creativity that would lighten the gloom of post-war austerity Britain, a

23   Ibid.

public event that would capture something of the heroic spirit for the age, in building peace rather than making war. The 1948 Olympics presented the opportunity for a reconfiguration of Britishness, in which the BBC was strongly implicated.

The BBC external services were the centre of the media coverage of the games. The scale and the scope of coverage, given the economic and technological limits of the era, were immense. The BBC alone was broadcasting the games on its Latin American, Arabic, Turkish, and English to India, Eastern, Far Eastern, North American, Pacific, South African, Colonial, and European Services. The Far Eastern Service was broadcasting in seven languages – Korean, Kuyou, Chinese, Japanese, Siamese, Burmese, Malay, the European service in twenty-one languages. The Overseas Service transmissions exceeded all other broadcasters combined and foreign radio stations were rebroadcasting BBC material, which was played daily on over 100 Latin American stations including many who had their own representatives at the Games as well.[24]

In spite of its dominance in the post-war era, the BBC external service adopted a remarkably open minded attitude to its role. The traditional purposes of the service were emphasized in a Memo from the head of the European Service, who argued that the BBC should be able, 'to reflect in its output the great international sporting event taking place in Britain and to provide a service for European broadcasting organizations by enabling their reporters to cover the games'.[25] This was immediately counterbalanced by the note, 'our commentators should try to give a balanced picture of the whole games... always bearing in mind that our reporting must not be on narrow nationalistic lines'.[26]

John Arlott of the Eastern Service stressed that it was the intention to establish at the outset of the games to broadcast specifically the views of the games most interesting to India and Pakistan and to place himself above all Indian and Pakistani listeners, to identify himself with them, to make it clear that he was catering for them only.[27] Impartiality involved

24   BBC WAC R30/2,060/1 Olympic Games 1948.
25   BBC WAC R30/2,046/2 Olympic Games 1948, File 1B.
26   BBC WAC R30/2,046/2 Olympic Games 1948, File 1B.
27   BBC WAC R30/2,046/3 Olympic Games 1948, File 2.

endeavouring to enable full access to a range of listeners as possible, or at least the acknowledgement that the listening constituency does not only comprise expatriate communities.

The 1948 Olympics were probably the high water mark of the BBC as a sports broadcaster. Comparison with later games suggests a diminished role, registering the impact of transformations in networks of power that occurred across the globe and especially the decline of empire. 1948 offered a unique historical moment: not only did the BBC have the best technical facilities, they also had the legitimacy conferred by their role in the defeat of Nazism, reflecting Britain's post-war position as a victor who fought for a culture that embodied fair-play, impartiality and civilized values (Germany and Japan had been excluded from the Games, while the USSR boycotted them). The dismantling of formal properties of empire, for example through the independence of India, did not of course diminish many of the political and cultural forces of imperialism and the BBC retained the authority to speak on behalf of and to the rest of the world.

Twenty years later in Mexico it was a different story. Britain's Imperial power had receded in the intervening years while the globalization of sport had continued at a rapid pace. The gulf between the BBC's perception of its mandate and the actuality of a post-colonial world widened. This, combined with the arrival of television, which accelerated the global appetite for sport and the spread of the technologies to disseminate it, gave rise to a much altered scenario in the preparations for 1968, where decisions about coverage were influenced by machinic technologies as well as political considerations.

The European Broadcast Commission, which had organized a consortium of European broadcasters to carry coverage of the 1964 games in Tokyo, presented a rival service. The BBC refused to join, preferring to remain aloof of this organization and to differentiate itself from the European venture while stressing the singularity of the British project; a trend that was confirmed by the BBC's decision to form a separate Commonwealth Pool.[28]

28   R30/4502/1=Olympic games summer 68, EBU.

The heavily paternalistic tone appears in Max Muller's comments regarding their European rivals, 'If it is felt that BBC Radio must work through the EBU, I suggest that some safeguard should be made for other Commonwealth members not in such a strong position as ourselves.'[29]

At an EBU meeting of the Sound Broadcasting Committee, an Expert Working Party on the Mexico City Olympics 1968, held in Geneva on the 22nd Sept 1965, including German, Belgian, French, Italian, Norwegian and Swiss representatives, Muller argued for and won special consideration from the Commonwealth. Assuming there would be another broadcasting pool, the minutes noted that 'bound by a common language, the Commonwealth Group would like its own representative in the EBU Operations Group, so that not only could facilities be negotiated for it but also… a steady flow of relevant information could be continually fed to its members.'[30]

Having chosen an Australian as Operations Manager, Arthur Povah of ABC, the BBC then opted out of the EBU in the early 1967 to run the Commonwealth Pool, still confident that the former colonies would rally round the flag. The initial feedback was encouraging if not a stampede of interest, as noted in a report by the Commonwealth Broadcasting Conference Secretariat, of the 19 Commonwealth Broadcasting organizations consulted four (Cyprus, Malawi, Sierra Leone and Tanzania) were unwilling to participate; two (Kenya and Pakistan) made no reply at all: five (Ceylon, India, Malta, Uganda and Zambia) were agreeable in principle but were considering the cost factor in relation to national participation and policy etc: and eight (Australia, Britain, Canada, Ghana, Jamaica, Malaysia, New Zealand and Nigeria) definitely supported the project. However, he was confident that the seven neutral states would comply.[31]

The reality was somewhat different in a world of emergent nations shrugging off their colonial heritage, more complex and harder to predict. Muller conceded in a report written after the Games, 'the response from Commonwealth organizations in the end was disappointing'. Only four

29   Ibid.
30   R30/4503/1-Olympic games Summer 1968, EBU.
31   Ibid.

members joined with the BBC, the Australian Broadcasting Commission, New Zealand Broadcasting Corporation, All India Radio, Jamaica Broadcasting. This put pressure on resources and staffing leading to the minor humiliation of working very closely with the European Broadcasting Union. Although Muller admitted that 'in many instances this was of considerable benefit', he was quick to remind us that it was also of 'considerable benefit' for the Pool members 'not to be tied to the much larger EBU operation'.[32] This was a turning point in the BBCWS's sports coverage.

Test Cricket: the Game of Empire?

The files on the BBC External Services' coverage of Test Match cricket, particularly the tours of overseas teams to the UK are amongst the richest and most complete in the archive reflecting the high level of coverage accorded these events and the high prestige in which they were held at home and abroad. Cricket also offers the closest links between colonialism and Britishness, largely encoded as Englishness. Despite the huge popularity of football in the post-war period, the Football League recording record levels of attendance for five years after the end of the war, its place as the national game was challenged by cricket. The scheduling dominance of cricket and its coverage suggest that the game more effectively embodied the national character than football. Writing in the 1930s, Neville Cardus, the music and cricket correspondent for the *Guardian*, was able to write, 'If everything else in this nation of ours was lost but cricket – her Constitution and the laws of England – it would be possible to reconstruct from the theory and the practice of cricket all the eternal Englishness which has gone to the establishment of that constitution and the laws aforesaid'.[33]

32   Ibid.
33   N. Cardus, *Cricket* (London: Longman, 1930).

However, in cricket there had been for some considerable time a sense that the game was part of the cultural fabric of the wider British Empire. Englishness and Britishness elide frequently in these sporting stories and it is not by chance that it is English cricket with its histories of gentlemen and players and the English cricket team, rather than teams of any of the nations that make up the UK that carries the most powerful imbrications of empire. Australia had demonstrated the potency of colonial cricket over sixty years before when they won the first Test Match series against England. Since then South African, Indian, West Indian and New Zealand teams had all shown considerable prowess in the game, and had amongst the elite of commentators, demonstrated their own distinctive styles of playing the game.

Given cricket's central place in the construction of both national and imperial identities, it is hardly surprising that the 1946 tour by the All-India side attracted considerable interest and ideological baggage. At a point of political disruption wrought by the processes of decolonization and fragmentation along religious and ethnic lines, the all India team's tour was emblematic of both Indian unity (the ethnic maker of the team was remarkably balanced drawing on Hindus, Christian and Muslim) and the umbilical linkages between centre and periphery.[34]

It was an event of sufficient importance and interest inside the BBC for a memo to be issued stating that for reasons of expense and time only a very limited number of people would actually be able to attend the Indian team's arrival. Coverage of the tour began on the team's arrival in London with a special broadcast of fifteen minutes consisting of personal messages. It would continue through the summer with daily reports, on-the-spot interviews and summaries being delivered, in three languages, from all the team's Test Matches as well as a considerable number of games against the MCC, Oxbridge varsity sides and county teams. The following year, the external service would broadcast the South African Tour at an even higher level of coverage including games against the combined services team and all three days of the Gentleman vs. Players game at Lords as well. Com-

34   Guha, *A Corner of a Foreign Field.*

mentary and summaries were broadcast alternately in Afrikaans and English on the African service, in three languages on the Eastern services as well as specially tailored reports in English for the Pacific and General Overseas networks. The appetite for cricket was so great that only the most minor of matches were deemed superfluous. The DCA noted that 'the African service is approaching saturation point with cricket and suggests that unless you have strong feelings about it, we should tell Northern Ireland we have decided not to broadcast'.[35]

A January 1946 memo from the Director of Eastern Services to the Director of Outside Broadcast noted 'the tour of the all-India team this summer is going to be matter of outstanding interest for our broadcasts to India. We are already getting correspondence asking for maximum coverage in Eastern Services'.[36]

India was not the only place calling for more cricket on the radio. The next decade saw a steady growth in the level of cricket coverage on the BBC's domestic and external services. By 1951 the corporation had begun to experiment with ball-by-ball commentary of test Cricket. Parts of the 1951 South African tour received this treatment as did the 1953 Australian tour. By 1957 the format had been settled and *Test Match Special* was launched offering all-day, ball-by-ball coverage on both domestic and external services, while in 1959 the England tour to Australia was the first 'overseas tour' broadcast back to the UK and around the world.

Cricket carried diverse sets of meanings in different parts of the Commonwealth and what was left of the empire, but the External services were alert to the sensitivities of India. In the same memo the New Delhi office says, 'Cricket commentaries, especially in English, creating greatest interest yet in Eastern Service programmes and widely acclaimed and publicized. Will cable further reactions but already obvious Hindustani commentaries high prestige value'.[37]

---

35   BBC WAC R30/3081/1 – Cricket, South African Tour 1947.
36   BBC WAC R30/1319/1 Indian Cricket Touring Team.
37   Ibid.

That value was in part political, recognizing 'that a very high proportion of the listeners to our Eastern Service in English are Indians; and that at the present time there are genuine and urgent reasons for fostering anything which promotes goodwill towards Britain amongst Indians, even in the modest realm of sport'.[38]

The recognition of the political and cultural value of these cricket broadcasts to Britain suggests, at one level, a direct and instrumental imperialism. However, the most revealing document in the files suggests quite the contrary. An internal memo written in January 1946 raises the idea that the BBC Eastern Service could round off the tour of the Indian cricket team by holding a studio based discussion comparing and contrasting Indian and English cricket.[39] The proposed members of the panel were Prof D. B Deodhar, Abdul Hamid, John Arlott, Arthur Russell, and as Chair of the conversation, black Caribbean cricketer Leary Constantine then playing professionally in the Lancashire cricket leagues. It is not clear from the files whether the programme was made, though notes in the margins suggest general approval. More significantly, it is hard to imagine anywhere else in the British public sphere in 1946, that a conversation could be held between Indians, Britons and a black West Indian within so equitable a framework of expertise.

The balance of power had shifted even further by 1952. Five years after Indian independence, Rex Alston, the Director of Outside Broadcasts sent a memo to commentators and announcers at the BBC covering the Indian cricket tour that summer: 'the Anglo-Indian fraternity is both irritable and vociferous and we shall cause much annoyance both at home and overseas if we do not adopt it'.[40]

A similar sensitivity can be detected in the discussion notes of the 1951 South African tour which made clear that the sound of Bow Bells was not be broadcast on the Afrikaans service.[41] In addition, the desire not to antagonize the subcontinent's enormous cricket audience was expressed in a memo considering the first test tour to England by Pakistan in 1954.

38   Ibid.
39   Ibid.
40   BBC WAC R30/1319/2 Indian Cricket Touring Team.
41   BBC WAC R30/3018/1 Cricket: South African team.

A final coda in the files to this steady drift of opinion with the external services comes in an exchange of letters in 1959 over the employment of Indian commentators and summarizers on the English-language world service coverage of India's tour of England including the Maharajkumar of Vizzianagarm and Pearson Surita. Vizzianagarm was successful but Surita, in a complete reversal of the older colonial expectations, was deemed too English for the role. A senior figure wrote that 'although he is by far the best commentator, I can see little point in your using him in GOS [General Overseas Service] as he sounds like a "retired Indian colonel"'.[42]

The archive reveals both perceptive awareness of the wider social and cultural context, as well as the assumed reiteration of very traditional British values, through the enormous attention to detail in the decision-making process to ensure what is stated as fair treatment in accordance with the principles of the service. Britishness and Englishness elide in cricket more than in many sports, for example rugby, which is not only played by Wales, Ireland and Scotland, but also has different meanings in relation to social class in these nations and between union and league. Cricket is implicated in a particular version of empire, but the earlier discussion of the need to accommodate different diasporic audiences prefigures more recent, twenty first century shifts in the power geometry of sport towards the Indian sub-Continent.

Coverage of sport demonstrates the ambiguities of fair play; the divisions of class, gender, race and ethnicity muddy the field and it is these tensions with which the World Service has to deal. These factors articulate together, but there are moments in which sport offers more opportunities for democratization and broadcasting space opens up possibilities for different voices to be heard. The impartiality that is pivotal to the version of Britishness promoted by the BBCWS opens up some possibility of disruption and transformation and is often played out through the inclusion of these new inflections.

---

42   BBC WAC R30/1319/3 Indian Cricket Touring Team.

Conclusion

Our timescale predates the transforming and often liberating technologies of the Internet, but sport is both typical and enduringly distinctive of the BBC World Service; something that is part of a wider picture but also an area of experience with a life of its own. The World Service has travelled in its engagement with sport through the legacy of empire and patriarchy and the multiplicities of change in the re-construction of Britishness. Diasporic audiences have transformed the relationship between local and global and between the UK and its place in the world. In 1948 the world came to London for the Olympic Games; in 2012 the world is already in the UK. The heritage of Britishness on the BBC World Service gives particular emphases to fair play and to impartiality as well as, sometimes overtly, sometimes implicitly, representing a colonialist discourse of imperialist identifications.

The BBCWS has played a key role in framing and shaping diasporic contact zones, through the diversity of the diasporic audience and the reiteration of the need to engage with the dynamic of change, in sport and in social relations. The process is dynamic because sports generate their own versions of fair play, ranging from the gentlemanly practices of cricket to the raw, polarized combat of boxing.

Coverage of big events was maintained through the 1930s and into the 1960s in the development of the BBCWS. However, it is not only the global dimensions of sporting events that are taken for granted, so too are national identifications, with Britishness or Englishness, all under the aegis of an assumed impartiality of 'playing by the rules' and the fair play of sport. The superiority of British/English sport is naturalized through its dominance of the BBCWS airways, but the possibilities of re-interpretation and re-accommodation are also made possible. The major period covered in the paper demonstrates that the changing place of sport in the BBCWS can only be understood with reference to wider changes in the relationship between broadcasting and sport and demonstrates the powerful synchronies between social, political, technological, economic and cultural factors, even at historical moments, such as during the Second World War when the Empire Service played a particularly important and didactic role in communicating home to the military. However, the narrative of change is not linear and can be more usefully understood as manifesting multiplicities that encompass disruptions and accommodations and, most importantly, the BBCWS provides a space for the pursuit of sporting interests and engagement with the politics as well as the pleasures of sport. Diasporic audiences shape the schedule and so does what is broadcast. There is no single voice of the BBC in sport.

There are silences, notably in women's sport; sport is a patriarchal field, but different strands interweave through the imperial genealogies of sport inextricably entwined with the social, political and cultural changes taking place in the wider world. There is no detectable linear narrative but rather a series of tensions and contradictions that are reflected up and reconfigured in the texts in which deliberations are made. The relationship of the BBCWS with its listeners is dialogic rather than presenting a univocal imperative expressing the voice of empire in a one way narrative.

Sport is played through the genealogy of colonialism, but there are disruptions that represent change and the emergence of more democratic versions of Britishness. The over pervading ethos of the archive material is detailed discussion and engagement with 'fair play' on all counts. Before equal opportunities or diversity policies had been put into discourse the BBCWS was nonetheless concerned with social inclusion, if only because the service has always been responsive to its listeners and also because sport has the potential to open up new, transnational, democratic sources of identification.

AMY VON HEYKING

10 'Proud to call themselves Englishmen': Representations of Britishness in Twentieth Century English-Canadian Schools

At the beginning of the twentieth century, English-Canadians had a strong sense of connection to Britain; indeed they were Britons. While many Canadian historians have traditionally seen the twentieth century as the story of Canada's progress from colony to nation and of the evolution of its unique national identity, some are now acknowledging that 'English-speaking Canadians had no difficulty in holding multiple identities. They saw themselves as both British and Canadian, and they saw the empire as belonging to them as well as to the British who lived in the mother country'.[1] The Britishness of English-Canadians endured well into the twentieth century, even into the 1960s. What Britishness was, however, and what it meant within the context of an emerging Canadian national-ism, changed over time. One interesting source of information about the nature and evolution of Britishness for English-Canadians is the school curriculum.

This chapter is an historical examination of representations of British-ness in English-Canadian schools throughout the twentieth century. It relies on a content analysis of curriculum documents and sixty textbooks used in literature, history, civics, geography and social studies courses in English-Canadian elementary and secondary classrooms. These courses have always represented an official understanding of Canadian identity. They transmitted messages about what it meant to be Canadian to generations of students.

---

1   P. Buckner, 'Introduction,' in P. Buckner, ed., *Canada and the End of Empire* (Vancouver: University of British Columbia Press, 2005), 3.

In Canada, education was and is a provincial responsibility. However, curricular decision-making was centralized in the sense that officials in the provincial education ministries wrote programmes of study for schools and authorized specific textbooks to support the teaching of the programmes and Ministry officials often commissioned accompanying textbooks and provided copies to schools. Several provinces have monitored course content by setting school-leaving examinations based on the textbooks. In other words, we can analyze the content of textbooks with some assurance that they represent the content of the courses.

This analysis demonstrates that in English-Canadian schools, Britishness referred to a dynamic set of values and beliefs that informed Britons' ways of being in the world. These values were shared by Britain and its dominions, and they were explicitly taught in schools as long as they understood themselves as members of the same family. They declined in importance in English-Canadian schools as the country distanced itself from the legacy of the empire and sought to redefine itself after 1970. A clarification of the values and beliefs fundamental to Britishness, however, indicates that they remain relevant, if not to Canadians' national identity, then to the institutions that govern them and the ideas that inform their ways of living in unity within a diverse community.

They Were Britons: 1900 to 1945

At the beginning of the twentieth century, English-Canadian schools attempted to create citizens of good character who were loyal to a Canadian nation defined by its membership in the British Empire. The reaction of English-Canadians to Britain's call to arms at the outset of the First World War indicates the extent to which they saw Britain's interests as their own, the extent to which they identified with Britain. As historian James Belich says, like New Zealanders and Australians, during the First World War,

'Canadians fought like Britons because they thought they were Britons'.[2] Canadian historians have long argued, however, that Canada's experience in the war triggered the first serious attempts to establish a national identity separate from Great Britain. Canada's role in the treaty negotiations and its insistence on separate and independent membership in the League of Nations represented the end of dreams of imperial federation and beginning of Canada's commitment to shaping its own national identity and national destiny.

But the First World War did not end Canada's identity as a British nation. Indeed there is a growing understanding among historians that the country's emerging sense of national identity was not anti-British or anti-imperial. Indeed Canadian nationalism in this period included a loyalty to Empire and to British institutions; it was entirely consistent with a liberal imperialist point of view. English-Canadian identity was so closely identified with a British identity that in the 1920s immigrants from the British Isles did not have to be naturalized in order to receive the benefits of citizenship. In the census, people born in Canada or the British Isles were all identified as British born.[3]

In the period before the Second World War, a British liberal imperial ethos permeated all subjects of the school curriculum. The content of school readers was almost exclusively drawn from English literature. Children read stories about the Knights of the Round Table, the Battle of Blenheim and heroes of British history such as Lord Nelson.[4] Geography classes in the intermediate years emphasized the resources and industries of the British

2   J. Belich, 'The Rise of the Angloworld: Settlement in North America and Australasia, 1784–1918,' in Phillip Buckner and R. Douglas Francis, eds, *Rediscovering the British World* (Calgary: University of Calgary Press, 2005), 49.

3   M. Barber, 'Nation-Building in Saskatchewan: Teachers from the British Isles in Saskatchewan Rural Schools in the 1920s,' in P. Buckner and R. D. Francis, eds, *Canada and the British World: Culture, Migration, and Identity* (Vancouver: University of British Columbia Press, 2006), 216.

4   N. J. Sheehan, 'Character Training and the Cultural Heritage: An Historical Comparison of Canadian Elementary Readers,' in G. Tomkins, ed., *The Curriculum in Canada in Historical Perspective* (Vancouver: Canadian Society for Studies in Education, University of British Columbia, 1979), 77–84.

Isles, and the vastness and diversity of the global British Empire.[5] Civics
lessons celebrated the benefits of British parliamentary democracy and
Canada's status as a dominion, ruled by the Mother of all parliaments.

Though students received lessons in Canadian as well as British history,
a prominent Canadian historian later recalled the nature of those lessons: 'I
don't think anybody ever suspected that there was any other kind of history.
And we had history in the public school, we had history in the high school,
and we had history in Varsity, and it was all English history'.[6] Clearly, to learn
British history was to learn what it meant to be Canadian: 'The important
thing in the study of history is not the acquisition of a stock of facts, but
the development of an intelligent interest in the past of one's country and
one's race'.[7] The amount of British content and the nature of the messages
embodied in the literature, geography, civics and history lessons supported
the fundamental purpose of schooling in this era: to create citizens with a
specific set of virtues associated with Canada's Britishness.

According to English-Canadian schools, the people of the British
race were, firstly, reluctant imperialists. One text, *The Story of Our People*,
explained, 'Let us begin our story by telling how it came about that Englishmen left their island home, crossed the wide seas to far-distant lands,
and, in an attempt to make themselves rich, unwittingly founded a great
Empire'.[8] But for a people who took on the burden of colonization reluctantly, they were generally portrayed a having a natural talent for it: 'They
early developed a genius for colonization and a power of adapting them-

---

5   See for example, A. McIntyre, *World Relations and the Continents: An Elementary
     Geography for the Junior and Middle Grades of the Public Schools* (Toronto: The
     Educational Book Co., Limited, 1911); *New Canadian Geography, North-west
     Territories edn* (Toronto: W. J. Gage and Company Limited, 1899); G. A. Cornish,
     Canadian Geography for Juniors (London: Dent, 1927).

6   A. R. M. Lower quoted in P. T. Phillips, *Britain's Past in Canada: The Teaching and
     Writing of British History* (Vancouver: University of British Columbia Press, 1989),
     4.

7   W. S. Wallace, *A New History of Great Britain and Canada* (Toronto: The Macmillan
     Company of Canada, 1934), vi.

8   G. Paterson, *The Story of Our People* (Toronto: The Ryerson Press, 1933), 404.

selves to conditions in new lands, which has made them, perhaps, the greatest colonizing nation that the world has ever known'.[9]

This empire that Britain so reluctantly took on, but brilliantly governed, was always portrayed as a force for good: '[England] still leads all peoples in the struggle against vice, ignorance, and tyranny'.[10] Her history was presented as 'the story of how we became free,' tracing the development of parliament from Magna Carta to Walpole's ministry.[11] Canada's history too was presented as the growth of freedom through the establishment and growth of British rule, the story of 'French failure through the folly of absolutism, monopoly, and feudalism; of British success through the wisdom of self-government, freedom and equality'.[12]

In the English-Canadian schools of this period, Britishness represented fairness, even magnanimity. As the British extended their Empire, children were told, their rule was characterized by a respect for conquered people and their fair treatment. After the British Conquest of Canada, 'The military officers in Canada were instructed, not only to administer the old French laws, but also, as far as possible, to leave their enforcement in the hands of the Canadians themselves. The soldiers were particularly forbidden to comment unfavourably upon the habits and customs of the Canadians or worst of all, to cast reflections upon the religion they professed'.[13] Britishness meant freedom, fairness, and generosity.

9   *Public School Geography for Alberta* (Toronto: W. J. Gage, 1925), 219.

10   W. J. Robertson, *Public School History of England and Canada* (Toronto: Copp Clark Company Limited, 1902), 195.

11   See for example, Paterson, *The Story of Our People*, 181–223.

12   D. M. Duncan, *The Story of the Canadian People* (Toronto: The Macmillan Co. of Canada Limited, 1916), v.

13   W. H. P. Clement, *The History of the Dominion of Canada* (Toronto: William Briggs, 1897), 91. See also *Ontario Public School History of Canada* (Toronto: Macmillan Company of Canada Limited, 1912), 106, and Robertson, *Public School History of England and Canada*, 219.

Other qualities of character were associated with Britishness in the period before the Second World War. They were always described as 'industrious and energetic'.[14] They were a martial people, courageous and inventive in battle. Canadian soldiers' efforts in the Boer War were celebrated because their heroism proved them the equals of their British peers: 'In marching, scouting, and fighting, the Canadian troops proved themselves worthy sons of the Empire, and in several hard-fought engagements bore themselves with credit beside Britain's most honoured regiments'.[15]

The British were portrayed as persistent, honourable, and capable of self-sacrifice. Readers included the story of Captain Scott's last voyage to the South Pole. When Oates walked out into a raging blizzard to die quickly rather than burden his colleagues' progress, it was described as 'the act of a brave man and of an English gentleman'.[16] Love of liberty, fairness, vitality, sportsmanship, valour, honour: these were the qualities of character that defined Britishness and defined good citizenship in the English-Canadian schools of this period. That these were specific British qualities of character was taken for granted. That they were embodied in the Empire was assumed. And in the period before the Second World War English-Canadian schools took their responsibility for the survival and success of the Empire very seriously.

Belonging to the Family of British Nations: 1945 to 1970

In Canadian historiography, the Second World War is generally seen as a turning point in the country's emerging national identity, marking the end of its subordinate relationship to Great Britain and firmly identifying it as

14   W. D. McDougall and G. Paterson, *Our Empire and its Neighbours* (Toronto: The Ryerson Press, 1937), 9.

15   *Ontario Public School History of Canada*, 249; See also Robertson, *Public School History of England and Canada*, 277.

16   *The Canadian Readers, Book V* (Toronto: T. Nelson & Sons, 1928), 26.

a North American nation.[17] Indeed in the period after the Second World War, a combination of economic, political and military factors turned Canadians increasingly toward their neighbour. But, as historian Phillip Buckner has stated, in many ways the Second World War strengthened English-Canadians' sense of belonging to a family of British nations. Half a million Canadians had lived in Britain during the war and many brought British wives back to Canada.[18] Moreover, between 1945 and 1970, 28 per cent of all immigrants to Canada (over 900,000) came from the United Kingdom, making it its principal source of immigrants.[19]

Diplomatic tensions between Canada and Britain that had become apparent during the Suez Crisis in 1956 were heightened in the 1960s by differences of opinion on a range of issues from South Africa's continued membership in the Commonwealth to Britain's attempt to seek membership of the European Economic Community.[20] In 1967, Canada's newly-appointed high commissioner in Britain commented that 'we and the British were excellent friends who had known each other for a long time, but we were no longer members of the same family'.[21] This would certainly seem to support the view that the 1960s saw the end of 'English-speaking Canada's self-representation as a "British" nation'.[22]

The vigorous debate surrounding the adoption of Canada's new flag demonstrated, however, that if Canada's politicians were prepared to say goodbye to the British world, in 1964 a sizeable proportion of Canada's

---

17   J. L. Granatstein and N. Hillmer, *For Better or For Worse: Canada and the United States to the 1990s* (Toronto: Copp Clark Pitman Ltd., 1991), 162.

18   P. Buckner, 'The Long Goodbye: English Canadians and the British World,' in Buckner and Francis, *Rediscovering the British World*, 200.

19   Ibid.

20   See J. Hilliker and G. Donaghy, 'Canadian Relations with the United Kingdom at the End of Empire, 1956–73,' in P. Buckner, ed., *Canada and the End of Empire* (Vancouver: University of British Columbia Press, 2005), 25–46; and, A. Benvenuti and S. Ward, 'Britain, Europe, and the "Other Quiet Revolution" in Canada,' in Buckner, *Canada and the End of Empire*, 165–82.

21   Quoted in Hilliker and Donaghy, 'Canadian Relations with the United Kingdom at the End of Empire, 1956–73,' 40.

22   Benvenuti and Ward, 'Britain, Europe' 166.

English-speaking population still felt a lingering attachment to its British roots. They 'saw their ethnicity as British as well as Canadian' and believed 'that the nation's symbols should incorporate that sense of a British-Canadian identity'.[23] Representations of Britishness within the school curriculum are helpful in the sense that they help us understand one significant force that shaped this continued attachment to Britain that many English Canadians still felt.

From 1945 to 1970 the curriculum for good character was replaced with education for democracy. English-Canadian schools put less emphasis on the virtues associated with British gentlemanly conduct and instead attempted to prepare students for the ideological battle of the Cold War. To that end, provinces across Canada revised their school curriculum to increase American content in geography, history and social studies courses.[24] The treatment of the United States in the curricula and in texts reflected its global profile as a champion of democracy. Enhancing Canada's relationship with the United States was seen as an important objective in history courses. The most popular Canadian history textbook used in this period explained that in this book, 'a serious attempt has been made to correlate the story of our own country with that of the United States, and to impart sympathetic understanding of our relations with our neighbour'.[25] In the name of such sympathetic understanding, texts even included obvious errors such as, 'more people have come to Canada from the United States than from any other country'.[26] But the increase in American content and the generous treatment of the United States in English-Canadian schools did not contradict the fundamental vision that Canada belonged to a British family of nations, and that its Britishness was defined by a heritage of liberty and the values associated with parliamentary democracy.

23   Buckner, 'Introduction,' Canada and the End of Empire, 7.
24   For a detailed treatment of the changing images of the United States in English-Canadian schools, see A. von Heyking, 'Talking About Americans: The Image of the United States in English-Canadian Schools, 1900–65,' History of Education Quarterly 46 (3) (2006): 382–408.
25   G. W. Brown, E. Harman and M. Jeanneret, The Story of Canada (Toronto: Copp Clark, 1950), vii–viii.
26   A. Garland, Canada Then and Now (Toronto: The Macmillan Company of Canada Limited, 1954), 374.

The English-Canadian school curriculum firmly placed Canada in a British family of nations. However, while previous generations defined themselves as 'Britons' and therefore took the study of British history for granted, the textbooks after the Second World War acknowledged the new forces shaping Canada and explicitly addressed the question of the relevance of Britain's history for young Canadians:

> [Canadians] live in a country where Washington is closer than London, England. ... Canada's own population includes an ever increasing proportion of citizens who are not British born. Canada, herself, is striving for a distinct national destiny and, as never before, Canadians are aware of this. Well may they ask, 'Why study British history?'

> The answer is simple. In a world increasingly threatened by tyranny, our priceless liberties and institutions, to a great degree, come from Britain. Our system of popular responsible government, our tradition of individual freedom, our incorruptible law courts, the useful and often beautiful English language, the bonds of Commonwealth and our beloved monarchy – all these heritages were founded in Britain. To protect them, we must understand them.[27]

In the era of the Cold War, the English-speaking countries were described as the defenders of political liberty and personal freedom. The history of Great Britain, the United States and Canada was told as a history of democracy. Indeed the countries had no separate histories; rather, 'there is a history of the English-speaking peoples serving to maintain and promote good ways of life for all'.[28]

After the Second World War, Britishness was still conceived of in genetic terms, as a set of values that could be passed on to 'kin'. It is significant that in English-Canadian schools, the United States was always seen within the context of this British family. In the texts of the earlier period, authors had stressed the distinction between the United States and Canada, explaining that after the Revolutionary War, 'when Great Britain, our Mother Country, lost the United States, Canada remained

27   R. S. Lambert, *The Great Heritage: A History of Britain for Canadians* (Toronto: The House of Grant, 1958), v.

28   J. C. Ricker, et al, *The British Epic* (Toronto: Clarke, Irwin & Company Limited, 1959), 417.

British,'[29] After the Second World War, rather than emphasizing American republicanism, the texts explained that like a family tree, 'the roots of Magna Carta had grown branches that did not restrict their growth to those areas in the British Empire or Commonwealth.'[30] Conflicts among the members of this family, such as the American Revolutionary War, were described as 'family quarrels.'[31] Ultimately the British acknowledged the independence of the United States because 'the British had not enjoyed fighting people of their own race. It was too much like brother fighting brother.'[32]

But if Britain and the United States were brothers, there was a definite hierarchy among the members of the Commonwealth family. It was assumed that the role of the senior member, indeed the purpose of the Commonwealth, was to spread British civilization and so to prepare junior members for independence. As textbook author W. D. McDougall stated: 'British traditions, customs and institutions have been transplanted overseas to change the ways in which native peoples think and act about many important problems.'[33] Texts listed and described all the self-governing dominions, and then many of the dependencies, insisting that 'the United Kingdom is helping these races to learn the ways of our civilization, so that one day they will be able to govern themselves.'[34] Britishness in this era consisted of a commitment to the ideals of liberty and freedom, and to institutions that embodied those ideals. Other than the example of the United States, however, those ideals and institutions were not adaptive to new environments or particularly respectful of other cultures. The genius of the British 'political evolution' that was celebrated in the textbooks consisted of the peaceful imposition of those institutions and the development of greater self-government along specifically British lines.

29   McIntyre, *World Relations and the Continents*, 67.
30   Lambert, *The Great Heritage*, 417.
31   W. D. McDougall, *The Commonwealth of Nations* (Toronto: The Ryerson Press, 1952), 180.
32   G. E. Tait, *Fair Domain: The Story of Canada From Earliest Times to 1800* (Toronto: The Ryerson Press, 1960), 365.
33   McDougall, *The Commonwealth of Nations*, xii.
34   H. W. Brown, et al, *The Story of the Commonwealth* (Vancouver: Copp Clark Publishing Co. Limited, 1954), 11.

Textbooks continued to celebrate the traditions that bound the members of the British family together. Particularly in texts published at the end of or just after the Second World War, the Crown was seen as a symbol of 'unselfish devotion' and 'dedicated service' to the people of the Commonwealth.[35] The English language was another symbol of unity and civilization. Children learned that 'wherever educated men meet, English is likely to be the only language they have in common.'[36] English-Canadian students were assured that the works of Chaucer, Shakespeare, Dickens, Tennyson and Eliot were their inheritance, indeed 'these are but a small part of the priceless treasure which is the birthright of every English-speaking person.'[37] A common language and familiarity with the classics of English literature were still fundamental for members of the British family of nations.

The most important inheritance for English-Canadians, however, stressed by every textbook, was 'British ideas of justice, freedom and democracy.'[38] The British family was characterized by a love of liberty. This was not the result of an act of Parliament or the evolution of specific political institutions. According to a British history text, it was a genetic inheritance, 'it is part of the general make-up of the British character. The Englishman has learned from history that it does not pay to meddle unnecessarily with other people's affairs. Equally, he resents any unjustified meddling with his own. ... Many of the famous figures in British history are men who have resisted oppression, or have obeyed conscience rather than authority.'[39] The British history textbooks celebrated the men who symbolized advances in freedom, such as John Wilkes, those who fought for or taught others about freedom and equality, such as William Wilberforce and John Wesley, and those who led governments committed to political and social reform, such as William Gladstone. Students learned that individual liberty and equality

35   G. W. Brown, *Building the Canadian Nation* (rev. edn) (Toronto: J. M. Dent & Sons, 1950), 479; See also D. A. McArthur, *A History of Canada for High Schools*, rev. edn (Toronto: W. J. Gage, 1944), 493, 496.
36   Ricker, et al, *The British Epic*, xii.
37   Lambert, *The Great Heritage*, 5.
38   M. A. Kostek, B. W. Braund and J. K. Woods, *The Modern Commonwealth* (Toronto: McGraw-Hill, 1963), 91.
39   Lambert, *The Great Heritage*, 6.

were embodied in British law and the court system, and that important legal rights – trial by jury, freedom from unjust arrest – protect all members of the Commonwealth.[40] Respect for the law and faith in a British system of justice were hallmarks of Britishness in this era.

All of the history courses taken by English-Canadian students recounted the growth of Parliament beginning with its roots in medieval England, because 'Canada owes so much of her own system of government and so many of her institutions to Great Britain that to obtain a clear understanding of Canadian forms it is necessary to study the British models'.[41] Indeed the courses on British history were structured entirely around the advance of democracy as represented by the development of modern parliamentary democracy. In their Canadian history courses students learned how the process was transposed in a new land, and how when Canadians felt compelled to rebel against the colonial government in the 1830s, wise men understood that 'the answer to Canada's problems was to establish a system of government more nearly like that of Great Britain'.[42] Britishness, then, consisted of political institutions that could change over time, and could be imposed on new territories, but would not be transformed by them.

In the textbooks after the Second World War, there were some qualities of British gentlemanly virtue that carried over from the previous era. For example, the British were described as a 'sturdy, intelligent and courageous people' who were daring and adventurous in their exploration and settlement of lands far away.[43] British seamen, such as Sir Francis Drake, and empire-builders, such as Robert Clive were still described in romantic terms. Descriptions of the Second World War now provided opportunities for textbook authors to celebrate the traditional valour of the British:

---

40   See Ricker, et al, *The British Epic*, xii; Brown et al, *The Story of the Commonwealth*, 12.

41   B. Lawrence, L. C. Mix and C. S. Wilkie, *Our European Heritage* (Toronto: J. M. Dent, 1962), 336. See also W. G. Hardy and J. R. W. Gwynne-Timothy, *Journey Into the Past* (Toronto: McClelland and Stewart Limited, 1965), 402–3; and McDougall, *The Commonwealth of Nations*, 34–45.

42   Garland, *Canada Then and Now*, 264.

43   Ricker, et al, *The British Epic*, 326.

At Dunkirk, on the African deserts, and in the icy waters of the North Atlantic, British soldiers, sailors and airmen again proved they were able to rank beside the legendary heroes of Britain. Though they did not have to fight on their own beaches, they fought elsewhere as men of the British race have always fought, proudly, courageously, doggedly, until victory was won.[44]

In Canadian history texts, Canadians were described in contrast to Americans, and that contrast was always attributed to Canada's Britishness. So, for example, while both the United States and Canada depended on the initiative and energy of pioneering people, in Canada this was tempered by 'moderation and patience'. Both North American countries required self-reliant individuals, but in Canada that individualism was always 'accompanied by a tradition of respect for the law and of faith in the operation of the British system of justice'.[45] English-Canadians exhibited uniquely British traits of honour, stability and moderation.

New in the textbooks of this era was a sense that the global profile of Britain had come to an end. This was acknowledged with regret, but also with a sense of acceptance. Texts claimed that the Second World War exhausted Britain and while she had fought with courage and led the victory, she had paid 'a terrible price'.[46] But if the twentieth century had exhausted Britain and unravelled the empire, 'Britain still remains as a significant power, representing a force for good in the world today', claimed one text. 'She stands with other Western nations as a democratic bulwark against the threatening spread of communism'.[47] Within the context of the Cold War, English-Canadian students understood that 'justice and freedom, liberty of speech and religion, fair play and fair treatment for all men... are precious to all people. Without Britain they would vanish from large sections of the earth'.[48]

44 W. D. McDougall and E. R. Moore, *The Commonwealth of Nations*, rev. edn (Toronto: The Ryerson Press, 1966), 140.

45 E. McInnis, *North America and the Modern World* (Toronto: J. M. Dent & Sons Limited, 1945), 277.

46 Lambert, *The Great Heritage*, 416.

47 Tait, *Proud Ages*, 389.

48 McDougall and Moore, *The Commonwealth of Nations* (1966), 484.

In the period 1945 until 1970, Britishness in English-Canadian schools was fundamentally associated with a heritage as a free people. Britishness was also connected to the Commonwealth, the family of nations that had grown out of the Empire and that had been given the political institutions that embodied this freedom. But when English-Canadians no longer identified themselves as 'British people' and the legacy of the Empire became one of embarrassment and guilt, the interpretation of Canada's British connection had to be redrawn in English-Canadian school curriculum and textbooks.

Broken Free: 1970 and beyond

By 1970, the school curriculum that celebrated Canada's place in a family of British nations seemed out of date. Britain's military and economic power had largely collapsed. The Empire was gone. She had turned firmly toward Europe. Canada had changed too, losing its emotional tie to a British world. Many immigrants of non-British origin had settled in Canada. Moreover, those Canadians who were of British origin were so many generations removed that there was little sense of connection to their British roots. An emerging Quebecois nationalist movement aggressively challenged the belief that Canada was part of a British world. American influence over the Canadian economy, its defence and its popular culture dominated discussions and concerns about Canada's national identity.

National research studies undertaken in the late 1960s lamented the abysmal state of history teaching and citizenship education in Canada. Researchers argued that the content of history and social studies courses was irrelevant for young Canadians and exacerbated linguistic and ethnic divisions in the country.[49] The courses in British history and the 'pro-British' tenor of traditional Canadian history courses were particularly

49   A. B. Hodgetts, *What Culture? What Heritage? A Study of Civic Education in Canada* (Toronto: Ontario Institute for Studies in Education, 1968).

singled out in this regard. As a result, the federal government funded initiatives that provincial ministries of education took up to increase Canadian content in schools. Provinces across the country revised school curricula to better reflect the issues dominating Canadian political and cultural life at the time: enhanced understanding of French-Canadian aspirations within Confederation; regional identities, particularly related to the western provinces; and, the maintenance of Canadian sovereignty in the face of the financial, political, military and cultural might of the United States. And given the emerging emphasis on global as well as national citizenship, issues such as the nuclear proliferation, overpopulation and racial conflict were also integrated into citizenship education courses such as social studies. British and Commonwealth history was was replaced by courses on 'Canada in a North American Perspective' or Canadian-American relations and with social studies courses that examined selected countries in Asia, Africa and the Middle East as case studies of Third World nationalism and modernization.

The only courses in which English-Canadian students received any British content were the Canadian history courses they took. These courses were dominated by the story of Canada's evolution from colony to nation. They demonstrated how Canada disentangled itself from its British roots and therefore how its Britishness became less and less relevant to Canada's contemporary identity. Gone were the images of 'the Motherland' providing protection and wise counsel. Now the texts celebrated Canadian politicians who refused to be bullied by the British. For example, one text in describing Canada's response to Joseph Chamberlain's attempts to create a united, imperial foreign and defence policy at the 1902 Colonial Conference, said:

> Chamberlain was more aggressive and demanding than he had been five years before, Laurier was even more determined to resist. With Canada's refusal to submit, imperial federation was finished. Canada's control over it [*sic*] own affairs would continue to grow as Canadians of all backgrounds developed pride in their own country and its achievements at home and abroad.[50]

---

50   H. H. Herstein, L. J. Hughes and R. C. Kirbyson, *Challenge and Survival: The History of Canada* (Scarborough: Prentice-Hall of Canada, 1970), 308.

In the history texts after 1970, Canadian nationalism was always portrayed as incompatible with loyalty to or pride in the British Empire. The First World War was described as a crucial step in the distancing from Britain. The war was described under headings such as 'Canadian Sovereignty: A Nation Forged in Fire,'[51] The history of the interwar period was presented as a series of steps that increased the pace of Canadian sovereignty: the Chanak Affair, the Halibut Treaty, the Imperial Conference of 1926 and finally the Statute of Westminster in 1931 demonstrated that 'British interests and Canadian interests were growing increasingly divergent. Greater Canadian independence appeared to be essential, if not inevitable, to progress.'[52] Canadian efforts in The Second World War were also detailed under headings such as 'Canadian Sovereignty: A Nation Comes of Age.'[53]

The adoption of the new Canadian flag in 1965 is an example of how events were now presented as a process of saying goodbye and good riddance to the British connection: 'Pearson acted on a long-standing complaint in Quebec that Canada's symbols were too British... Pearson chose the maple leaf as the symbol for the new flag because it seemed to represent all Canadians.'[54] Opponents of the change were described as out of touch with contemporary Canada as after 1970s, Canada's British identity was history.

Canadian history courses now stressed the country's multicultural identity and this was not presented as a twentieth century development. Canada was described as a 'country of immigrants,' even characterizing aboriginal people as 'the first immigrants to come to Canada.'[55] Chapters on contemporary, multicultural Canada included census statistics that demonstrated that over 40 per cent of Canadians identified themselves

51   D. Eaton and G. Newman, *Canada: A Nation Unfolding* (Toronto: McGraw-Hill Ryerson, 1994), 176.
52   Herstein, Hughes and Kirbyson, *Challenge and Survival*, 355.
53   Eaton and Newman, *Canada: A Nation Unfolding*, 280.
54   Colin M. Bain, et al, *Making History: the Story of Canada in the Twentieth Century* (Toronto: Prentice-Hall, 2000), 257.
55   A. D. Hux, *Canada: A Growing Concern* (Toronto, ON: Globe/Modern Curriculum, 1981), 328.

as of British origin, but when texts included the 'immigration stories' of Canadians, those of British origin tended to be senior citizens recalling their ancestral connections to settlement communities of the nineteenth century, like the Red River settlers of 1813.[56] In all the texts, Canada was portrayed as a nation of immigrants, not of colonists. In this way the British contribution to Canada's identity was reduced to the equivalent of any other immigrant or ethnic group.

Occasionally a traditional or stereotypical description of Canada's Britishness would emerge in the texts. For example, one text in describing Canada's British heritage pointed out that 'In Canada, peace, order, and good government are considered very important. Canadians are known to be polite, obedient, helpful, and pleasant.'[57] Descriptions of Britain's war efforts during World War Two still provided opportunities to applaud the courage and persistence of the British, but traditional British heroes in Canadian history were now described as the exception to the rule. For example, Sir Isaac Brock, Commander-in-Chief of Upper Canada during the War of 1812, was described as 'a gallant soldier and brilliant strategist,' but significantly this was 'unlike many of his fellow officers.'[58] The motives of the British in passing the Quebec Act were no longer described as generous or compassionate. One text described the background to and contents of the Act, and then asked students: 'Do you think the British were being wise or cynical in passing the Quebec Act?'[59] Gone too were descriptions of the political genius of the British in their rule over other imperial possessions in Asia and Africa. One modern history text acknowledged that the British tended to rule more indirectly than other European powers and tended to place less emphasis on cultural assimilation, but explained, 'The British had practical reasons for using indirect rule. ... A small nation, Britain, did not have enough officials or soldiers to control its huge empire without the

56   See for example Chapter One in E. Deir, et al, *Canada: The Story of Our Heritage* (Toronto: McGraw-Hill Ryerson Limited, 2000).
57   Deir, et al, *Canada: The Story of Our Heritage*, 19.
58   Ibid. 193.
59   Ibid. 143.

help of local leaders'.[60] After 1970, English-Canadian textbooks reflected the fact that the legacy of empire was embarrassing. They stressed the fact that Canadians were colonized; they downplayed the fact that some were enthusiastic participants in the imperial project.

Textbooks portrayed Canada's British connection not as a heritage of liberty, but as an authoritarian regime from which Canadians needed to free themselves. Rather than embodying liberty, the British represented aristocratic privilege and an anti-democratic impulse. Sir Guy Carleton, it was explained, supported the French Canadians after the Conquest because 'he had an aristocrat's sympathy for the seigneurs'.[61] The governors and colonial elites who ran the British North American colonies in the 1830s before attempted rebellions, were particularly criticized for their anti-democratic views. One text explained that 'they thought that because they were wealthy and better educated, they were much better able to govern the colony than ordinary people were'.[62]

In contrast to the textbooks of previous generations, texts now characterized American and European immigrants as better than British immigrants because of their farming experience. While authors acknowledged that the British were the largest group of immigrants to the Canadian prairies, they rarely provided detailed information about them. Instead, case studies of Scandinavians, Ukrainians and Mormons were often featured. When British immigrants were included, they were often characterized as ill-prepared for the harsh climate and for the difficult physical labour required in the first years of settlement. They were no longer praised for their gentlemanly accomplishments; now these were qualities they needed to overcome in order to be successful settlers in Canada.

So if the British connection was generally portrayed as negative in the colonial period, how were Canada's current British connections seen? In

60   B. F. Beers, *World History: Patterns of Civilization* (Toronto: Prentice-Hall, 1989), 156.

61   D. C. Willows and S. Richmond, *Canada: Colony to Centennial* (Toronto: McGraw-Hill Co. of Canada, 1970), 101.

62   J. B. Cruxton and W. D. Wilson, *Flashback Canada*, new edn (Toronto: Oxford University Press, 1987), 21.

textbooks that included information about Canada's government structure, there was no reference to the roots of parliamentary democracy in
Great Britain. References to the monarchy were quite interesting. One text
referred to our 'royal,' rather than our 'British,' heritage being evident in
the naming of our military units and on our currency.[63] All downplayed
the importance of the monarchy, calling it 'symbolic and ceremonial'.[64]
Rather than describe the monarchy as a symbol that unified Canadians,
textbooks acknowledged that Canadians were divided in their opinions
about the relevance of the monarchy and set tasks that encouraged students
to explore the debate.

The future of the Commonwealth was also presented as an issue to be
debated or described under a heading like 'Is the Commonwealth Worth
It?'[65] The Commonwealth was portrayed as an association of countries
that were once members of the British Empire but were now committed to 'ideals of democracy, human rights, racial equality, and sustain-
able development'.[66] One text suggested that its major value lay in the fact
that 'it is the largest and most important international organization not
dominated by the United States'.[67] All the textbooks discussed Canada's
involvement in the Commonwealth beside or in partnership with Canada's
membership in La Francophonie, emphasizing the equality of its two linguistic communities.[68]

In high school courses on twentieth century global politics, Britain's is
a story of decline. Decimated by the First World War, Britain was paralyzed

63   A. L. Scully, C. F. Smith and D. J. McDevitt, *Canada Today*, 2nd edn (Scarborough:
     Prentice-Hall Canada Inc., 1988), 90.
64   Eaton and Newman, *Canada: A Nation Unfolding*, 14.
65   R. Kolpin, *Global Links: Connecting Canada* (Toronto: Oxford University Press,
     1999), 82. See also 'Should the Commonwealth Be Abolished,' in J. Ruypers, et al,
     Canadian and World Politics (Toronto: Emond Montgomery Publications Ltd.,
     2005), 314–15.
66   Ibid.
67   Ruypers, et al, *Canadian and World Politics*, 309.
68   See J. B. Cruxton and W. D. Wilson, *Spotlight Canada*, new edn (Toronto: Oxford
     University Press, 1988), 364–5; Kolpin, *Global Links*, 82–3; Ruypers, et al, *Canadian
     and World Politics*, 309–16; Bain, et al, *Making History*, 333–4.

in the interwar period by economic depression and political division. Burdened by domestic problems and 'encumbered with an empire whose views on international affairs had to be taken into account,' British politicians were responsible for the policy of appeasement of Nazi Germany. After the Second World War, Britain 'had to struggle to come to terms with its diminished role in Europe and the world at large'.[69] It coped with problems associated with decolonization in the Middle East, Asia and Africa, and finally was integrated in the 'New Europe' that emerged in recent decades. The textbooks acknowledge that Britain has had to redefine, even reinvent, itself in the aftermath of this collapse, but it is clear that whatever Britishness now means to the British, it has little to do with Canadians.

Conclusion

Canada's, or at least English-Canadian schools', rejection of Britishness as a set of values and beliefs that informed, let alone continue to inform, their way of being in the world has resulted in at least two problems. The first is that Canadians, by rejecting their British connection, have failed to come to terms with their imperial past. Or perhaps more accurately, the understanding of Britishness that dominated English-Canadian schools has allowed Canadians to cast themselves as the colonized, rather than as imperialists. This has, among other things, prevented Canadians from dealing constructively with the legacy of imperialism for our aboriginal communities.

Second, English-Canadian schools' identification of Britishness and British political ideals with the Empire also meant that when the Empire and Commonwealth disappeared from the curriculum, so did any opportunity

69   A. Mitchner and J. Tuffs, *Global Forces of the Twentieth Century* (Edmonton: Reidmore Book Inc., 1991), 54; V. Zelinksi, et al, *Twentieth Century Viewpoints: An Interpretive History* (Toronto: Oxford University Press, 1996), 223.

to learn about the ideas and institutions of liberal democracy as they developed within the parliamentary system. English-Canadian students today learn about the structure and function of Canada's government, but they do not learn about the roots of that system and its evolution over time and in many different countries. They never have an opportunity to learn how parliamentary structures and traditions were not just transposed to new places but transformed by them. Surely current low levels of civic engagement among Canadian citizens and their increasing cynicism about the political process are in some way connected to the fact that we have neglected to teach our children about the dynamic and adaptive nature of parliamentary democracy.

Canadians may benefit from reimagining their British connection, their Britishness, in terms of an historical dialectic: a creative tension between forces such as freedom and authority, liberation and oppression, equality and elitism, innovation and tradition. Encouraging Canadian students to engage thoughtfully with our British connection in these terms would afford us the opportunity to appreciate how this creative tension has helped us find respectful and empowering ways for diverse people to live together. It would help us articulate an authentic set of Canadian values and beliefs that would help us navigate our future as a nation and in the world.

Brits Abroad: Travel and Migration

THOMAS THURNELL-READ

11 'Here Comes the Drunken Cavalry': Managing and Negotiating the Britishness of All-Male Stag Tours in Eastern Europe

Although often overlooked in discussions of local, national and regional identity, tourism and the activities and experiences in which people partake when they interact with, or themselves become, tourists can be seen to play a significant role in contemporary negotiations of identity. Such encounters provide a site of interactions which are at times beneficial and at others antagonistic. What is significant, however, is the way in which tourist spaces and the interactions which take place in them can be seen to allow for complex negotiations of various identities. Indeed, we might say that tourism provides many Europeans with 'their only first-hand knowledge of their apparent co-citizenship in any future European polity'.[1] It is therefore unsurprising that when considering Britishness and its relationship to the wider world we might seek some insight from both the behaviour of British tourists and, importantly, the perceptions of that behaviour which in turn feeds into the ongoing constructions of Britishness.

This chapter explores the phenomenon of British all-male premarital stag tours to Eastern European cities to highlight the fine balance between acceptance and antagonism and between benign and malign intercultural interactions which take place in such touristic settings. Taking the Polish city of Krakow as a case study, the behaviour of British stag tourists and the perception of that behaviour by others illustrates how understandings of British national identity and Britishness are negotiated and constructed in various ways. The notoriety of British stag tour groups and their drunken,

1   D. McNeill, *New Europe: Imagined Spaces* (London: Arnold, 2004), 128.

boisterous, and frequently transgressive behaviour mean that the linking of such behaviour to understandings of Britishness creates a problematic ground for the discussion of national identities. The chapter considers two locations of this dynamic; firstly, coverage of and the response to British stag tourism by Polish media and, secondly, the role of stag tour company guides as cultural intermediaries in their interactions with stag tour groups in the tourism setting.

British Identity and Tourist Spaces

One way of framing stag tourism is to see it as part of a perceived 'Brits abroad' problem. There is a need, however, 'to unpack these stereotypes which tell us more about those who construct them than about those they pretend to describe'.[2] Thus, the 1980s moral panic relating to British tourists and expatriates in Spain stemmed from worries that 'these British representatives of our once-great nation were considered to reflect decadence in British society as a whole'.[3] Hazel Andrews has shown that in the Mallorcan resorts of Magaluf and Palmanova the inscription of Britishness and national identity is evident in the names of pubs and bars, the foods and beer consumed and the bodies that consume them.[4] It can therefore be suggested that tourist spaces represent sites for the at time problematic enactment of national identity.

Many of the seminal attempts to address the nature and importance of contemporary tourism have, either implicitly or explicitly, directed

2   K. O'Reilly, *The British on the Costa del Sol: Transnational Identities and Local Communities* (London: Routledge, 2000), 2.
3   Ibid. 19.
4   H. Andrews, 'Feeling at Home: Embodying Britishness in a Spanish Charter Tourist Report', *Tourist Studies* 5 (3) (2005), 247–66; H. Andrews, 'Consuming Pleasures: Package Tourists in Mallorca' in K. Meethan, A. Anderson and S. Miles, eds, *Tourism, Consumption and Representation* (Wallingford: CABI, 2006), 217–35.

their attention towards a mythical ideal type, the male Western tourist.[5] Thus, with some notable exceptions, few studies have sought to focus on specific national and gendered variations of tourist behaviour. The tourist, for many theorists, is implicitly a male individual and, yet, both the specifically gendered nature and the common collective aspect of much tourist experience have been overlooked. In the case of stag tourism, the foregrounding of both national identity and gender, in the form of Britishness and masculinity respectively, are essential to any understanding of the phenomenon.

The experience of being a tourist has been described as a socially inscribed practice of gazing upon that which is marked as extraordinary rather than ordinary.[6] This means it is a problematic quest for authenticity as an antidote to the restrictions and banality of modern life.[7] However, it can be argued, these conceptualisations of tourist behaviour and practice fail to address the innumerable tourists, such as stag tourists, who seek not to gaze but to do and to consume. Moving away from the focus on the visual acting of gazing, therefore, involves a necessary focus on the body and the senses; on what the tourist does, as 'the tourist "doing tourism"'.[8]

A more recent trend is to consider tourism as a liminal state, neither home nor ever fully away. In terms of place, time and selfhood, then, tourists can be said to inhabit a liminal stage between home and away, acceptance and rejection.[9] It is within this ambiguous space and time that tourist experience represents a significant insight into understandings of national

5   Most notable of the early theorisations of tourism in this regard are: D. Boorstin, *The Image: Or, Whatever Happened to the American Dream* (London: Weidenfeld and Nicolson, 1961); D. MacCannell, *The Tourist: A New Theory of the Leisure Class* (New York: Shocken Books, 1976); J. Urry, *The Tourist Gaze: Leisure and Travel in Contemporary Societies* (London: Sage, 1990).
6   Urry, *The Tourist Gaze*.
7   MacCannell, *The Tourist*.
8   D. Crouch, L. Aronsson, and L. Wahlstrom, 'Tourist Encounters', *Tourist Studies* 1 (3) (2001), 254.
9   T. Selänniemi, 'On Holiday in the Liminoid Playground: Place, Time and Self in Tourism' In T. G. Bauer and B. McKercher, eds, *Sex And Tourism: Journeys of Romance, Love, and Lust* (Binghamton, NY: Haworth, 2003).

and personal identity. Tourists do, when not corralled in prefabricated resort environments, frequent spaces that are, to the day to day inhabitants, home. What we see is therefore a perhaps unavoidable clash between competing definitions of such spaces. For stag tour groups, cities such as Krakow are demarcated as sites for escape and for play verging on hedonistic abandon. For locals, however, these sites are still locations for business, leisure and family life. Such tourist settings, therefore, invariably involve some degree of antagonism or what we might call performance conflict.[10] Further, access to such sites and usage patterns may be highly spatialised along lines of class, ethnicity, gender and religion.[11]

This focus on tourist space and its relationship to tourist behaviour allows the excesses of stag tourism to be understood as part of the disinhibiting power of tourist practice; as social propriety is loosened and release and escape encouraged, identities become more salient or reworked in new ways. The term 'pleasure periphery', to borrow from the early tourism scholars Louis Turner and John Ash, captures this sense of a pre-designated space, which is 'both social and geographical', within which specific touristic behaviour can be undertaken.[12] Similarly, Rob Shields notes the power of such 'places on the margin' as highly symbolic and predicating certain, often transgressive, behaviour.[13] These sites, then, can offer the chance for aspects of behaviour and habit to be destabilised in a carnivalesque renegotiation of identity and values.[14] In relation to national identity, it can be

---

10   Significant contributions to the understanding of tourism as a spatial and performative practice include: T. Edensor, *Tourists at the Taj: performance and meaning at a symbolic site* (London: Routledge, 1998); T. Edensor, 'Tourists at the Taj: walking and gazing' in S. Taylor, ed., *Ethnographic Research: a reader* (London: Sage, 2002); T. Mordue, 'Tourism, Performance and Social Exclusion in "Olde York"', *Annals of Tourism Research* 32 (1) (2005), 179–98.

11   R. Preston-Whyte, 'Constructed leisure space: The seaside at Durban', *Annals of Tourism Research* 28 (3) (2001), 581–96.

12   L. Turner, and J. Ash, *The Golden Hordes: international tourism and the pleasure periphery* (London: Constable, 1975), 11.

13   R. Shields, *Places on the Margin: alternative geographies of modernity* (London: Routledge, 1991).

14   L. Malam, 'Performing Masculinity on the Thai Beach Scene' in *Tourism Geographies* 6 (4) (2004), 455–71.

observed that peripheral regions in general can often prove problematic. Thus, Robin Cohen has noted the 'fuzzy frontiers' of identity, between England and the Celtic fringe and between England and Europe and it is perhaps in a similar mode that the peripheral zones of many tourist spaces provide spaces in which Britishness is enacted but also contested.[15]

However, we might also consider a more optimistic view that 'tourism can be a bridge to an appreciation of cultural relativity and international understanding'.[16] Tourism as intercultural exchange therefore involves the interaction between tourists, other tourists, hosts and locals and also in the simultaneous destabilising of habits and packing and unpacking of both material and non-material cultural objects.[17] A given setting of tourist experience, such as the old town centre of Krakow, might therefore be understood as a 'contact zone'.[18] It could also be understood as 'a (neo) colonial location where formerly separated groups come into ongoing physical relation, predicated on complex structures of economic, social, and symbolic'.[19] Following from this, we might suggest that Europe, therefore, might be seen as 'a series of spaces of encounter' where the interactions taking place have a significant impact on the processes or reimagining Europe and European identity.[20] Much more than mere locations of hedonistic escapism, touristic spaces can become sites for the complex negotiation of identity and changing relationships between different groups.

15   R. Cohen, *Frontiers of Identity: the British and the Others* (London: Longman, 1994).

16   V. L. Smith, *Hosts and Guests: The Anthropology of Tourism* (Oxford: Blackwell, 1978), 8.

17   G. Jack and A. M. Phipps, *Tourism and Intercultural Exchange: Why Tourism Matters* (Clevedon: Channel View, 2005).

18   M. L. Pratt, 'Arts of the Contact Zone' in *Profession* 91 (1991), 33–40.

19   M. Bunzl, 'The Prague Experience: Gay Male Sex Tourism and the Neo-colonial Invention of an Embodied Boarder' in D. Berdahl, M. Bunzl and M. Lampland, eds, *Altered States: ethnographies of transition in Eastern Europe and the Former Soviet Union* (Ann Arbor: University of Michigan Press, 2000), 72.

20   D. McNeill, *New Europe*, 121.

On the basis of the above, tourism is one of many processes which contribute to the reimagining of Europe and, in this case specifically, positioning notions of Britishness within it. Peter Preston offers an account of developing ideas of European identity which provide space for a renegotiation of notions of English and British national identity, rather than simply a threat to them. He states that 'it is in the context of new ideas of Europe that we might find new expressions of Englishness'.[21] Further to this, it is worth quoting John Urry:

> In the current reworking of social identity, the changing relations between place, nation and Europe, travel is an element which may be of great importance in constructing/reinforcing novel identities. The development of a possible 'European Identity' cannot be discussed without considering how massive patterns of short-term mobility may be transforming dominant social identities.[22]

Tourist mobilities, for Urry, are an important element of the contingent mixing of local, national and European identity. Tourism mobility and tourist space creates stages for both positive and negative interactions and negotiations which have the potential to impact significantly on contemporary notions of personal and national identity.

What is immediately striking about the stag phenomenon is the apparent strong, yet narrow, conception of Britishness involved. As such, the Britishness associated with stag tour groups is frivolous, predominantly white and fixated by the masculine trope of girls, booze and the pursuit of risky or exciting behaviour. The various concerns and controversies which readily attach themselves to the stag tour phenomenon reflect a concern not just with Britishness but, specifically, with British masculinity stemming from a 'lad culture' seen as a backlash against feminism and changing gender relations and 'retro-sexist' in its retreat from responsibility.[23] As such, the knowing, self-referential, irony of lads' magazines represented

21   P. W. Preston, *Relocating England* (Manchester: Manchester University Press, 2004), 5.

22   J. Urry, *Consuming Places* (London: Routledge, 2005), 169.

23   I. Whelehan, *Overloaded: Popular culture and the future of feminism* (London: Women's Press, 2000), J. Beynon, *Masculinities and Culture* (Buckingham: Open

and, in a more diluted sense, still represents a very British sense of the things young men should think, want and do.[24] The perceived image of British-ness which becomes apparent through various reactions to the stag tour phenomenon, in the media and in popular discourse, is therefore heavily inflected with normative understandings of gender.

What the above serves to illustrate is the complexity of linkages between space in this case the spaces occupied by tourists, and identity. Touristic settings such as the Krakow old town, its streets and squares, pubs, cafes and nightclubs, give rise to spaces within which the behaviour of individuals and wider understandings of national identity are vividly and lively acted out. Considering firstly the coverage of the stag tourism phenomenon by Polish media and, secondly, the precarious role of stag tour company representatives who work as group guides and, it will be suggested, cultural intermediaries, the remainder of this chapter will discuss how varying constructions of Britishness are central to the stag tour phenomenon.

Stag Tourism, Britishness and the Media

In order to provide an insight into some of the ways stag tourism is represented and used to discuss understandings of Britishness this chapter considers a selection of articles taken from the Polish press.[25] Themes emerging from this media coverage highlight not only how the malign behaviour of stag tourists is constructed as linked to a negative conception of Britishness but that the media coverage itself represents a site for

University Press, 2002), B. Benwell, *Masculinity and Men's Lifestyle Magazines* (Oxford: Blackwell, 2003).

24   B. Benwell, 'Ironic Discourse: Evasive Masculinity in Men's Lifestyle Magazines' *Men and Masculinity* 73 (1) (2004), 3–21.

25   All extracts from Polish media sources have been translated to English from the original Polish.

the discursive construction of notions of national identities. It is possible, therefore, to discern three apparent facets of Polish media coverage of British stag tourism: that there is an overwhelming sense for the need for protection against an invading 'horde'; that there is a frequent deployment of difference and division to separate the reader from the foreign other; and, importantly, that there is an evident normative discursive quality to much of the coverage providing a space in which notions of both British and Polish identity are negotiated.

Throughout much of this media coverage there is a common motif of threat or invasion. There is an evident perception of loss of control over physical space and the sorts of behaviour that happens in those spaces. Further, the articles predominantly pose the phenomenon as a recent issue which calls for some reaction or resistance. Immediately apparent is the opinion that the city 'has to take the force of inebriated Brits' and withstand 'the onslaught of drunk Englishmen'.[26] Furthermore, the title of this chapter, 'here comes the drunken cavalry', comes from a comment overheard during an early field trip that seemed to acutely summarise this feeling that the town is being overrun largely against the will of the majority of locals.

The disruptive behaviour of stag groups is highlighted as the central theme where there is a loss of control over public spaces and local sensibilities are ignored. As such, one article describes stag behaviour as 'pulling down one's underwear, loud drunken singing, peeing in beer mugs – all in the centre of Krakow. This is the behaviour of a large number of English tourists, who, within the last year, have numbered in the hundreds of thousands in Krakow.'[27] Again, the overwhelming growth in stag tourist numbers is stressed along with the clear insinuation that such behaviour is not acceptable *all in the centre of Krakow*.

An important element of many of the articles considered is the establishment of a division between the reader and the foreign subject. Thus, there is surprisingly frequent use of words such as English, British, foreigners, islanders, Brits, travellers, tourists. Such descriptive terms are often

26   'Stag Parties in Krakow', *Radio Polonia, Europe East* item (21 August 2006).
27   'The Brits are at it again, but not in Krakow?' *Gazeta Wybrocza* (13 August 2007).

applied with judgements such as 'cheap', 'fourth-class' and 'drunken', clearly indicating the negative perception of a group marked as different. There is an almost inescapable descriptive division between tourist or foreigner and resident or local. For example, in one article from the Polish press, a senior civil servant refers to 'fourth class tourists, who just want to come and get drunk' while the article's author continues that 'renting the cheapest hotels, they set off on nightly pub crawls of the city. If they do see any historical sites, it happens on the way to the night clubs'.[28] We see a clear distinction here that positions stag tourists as bad tourists who are as 'alcohol-and-sex-crazed' and 'cheap'.[29]

As noted above, press coverage frequently mobilises negative aspects of stag tourist behaviour in order to establish stag tourists as a foreign and disreputable 'other'. Further to this, such articles might be seen as a site for discussing national characteristics and identity. Britishness is constructed as something irresponsible and negligent with the implicit counterpoint being that Poles are restrained and respectful. Interestingly, one radio article comments that 'many bartenders criticise the English for drinking too fast: a trait caused by restrictive licensing laws in the UK, which simply do not exist in Krakow, where many bars are open until the last customer standing'.[30] We therefore see that stag behaviour is rarely addressed as a problem involving irresponsible individuals, more over, disruptive stag tourist behaviour is seen as symptomatic of a wider problem with British drinking culture or Britishness as a whole.

It can therefore be suggested that these articles that address stag tourism are actually an important site for discussing both Polish and British national characteristics. Indeed, the nub of many of the articles considered was, put simply, what does stag tourist behaviour tell the author and the reader about Britishness? Thus, a British resident and editor of a Krakow tourism and cultural website says, 'how many of them are just yelling drunken assholes? I'd say 10–20 per cent, seriously. The rest are calm, easy-going, serious people, who just came to see another corner of the world. And for

28 'The drunken English are causing a stir in Krakow', *Gazeta Wybrocza* (20 July 2006).
29 'Krakow Not a Party Joint', *Gazeta Wybrocza* (6 February 2008).
30 'Stag Parties in Krakow', *Radio Polonia, Europe East* item (21st August 2006).

the 10–20 per cent, the English are known around Krakow as a bunch of drunken, loudmouthed eejits.'[31] What becomes apparent is that a sense of Britishness is being negotiated. This negotiation is inescapably relational. He continues that 'the Polish are truly an open nation, as are the English. We are getting to know one another even better, and no drunken fool could ever change that'.[32] The optimism of this person's viewpoint is clearly one which fully frames the stag phenomenon as a meeting of different nations and different cultures and of benign intercultural interaction.

This discursive element to the coverage of the stag tour phenomenon in Poland is illustrated by a Polish news site running a survey of reactions to stag tourism. Again, lack of decency and taste emerge as frequent motifs in discussions. Thus, one respondent asked 'does drinking have to be synonymous with lude, crude, aggressive behaviour? Have some decency, boys!'[33] Another warns stag tourists to 'know your limits and have a bit of taste'.[34] Also apparent here is an implicit balance between material capital and social capital where stag tourists are perceived as flaunting financial wealth while lacking common courtesy and restraint. Thus, one respondent complains that some treat the city and its inhabitants 'like a third world country'.[35] Similarly, another respondent states: 'I don't agree with these comments that they can do anything they want as long as they're paying for it. Money isn't everything. I believe there is something more important like personal dignity'.[36] Once more, the negotiation of national characteristics and identity is clearly relational. The apparent lack of restraint and cultural sensitivity exhibited by stag tourists is therefore perceived as an affront to Polishness.

---

31   'The English Bachelor', *Gazeta Wyborcza* (3 July 2007).
32   Ibid.
33   Survey conducted for Nasze Miasto (http://www.naszemiasto.pl/) 'Are you bothered by the behaviour of English "tourists" in Krakow?' Comment posted 26 October 2007.
34   Ibid. Comment posted 3 October 2007.
35   Ibid. Comment posted 15 September 2007.
36   Ibid. Comment posted 27 September 2007.

Guiding Stag Tours, Managing Britishness

It is observed above that, rightly or wrongly, much media coverage of British stag tourists focuses on behaviour which is seen as unacceptable and, further, to be symptomatic of a wider, malign, British identity. With this given, we may now consider the role of companies providing guided stag tour packages and, importantly, the guides they employ to this end. One immediate contrast, then, is between guided and non-guided groups in that the stag tour representative, invariably a young local female, is positioned in a role which involves controlling and managing the groups' behaviour and experiences.

The detection and avoidance of troublesome behaviour is a stated priority of stag tour guides. The ability to monitor and prevent trouble from occurring demands that the rep or guide develops an ability to control the group and a repertoire of techniques for dealing with possible transgressions. Thus, during an interview, tour guide Magda reflected:

> Like, you know, 'mama Magda!', like children everywhere, like a class room, counting all the time, are they still here? Are they coming or are they going or they stay or they're too drunk to go anywhere else. All this time even if I'm a little bit drunk I always have to remember that at any time if he doesn't really look good, taxi home. It's over for you for tonight.[37]

Here the guide is clearly in a position of some authority over the group, maintaining control and attempting to monitor the somewhat troublesome elements of group behaviour. Indeed, we see that the guide is in a position to curtail an individual's participation in the night's activities if he is deemed too drunk to toe the line. Similarly, Paulina, a former stag tour guide and now a tour company office manager, observed that:

> If they come with us they know the rules, they know how it works and if they behave so bad they will be thrown out of the hotel, something like that. Sometimes going into the clubs someone is too drunk or something like that but that is the reason why the rep all the time is out with the groups, it's hard to say, but our groups are ok.

---

37   All names of all tour company representatives have been changed to preserve anonymity of research participants.

As with the comment made by Magda, Paulina reflects on the role played by the stag tour guides in ensuring stag group behaviour is acted out within acceptable limits and that the potentially negative effects of unruly stag behaviour can be controlled and anticipated.

Interestingly, rather than being an outright rejection of the need to consider how they represent Britishness, many stag tourists are highly conscious of their potential to cultivate either good or bad reputations of British men. As another guide Marta noted, this can be shrewdly used to the guide's advantage in controlling group behaviour:

'I mean, I don't think we've ever had a situation where our groups have gotten kicked out of any club. Usually we're able to handle them and talk to them... especially now they're worried about the bad press that if you just tell them, remind them you know just "hey, remember!" then they're ok with it'.

Evidently, in this case, the threat of adding to negative stereotypes is at the forefront of the minds of both stag tourists and stag tour reps and can therefore be employed as a strategy using a concern with possible negative images of the British as a way to control behaviour.

In many ways, tour guides play a pivotal role in controlling, restraining and, sometimes, encouraging certain behaviour. Further, there is a clear awareness expressed by tour guides during interviews that much of this behaviour is seen as distinctly British. One guide also perceived that the reaction to that behaviour is based on clashing cultural expectations between stag groups and locals. Thus, Magda stated that:

> Last year it was perfect everyone loves them, everywhere... but there were a few acci-
> dents, not so much with our groups, but they were fighting or naked wrestling on
> the main square next to the cathedral and everywhere in places where they should
> behave. Not even in the clubs but outside, in the main square. Those were things
> that the locals don't really like about it. Most of the time it is fun but when they
> behave in the wrong way and sing too loud or... because your culture is different
> isn't it, where you sit in a pub you can sing and make noise and everything, in here
> it is just a little bit quiet.

This observation of difference highlights potential antagonism stemming from bad behaviour as well as a clear sense that the relationship between groups and locals in Krakow is moving from one of acceptance to rejection.

This rejection is clearly based on certain instances of behaviour which transgress social expectations. As with media coverage explored in the previous section, here the understanding of Britishness is relational; British drinking culture is loud while local, Polish, drinking culture is quieter and, as such, more acceptable.

Another example of how antagonistic behaviour transgresses social expectations, as well as how these transgressions are seen as inescapably indicative of national characteristics, is raised by another guide, Anna, who observed that:

> There is an opinion about Polish people, that we are alcoholics, but English people, how English people are drinking. You know, what is the difference, when Polish people are going to the nightclub, and they are really drunk, like a girl is really drunk, she is not staying, not sleeping, not throwing up, she is just taking a taxi and going home. And this is the difference between Polish and English people, they are staying and making a mess.

Again, there are similarities with the press articles considered above which act as a platform to discuss normative understandings of national characteristics. We see a clear conflation of individual recklessness with collective lack of decency. In short and, perhaps, understandably, the social transgressions of even one stag tourist can become a lightning conductor for a constellation of assumptions, expectations and feelings relating to national identity.

However, that is not to say that tour reps act solely to restrict or limit behaviour. Conversely, tour guides played a significant role in encouraging playful behaviour and were an integral and expected part of the stag tour package sold on notions of boisterous escapism. Thus, it was often observed that tour guides would act to bring those not involved with the immediate activity into line with the leading definition of the situation as one of playfulness and fun. This was confirmed by several tour reps during interviews. For example, Paulina explained that 'one of our rules is you can't stay with one guy on the group because he likes and does everything and he enjoy all the time, you need to find the most sad person in the group and try to persuade him to join in everything. That is the reason they are searching, searching all the time.

On the basis of this it is fair to assume that while certain behaviour is considered to be unacceptable, and certainly any behaviour which might risk a hostile response from local police or nightclub security is to be actively discouraged by guides, a lot of other behaviour is considered to be desirable and expected. The guides exhibited a strong knowledge of this and sought to help individuals achieve the feelings of release and playfulness desired. Engaging with quieter members of the group, perhaps offering to dance with them or encouraging them to drink shots of vodka, allowed tour guides to foster a collective sense of excitement and group cohesion. We can therefore see the guide as working a fine line balancing the groups within the liminal zone of acceptable and unacceptable behaviour. Thus, all those interviewed showed a keen awareness of liminal behaviour as desirable for groups to the point were encouraging such is a central role to their work, while, at the same time, restricting certain more flagrant social transgressions.

Given the concerns, highlighted earlier, of much tourism studies literature with the nature of cultural exchange created within tourist environments, it is apparent that stag tourist destinations create a highly gendered landscape of social interaction. Indeed, given the all-male nature of British stag groups, coupled with the frequently voiced motivation for travelling being to meet local women, it is unsurprising that specifically gendered interactions should be a feature of stag tourist experience. With this given, it soon became apparent during interviews that stag tour company staff were keenly aware of the complex relationship between the British men who participate in stag tours and the local women with whom they came into contact. Furthermore, they were eager to facilitate positive but limit negative interaction. An example of this understanding is given by Magda:

> You know what, first, English guys are much different to Polish guys. There's something different. How they look, how they dress on the night, they're not wearing T Shirts, like every day, they treat it like something special. Shoes, shirt and that's the way of doing it. And that's 'wow' alright, that's nice. Polish girls like it. But, here there are hundreds of them now.

In this case, we see British, or English, masculinity being perceived as different and, in this sense, desirable. However, it is clear that as with the more general move from acceptance to rejection outlined above, the specific interactions between British men and Polish women have changed as Krakow, as a stag tourism destination, becomes saturated. Thus, Anna observes: 'Polish girls do not like it anymore, too much yeah. Because you know, at the beginning when the guys were coming here the girls were happy, yeah, because it was something else, different. And now, they hate, especially when the guys are coming here and flashing the money'.

Significantly, the masculinity of British men is also contrasted with the masculinity of local, Polish men. As such, Paulina reflects on the perceived difference between English and Polish men by saying:

> Yeah, because you know sometimes the girls are happy when English guys are coming and, you know, English guys can join everything and can have fun all the time, that's the reason, because when you are going out in the evenings all the time they are having good time, laughing, drinking, everything, and they are loud and maybe that's the reason that sometimes the Polish guys don't understand that.

However, what perhaps is more telling is that, given the circumstances in which stag tours take place is written through with a pervasive script of fun and playfulness. In this sense, the liminal zone which these men occupy as stag tourists allows them to enact a playful masculinity which is here deployed by Paulina in contrast to the masculinity of Polish men.

Beyond their direct contact with groups, tour guides and those involved in the stag tour industry play a wider role as intermediaries in the perception of British stag tours. Thus, several of those interviewed spoke of ongoing attempts to rationalise the behaviour of stag groups to friends, family and, in some cases, the press. This example is from an interview with Paulina:

> I try to explain to my friends, because something, you know, for example, in Poland when in Krakow many people are coming to study from home village or something like that, so when they're going out from their home and from their family and going to study in Krakow they feel like free for the start and for the first year of study they feel like animal, you know, drinking, yeah, party everything, check it out... and for me, English guys, sometimes they behave similar, because the feel like they can do everything they want and they are not in their city nobody will notice nothing.

In this light, there is some mileage in suggesting that stag tour guides and companies engage in a considerable amount of discursive work in negotiating the perception of Britishness that stag tourists represent. Indeed, all those interviewed were quick to point out that the negative reputation of stag tour groups was at times vastly exaggerated and report that they had, at various times, attempted to make this clear to friends and family. As an example of this, one interviewee, Marta, said: 'I mean the idea that the media put out here in Krakow is that they're just here to rape our women and dirty our streets, but its not like that at all'.

Further to this, all those interviewed readily attested to the positive aspects of stag tourism and sought, to an extent, to dispel what was perceived to be a falsely exaggerated image of stag tourists. A large part of this was seen to counter the normative distinction between good and bad tourist, by referring to an openness and cultural awareness that most would associate with 'good' forms of tourism, but not stag tourism. For instance, Magda reflected that she was 'always amazed they are really interested in culture. Fifty per cent of guys before they come here they know a few words, they're learning words, and they know about the history of Krakow'.

In terms of national identity, then, the Britishness represented by stag tourism, at once playful and readily typified as disruptive and often lacking in restraint, must be placed within a current of change and negotiation. Here, Marta draws an interesting contrast between stag tourism and previous assumptions about British identity based on a very narrow range of cultural representations, primarily certain British comedy series: 'The thing is about the British comedies they play over here are like *Mr Bean*, you know, the nerd in the suite or *Keeping Up Appearances*, you know, that's probably what they think the British are like and they see these guys come over and party and they're just not like that at all'.

From this we can see that assumptions and expectations about Britishness are being articulated in numerous dynamic ways. Through its visibility, ability to court controversy and insight antagonism, stag tourism evidently plays a significant role in the current production of understandings of what it means to be British and, importantly in this case, how British national identity is perceived and thought about abroad. As such, the new patterns of mobility which abound in the contemporary European setting do indeed produce new and varied sites for contact, interaction and negotiation.

Conclusion

This chapter has explored the ways in which stag tourism in Eastern Europe and, more importantly, the perceptions of and reactions to the phenomenon might inform our understandings of how Britishness is constructed. In this sense, looking to tap into a 'view from abroad' necessarily considers an element of Britishness from which many would seek distance. Indeed, the division between what is perceived to be good and bad tourist behaviour is paralleled by notions of good and bad Britishness. How these normative distinctions are discussed in the media and through the work of those who can be seen as positioned as cultural intermediaries such as stag tour company staff occupies an interesting location at the centre of contemporary debates about Britishness.

What becomes apparent is that the construction of perceptions of national identity is not merely a static object nor is it something subjectively possessed by an individual. Rather, we must look at the spaces, both physical and imagined, within which multiple actors influence how Britishness is understood and related to. There is considerable scope for suggesting that tourism and tourist destinations can produce spaces for the enactment and renegotiation of identity through, at times, antagonistic cultural interaction. As such, we see that stag tour representatives play an important role in restricting or, at times, encouraging certain behaviour. Further still, tour guides, acting as cultural intermediaries, are often at the epicentre of the discursive negotiation of identity. Similarly, we see that media representations of stag tourism are replete with both overt and implicit discussions of what Britishness is and how it might be normatively responded to by the reader. As a contemporary phenomenon, then, stag tourism in Eastern Europe tells us, amongst other things, a great deal about Britishness and the way it is perceived when abroad and from abroad.

A. JAMES HAMMERTON

12 'Thatcher's Refugees': Shifting Identities among Late Twentieth Century British Emigrants

> I exist now in a state of limbo. I've lived in New Zealand for nearly four years, which my Wellington friends assure me is no time at all. I still have an English accent and gravitate without intention to other English people. But I don't feel English anymore. I don't read the English news or support England against New Zealand in sport. I knew more about the All Blacks than I did about the British Lions on their recent tour, but I'm still not a Kiwi. My friends mention cultural icons they've known since childhood and I have no idea who or what they are. I haven't acquired the deep cultural understanding that goes with growing up in a particular place.
>
> I'm a citizen of both countries and a native of neither, but it doesn't matter to me at all. I finally feel like I belong somewhere. ... It's not who I am or what I do that determines the quality of my life, but where I am that is the difference between sun and shadow, living and just making it through each day.

These reflections are from a young British woman, Tanya, who emigrated to New Zealand in 2001; she was a trans-migrant through Australia, who had also, in 1989 as a late teenager, accompanied her parents on their migration to Italy.[1] The Italian venture was, in her mother's words, an escape, 'to get away from England, and get away from Thatcher, and we just wanted

---

1   Interview and written account, Tanya Piejus, Wellington, New Zealand, 30 November, 2006, LU DP15. All references to personal testimony draw on the La Trobe University British post-war migration project, History Programme; the files consist of interview transcripts and autobiographical written materials.

to just go out, you know, go somewhere different. ... We couldn't stand
the woman. And I mean it was that bad, you know, we just wanted to get
away from her'.[2] While the Italian sojourn was for only two years, both
mother's and daughter's restlessness persisted; her mother and stepfather
also moved to New Zealand in 2001, where within two years they were
farming alpacas. For Tanya it was contempt for the values of middle-class
England, rather than any political regime, which drove her away. Referring to her parents' friends' status aspirations for the large house, two cars,
double garage and tennis club, 'it was just the whole middle class thing I
just found very bland and very superficial and I just didn't *like* that at all, I
just didn't feel that I really want to be part of that'. So in eschewing middle-
class England Tanya came also to eschew any concrete sense of English
identity, as conveyed in the opening text, retaining a residual attachment
only for the history, architecture and countryside of her native land, but
more as a tourist than a native.

What emerges here as a casually discarded English loyalty and identity
certainly does not typify the enormously diverse attitudes of two generations of British emigrants since 1945, but it does raise questions about the
impact of the migrant experience on their attitudes to national identity,
heritage, citizenship and loyalty in the latter decades of the twentieth century. In old white settler receiving countries, like Australia, these attitudes
invariably have been stereotyped, often in contradictory ways. Hence the
British, sharing the advantage over other migrants of the foundational
culture and first language, have been seen to adjust to the new country
seamlessly without suffering the trauma of other migrants. At the same
time they have been castigated as 'whingeing poms' or limeys and scorned
for their ungrateful propensity to complain and return home at the least
discontent.[3] Their slowness to take out local citizenship, too, has invariably been regarded as a reluctance to let go of their British attachments

---

2   Interview and written account, Barbara Ingram-Monk, Picton, New Zealand, 29
     November, 2006, LU DI05.
3   A. J. Hammerton and A. Thomson, *Ten Pound Poms: Australia's Invisible Migrants*
     (Manchester, Manchester University Press, 2005), 12–13, 340–5. J. Jupp, *The English
     in Australia* (Melbourne, Cambridge University Press, 2004), 194–5.

and identity, taking the durability of their Britishness for granted while claiming the advantages of residence, thus wishing to have the best of both worlds but without commitment to the new country.[4] Recently some whiteness studies scholars have elaborated these attitudes in Australia to extend to their racial implications, so that, referring here to Aboriginal-white relations, British migrants are most easily able to 'absolve themselves of responsibility for Australia's past at the same time as they accord themselves full rights of participatory belonging on the basis of their privileged origins at the heart of white modernity'.[5]

Simply on the grounds of the diversity and shifting nature of the British emigrant population since 1945 these claims can be shown to be gross oversimplifications and of diminishing relevance to the British migration of modernity. In our recent work on the 'ten pound poms' generation up to the 1970s, for example, diversity was the dominant theme from oral testimony on issues of belonging and national identity. Robust Australian commitment appeared alongside stalwart loyalty to British heritage and citizenship, whilst anger at Britain's rigid class structure and criticism of everything British coexisted with veneration of the homeland and British citizenship. Most revealing, perhaps, was the slight majority of our informants in favour of an Australian republic.[6] By contrast this plurality is not the impression that emerges from scrutiny of more institutional expressions of British migrant identity. These can be found in British loyalty organizations like, in Melbourne, the 'British Australian Community', various 'St George's societies' and more significantly in recent years the proliferation of websites devoted to British expatriates and migrants, like 'Brits Abroad'. Here, among a range of opinion, one is most likely to find the most extreme expressions of white British sentiment, often bordering on xenophobia.[7]

---

4   S. Schech and J. Haggis, 'Terrains of Migrancy and Whiteness: How British Migrants Locate Themselves in Australia', in A. Moreton-Robinson, ed. *Whitening Race* (Canberra, Aboriginal Studies Press, 2004), 188. Jupp, *English in Australia*, 197–9.
5   Schech and Haggis, 'Terrains of Migrancy and Whiteness', 191.
6   Hammerton and Thomson, *Ten Pound Poms*, 9–11, 14–17, 331–4, 340–5.
7   See, for example, the British Australian Community's Melbourne based website: www. geocities.com/endeavour_uksa/uksa.html; one of the numerous Canadian St George's

But even in the 'ten pound poms' generation we found this to be a tiny minority of British migrant sentiment, with most informants expressing lack of interest or contempt for such organizations.[8] Oral and written testimony based on extensive life histories is likely to provide a corrective to such minority expressions, and this chapter draws on a large survey of post-1960s British testimony in the main Commonwealth countries of immigration.[9] The focus in this chapter is on one particular decade, the 1980s, when emigration began to be influenced by a new ideological and economic framework. Migrant experience here is interpreted from the migrants' telling of their life stories and their responses to questions about the meaning of British identity.

Thatcher's Refugees

The experience of a young woman who emigrated twice to Australia, in 1982 and 1984, settling permanently in Sydney after her second migration following some internal moves between Sydney and Melbourne, points the way. Viviane, born in 1959, was the epitome of the young single British sojourner migrant of the modern era.[10] A middle-class tertiary educated woman from the south of England who eventually completed a BA and MA in French Studies and Politics at the London School of Economics,

---

societies (in Vancouver): www.stgeorgebc.ca/about.html; the British Expat Forum, one of the less ideologically focused websites: www.BritishExpats.com; and the more robust Brits Abroad, which is no longer active but retains a web presence: http:// myweb.ecomplanet.com/lepo6596/. See also Ben Wellings' chapter in this volume.

8   Hammerton and Thomson, *Ten Pound Poms*, 334–7.

9   The project has built a database of 179 informants in Australia, New Zealand, Canada, Hong Kong, one in the USA, and Britain. 131 of these were interviewed and most provided a written account. Their migration departures span the 1950s to 2005, with most dating from the 1970s and many with a record of 'serial migrations' which testify to the 'mobility of modernity'.

10   Interview, Viviane King, Sydney, 23 March, 2007, LU DK20.

she was ambitious, well qualified and politically conscious. She was typical of her middle-class cohort in her family's routine mobility outside Britain, with regular holidays in France, and in her first independent holiday trip to the United States, aged 17. She was untypical in having a French mother, which caused her to feel something of an outsider among her childhood peers, and significantly her closest school friends also had a French or Italian parent. But while her attachment to France and things French was unique in stemming from her family inheritance (she managed to complete one year of her university studies on exchange in Grenoble), her passion for Europe generally and France in particular was, by the 1980s, increasingly common among her generation, and it is from this time that the proportion of British citizens residing permanently in countries like France, Spain and Italy began to increase significantly, one of the early social consequences of European Union membership.

Viviane's background predisposed her to future mobility, but certainly did not make it inevitable, and she describes her departure for Australia in 1982 as a clear matter of circumstance; underplaying the role of explicit original intention at her departure, she insisted that 'I never set out to emigrate to Australia, it happened by stealth'. Graduating with her BA at the end of 1981, her employment prospects in England were dismal. At the suggestion of a boyfriend she embarked on an 18 month working holiday in Sydney and Melbourne, which provided better opportunities, but after returning to LSE for a year to complete her MA the work prospects in Britain were even worse, and so by 1984 she was back in Melbourne, where she thrived as a research officer. She later moved to Sydney, worked for politicians, married and gave birth to a daughter. The British political background to these moves, still palpable in Viviane's memories of her migration, was, of course, the regime of Margaret Thatcher throughout the 1980s. This led Viviane to describe herself as a 'refugee from Thatcherism'. As she explained it,

> I realised that there were far more opportunities here [in Australia], I mean I'm an economic migrant, there's, there's no doubt about that. ... Because of the unemployment I mean I consider myself as a refugee from Thatcherism, but... I suppose the fact that I'm a refugee stemmed from the fact that there really was nothing for me in, in England. ... Look if, if there had been something that would have offered a

career-path in, in London, it would have had to have been very good, to compare with the lifestyle that I had in Australia. ... I think like most other people, you know, everyone's got their price, I could have been bought, you know, at the right price, there was nothing that I could see that I could do in London. Even when I went back for the year to do the Masters degree I... looked around to see if there was anything that I could do and really, there was nothing, at that point I think unemployment was probably closer towards the four million, and it was harder still. And I just did not see that I could do anything that would be a reward for the skills that I had gained, and that could give me a lifestyle that I suppose I figured that I should have been able to earn myself.

While Viviane underplays the ideological factor here in driving her migra-tion, she also acknowledges a political motivation, recalling her excitement at arriving in Melbourne which contrasted with Britain. Migrant excitement at arrival is traditionally recalled through impressions of the surrounding environment, the weather, or a friendly reception; Viviane, recalling the new governmental landscape she encountered in Australia, remembered hers through a political lens:

It was, you know, it was such a contrast. John Cain [Premier of Victoria] had just come in when I arrived, in '82 and that was after twenty something years of a state Liberal government. Bob Hawke, well Fraser was still in for one more year after I arrived but the ALP was on the ascendancy federally, and you could just see that, you know, Australia was, was changing, and you could see, you know from the noises that the ALP was making, that they were going to try and transform Australia and, and bring it really kicking and screaming into the twentieth century.

A woman who worked for politicians and in policy development, Viviane might seem to be exceptional in her political motivations. Yet while not all youthful emigrants of the 1980s were so political, and some claimed emphatically to be Thatcher's beneficiaries, the 'Thatcher refugee' theme is a consistent one, across class, down to the early 1990s, encompassing both the high unemployment rate of the early 1980s and an ideological revulsion to the regime. Catherine and her husband, both middle-class Scots, left Edinburgh in 1982 with a sense of a bleak future for Britain. 'People were suffering, before even *we* left', she recalled, 'and we thought "everything's going to go backwards in Britain'".[11] John, a boiler-maker from Barrow-in-Furness, described the Thatcher victory as 'the last nail in the coffin' for him, which provoked his family's migration in 1981.[12] Adam, from Manchester, completed his tertiary education in the 1980s and became a teacher before he began his 'serial migration' in 1993, first with an expatriate position in Brunei, later moving to Australia with an Australian wife, but he places his departure firmly in the context of political alienation, which began with the Falklands War: 'I was sixteen in 1982 when the Falklands happened and I was disgusted and appalled by it and I still remain to this day. ... It turned me against cheap nasty jingoism. ... My reaction was to get out, I just thought, oh, I just didn't see that there was any particular way back for Britain by that point'.[13] These examples illustrate how ideological hostility could pave the way for lasting antagonism to Britain and so stimulate a more mobile future and an ambiguous attitude, at least, to British heritage and identity.

It is no surprise that the forthright expression of political and ideological motivations for migration among these tertiary trained and youthful emigrants of the 1980s and 1990s coincided with the period in the early 1980s when, demographically, the proportion of British emigrants classified as 'professional and managerial' decisively overtook the traditionally largest cohort, the 'manual and clerical'. That is, the post-1970s emigrant generation became distinctively more middle-class, even allowing for the changing profile towards a middle-class preponderance in the British population overall in the same period.[14] But if an anti-Thatcher mindset is far from being the whole story of this 1980s and early 1990s generation, it does provide a hint of the changing profile of these younger, more professional and largely more urban and cosmopolitan migrants, with little interest in sustaining a collective sense of British identity, which distinguished them

11   Interview, Catherine Taylor, Melbourne, 22 August, 2006, LU DT10.

12   Interview, John and Ann Whiteside, Wollongong, NSW, 18 July, 2006, LU DW45/50.

13   Interview, Adam Salt, Melbourne, 21 September, 2005, LU DS10.

14   D. Sriskandarajah and C. Drew, *Brits Abroad: Mapping the Scale and Nature of British Emigration* (London, Institute for Public Policy Research, 2006), 22–5.

from their parents' generation. Viviane, for example, is no longer unusual in holding three passports, British, French and Australian, the first two of which she kept for convenience rather than commitment or patriotism.

An explicit commitment to a preferred lifestyle also accompanied the cosmopolitan outlook from the 1980s. It was significant that Viviane's interview took place in her home in a city centre apartment in Sydney, which she shared with her Australian husband and nine year old daughter, then attending an inner city French immersion school. In Australian cities especially, despite its growing popularity, this remained a relatively rare choice compared to inner or outer suburban living, especially for those with children. Yet increasing numbers of interviews for the project took place in such inner city dwellings rather than the suburbs, which was almost universal among the migrant generation up to the 1970s. For Viviane this was an act of deliberate choice, partly in opposition to suburban living, but more emphatically in reaction to her upbringing in the socially and culturally conservative provincial English town of Maidenhead. She commented that 'growing up in "white bread" England in the sixties I might as well have come from Mars', and that she fled as early as possible to life in London, a prelude act of migration to international mobility. But her Australian choice was also driven by a choice of lifestyle linked to memories of her cosmopolitan past in London, so that Sydney became for her 'that opportunity I suppose to go back to the, you know, the lifestyle that I had when I was a student in London living in the apartment in central London'. It is an irony that she sought and re-discovered her cosmopolitanism in Australia, since the previous generation of urban migrants had commonly expressed horror after arrival at the narrow conservative provincialism of Commonwealth cities like Melbourne, Perth, Toronto, Vancouver, Auckland and Wellington.[15] Notably this cosmopolitan theme in migration coexists with a sharp counter trend among late twentieth century migrants, what has been called 'treechange' and 'seachange' phenomena. This refers to the use of migration to effect a major lifestyle change by avoiding the city life migrants had known in Britain in favour of movement to rural bush areas, often with an ecological land care agenda, or to coastal areas with an

---

15   Viviane King, LU DK20; Hammerton and Thomson, *Ten Pound Poms*, 132, 139–41.

accent on escape to a beachside lifestyle. This is the subject for a separate discussion, but it too is characteristic of the mindset of the Thatcher generation of young middle-class emigrants whose ideology influenced their migration choices. In these ways 1980s lifestyle choices were coming to be more thoroughly bound up with migration decisions and places of settlement. These migration choices are where we can see how, in some respects, western migration began to take on characteristics of consumerism, a distinguishing feature, perhaps, of modern migrations of prosperity.

It is no accident that a woman like Viviane King best illustrates some of the striking themes of cosmopolitanism and the changing meaning of British migration in the 1980s, because it is among women that some of the dramatic social changes of the late twentieth century have impacted most starkly on their profiles as migrants. In the 1950s and 1960s the classic profile of the British single female migrant was of a woman with a mobile occupation like nursing, physiotherapy, hairdressing or secretarial work, intent on a two-year working holiday, although often 'hijacked' in midstream by marriage to a local.[16] By contrast, the tertiary educated Viviane was pursuing career development. This was an increasingly common theme by the 1980s. Another young woman, Beth, with postgraduate qualifications in pharmacology, emigrated to Melbourne in 1988 after some global travel. She too admitted to some 'Thatcher refugee' motivations alongside personal ones, but she pursued her career and further global travel with determination until, in the early 1990s a 'new age' epiphany and marriage to an American immigrant brought further change with a career switch into naturopathy and massage and a 'treechange/seachange' move to the highly receptive territory of Byron Bay in coastal New South Wales. Her spiritual transformation accompanied a corresponding distancing from any explicit English or British identity: 'I'm more interested now in finding like-minded community in different parts of the world... the connection with the planet. ... I don't consider myself particularly British or particularly Australian, I mean I know I have *huge* English influences, I'm aware of them, but I don't wear it like a badge, it's not an identity for me.'[17]

16   Ibid. 248–63.
17   Interview, Beth McIntosh, Billinudgel, NSW, 1 July, 2006, LU DM65.

A variation on this theme is represented by an Australian journalist, Sushi Das, who is well known in the Melbourne public domain.[18] Sushi stands out as an example of the recently noticed development of those post-war British non-white 'immigrants who become emigrants'. That is, she was born in India in 1964 but went to England – Twickenham, an all white suburb of London – with her family at the age of three. She became a rebellious teenager, defied her parents' schemes for arranged marriages with various Indian suitors, and, at university in the 1980s, became highly politicised in the anti-Thatcher university environment of the time. But from an early age she was driven by an ambition to become a journalist, and while she sustained her left-wing politics from the 1980s, when she emigrated with her British academic husband to Melbourne in 1991, it was he who carried the most powerful 'Thatcher refugee' mentality, while she was preoccupied with career advancement. Her journalism came to focus emphatically on issues of migration and race and she was one of the regular irritants for a succession of Australian immigration ministers under John Howard's government. Still, her career success in Australia, and her second marriage to an Australian and a baby born in Australia, did not extinguish an abiding English identity, expressed mostly in passion for the excitement of London, the place of her memories of youth, and like so many modern migrants she remained open to further moves and especially a return to Britain, which she still described as her cultural home. But in extended discussion about her identification with England the story became more complex, where an English/British identity became only one extension of a global outlook of non-belonging alongside her Indian ethnicity:

> This is a *very* hard question because of course it's the kind of question you're trying to answer all your *life*, I don't feel, and I never have felt, that I belonged, specifically, *anywhere*, and that's a real, a real problem, in terms of coming up with your identity, I think. However, I do feel more British than Indian sometimes, simply because of where I went to school, my friends, and the kind of value-system, and what's important to me, that kind of stuff, but of course every time I look in the mirror, I can't get away from the fact that I'm Indian too.

18   Interview, Sushi Das, Melbourne, 18 September, 2007, LU DD07.

Well, I've always felt British, I still feel British, I've been here 16 years and I reckon I'm going to feel British, until I die, okay, because my *youth* was there, and my teenage years were there, and those years I think are important, they *form* you, my 20s were there, and I think those years are important because they *make* you, in so many ways, they make, they mould the core of you, and so that's why I think I'm always going to feel British, I think partly because I left, left reluctantly, with always a view to going *back*, and for me it feels unfulfilled, that I didn't go back. ... I'm fearful of losing my *British* identity, I know I can never lose my Indian identity, because it's in my skin, but I'm fearful of losing my British identity because well, that's not on my face, do you know what I mean?

I think that we're moving into a new phase where people can't comfortably *say* any more that: 'I belong to this country because we come from so many *different* places'. So I think that people, because of their eagerness to belong *somewhere* are, are now beginning to say things like: 'Oh, I'm a global citizen, because now, if you can't belong to a country, well we'll belong to the world... and, you can't take that away from us, and there's no borders on that'... and maybe that's a good thing, maybe once we all start seeing ourselves as earthlings, there might be *less* division, between us all.

These thoughts are the product of deep reflection about identity and belonging, but they are also powerfully subjective, far removed from the overt patriotism and communal networking often associated with collective British identities abroad. They do not easily lend themselves to claims about the resilience of Britishness among modern migrants. Moreover, Sushi Das's forthright English identity contrasts with a different tendency of British emigrants since the 1970s to spurn it, not necessarily in favour of attachment to their adopted country but rather for a commitment to a 'European' belonging, a variation on the transnational 'citizen of the world' identity. Alongside those sentiments which resist robust assertions of British migrant identity we encounter what is perhaps the most dominant political outlook of all, which is an aversion or lack of interest in national identity at all. Frequently a by-product of an apolitical outlook generally, it can also accompany varieties of 'rugged individualism' which can find fertile ground in immigrant countries like Australia and Canada, especially for men. For example, Andrew, a 1992 immigrant to Australia, protested utter lack of interest in the politics of identity, preferring, even as a husband and father, to prioritize his life around long-distance yachting activities which sustained his independence from any attachment to nation.[19] More commonly a lack of interest in British or other national commitment is likely to be associated with what commentators usually describe as political apathy, or a greater interest in just getting on with life.[20] This is not inconsistent, it should be noted, with regular visits to what has become a burgeoning growth of 'treats from home' and 'best of British' type shops around the Commonwealth catering to Britons' tastes for such delicacies as Bisto Gravy, boiled sweets and Yorkshire tea, frequented especially by British tourists. [21]

Thatcher's Beneficiaries

Political alienation, 'new age' lifestyle transformations and global identities easily complemented each other, but these were far from being the whole story of 1980s emigration. Thatcher's refugees, for example, were balanced by quite self-consciously described Thatcher's beneficiaries and supporters, sometimes a simple outcome of conservative background, ingrained political instinct and ideology, but equally a matter of self-interested calculation among budding elites and professionals in emerging industries. Aspiring entrepreneurs, normally part of the Conservative Party's bedrock support, were likely to feel particularly strongly about Thatcher's reforms, often fuelled by resentment against a high taxing welfare state, but this did not necessarily translate into robust British loyalty or patriotism.[22]

19   Interview, Andrew Mackie, Melbourne, 23 November, 2007, LU DM15.
20   For discussion of this view in the context of a woman migrant to Australia from the 1920s see S. Constantine '"Dear Grace... Love Maidie": Letters from Australia, 1926–1967', presented to British World Conference, Bristol University, 11–14 July, 2007.
21   For example 'Treats from Home' outlets in Sydney and Melbourne, 'Best of British', Perth and 'Cool Britannia', Wellington.
22   See, for example, Michael Whitley, an entrepreneur from a traditional Conservative family, who welcomed Thatcher's reforms but in Australia had little time for identity politics, describing himself alternately as 'international' and an 'Auspom'. Interview, Michael Witley, Sydney, 14 July, 2006, LU DW55.

Stories from a younger generation, without prior political commitment, underline global tendencies in common among young migrants
of the 1980s regardless of political orientation. Mark, for example, was a
child of the rapidly developing revolution in computer technology, with
a sharp eye for new opportunities beyond the modest white-collar career
of his father. He seized one of the limited prospects for tertiary study of
computer science in the early 1980s at Sunderland Polytechnic and, after
a number of promising positions with county councils in his native Mid-
lands, pursued fixed term contracts, which by 1987 took him to London
for lucrative work in financial services. The money, he recalled, 'was just
flowing around the place', and even after the market crash of that year the
work 'just kept going'. So when, quite unexpectedly in 1988, he received
an offer of a year's contract as a computer programmer in Melbourne,
this was simply a continuation of a regular succession of challenging job
opportunities. In early 1989 he and his girlfriend moved to Melbourne.
For Mark much of this easy success was attributable to Thatcher's policies,
making him conscious of the huge leap he had made from his origins when
his family lived in a rented Council flat in Derby. 'I certainly profited,
without a doubt, from Thatcher', he reflected, 'I mean Thatcher, Thatcher
liberated the financial services sector, and I certainly profited from that'.
But his political endorsement was equivocal. Given his background, and
his origins around Derbyshire mining districts, it is not surprising that the
intense conflict between Thatcher's government and striking miners in
the early 1980s caused him some misgivings and political doubts. A keen
football fan, he was disturbed to find that police tactics towards the miners
resembled those used against football supporters. But with an eye to the
larger picture, 'from a political perspective I felt that it had to be done,
what Thatcher was doing after all had to be done because things certainly
were atrocious under Callaghan before her'.

Mark projected an element of political ambivalence here, and in this
respect his attitude characterizes that of a young generation of educated and
ambitious migrants in the 1980s, for whom political identity, whatever its
colour, was secondary to career ambitions, travel and 'lifestyle'. Reflecting
on his story, Mark traces his mobile instincts to a tendency to 'wander' as a
young boy, but with a practical purpose. His wandering, while always 'a bit
of a yearning of mine, I've always been one that's, that's travelled a little bit',

was emphatically not wanderlust, 'because wanderlust to me is something that you do without a purpose, and my travelling always to me seemed to have a purpose, I was never one that looked at the back-packer trail with any sort of envy... there's always been a purpose to the travelling, even if it meant taking myself off to Nottingham as a twelve year old because I used to do *that* quite often on a Sunday, just go round the museums and that sort of thing as well, but to me again that served a purpose'. In his migration that 'purpose' was largely career driven, and lacked the impetus to flight evident among Thatcher's refugees, but it also drew on similar lifestyle quests that we saw in Viviane's devotion to London.

By 1995 Mark was married to an Australian, Junette, and in the process became stepfather to her three children. The attractions of family life and domesticity confirmed his feeling that Melbourne was now home, but homesickness for England persisted. Long after leaving his original home, in Derby, he had retained a strong attachment for his local origins. But paradoxically his drive to return stemmed from nostalgia for his time in London. Like Viviane the memory of a free-wheeling single life in the metropolis exercised a powerful attraction, and although Junette was not keen to leave home, they were sufficiently well off to undertake a London trip for an agreed twelve months. He reflected on the way his nostalgia evolved:

> I think, looking at it afterwards, what I missed is a certain lifestyle, it wasn't home-sickness per se, although I really missed the lifestyle that I had in London, and I think I say I was *never* homesick, ... which was strange, because I've never consid-ered myself a Londoner, and yet I missed that, that *lifestyle* which London offered, which was a hard-working, hard playing, hard drinking, single lifestyle, and it was, it *was* very much that single lifestyle which I missed, and it was only when I actually went back that I was able to realise that it was the lifestyle that I missed rather than individuals or places.

In the event Mark left Australia first to arrange housing, and by the time Junette and the children arrived he felt his passion for London had been satiated. When the contract expired after ten months he was relieved to return to Melbourne, although now London had exercised its charms on his wife, so that 'we had to drag Junette onto the plane back to Melbourne!'

For Mark the return sojourn worked its way in what is a familiar return migrant story, becoming

> the actual catharsis for me, it was at that point that I knew that my whole future lived, lay here, yes. ... I very quickly realised that the lifestyle that I missed, and was feeling homesick for, was very much *not* the person that I was *now*, and that London was, London was not necessarily the sort of place to have... a nine year old to be going *into* this sort of thing, ... So by the time they arrived which was New Year's Day, 1996, I'd almost decided that London wasn't home.

If Mark's story began as a successful career narrative driven by opportunities created by Margaret Thatcher's policies, it never took on the strong political flavour evident among Thatcher's refugees. Indeed, Thatcher's 'revolution' did nothing to prevent him from criticizing the quality of life in England by contrast to what he enjoyed in Melbourne; 'I just find the lifestyle a little insular over there', he remarked. In its greater preoccupation with travel, return experience, lifestyle quests and identity his story speaks for those of the young migrants of the 1980s more generally. Spurred initially by youthful ambition, in the end the story was dictated by family priorities, and Mark attached particular importance to the fact that he married into an existing family, to a mother with three children. 'I was very much aware of the fact that I *was* moving into a family, and, and so my future very much was shaped along the *family* lines whereas if [Junette] was another single person, I think my life would have taken a different turn again, but because I was moving into a family that sort of shaped it as well'. Mark's family emphasis accompanied an identity that remained intensely local, with high valuation of his Derbyshire football loyalties and similar devotion to Melbourne sporting teams, but indifference to any larger British identity or patriotism; indeed, national identity of any kind was of minor importance compared to the imperatives of family and the pleasures of lifestyle.[23]

23   Interview, Mark Waite, Melbourne, 29 April, 2006, LU DW05.

Conclusion

Ideological motives for migration in the 1980s highlight a range of new factors which mark dramatic shifts in the ways we have come to emigrate in the developed world over the last half century and which cast doubt on claims for the resilience of British identities in the British world. At the same time it must be stressed that such ideological motivations for migration were not new, seen previously, for example, in the thinking of many post-war migrants of the late 1940s who spoke with some bitterness of their disillusion with the nationalisation policies of the Attlee Labour government alongside conditions of acute austerity. The parallels and continuities are important in migration history, but close scrutiny of migrant testimony illustrates some vital differences setting in powerfully from about the 1980s. Pre-eminent among these is a global or transnational 'citizen of the world' outlook which resists patriotic attachment, and in the specific context of the 1980s was fostered in part by political and cultural alienation. Since the 1980s this global identity has been nurtured further by environmental commitments of migrants, often in search of 'treechange/seachange' life transformations, evident even in the 'grey nomad' phenomenon, which often transcend national identities and attachments. This modern generation of migrants, young and old, might, then, suggest that under the pressures of global identities the resilience of Britishness is soon diluted. These are some of the ways in which the mobility of modernity has brought new meanings, at the expense of national identity, to the act of migration.

BEN WELLINGS

13 The English in Australia: A Non-Nation in Search of an Ethnicity?[1]

Australia boasts many impressive tourist attractions. Sydney Harbour, Uluru and the Great Barrier Reef are must-see destinations for any tourist venturing 'Down Under'. Less well known, though no less important for the purposes of this essay, is Cockington Green. Located in the north of the Australian Capital Territory, Cockington Green opened its doors to the public in 1979 and has been one of Canberra's most popular tourist attractions ever since. Inside the grounds, the visitor will find a miniature English village, complete with miniature church, miniature pub and miniature football ground. A miniature train trundles past a miniature Stonehenge and this entire simulation of English country life is situated within an impressive life-size English garden.

The idea for Cockington Green came to its founders, Doug and Brenda Sarah, after a visit to England in 1972, when they visited a similar model village in Torquay, Devon. In this sense, Cockington Green is emblematic of the links that exist between England and Australia and the important legacy of English migration to Oz. Although Australia is often portrayed as the most 'Catholic' or 'Irish' of all the former British Dominions, the impact of migration from England is statistically greater, although less explicitly stated and organized in public life. In 1901 English-born residents of Australia totalled 393,211 people, over 10 per cent of the Australian population of 3,773,801. Although as a percentage, the English-born declined as the century drew on they were still the largest overseas-born nationality in Australia at the time of the 2006 census (representing 4.3 per cent

1   I would like to thank Ms Natassja Hoogstad-Hay for her research and Dr Shanti Sumartojo for her support in the production of this chapter.

of the total population).[2] Despite this numerical preponderance, James Jupp has noted that 'the outstanding characteristic of the mass, mainly working class, migration of the 1950s and 1960s is that it has not created a viable English community', noting that 'English organisations are few and far between'.[3] This has led other experts to characterize the English as 'Australia's invisible migrants'.[4] However, there is an extra dimension to understanding the English in Australia and that is the self-awareness of the English themselves as a distinct national, cultural or even ethnic group. This paper will argue that the English in Australia occupy a strange sort of no-man's land in multicultural Australia. During the largest, sustained period of immigration from the British Isles to Australia, from 1947 to 1983, the English were told by their old and new governments that they were British and hence that they and the Australians were essentially the same, racially and linguistically. This message contrasted starkly with the reception, both material and personal, that some migrants received when they arrived in their new land. Furthermore, when the policy of assimilation shifted to one of official multiculturalism in the 1970s, the English were not well equipped as a collectivity to adopt the new language of ethnicity or to consider themselves a minority in anything other than a defensive sense of a group having been denied rights and a 'fair go'. By examining official records and looking at the activities of organizations established to help new arrivals from the United Kingdom, this paper hopes to illustrate why many English people in Australia felt neither Australian nor merely as if they were 'just another ethnic group'.

2   Australian Bureau of Statistics, Australian Historical Population Statistics (cat. 3105.0.65.001, 5 August 2008), http://www.abs.gov.au/AUSSTATS/abs@.nsf/Web+Pages/Population+Clock?opendocument#from-banner=LN, accessed 27 May 2010.

3   J. Jupp, The English in Australia (Cambridge: Cambridge University Press, 2004), 199.

4   J. Hammerton and A. Thompson, Ten Pound Poms. Australia's Invisible Migrants (Manchester: Manchester University Press).

Ambiguous Immigrants

There is, of course, a word for all of this: 'pommy'.[5] An examination of the etymology and usage of this word sheds light on two main issues. The first of these is the ambiguous nature of the word itself and hence Australian attitudes towards English people in general and the second is the close relationship between the development of a nativist Australian nationalism, particularly from the later nineteenth century part of which was imagined against an English or British 'other'. The *Oxford Australian Dictionary* defines POMMY as:

> A. *n.* An equivocal term for an immigrant from the British Isles; applied also, more recently, to an inhabitant of the British Isles (esp. of England)... See also POM and WHINGEING POM.
> B. *attrib.* or as *adj.*
>   1. Of or pertaining to a 'pommy'; British, English. Esp. (often as a term of affectionate abuse) as pommy bastard.

However, the Oxford English Dictionary Online is less enamoured with the term:

> Pom, n.[2] (and *adj.*)
> *Austral.* and *N. Z. colloq.* (usu. *derogatory*).

Differing interpretations of the meaning behind the word were brought to public attention in the summer of 2006–7 by an advertising campaign for an Australian beer ahead of the England cricket team's Ashes tour of that summer. The advert in question was for Tooheys New Supercold, described by the beer's brewer, Lion Nathan, as 'product innovation' which meant that Tooheys New could now be bought and consumed at near sub-zero

---

5   It is interesting to note that the header entry 'pommy' is followed by 'poofter' in the Oxford Australian Dictionary. The entry for 1985 hints at the relationship of these two concepts in the Australian idiom: *Sydney Morning Herald* 20 June 11/6 '[Joseph] Banks was a pooftah'. 'Have you got any proof of that?' 'He was a botanist and a pommy – what more proof do you want?'

temperatures. The advert featured a glass of Toohey's New Supercold along-side various slogans such as 'Let the whingeing begin. It's a Pom's worst nightmare' and 'Sends shivers down a Pom's spine'.[6] A complaint was brought against Lion Nathan under section 2.1 of the Advertising Standards Code (Discrimination or Vilification of Nationality) by a group named British People Against Racial Discrimination (BPARD) from Western Australia and Victoria whose members stated that 'the racial terminology POM is offensive to us personally and to a significant number of English people generally'.[7] The complaint was picked up by the press on both sides of the Australian continent and was sympathetically viewed by Western Australia's Ethnic Community Council (ECC). The ECC president, Ramdas Sankaran, was quoted as saying that 'The word Pom is no better than other racial slurs used to describe ethnic groups or indigenous people and it has no place in Australia'.[8] However the Advertising Standards Bureau (ASB) dismissed the case, concluding that 'the term is used largely with non-hostile, playful and often affectionate intentions'.[9] The ASB's director, Mr Mark Jeannes argued that 'Pom could not be compared to harsher monikers like wog or coon and is probably closer to calling someone a Kiwi or Aussie, especially when more often than not in Australia it is used in an affectionate manner'.[10] But when Lion Nathan rolled out a radio advert which featured men singing 'Land of Hope and Glory' but with revised lyrics such as 'whinge, whine, bang-on, gripe, grumble', the ASB upheld BPARD's second claim under Section 2.1. Stating that 'racial terminology should not be used to advertise products', BPARD's director, Mr Dave Thomason argued that 'contrary to the belief of many Australians, the word "'Pom'" was, has and still is being used as a racist slur. It is not and never will be a term of endearment'.[11]

6   Advertising Standards Bureau, 488/06 (12 December 2006).
7   Ibid.
8   P. Lampathakis, 'No racial slurs please, we're British', *perthnow.com* (18 November 2006), http://www.news.com.au/perthnow/story/0,21598,20780264–5008620,00. html, accessed 22 April 2008.
9   Advertising Standards Bureau, 488/06, 12 December 2006.
10   J. Lee, 'First the Ashes, now the Pommy bashers', *The Sydney Morning Herald* (21 December 2006).
11   E. Gosch, 'Protesters take their "Pom" whinge to the UN', *The Australian* (27 January 2007).

Empire, Australia and England

According to the *Oxford Australian Dictionary*, the first recorded use of this ambiguous term 'Pom' was in November 1912, when it appeared in two Sydney newspapers, *The Truth* and *The Bulletin*.[12] The latter, known colloquially as 'the Bushman's Bible', had been at the mouthpiece of a nativist, republican nationalism during the early 1890s.[13] The date 1912 is significant since it locates the development of 'Pom' at an interesting juncture in the development of nationalism in Australia. The word itself is an abbreviation of 'pomegranate' which was itself a play on the word 'immigrant' which was used to refer to the reddish complexion of new, sun-burnt arrivals. During the nineteenth century the tern 'New Chum' was more common, but 'pom' made its appearance just as the movement for Federation had achieved its major goal. The six Australian colonies federated in 1901 around the issues of trade and defence, bound to each other and the British Empire through ties of race, as well as notions that becoming a nation would eradicate the 'convict stain' which some believed blighted the character of the descendents of those people transported to the Antipodes. November 1912 was also barely two years before the outbreak of the Great War. It was this war which reinforced the equivocal relationship to England and Britain within Australian nationalism. The landings in the Dardanelles of 25 April 1915 provided subsequent Australian nationalists such as the official war correspondent CEW Bean or the film maker Peter Weir with ample material by which to contrast Australians and Britons. In a nationalist twist on the 'lions led by donkeys' interpretation of the First World War, narratives such as Bean's and Weir's put forward a case for *British* military incompetence resulting in the death of *Australians*. However, unlike national founding moments in the United States, India or Ireland, here was a war of national birth fought *with* an imperial power rather than against it. No less important than these national narratives

---

12   *Oxford Australian Dictionary*, 1988.
13   M. McKenna, *The Captive Republic. A History of Australian Republicanism, 1788–1996* (Cambridge: Cambridge University Press, 1996).

were the experience of diggers on leave in England itself. Kosmas Tsokhas has argued that 'for many Australian troops during World War I, the more they were exposed to the British class system, to the sharp inequalities and layers of poverty in British industrial cities, the more they came to realize that Britain was not home'.[14] Nevertheless, the experience of fighting a common enemy in Europe and the Middle East did engender fellow feeling in many Australians, so that by the war's end, resentment and affection existed side-by-side.

Similarly equivocal relations were produced by the battles of the Second World War, particularly the conflicts in south-east Asia and the Pacific. As the war in the east opened for the western Allies in December 1941, it was clear that this would have major implications for Anglo-Australian relations. On 27 December 1941 the Melbourne *Herald* published an article written by the Labor Prime Minister John Curtin. In this article entitled 'The Task Ahead' Curtin laid out what he saw the next year bringing and noted pointedly that 'Without any inhibitions of any kind I make it quite clear that Australia looks to America, free of any pangs as to our traditional links of kinship with the United Kingdom'.[15] It was the asymmetrical nature of the relationship between Australia and the United Kingdom which led to a growing sentiment of suspicion towards Britain and its government's motives. Curtin continued: 'We know the problems that the United Kingdom faces. We know the constant threat of invasion. We know the dangers of dispersal of strength. But we know too that Australia can go, and Britain can still hold on'.[16] When Malaya and Singapore fell to the Japanese in February 1942 and Australia and New Guinea were themselves attacked a sense of betrayal developed. But despite these difficulties political and cultural ties between Australia and Britain were strengthened as the war entered its final phases. This cooperation was deepened in the post-war years, witnessed by the testing of Britain's nuclear weapons at Maralinga in South

14   K. Tsokhas, *Making of a Nation State. Cultural Identity, Economic Nationalism and Sexuality in Australian History* (Carlton: Melbourne University Press, 2001), 151.

15   J. Curtin, 'The Task Ahead' cited in S. Alomes and C. Jones, *Australian Nationalism. A Documentary History* (North Ryde: Angus & Robertson, 1991), 264.

16   Ibid.

Australia and by the young Queen Elizabeth's Royal Tour of 1953–4. It was the latter – according to the souvenir programme produced for sale to the millions of Australians, New Zealanders and Pacific Islanders who had seen the Queen during the months of her visit – that brought 'her antipodean peoples into more intimate unity with the crown', whilst 'for her part, the Queen soon found herself more closely identified with the loyal peoples of the Pacific who have contributed much that is fresh and vigorous to the unique comity of nations which is the British Commonwealth'.[17] Thus in the years following the war, a newly imagined Australian nationalism sought to assert a greater degree of independence from Britain, but still operated within the bounds of Britishness. In this way, Australian nationalism was situated within wider categories of belonging – and in particular race – which provided a framework for articulating distinctiveness from Britain whilst still retaining elements of commonality. As the Foreword to a book produced in 1945 aimed at promoting Australia to foreign visitors put it: 'Out of nothing – it may be said – men of the British race have built up the Nation the Anzacs have made famous; and our pioneers, in the face of great perils in a new and strange land, have made progress of which we have every reason to be proud'.[18]

One reason for adopting the language of race at this historical moment was to legitimise the massive inflow of migrants that the Australian government deemed necessary for the development and defence of Australia, so it was into this ambivalent attitude towards Britain that the Assisted Migration Scheme began operation in 1947. Writing in the first edition of *Tomorrow's Australians* in a column entitled 'Settling In', Larry Boys painted a picture of Australia as a refuge from post-war Europe, one particularly suited to migrants from Britain:

17   K. Bourne, ed., *The Royal Tour of Australia and New Zealand* (Melbourne, Colour Gravure, 1954), 2.
18   The Australia Story Trust. *Displaying Australia and New Guinea, A Pictoral Survey of the Progress of a Young Nation* (Sydney: The Australia Story Trust, 1945), 9.

> The urge to emigrate after a war is an almost racial instinct in Europeans. British-
> ers are no exception. They sell up their house and furniture, relinquish their little
> grocer's shop or their safe job on the Town Council, and join a queue for a migrant
> ship... Quietly, unostentatiously, they are settling down happily to become good
> Australian citizens.[19]

The theme of Australia as a land almost reserved for migrants from the British Isles was underlined by the Minister for Immigration, Arthur Calwell.
However, this special status for migrants from Britain had to be underlined
whilst at the same time admitting that there were simply not enough potential migrants in Britain alone and that the Australian government would
need to look elsewhere in Europe in its bid to populate Australia's wide
spaces with twenty million people by the end of the twentieth century. This
dilemma was particularly acute in the first years of the migration scheme
when the demand for labour in Australia was high, but the available shipping on the UK-Australia run was low. In the first edition of *Tomorrow's
Australians* Minister Calwell was quoted as saying, 'I give this assurance to
the people of Britain and their kinfolk who are awaiting them here, that no
British subject wishing to migrate to Australia will be denied a berth by the
sailing of a non-British migrant'.[20] In contrast to 2006, when the terminology of race was deployed by BPARD as a means of *distinguishing* British
migrants and Australians, race was used in the post-war period as a means
of *overcoming* divisions or suspicions between established settlers and new
arrivals. In a letter written for the London *Daily Graphic* and re-printed in
Tomorrow's Australians in August 1948, Calwell argued that 'Every individual Briton has a stake in Australia whether he is aware of it or not', adding
'I, and all Australians, believe that if anyone should share in our national
destiny it is our kinsmen from the little islands of our forefathers'.[21] But
these assertions of kinship between Australia and Britain existed alongside
articles designed to allay fears and thus contributed to the communication

---

19   L. Boys, 'Settling In', *Tomorrow's Australians. Bulletin of the Department of Immigration*,
      No.1 (12 April 1948). Canberra: Department of Immigration.
20   A. Calwell cited in 'Migrant flow twenty five times greater than year ago', *Tomorrow's
      Australians*, No. 1 (12 April 1948).
21   A. Calwell cited in 'Immigration minister tells what migrant types we want', *Tomorrow's
      Australians* (9 August 1948).

of mixed messages in the pages of promotional literature such as *Tomorrow's Australians*. The attentive reader could discern straws in the wind regarding the attitude of some Australians towards new arrivals. 'We Australians are prone to frown upon the advent of "the foreigner"', wrote Mr P. Wilkins, Federal Secretary of the Associated Chambers of Commerce of Australia and member of the Commonwealth Immigration Advisory Committee. 'Because of our geographic isolation we are possibly more insular than our British kinsfolk, whose proximity to the Continent makes them far more tolerant of the foreigner than Australians.'[22] The prospective migrant from the British Isles might have been forgiven for asking if he or she was indeed a 'foreigner' or not. Certainly, the advent of Australian citizenship in 1948 did not affect the status of Australians as British subjects and technically the 'alien-born' were not those born in the United Kingdom, a situation that persisted legally until 1999. So the prospective migrant would have had to look at more popular responses to discern the nature and extent of their inclusion and exclusion in the Australian community. Larry Boys brought up this subject on the pages of *Tomorrow's Australians* in June 1948. 'A correspondent has asked me what we are to do about ironing out expressions like Reffo, Dago, Eyetie, Yid and Pommy', concurring with the letter writer that 'tagging offensive names onto newcomers is one sure way of retarding their assimilation into the Australian community'.[23] However, Boys elides the disturbing implication that pommies could be lumped in with precisely the type of foreigner that English people themselves may have looked down upon in their homeland. This is not to say that all migrants from England experienced negative attitudes on their arrival in Australia. Hammerton and Thomson's research shows that for many English and British migrants, emigration to Australia was a liberating experience. Nevertheless, their research has also shown that a significant minority of 'ten pound poms', up to 25 per cent of all assisted migrants, returned to England for a variety of reasons, some disappointed with their time in Australia.[24]

22   P. Wilkins, 'Now is our golden opportunity to obtain needed population', *Tomorrow's Australians*, No. 2, 10 May 1948.
23   L. Boys, 'Settling in', *Tomorrow's Australians. Bulletin of the Department of Immigration*, No.3 (14 June 1948). Canberra: Department of Immigration.
24   Hammerton and Thomson, *The English In Australia*, 264.

England's Elusive Nationalism

It will be useful at this stage to introduce some discussion of the ways in which Englishness has been analysed in recent years in order to help explain the post-war English experience in Australia. In his *The Making of English National Identity*, Kumar argues that the English, to some extent consciously and systematically, played down their own sense of nationality because to emphasise their own nationality would have been a threat to the running of the multi-national state and empire of which they were the 'core nation'. Thus for Kumar, nation and empire are broadly incompatible and we see the emergence of a truly and explicitly English nationalism only at times when the empire was in crisis – especially the 1890s – and when the British state itself was undergoing significant constitutional change in response to nationalist pressures – as in the 1990s.[25] In short, empire inhibited English nationalism.

Kumar's argument has been extensively and robustly critiqued.[26] What is of value to this discussion of the English in Australia is Kumar's concept of the 'imperial nation', albeit with some modifications. 'Empires', writes Kumar, 'though in principle opposed to claims of nationality, may be the carriers of a certain kind of national identity which gives to the dominant groups a special sense of themselves and their destiny'.[27] Kumar cites several examples of this type of imperial nation in support of his argument: the Turks; the Austrians; the Russians and, of course, the English. We should, however, nuance this concept in two ways. Firstly, the idea of 'core' and 'peripheral' nations needs to be treated carefully. We should not always see the English as dominant, particularly when compared to other powerful national groups within the British state and Empire. Nor should we see places such as Australia as necessarily peripheral when it comes to the

25 K. Kumar, *The Making of English National Identity* (Cambridge: Cambridge University Press), 2003.
26 See for example the discussion of Kumar's arguments in *Nations and Nationalism*, 13 (2) (2007), 179–204.
27 Kumar, *The Making of English National Identity*, 33.

construction of Britishness. Paul Pickering has shown that where the Chartists failed in Great Britain, they succeeded in Australia, establishing the payment of MPs, the secret ballot, three-year (if not annual) parliaments and other aspects of the Chartist programme by the end of the nineteenth century.[28] In this way, ideas about liberty and democracy were not simply minted in England and exported to the Empire; they existed in a mutually reinforcing way which served to suggest that Empire, liberty and nationality were quite compatible.

Elsewhere, I have tried to argue that in Empire, Britishness and Englishness were not uneasy bedfellows, but were in fact merged.[29] The evidence from the English experience in Australia would seem to support this, in as much as English people were encouraged – when they thought about it at all – to think of themselves as part of a wider category of belonging than just the 'merely' national. It was membership of this wider community of Britons that allowed English people benefits such as subsidized migration to lands where meat was plentiful, housing was spacious and affordable and the sun made a regular appearance in the sky. In this way, 'the Empire' helped contribute to a general sense that England and Australia blended together in imperial and racial commonality.

Anglo-British Australians

For the English in Australia, this conception of Englishness and its relationship to other nationalities in the Empire or Commonwealth had two important consequences. The first was that some people did indeed fit in very quickly and unostentatiously. The other stemmed from a sense

28   P. Pickering, 'A wider field in a new country: Chartism in colonial Australia' in M. Sawer, ed., *Elections, Full, Free and Fair* (Annandale: The Federation Press 2001), 28–44.

29   See B. Wellings, 'Empire-nation: national and imperial discourse in England', *Nations and Nationalism*, 8 (1) (2002), 95–109 and B. Wellings, 'Rump Britain: Englishness and Britishness, 1992–2001', *National Identities*, 9 (4) (2007), 395–412.

of betrayal that the reception of English migrants was not was expected from 'kinsmen' such as Australians and that the English should not be considered as just another minority group. This position is underlined by looking at the United Kingdom Settlers' Association (UKSA) from its establishment in 1967 to the present day. UKSA was created as 'a non-political and non-denominational organization to represent the interests of all settlers from the United Kingdom'.[30] Here again was a capacious understanding of nationality. Unlike the Caledonian Society or other national societies, UKSA was 'non-denominational' and was designed to assist people from all over the British Isles. Some of its initial aims were practical, such as campaigning for the acceptance of UK degrees, diplomas and technical qualifications in Australia. Other aims were more open-ended such as 'cooperating with Federal and State Governments and Australians in general, with a view to overcoming prejudice and misunderstanding between settlers and existing residents'.[31] It was this latter concern that would dominate UKSA by the turn of the century.

One recurring theme of the first three years of UKSA's existence is that of the difficulty of mobilizing settlers from the UK into the organization. The Association struggled for support – literally at times. The 'Soccer Club News' from May 1970 bemoaned that 'the very few members who took the time and trouble to support their team saw a good game of soccer and thoroughly enjoyed themselves at the Supper Dance provided by the Yallourn Branch of UKSA'.[32] Cartoons and commentary in other newsletters worried at the lack of people acting as welcoming committees for new arrivals and a survey conducted by UKSA found that although recent arrivals on the piers at Melbourne's docks were pleased to see the UKSA Welcoming Group, 'the meeting on the pier did not register a lasting thought of the UKSA' and that 'not many people in the hostels join' the Association.[33]

---

30 *United Kingdom Settlers' Association Newsletter*, July 1969, National Archives of Australia.

31 *United Kingdom Settlers' Association Newsletter*, July 1969, National Archives of Australia.

32 *United Kingdom Settlers' Association Newsletter*, May 1970, National Archives of Australia.

33 *United Kingdom Settlers' Association Newsletter*, May 1970, National Archives of Australia.

The reason given for the latter observation was the not many people in the Commonwealth Hostels had access to a car and were therefore unable to get to UKSA social and administrative functions. Changing modes of transport may also have affected UKSA's ability to recruit lasting members. UKSA was established at the time when jet airliners started to replace sea liners as the main means of reaching Australia. Cheaper fares and shorter times to return 'home' may have weakened the cohesiveness of any incipient English or British group in Australia. One of UKSA's main roles in its early years was the arranging of charter flights back to the United Kingdom. Writing after a return to the UK for Christmas in 1968, the Association President Mr G. A. Howard, wrote that

> It was with deep pride that my wife and I greeted the Christmas Charter Flight when it arrived in London, I am sure that with the excitement of arriving and the frantic looking for relations we were not much noticed, but we did get some good films of the Members coming through the Customs Hall and with faces beaming, greeting their loved ones and friends.[34]

Such an oversight of the UKSA representatives might be understandable after a long flight on a Boeing 707, but the problem seemed to haunt UKSA. In July 1970, Howard wrote in the 'President's Message' that 'I am disappointed, however, with so few replies on the subject of "Headquarters" for the Association... and it surprises me that over 7000 members must feel indifferent to such a significant issue that concerns them. I am positive that ALL our members' interests are not solely on concession flights...'[35] This seeming difficulty for the Association to attract and interest membership beyond returning home does suggest a lack of cohesion amongst the target audience in Australia and one which can be explained beyond structural changes such as improving transport links between the England and Australia, and one on which the concept of England as an 'imperial nation' helps shed light.

34 *United Kingdom Settlers' Association Newsletter*, February 1969, National Archives of Australia.
35 *United Kingdom Settlers' Association Newsletter*, July 1970, National Archives of Australia.

Multiculturalism and the English

However, England was only one of the donor countries for migration into Australia in the decades after World War Two. Significant immigration also came from countries such as Italy and Greece as well as regions such as the Baltic States and Balkans. Initially, the policy of successive Australian governments was that of 'assimilation', whereby the migrants would ultimately speak English and abandon their own cultures in favour of an Anglo-Australian one.[36] As late as 1972, Prime Minister William McMahon re-stated the aims of Australia's immigration policies in the following terms:

> the aim of immigration policy remains the preservation in Australia of an essentially homogenous society. That means a society that does not have permanent minorities of people with extremely different backgrounds that will resist integration in the long-term. We want one Australian people, one Australian nation.[37]

However, this official policy of assimilation changed after December 1972 with the election of the reforming Labor government under the leadership of Gough Whitlam. Although the Whitlam government was ousted in 1975, the policy of 'multiculturalism' that replaced assimilation received bi-partisan support until the mid-1990s with the election of the Liberal-National Coalition in 1996. During this period, multiculturalism became an important feature of Australian society and politics, but one which conservatives feared would rob Australia of a strong sense of national community. In order to allay such concerns the National Agenda for Multicultural Australia of 1989 re-stated the fundamental position of the Australian government as such: 'Our British heritage is extremely important to us. It helps us define an Australian. It has a created a society that is remarkable

---

36   A. Davidson, *From Subject to Citizen. Australian Citizenship in the Twentieth Century* (Cambridge: Cambridge University Press, 1997), 122.

37   National Archives of Australia, File Name Immigration Policy (Part 10), 'Statement by the Prime Minister William McMahon, 4 May 1972'. Series Number A1838/399.

for the freedom it can give to its individual citizens. It is a large part of what makes Australia attractive to migrants and visitors.'[38] The report also emphasized that the purpose of policies of multiculturalism were not to dilute or undermine Australian national identity, but government and the bureaucratic capacities to 'respond flexibly to the needs of an ethnically mixed population.'[39]

This passage illustrates some of the difficulty that the English in Australia confronted when multiculturalism became established policy. Australia's British heritage meant that people from the Britain were already part Australian, a message that remained constant since the beginning of the assisted migration scheme in 1947 until the High Court's ruling in the *Sue v Hill* case of 1999. But their experience of migration often suggested otherwise. Furthermore, now that government policy was oriented towards the provision of services through organizations based on ethnic affiliation, the English, who never seemed to have considered themselves as an ethnic group, were ill-equipped to operate in such an environment. In a society where ethnicity and identity were important social categories, resentment emerged on behalf of groups who could not conceive of themselves easily in such terms. In late 1990s the UKSA changed its name to the British-Australian Community and shifted its activities from the 'non-political and non-denominational' organization of 1967 to promoting 'the past and present culture of the British Isles... with a view to overcoming prejudice and misunderstanding regarding British people and their descendants.'[40] The UKSA had drifted into a defensive posture, aimed at countering perceived Australian prejudice and an organization which, like BPARD in 2006, understood this discrimination in increasingly racial terms.

---

38   A. Davidson, *From Subject to Citizen*, 167.
39   Ibid.
40   British Australian Community, 'Constitutional Objectives', 2005. http://www.geocities.com/eandeavor_uksa/constitutional_objectives.html?200822, accessed 22 April 2008.

Home and Away

It is interesting to enquire as to how this reversal of race, from an ideology which initially bound Britons and Australians to one which ultimately divided them, came about. As the Assisted Migration Scheme continued, the English conception of themselves altered back in the 'home country' too. The issue of mass immigration *into* England, also from the late 1940s, started to play an important part in British and especially English self-identification. The English now began to see themselves, at times somewhat reluctantly and certainly resentfully, in more ethnic and racial terms. Enoch Powell, himself a one-time resident of Australia, reflected in 1958 on the emerging difference between the patterns of migration to Australia and the United Kingdom. 'Finding herself providentially lacking the elements of racial division,' wrote Powell on the twentieth anniversary of his arrival in Australia as Professor of Greek at Sydney University, 'yet able to achieve her national development without creating them, Australia would be worse than foolish if she did not jealously preserve the advantage of an all-white population', adding that 'there will be problems enough in the assimilation of the "new Australians" from Europe'.[41] From the 1960s Powell was instrumental in articulating the new way that race was situated within a national framework in England and Britain and it was this new, narrower deployment of race within rather than beyond national boundaries which began to impact on Anglo-British self-conceptions in Australia.

In the 1990s a newer sense of being English emerged in addition to this racialised one and one which was, in large measure, a response to the success of home rule and nationalist movements in Wales, Northern Ireland and Scotland. On a cultural level, much of this Englishness found expression in a carnival-esque support for the England football team, although some authors dispute that this support is anything more than ephemeral and is actually subordinate to stronger sources of identification with nationally-

41   E. Powell, 'Development Down Under', *The National and English Review*, August 1958: 67.

diverse football clubs providing a local loyalty or brand allegiance.[42] Unlike racially-derived notions of Anglo-Britishness, this newer form of identification did make the distinction between being English and British. It was also during the 1990s that the English in Australia did begin to organize themselves as explicitly English rather than British, notably as the group The English in Australia (TEA). TEA was formed in the mid 1990s coalescing around the concrete issue of non-transferable pension rights from the United Kingdom to Australia. Unlike the Royal Society of St George which was established in Melbourne in 1848 as an empire-loyalty organization, TEA is post-imperial and post-Assisted Migration. Another issue around which British identities in Australia became prominent was the so-called 'Forgotten Generation' of the estimated 150,000 children who were sent to Australia and other dominions under the Child Migrant Scheme, many of whom suffered emotional and physical abuse as a result and to whom Prime Minister Gordon Brown extended an official apology in February 2010.[43] But other expressions of a newer, merged Australo-Britishness were evident in the first decade of the twenty-first century. The Perth-based magazine, *Whingeing Pom*, set out to cater for migrants from the United Kingdom and introduced the notion of a 'Possie' (someone who holds dual nationality rather than being a permanent resident), a category which was explicitly framed in post-Assisted Migration terms:

> It is important to remember that a Possie is not a Pom. Poms are a purely migratory species that visit these shores only temporarily before returning to Britain. Possies, on the other hand, make the long flight just once, lured by the thought that whole swathes of land in Western Australia can be purchased for the price of a downstairs toilet in London.[44]

42   J. Abell; S. Condor; R. Lowe; S. Gibson; R. Stevenson, 'Who Ate All the Pride? Patriotic Sentiment and English National Football Support' in *Nations and Nationalism*, 13 (1) (2007), 97–116.

43   ABC News Online, 24 February 2010.

44   I Gerrard, 'I Possie', *Whingeing Pom*, March/April 2009: 80.

But even modern Possies felt the strain of the similarities between England and Australia, which set them apart from other migrant groups. 'We'll be buggered if we've moved 10,000kms away from friends and family,' wrote the *Whingeing Pom*'s editor Simon Hollway, 'only to end up in a sunnier version of Watford'.[45]

Conclusion

The conflated sense of being English and British became doubly important for the English in Australia. Encouraged in the post-war years to consider themselves British in order to ease their transition from England to Australia, English migrants were not in the habit of thinking of themselves as a distinct ethnic group. Rather, they were part of the 'imperial nation', one which had merged its sense of nationality with wider categories of belonging. Once the official Australian immigration policy and its attendant notion of social cohesion shifted from 'assimilation' to 'multiculturalism' in the 1970s, the English were ill-placed to fit into this new accommodation of difference in Australia. Thus even today, the English in Australia remain 'the same, but different'; keen to assert their difference, but reluctant to organize as an ethnic group. Their own post-war collective experience and the existing frameworks of their nationality have contributed to their ambiguous status in contemporary Australia's multicultural make-up.

45   S. Hollway, 'Welcome', *Whingeing Pom*, March/April 2009, 1.

TAMARA VAN KESSEL

14 'Britishness' as promoted by the British Council in the 1930s and 1940s

In 1934 the British Committee for Relations with Other Countries – soon known as the British Council – was created. Germany, France and Italy had already embarked in foreign cultural policy before the turn of the century by setting up cultural organizations which had comparable goals and which professed to be apolitical, non-governmental and of no religious denomination while each being to some degree co-financed by government funds. The British Foreign Office was well aware of the foreign cultural promotion other European states were engaged in, and gathered information about how much these spent in that field.[1]

Nevertheless, the unrestrained use of propaganda techniques by the British government in the First World War had made government involvement in cultural propaganda seem rather disreputable. During the First World War the House of Commons had questioned the appointment of Lord Beaverbrook, owner of the *Daily Express*, as Minister of Information and of two other press barons as directors of propaganda in enemy and allied territory. After the war, publications such as *Falsehood in War-time: Propaganda Lies of the First World War* (1928) by Arthur Ponsonby, caused a commotion by revealing how much false information had been spread in order to gain support for the British intervention and to incite hatred towards 'the Hun' (as the German enemy was portrayed).[2]

---

1   P. M. Taylor, *The Projection of Britain, British Overseas Publicity and Propaganda 1919–1939* (Cambridge: Cambridge University Press, 1981), 135–9.
2   A. Ponsonby, *Falsehood in War-time: Propaganda Lies of the First World War* (London: George Allen & Unwin, 1928). See also: G. S. Messinger, *British Propaganda and the State in the First World War* (Manchester: Manchester University Press, 1992);

Cultural affairs were on the whole seen as a matter of private initiative, not to be sustained by the state. Furthermore, there was a tendency to think that British international supremacy already spoke for itself and that boasting about cultural achievements was superfluous.[3]

Specific commercial and political motives eventually made the promotion of British culture abroad seem sufficiently necessary for the Treasury to agree with government investment in the creation of the British Council. The *D'Abernon Report* (1929), giving an account of a trade mission in South America, revealed that British commercial interests on that continent were waning because of the French, German, Italian and American active cultural penetration there. Concerns about Britain losing its prime position in the world were subsequently aggravated by the emergence of dictatorial regimes that threatened to endanger the stability of the European continent. Whereas the Council's above-mentioned European equivalents were formed in the hey-days of nationalist expansionism, the British organisation for cultural promotion became only feasible in the 1930s: that is, precisely in a decade that Britain witnessed acute ideological tensions in Europe and when the British Empire was undeniably in decline.[4]

The Council was created as a non-governmental body yet it fell under the wing of the Foreign Office. In time, the expectation was, the organization would be able to gather sufficient private funds to no longer need government grants. Now we know that it was to remain fully dependent on the Treasury for its existence. This meant that the Council officials had to keep convincing the Chancellor of the Exchequer that despite the economic hardship caused in part by the Great Depression, it was worth investing

M. Sanders and P. Taylor, *British Propaganda during the First World War, 1914–1918* (London: Macmillan, 1982).

3   R. A. Leeper, 'British Culture Abroad' in: *Contemporary Review* 148 (August 1935), 201; Harold Nicolson, 'The British Council 1934–1955', *Twenty-first Anniversary Report* (London 1955), 4.

4   Taylor, *The Projection of Britain*, 173; P. W. Doerr, *British Foreign Policy 1919–1939* (Manchester & New York: Manchester University Press, 1998), 2; J. Edmunds and B. S. Turner, *Generations, Culture and Society* (Buckingham & Philadelphia: Open University Press, 2002), 80.

in foreign cultural policy.[5] One of the motors behind the creation of the Council was the civil servant Rex Leeper, who became head of Foreign Office's News Department in 1935. He was known to have an excellent relationship with Robert Vansittart (Permanent Under-Secretary to the Foreign Office from 1930 to 1938) and Anthony Eden (Under-Secretary of State for Foreign Affairs from 1931 to 1934, then Foreign Secretary until 1938). The most influential leader of the British Council, George Lloyd (Chairman from 1937 to 1941), had been Governor of Bombay and High Commissioner to Egypt. There was no denying that the Council's ties with the government, and in particular the Foreign Office, were strong. Unsurprisingly, the social background of most officials working for the British Council was similar to that of Foreign Office recruits, who in the interwar period still nearly all came from the pool of Eton and 'Oxbridge' as well as belonging for a large part to the British aristocracy or gentry. It is said of Vansittart's view of diplomacy that it was 'relentlessly Edwardian', perceiving the international arena 'as a vast extension of London's clubland, where all the members obeyed certain accepted rules'.[6]

This chapter explores the specific image of British culture that British Council promoted and considers how these images reflected the interests and political background of those managing the Council's cultural policy. For an organization that repeatedly claimed not to be engaged in propaganda but to merely 'make the life and thought of the British peoples more widely known abroad; and to promote a mutual interchange of knowledge and ideas with other peoples' the British Council presented a remarkably consistent image of what it considered to be Britain's essential qualities.[7] The icons of this constructed imago can be traced in two of the British Council's publications: the review *Britain To-day* and the series *British Life and Thought*.

5   F. Donaldson, *The British Council: The First Fifty Years* (London: Jonathan Cape, 1984), 29, 32, 57–63.

6   Doerr, *British Foreign Policy, 1919–193*, 137.

7   The British Council Report by The Rt. Hon. Lord Eustace Percy, M. P. of Activities from 1st April 1936 to 15th July 1937, BW 151, British Council Registered Files, The National Archives.

Format and Circulation of *Britain To-day*
and *British Life and Thought*

The first issue of *Britain To-day* appeared in March 1939. The purpose of
this review, as expressed in the foreword of its first issue, was 'to bring the
friends and, for that matter, the critics of Great Britain into closer touch
with current happenings in our country'.[8] As the title suggests, its prime
focus was on the current developments in British society, from innovative
approaches in industry and in local or central government, to cultural
movements. Providing this information was deemed beneficial for the
world at large, for were not all nations facing similar challenges of the
modern world? In spite of political and cultural difference, *Britain To-day*
argued, did not all countries have the task of: 'improving and adjusting the
civilization handed down to us by our ancestors: a civilization which has a
common basis although its expression takes different forms suited to the
genius of particular peoples'.[9] It was a question of sharing best practices
and of offering the fruits of British civilisation to its Dominions, Colonies
and the world at large. In giving such information, *Britain To-day* claimed
to be providing a background to the ordinary news.[10] In the foreword
there was also a clear invitation to send comments and suggestions for any
subjects that readers wished to see further explained.

Britain To-day generally contained three articles and a number of
photographs or drawings: in total sixteen pages of reading-matter and four
pages of illustrations. The articles were free of copyright, presumably with
the intent of encouraging the reprinting of the content by foreign press.
Initially it was a fortnightly publication, but as of January 1942 it became

8   Foreword, *Britain To-day*, Number 1 (17 March 1939) 1.
9   Ibid. 1. Note that this quotation seems to suggest there was some influence noticeable
     of the Boasian anthropological idea of the uniqueness of each culture, as opposed to
     the more traditional British concept of different stages of development in a universal
     human civilization. (See P. Mandler, *The English National Character* (New Haven:
     Yale University Press, 2006), 157–9.)
10   Ibid. 2.

an extended monthly publication. To start with, *Britain To-day* had a print run of five thousand and was distributed for free to 'carefully selected mailing lists'.[11] With 68,000 copies in 1941 and more than 120,000 in 1934, the circulation reflected a steady increase in popularity. The review was (in some cases intermittently) published in several languages besides English: French, German, Italian, Spanish and Portuguese. Most of its readers were located in Europe's neutral countries, the United States of America and South America.[12]

The projected series of brochures on *British Life and Thought* was first mentioned in February 1938.[13] The series was created by the publisher Stanley Unwin (a member of the Council's Books and Periodicals Committee) who was opposed to censorship and concerned about the rise of Nazi Germany. The brochures were meant to be readable, informative essays, written by experts on the subject matter, richly illustrated with photographs, and to be sold singly, at a shilling per booklet. In 1940 the first ten booklets appeared, all of them devoted to specific British institutions from the system of government to sport and games. Each booklet, as described on the back cover, was to be:

> complete in itself, and taken together they provide a unique account of the life and work, the ideas and ideals, of Britain today. The English reader will find them as informative as they are stimulating. For the foreign reader who has never visited Britain they are *the best substitute for such a visit, and they will go far to make plain to him how life is lived in this country, how the British Commonwealth of Nations is organised, and in what spirit Britain now stands for liberty and justice throughout the world.*[14]

11   D. Eastment, 'The Policies and Position of the British Council from the Outbreak of War from 1950', PhD thesis, University of Leeds, 1982, 58.

12   Ibid. 59–60; A. Byrne, '"Boosting Britain": Démocratie et propagande culturelle, Britain To-Day 1939–1954', PhD thesis, Université de Provence, Aix-Marseille 2010, 85–97.

13   Minutes of the 7th meeting of the Books and Periodicals Committee, 3 February 1938, BW 70/1, British Council Registered Files, The National Archives.

14   The Earl Baldwin of Bewdley, *The Englishman* (Edinburgh; Longmans, Green and Co. Ltd., 1940). Emphasis added.

Admittedly, these two publications give only the official view within the British Council of how British culture was to be presented to the outside world. Enough has been written about the propagandist nature of the review and about the controversies that this occasionally provoked among the Council staff.[15] However, though the archival sources do not give a complete picture of how the content of the publications was decided, we must assume there was some degree of consensus both among British Council staff and at the Foreign Office on the proposed image of British culture or else it would not have been so consistent. The focus here is this image and how it justified the promotion of British language and culture across the world.

The Ministry of Information, from which the Council was able to remain independent, was created in 1937.[16] Though being two different organizations, both had to appeal at least in part to the predominant ideals of the 1930s if their proposed icons were to be convincing. Hence it is not surprising that much of the imagery used by the British Council, though projected abroad, coincides with depictions of nationhood and British-ness used to motivate the British home front during the Second World War.[17] The recurring themes of this imagery and the portrayal of Britain and Britishness in the world will now be explored.

15   Byrne, 'Boosting Britain', 10–21; Eastment, 'The Policies and Positions of the British Council', 60.

16   In the summer of 1939 the British Council was able to reverse and hold back initial plans for it to be absorbed by the Ministry of Information (Donaldson, *The British Council*, 68–81; Taylor, *The Projection of Britain*, 283–4).

17   S. O. Rose, *Which People's War? National Identity and Citizenship in Britain 1939–1945* (Oxford & New York: Oxford University Press, 2003); W. Webster, *Englishness and Empire 1939–1965* (Oxford & New York: Oxford University Press, 2007) 19–54.

Britain and European or World Civilization

One recurring idea was that of Great Britain being the custodian and beacon of European civilization. As was emphatically stated in a 1939 issue of *Britain To-day*: 'It is not too much to say that, with the increasing pace of modern life, the people of Great Britain have become increasingly aware of the value to their own and to European civilization of maintaining the standards and the inheritance received from their forefathers'.[18]

Such references to the way Great Britain was to engage itself in defending European civilization stressed the *tradition* that it had to preserve but also called for the constant interaction with external cultural influences to maintain the *dynamism* of the civilization. This seemingly contradictory mission was, for example, illustrated by an editorial entitled 'In the Defence of Culture' which appeared in *Britain To-day* in April 1943, in the middle of the Second World War. It explicitly spoke of the rival claim among nations for primacy in creating what could be named European culture, Western culture or modern culture.[19] The author went on to say that this European civilization had always been subject to a rapid circulation of ideas and that it was indeed important to stimulate this openness. Such cultural dynamism coincided with the cultural mission expressed by the renowned Victorian poet Matthew Arnold, paraphrased in the editorial as 'a disinterested endeavour to learn and propagate the best that is known and thought in the world, and thus to establish a current of fresh and true ideas'.[20] European cultural heritage – defined as being based on the Roman conception of law, the Greek conception of freedom of thought, and the religious conception of love and the sanctity of the individual soul – could benefit from contact with the new worlds of North and South America, as well as with the ancient worlds of Russia and China.

---

18   Un-named author, 'Preserving the Past' in: *Britain To-day*, Number 7 (9 June 1939), 16.
19   The Editor, 'In the Defence of Culture' in: *Britain To-day*, Number 84 (April 1943), 3.
20   Ibid. 3–4.

By the end of the war, the literary scholar Benjamin Ifor Evans in an article entitled 'Great Britain and Western Europe' regretted the wartime isolation between countries in Western Europe and praised pamphlets such as *Britain To-day* that had tried to break through it by making known the new cultural climate in Britain.[21] It was in this crisis of Western civilization that, according to Evans, Great Britain had discovered her unique role. The 'prolonged stay within her shores of distinguished representatives of all the occupied countries' had made many British men and women aware, more than ever before in their lives, of 'their common heritage with Europe' and of the 'conception of Western Europe as a community with common spiritual origins'.[22] Whereas in peacetime the cultural agencies in any country would usually be in charge of presenting their own national history and cultural inheritance, a different task was now required from them.

> Rather than the discovery and the emphasis on what is best in the national tradition, there should be the exploration of what the common European inheritance possesses. ... England, by the very fact that its internal problems are momentarily less severe than those of other European countries, can serve Europe by being one of the prime participators, and the depository for the European idea.[23]

The British proposals for the setting up of a Conference of Inter-Allied Ministers and an Association of University Professors of the Allied Countries were to be seen against this background.

It was not only Europe that was seen to benefit from Great Britain's endeavours in the defence of European civilization; humanity at large was expected to be a grateful recipient of the fruits this would bear.[24] Evans sketched a world where technological advances had so greatly increased

21   B. Ifor Evans, 'Great Britain and Western Europe' in: *Britain To-day*, Number 112 (August 1945) 10–14.

22   Ibid. 12.

23   Ibid. 13.

24   Ibid. 10–14; 'Let us therefore look at the man who will take his stand for civilisation, not of his own country but of Europe: not of Europe, as will one day be recognised, but of the world'. Earl Baldwin, 'The Englishman' in: *British Life and Thought* (London, New York, Toronto; Longmans Green & Co. 1941), 458.

international contact that a mental and spiritual transformation towards worldwide cultural understanding was needed. Western European culture was not to be exclusive. Certain European principles, deriving from Christianity, such as the 'supreme value of the individual man' were considered by Evans as being by now so universally accepted that they could serve as a basis for humanity as a whole, no matter what religion.[25] However, part of the consistent image of Britain spread by the British Council was the belief that it did not wish to export abstract ideological principles, but rather good practice that had proven to be such simply through experience:

> He [the Englishman] has instructed other races committed to his charge in the only school with which he is familiar, the school of self-government, not from any high moral motives, but for purely practical reasons.

> Self-government is the Englishman's ideal because it seems to him more likely to work than government imposed from above. The Englishman is not interested in theories of government; he wants results. ... The English are varied in their practice, but uniform in their aim. They are the least ideological nation in the world, but they are the most consistent in pursuing their ultimate aims.[26]

And so with this same practical sense, the British 'preached' to other countries the 'cult of games and pastimes'.[27] Through the British Admiralty Charts they put their hydrographic information to the service of the whole world.[28] Similarly, it was seen as wisest in Britain's relations with the Commonwealth, to offer means by which the Dominions and the Colonies could learn to govern themselves and reach greater prosperity. The African 'native' had to be encouraged to 'rise in the scale of civilization' or else he would be doomed to an even more hopeless condition.[29] The British

25   Evans, 'Great Britain and Western Europe', 13.
26   'The English Way of Life' in: *Britain To-day*, Number 7 (9 June 1939) 1–3, 2.
27   B. Darwin, 'British Sport and Games' in: *British Life and Thought* (London, New York, Toronto: Longmans Green & Co. 1941), 279 and 295.
28   M. Lewis, 'British Ships and British Seamen' in: *British Life and Thought* (London, New York, Toronto; Longmans Green & Co. 1941), 345.
29   Unnamed author, 'British Rule in Tropical Africa' in: *Britain To-day*, Number 3 (14 April 1939) 1–8, 7.

Colonies would through self-government grow stronger in character and become more self-reliant, learning from their mistakes as they went along.[30] Nevertheless, although the Council publications underscored the image of Britain being 'the least ideological nation in the world', after a critical analysis of the themes they dealt with a number of values can be identified that were evidently considered typically British yet exemplary worldwide. We shall now have a closer look at these.

Freedom, Democracy and Peace

One of the essential values that British culture was felt to represent and that was considered of supreme importance for all civilization was that of freedom. It was portrayed as the guiding principle both within Britain's own system of government[31] and that of the British Commonwealth.[32] In *Britain To-day* it was emphasized that the communities of the British Commonwealth of Nations were 'freely and closely associated with one another' and that there was free co-operation but no compulsion.[33] Thereby the policy of the British Commonwealth was contrasted to that of the French, characterised as aimed at making the Africans adapt where possible to the social and cultural institutions of French civilization.[34] The Commonwealth was said to be built on the willingness to benefit from

---

30   A. Berriedale Keith, 'The British Commonwealth of Nations' in: *British Life and Thought* (London, New York, Toronto; Longmans Green & Co. 1941), 20.

31   W. A. Robson, 'The British System of Government' in: *British Life and Thought* (London, New York, Toronto; Longmans Green & Co. 1941), 80.

32   'Commonwealth', the author felt, was as term more preferable than Empire because it underlined the aspect of voluntary choice. (Keith, 'The British Commonwealth', 1 and 8.)

33   Unnamed author, 'The British Commonwealth of Nations' in: *Britain To-day*, Number 2 (31 March 1939) 1–7.

34   'British Rule in Tropical Africa', 6.

British cooperation, not on brutal conquest like the Empires of Alexander, Charlemagne, the Ottomans or Napoleon.[35] In the *British Life and Thought* booklet *British Ships and British Seamen*, glossing over many a historical fact, it was candidly stated that after having erroneously upheld Mercantile Theory, Britain discovered free trade and the concurrent need for freedom of the seas. The *Pax Britannica* had henceforth defended trade and worldwide freedom: Great Britain had become the 'policeman' of the seas, 'big and good-tempered' such as British police were, there to protect the public and prevent evil deeds.[36]

In this representation of things, Great Britain invested in the *Pax Britannica* not just in its own interest but in the interest of all nations.[37] Great Britain's global commitment to freedom was said to be demonstrated among other things by the leading role it played in the abolition of slavery: 'What the opening-up [of the "Dark Continent"] would have meant, not only to millions of coloured people who inhabit it, but also to world-civilisation as a whole, had slavery remained the normal procedure of the white pioneers, it is terrible to contemplate.'[38]

Britain saved the world from this 'by making the discovery, on the nick of time, that the Black Man has a soul.'[39] Besides mentioning the aid given to freedom-fighting Greeks and Italians seeking national independence, British love of liberty was also reflected in the contemporary dislike for dictatorship. Subtle references were made to the way in which British freedom was totally incompatible with dictatorial state systems. For example, the *British Life and Thought* booklet on British education, in stating that the mass production of ideas was entirely foreign to British culture, portrayed its education system as one of 'genuine freedom' and with which 'the State has no axe to grind.'[40]

---

35   Lewis, 'British Ships', 334.
36   Ibid. 334–6.
37   Ibid. 340.
38   Lewis, 'British Ships', 349.
39   Ibid.
40   Ibid. 351–3; J. E. Hales, 'British Education' in: *British Life and Thought* (London, New York, Toronto; Longmans Green & Co. 1941), 169.

The best safeguard for the freedom of the individual and the nation was held to be democracy. *The British System of Government* made very clear how central democracy was to what the British Council considered as being British. The sovereignty of Parliament was presented as 'the cornerstone of the British Constitution'. The ultimate sovereignty within Parliament belonged to the House of Commons, of which almost anyone could become a member. The author conceded that the House of Lords, with its privileged members, was something of an anachronism, but explained that no alternative to this body had so far been found that would suit all parties, thereby reiterating the positive notion of compromise.[41] In underlining the importance of debate and openly expressed criticism in Parliament, there was an overt reference to totalitarian states, where dictators were made to appear infallible and the media were prevented from voicing any criticism.[42] Even more explicit was the assurance that, unlike in totalitarian states, the citizen in Great Britain was free from fear of arrest by secret police, imprisonment without trial, unformulated offences and political censorship.[43]

Again, as in other institutions, the adage in democracy was that it was based on experience and not on an intellectual theory, and was the result of a compromise between ancient forms and modern needs. Hence, as was stated in an issue of *Britain To-day*, it was not because of some abstract theory that the British had chosen their political system but on the basis of present experience.[44] It was hereby repeatedly added that there was no wish to impose British views on others or to disparage other systems, but that it was simply 'from the evidence of fact' that British people knew that a democratic government had created the best opportunities, giving them the habit of enterprise and self-help: 'We speak for ourselves without wishing to impose our views on others – we have been brought by the facts

---

41   Robson, 'The British System of Government', 55.
42   Ibid, 61.
43   Ibid, 76.
44   Unnamed author, 'Democracy in a Changing World' in: Britain Today, Number 1 (17 March 1939) 2–3.

of to-day to a reaffirmation of our fundamental democratic liberties'.[45] By not being dependent on an authoritarian central authority, the British had become particularly capable of coping with crises.

However great the praise was for government institutions such as Parliament or the system of justice, a deep-seated belief in the importance of private initiative underpinned the way Britain was presented. In examining social services, the assertion was that 'in this respect the totalitarian countries differ from democracies not in the amount of "social service" provided, but in the methods by which this service is organized, the scope allowed to private initiative'.[46] Whereas under a totalitarian system social services were frequently used 'as instruments to create a servile mentality', in Great Britain they were 'the jealously guarded responsibilities of scores of democratic bodies and of tens of thousands of public spirited citizens'.[47] The leading idea in Great Britain was to diffuse the spirit of leadership instead of concentrating it, allowing a multitude of self-governing private initiatives to cooperate with State or local authorities. The contribution of private organizations, with or without state help or patronage, was commended as one of the most interesting and characteristic features of British democracy. An enormous number of voluntary associations were able to participate in shaping both legislation and administration, thereby teaching individuals 'a valuable lesson of self-government'.[48] This room for private initiative was a longstanding tradition, but also something that was regarded as the solution to the problems of the future: 'In our opinion, the future course of history in the twentieth century will be determined largely by the success or failure of this blending of public and private activity, of which we in Great Britain can show so many examples'.[49] Even the most

45   Ibid, 5.
46   Unnamed author, 'Voluntary Social Service' in: *Britain To-day*, Number 2 (31 March 1939) 13–15, 13.
47   A. D. K. Owen, 'British Social Services' in: *British Life and Thought* (London, New York, Toronto; Longmans Green & Co. 1941) 173–216, 186.
48   'Democracy in a Changing World, 4; 'Preserving the Past', 11; Robson, 'The British System of Government', 57.
49   'Democracy in a Changing World', 8.

vital infrastructure for British trade and for the Empire – the Navy – was
to a large extent dependent on the voluntary service of British seamen,
with as notable example the role ordinary British seamen had played in
the successful retreat from Dunkirk.[50]

What was purportedly the objective of letting the world know about
British attachment to (individual) freedom and democracy? Right from the
start, the British Council justified its existence by arguing that informing
people abroad about British culture and society and sharing ideas would
contribute to world peace. As stated in a policy paper of 1937: 'the Council's policy is inspired by their belief in the decisive contribution which
the character, ideals and achievement of the British people can make to
the cause of peace and peaceful trade; and by the desire that the nature of
this contribution shall be understood and appreciated by the rest of the
world'.[51]

This concept of *Pax Britannica* was part of the parallels that British
civil servants were taught to see between the Ancient Roman Empire and
the British civilizing mission in its Empire.[52] There is evidence however
of a preference in Council publications to emphasize the affinity with the
Athenian model of colonisation, to distance itself from the aggressiveness
of the Roman expansion. Hence the Commonwealth is described as having
since its earliest days 'had closer affinities to the Empire of Athens in the
fifth century B. C. than to that of Rome': at no times had it resembled that
of Rome, 'the result of the subjugation of foreign peoples' and control over
them by force.[53] This Athenian 'turn' was possibly a reaction to a revived
Pax Romana Mussolini aspired to in the context of Italian Fascism's cult
of 'romanità'.[54]

---

50   Lewis, 'British Ships and British Seamen', 331 and 356–7.

51   *The Work of the Council. Its History, Present Programme and Future Policy* (London,
     January 1937) 6 in: The National Archives, British Council Registered Files, BW
     2/112.

52   R. Hingley, *Roman Officers and English Gentlemen. The Imperial Origins of Roman
     Archaeology* (London & New York: Routledge, 2000) 9–10, 52–3 and 70–1.

53   Keith, 'The British Commonwealth', 8–9.

54   R. Visser, 'Fascist Doctrine and the Cult of Romanità' in: *Journal of Contemporary
     History* 27: 1 (1992) 5–22.

The Harmony of Hierarchy

Another value that the British Council publications were geared to underline was that of the social harmony of the British nation. In *The British System of Government* as well as *The Englishman*, such qualities as tolerance, justice and fair-play were attributed to the British as well as a willingness to take into account the voice of all minorities. This spirit of tolerance and consent was given as explanation for why the Marxist philosophy of class war had made little progress in Britain. In the field of industrial relations, for example, the voluntary negotiation between trade unions and employers' associations was said to have prevented any clashes from arising.[55] Hence, 'politics in England is one long essay in the gentle art of compromise, English education one long lesson in the business of avoiding extremes of conduct or thought'.[56]

The authors touching on the subject of class did not deny that there were huge differences between classes in British society, but nevertheless concluded that there was a fundamental harmony in this arrangement. There was in their view no hatred between classes.[57] The upheaval of the Cromwell period had made any notion of revolution repellent to the British ever since and had created a stronger sense of community. Subsequently the middle classes had recognized the need for social reform for the proletariat, just as the unions had regarded the weapon of the strike to be avoided at all costs. It was proudly pointed out that no major strike had taken place in Great Britain since 1926.[58] Gradual reform had been notable in the poor relief, in social housing and in education. All parties agreed that more was to be gained through constitutional means than through violence or revolution.[59]

55   Robson, 'The British System of Government', 77.
56   Ibid, 78.
57   The Editor, 'Step by Step' in: *Britain To-day*, Number 81 (January 1943) 1–4.
58   Ibid, 2–3.
59   Ibid, 3–4.

That not everyone agreed with this view of British society was proven by the need for Ernest Barker, in his review of *The English People: Impressions and Observations*, to deal with the accusation made by critics of English life that England failed as a social democracy because of its class-divisions, each class being identified through accent, manner of speech, posture or gesture.[60] Describing himself as 'one who was born and bred, and lived for a quarter of a century, within ten miles of Manchester, among cotton-factories and coal-pits (in which, by the way, his mother and father worked)', Barker put forward quite a different experience; that of an 'industrial democracy' where masters and men regarded one another 'as being of the same stuff'. The social structure was based on mutual respect and acceptance of each individual's specific position. Barker did not see this as being hierarchical or snobbish but in fact 'genuinely democratic'. Each had his or her pride in sticking to the position he or she naturally fell in, be it that of a domestic servant or that of a scavenger. These positions were part of 'the pageant, or solemnity, of English life', as old as the sixteenth century and as old as the English Book of Common Prayer which taught that each person had a duty assigned to him or her by God.[61] *The British System of Government* presented a less roundabout way of resolving the issue of class differences. While conceding that enormous inequalities of wealth, birth and opportunity existed in Britain, the conclusion drawn by the author was that the 'truth of the matter appears to be that the people of Britain do not care greatly for social and economic equality'.[62]

Besides this idea of harmony between social classes, British society was also portrayed as having peacefully incorporated different nations. Officially the United Kingdom of Great Britain and Northern Ireland

---

60   Ernest Barker, 'The English People' in: *Britain To-day*, Number 87 (July 1943) 15–19. *The English People* (New York: Alfred A. Knopf, 1943) was written by a Scotsman, Denis William Brogan, and was intended for the American public. No doubt the combination of these two factors explains Brogan's critical approach to British so-called social harmony.

61   Ibid, 17–18.

62   Robson, 'The British System of Government', 79.

encompassed English, Welsh, Scottish and Irish populations.[63] Did the British Council publications make its readers aware of the internal cultural diversity of what was frequently simply referred to as 'Britain'? The terms 'British' and 'English' were more often than not used as interchangeable qualifications, as if 'Englishness' was unquestionably the essence of 'Britishness'. This tendency to equate 'Britishness' with 'Englishness', whilst reducing the Welsh, the Scots or the Irish to the peripheral status of Celtic 'other', was part and parcel of identity building in the British imperial context.[64] One can also recognize in the Council's publications the idea of Britain being a racially-mixed nation, combining the racial virtues of the Britons, Romans, Danes, Saxons and Normans to forge a united Britain, in which however the English appear to have been the prime inheritors of Roman civilization.[65] However, the impression that the British Council was intent on presenting to the world 'this false idea of Britain as a "homogeneous" nationality which was, of course, entirely English in concept' needs a certain nuance.[66]

Even if nearly all articles of *Britain To-day* either dealt with British or with English matters, this review by no means presented Britain as a monolithic phenomenon. There was also occasional attention for the specifically Scottish, Welsh or even Irish heritage. For example, one article opened with the recent publication of the official biography of W. B. Yeats, arguing that it was hard to make a clear-cut distinction between English

---

63   The Act of Union of 1707 had unified the Kingdoms of England and Scotland, including also Wales, and was followed by another Act of Union in 1801 that added Ireland to this United Kingdom. Since 1927, the year in which the partition brought about by the Irish War of Independence was recognized by Parliament, this political territory became known as the United Kingdom of Great Britain and Northern Ireland.

64   Murray G. H. Pittock, *Celtic Identity and the British Image* (Manchester & New York: Manchester University Press, 1999) 6–12; Ian Baucom, *Out of Place. Englishness, Empire and the Locations of Identity* (1999) 80; Hingley, *Roman Officers*, 65–8.

65   Baldwin, *The Englishman*, 12. Compare with: Hingley, *Roman Officers*, 162.

66   Peter Berresford Ellis, 'When was the United Kingdom?', Lecture under the auspices of the University of Reading's Town Hall Lecture Series on The United Kingdom, Reading, 19 January 2004.

and Irish literature. Yeats' 'imagination in youth' was described as being 'fired by the Irish scene and Irish legend' and his concentration on Ireland undeniable, but it was added that he owed much to English poetry and the English writers with whom he interacted.[67] The Irish literary movement, in the words of the editor, was 'an expression of the distinctively Irish genius,' which contributed in its own way to British literature, yet would never have emerged without the background of English literature and in a way discovered itself through the awareness of being different, of having a separate individuality.[68] The author then went on to argue that just as there were rival claims among the English, the Irish, the Scottish and the Welsh regarding certain elements of British culture, so too different countries claimed their contributions to the creation of European culture. There was recognition of the fact that Great Britain was a composite of parts.

Admittedly such an article still implied that English culture stood above the rest. Rather like the different classes each had their own position within England, so too the different nations fitted into Great Britain. It is well imaginable how such thinking in terms of a harmonious hierarchy of classes or countries could easily be transposed to the Empire and Britain's relationship with its colonies, justifying in noble words what was in fact cultural domination. Yet there are equally examples of Council publications that recognised difference without obviously reducing it to a subjugated 'otherness'. For example, in *British Sport and Games* the author described rugby football in South Wales as giving vent to intense local patriotism and producing 'an almost religious enthusiasm', thereby confessing that he too having some Welsh blood in himself became wholly Welsh whenever he was at a match the involving the Welsh team.[69] It is perhaps useful to recall what the historian Linda Colley wrote in her much-praised *Britons. Forging the Nation 1707–1837* about the Scots being until this day unusually well represented in Britain's Foreign Office and its diplomatic service.[70]

---

67   The Editor, 'The Defence of Culture', 1.
68   Ibid, 1–2.
69   Darwin, 'British Sport and Games', 293.
70   Linda Colley, *Britons. Forging the Nation 1707–1837* (New Haven and London: Yale University Press, 1992; 2005) 132.

The effects of this phenomenon as well as the fact that Charles Bridge, the Council's Secretary General, was of Irish origin may have made it harder for the Council publications to ignore the 'Celtic fringe' entirely.

Contrasts between past and future, as well as between rural and urban life, are also ably reconciled by Council publications to form an impression of harmony. In British war propaganda the Southern English countryside was often conflated with Britain and made to represent 'authentic England' unchanged by time.[71] In a *Britain To-day* article tellingly entitled 'Preserving the Past', the English countryside was described as being 'studded with the remains of every period from prehistoric times onwards' and village names, their buildings and their boundaries as 'redolent of the past'.[72] This was attributed to the insular character of the nation and its relatively peaceful internal history. Concern was voiced about the damage the industrial revolution and the modern urbanisation could cause, for which the remedy was sought in educating town-dwellers to a greater degree about the unspoilt character of rural districts and in private as well as government initiatives to protect the landscape.[73] To interpret such portrayals of the English landscape as pure nostalgia would be to ignore the actual response to the changing of times that is expressed in the Council's combined attention for urban and rural planning.[74] Plenty of triumphant articles were dedicated to modern urban planning projects, to the development of new, functional housing and public buildings. For example, *Britain To-day* took the opportunity to present innovative projects in urban planning and reconstruction that had been executed or were intended for after the end of the war. Already in 1941, one could read that a new era in housing development would begin once the war ended. The destruction caused by the bombing of London and other big cities had 'provided an opportunity for creative town-planning and reconstruction unequalled since the aftermath of the Great Fire'.[75]

---

71   Rose, *Which People's War*, 198–218.
72   'Preserving the Past' in: *Britain To-day*, Number 7 (9 June 1939) 10–16, 10.
73   Ibid, 11.
74   In the 1930s and 1940s the campaigns for what was a modern experience of rural life went hand in hand with those for modern urbanity (David Matless, *Landscape and Englishness* (London: Reaktion Books, 1998) 32–3).
75   Owen, 'British Social Services', 205.

Truth Will Triumph

The British Council's motto was 'Truth will Triumph'. Propaganda was allegedly not needed; the facts would speak for themselves. Hence there was no wish on the part of *Britain To-day* to focus on the organization of defence in Great Britain, on the resources it possessed in its Empire and on its military endurance. Generally the review would provide 'a description of the more positive and fruitful developments in spheres of other activity than those of preparation to defend'.[76] Articles on military subjects and photographs of munitions factories, the British Navy and women involved in military activities were, nevertheless, certainly not lacking.

The Council strongly condemned the relentless German propaganda in the Middle East, which was spreading false rumours and news to discredit the British. In an article in the 1941 BBC Handbook, Harold Nicolson, Parliamentary Secretary to the Ministry of Information insisted that there had to be British propaganda too. However, instead of creating slavish, unthinking opinion and appealing to the lowest in human nature, as was the case with the deceitful German propaganda, the British democratic propaganda would be a long term one 'seeking gradually to fortify the intelligence of the individual'.[77] British propaganda would rest on truthfulness: 'It must seek to build up an unshakable edifice of ascertained fact which will defy falsification and rumour. ... Concealing nothing that can safely be disclosed, it invites the free-minded men to whom it appeals to form their opinion in the light of realities'.[78]

At the end of the Second World War, reflecting on how the age of internationalism had begun in 1935–9 and how more than ever people of all countries had found themselves talking about the same issues and challenges, the editor of *Britain To-day* concluded that the cure for the

---

76   'Democracy in a Changing World', 8.
77   Nicolson as quoted in: The Editor, 'Propaganda', *Britain To-day*, Number 50 (4 April 1941) 1–3, 2.
78   Ibid.

post-War world 'lies not in less but in more internationalism'. The press had to be free, intellectual, social and economic barriers removed and the 'malignant giants of ignorance' destroyed. This attitude implied a great confidence in the capacity of the individual to evaluate facts and in the notion that worldwide communication benefited from open cultural exchange.[79] The example of a totalitarian state in Germany had shown that spiritual slavery could be imposed whereas spiritual freedom could by no means be enforced. Although totalitarianism had been militarily defeated, its evil had not yet been entirely extinguished and 'complete victory remains to be won, not by force of arms, but by reason, by right thinking, by the persuasion of sound example'.[80]

Conclusion

The British Council publications consistently presented Britain as the custodian of European or Western civilization; a state free of authoritarian traits, wishing to bring the values of freedom, democracy and peace to the world. Arguing that contemporary technological advances in communication called for worldwide cultural understanding, the Council justified its presentation of British life and thought abroad as being part of this dialogue between nations. By subsequently paying attention to themes such as the voluntary participation of former colonies in the Commonwealth of Nations or Britain's tradition of harmonious cooperation between social classes as well as between private and public initiatives, the Council publications further solidified the myth of British disinterested engagement in international order. Given the trouble that Britain was having in

79   The Editor, 'Before War, And After' in: *Britain To-day*, Number 111 (July 1945) 1–4.
80   The Editor, 'The Mind of a Nazi – The Nuremberg Trials' in: *Britain To-day*, Number 122 (June 1946) 1–4,4.

maintaining its military and economic grip on important areas such as India and Egypt, it appears that the British Council came conveniently into existence just as Britain had to seek for new ways of legitimising its global power.

Simultaneously, the Council was set up in response to the active foreign cultural policy that especially Nazi Germany and Fascist Italy were developing in Britain's sphere of influence. Vansittart was outspokenly against the 'appeasement' policy that prevailed under Neville Chamberlain's premiership (1937–40) and instead wished to see Hitler firmly dealt with. Rex Leeper's close ties with Vansittart and the active engagement in the Council of critics of appeasement such as Harold Nicolson, would suggest that the Council was in favour of an anti-Nazi stance. However, Leeper's own conclusions on the question of ideology are indicative for the ambiguity that remained. For Leeper it was not ideologies that mattered most but holding back those countries whose nationalist ambitions threatened to bring war to Europe.[81] Nevertheless, despite all claims that the Council was not engaging in propaganda, that Britain was led by pragmatism rather than abstract ideas, and that it wanted truth to triumph, the images conveyed by *Britain To-day* and the *British Life and Thought Series* leave no doubt that with the creation of the Council Britain had joined the ideological battlefield.

81   Donald Lammers, 'Fascism, Communism, and the Foreign Office, 1937–39' in: *Journal of Contemporary History* 6 (3) (1971) 66–86, 72–3.

Post Imperial Citizenship: Homecoming and Identity

ALAN SEARS, IAN DAVIES AND ALAN REID

15 From Britishness to Nothingness and Back Again: Looking for a Way Forward in Citizenship Education

The London tube and bus bombings of July 7, 2005 were horrific and the level of concern in Britain was greatly heightened by the discovery that the bombers were not foreigners or immigrants but native-born British citizens. As then Chancellor of the Exchequer Gordon Brown said:

> We have to face uncomfortable facts that while the British response to July 7th was remarkable, they were British citizens, British born apparently integrated into our communities who were prepared to maim and kill fellow British citizens irrespective of their own religion ... We have to be clearer now about how the diverse cultures which inevitably contain differences can find the essential common purpose also without which no society can flourish.[1]

Shortly after becoming Prime Minister, Brown commissioned Lord Goldsmith to investigate British citizenship including attention to issues of diversity.[2]

About the same time as the London bombings, concerns about the challenges raised by increasing ethnic and social diversity in Australia motivated the federal government to introduce a national programme designed to foster the teaching of 'Australian Values' in schools. Brendan Nelson, the Education Minister of the day, asserted:

---

1   BBC News, 'Brown's speech promotes Britishness', (14 January 2006) http://news. bbc.co.uk/1/hi/uk/4611682.stm accessed 10 May 2008.
2   Lord Goldsmith QC, *Citizenship: Our Common Bond* (London: Ministry of Justice, 2008).

If you want to be in Australia, if you want to raise your children in Australia, we fully expect those children to be taught to accept Australian values and beliefs. ... We want them to understand our history and our culture, the extent to which we believe in mateship and giving another person a hand up and a fair go. And basically, if people don't want to be Australians and they don't want to live by Australian values and understand them, well basically, they can clear off.[3]

In 2007 the tiny Municipalité Hérouxville in rural Québec, Canada garnered international attention when it published a carefully crafted statement of standards targeted at potential immigrants 'so that the future residents can integrate socially more easily'. The statement referred to unacceptable behaviours including: 'killing women by lapidation or burning them alive in public places'; school children carrying 'any weapons real, fake, symbolic or not'; and hiding one's face in public except during Halloween.[4] These obviously target specific cultural and religious groups and ascribe extremist tendencies to whole communities. As *The Gazette* of Montreal reported, 'While the values espoused might be universal, the code has sparked an international controversy because the intention appears to be to scare off newcomers with a code that presumes the worst of them'.[5] Whether or not they wanted to 'scare off newcomers', the Mayor and council of Hérouxville made the primary intent of the statement explicit, 'We would especially like to inform the new arrivals that the lifestyle that they left behind in their birth country cannot be brought here with them and they would have to adapt to their new social identity'.[6]

The views of Gordon Brown, Brendan Nelson or the Hérouxville council are not reflective of a consensus of public opinion in their respective

---

3   A. Clark, *History's Children: History Wars in the Classroom* (Sydney: University of New South Wales Press, 2008), 55.

4   Municipalité Hérouxville, *Municipalité Hérouxville Publication of Standards* (2007), 1–3 http://municipalite.herouxville.qc.ca/Standards.pdf. accessed 31 January 2008.

5   R. Bruemmer and K. Dougherty 'Herouxville: Cause Celebre', The *Gazette* (2 February 2007) http://www.canada.com/montrealgazette/news/story.html?id=8af3c4eb-5bc7-40bc-ba38-93f785c5646a, accessed 31 January 2008.

6   Municipalité Hérouxville, Standards, 1.

countries. These vignettes do illustrate, however, the ubiquitous nature of concerns about diversity and social cohesion across the democratic world. The Commission struck in Québec partly in response to the Hérouxville incident commented, 'most Western nations are facing the same challenge, that of reviewing the major codes governing life together to accommodate ethnocultural differences while respecting rights'.[7] This is one of the central challenges for all Western democracies and, in particular, for their approaches to citizenship and citizenship education.

In this chapter we examine the role of citizenship education in addressing questions of identity, diversity and social cohesion over time and set out a possible way forward that will strike a balance between fostering a sense of collective – or perhaps national – identity and respecting the complex and overlapping sets of individual identities of individuals and groups in pluralist democratic societies. We draw particularly on examples from our own experience with Australia, Canada and England all of which have a considerable history of trying to foster a sense of 'Britishness'.[8] Prior to World War Two citizenship education was almost exclusively assimilationist in nature and, particularly in the immigrant societies of Australia and Canada, sought to create a common sense of national identity rooted in common allegiance to the Empire and/or Commonwealth. We trace the move away from overtly assimilationist approaches to citizenship education in the latter half of the twentieth century to more the more generic orientations. We argue that these fail to adequately account for national contexts and set out recommendations for developing citizenship education that pays attention to those contexts without stifling alternative individual or collective identities.

---

7 Commission De Consultation Sur Les Pratiques D'Accommodation Reliées Aux Différences Culturelles, *Accommodation and Differences Seeking Common Ground: Quebecers Speak Out, Consultation Document* (Québec: Gouvernement du Québec, 2007), vi.

8 For the most part our analysis of the British nature of Canadian citizenship education focuses on Canada outside Québec or what is sometimes referred to as 'English Canada'.

Britishness and the Assimilationist Past

Systems of universal public education arose concurrently with nation states and the creation of new political entities necessitated the creation of citizens of those entities. Curtis has carefully documented this process of *'public construction'* in Canada arguing that in establishing early public education the state was concerned with the overlapping functions of institution building and 'political characterization of the population'.[9] According to Curtis, the elites who pushed for, and achieved, universal public schooling in Canada in the nineteenth century were concerned about 'the creation in the population of new habits, orientations, [and] desires' that were consistent with 'the bourgeois social order' including 'respect for legitimate authority' and for standards of a 'collective' morality.[10] Bruno-Joffré writes, 'The public school was conceived as an agency for national unity and social harmony'.[11] In similar ways, the development of public education over the same period in Australia was largely focused on creating social order and social cohesion.[12]

Canadians and Australians were British subjects until the implementation of their respective Citizenship Acts in 1947 and 1949 and even then both Acts maintained the status of British subject alongside national citizenship for decades. In Canada, 'English speaking children were raised with the historical myths of British nationalism, as conveyed by adapted editions of the Irish National Reader and authors as diverse as MacCauly and

9   B. Curtis, *Building the Educational State: Canada West, 1836–1871* (London, ON: The Althouse Press, 1988), 111. Emphasis in the original text.
10   Ibid. 366.
11   R. Bruno-Jofré, 'Citizenship and Schooling in Manitoba Between the End of the First World War and the End of the Second World War', in Y. Hébert, ed., *Citizenship in Transformation in Canada* (Toronto: University of Toronto Press, 2002), 114.
12   D. Grundy, *Secular, Compulsory and Free: The Education Act of 1872* (Carlton: Melbourne University Press, 2002); P. Miller, *Long Division: State Schooling in South Australian Society* (Adelaide: Wakefield Press, 1986).

G. A. Hently'.[13] During the same period Australian school children at their weekly assemblies sang God Save the King/Queen and recited the Oath of Allegiance promising, among other things, to serve the monarch.[14]

Rosa Bruno-Joffre argues that citizenship education in Canadian schools, at least until the end of the Second World War, was focused on supporting this orientation. She writes, 'the aim of public schools in English Canada was to create a homogeneous nation built on a common English language, a common culture, a common identification with the British Empire and an acceptance of British institutions and practices'.[15] Similarly, Kennedy calls the period from 1901 to 1945 in Australian civic education, 'Australia and the Empire' and characterizes it as 'British in orientation and substance reflecting a tenuous independence from a still dominant colonial power'.[16]

Ironically perhaps, civic education in England was much less overt in its approach to fostering Britishness. As Kerr points out about the period prior to recent reforms in citizenship education, 'there is no great tradition of explicit teaching of civic or citizenship education in English schools' and it has more likely 'been located in the implicit or hidden curriculum rather than in the explicit or formal curriculum'.[17] That is not to say there was no concern for developing a sense of Britishness. Heath and Roberts make the point that rather than being overt, 'British identity was largely taken for granted'.[18]

13   D. Morton, 'Divided Loyalties, Divided Country?' in W. Kaplan, ed., *Belonging: The Meaning and Future of Canadian Citizenship* (Montreal and Kingston: McGill-Queens University Press, 1993), 55.

14   Education Department of South Australia, *Course of Instruction for Primary Schools* (Adelaide, 1953).

15   Bruno-Jofré, 'Citizenship', 113.

16   K. J. Kennedy, 'Civics' in B. Galligan and W. Roberts, eds, *The Oxford Companion to Australian Politics* (Melbourne: Oxford University Press), 104–5.

17   D. Kerr, 'Re-examining Citizenship Education in England' in J. Tomey-Purta, J. Schwille and J. Arnadeo, eds, *Civic Education Across Countries: Twenty-four National Case Studies from the IEA Civic Education Project* (Amsterdam: IEA, 1999), 204.

18   A. Heath and J. Roberts, *British Identity: Its Sources and Possible Implications for Civic Attitudes and Behaviour* (London: Ministry of Justice 2008), 5.

From the mid-1940s the assimilationist approach to citizenship education began to wane. First, as Western societies began to recognize the value of both indigenous and immigrant diversity, as well as some of the harm caused to these groups by previous policies, assimilation came to be seen as immoral and inappropriate. Second, attempts at assimilation simply were not working.

In regard to the former, Battiste and Semaganis describe something of the impact of the 'cognitive imperialism' of assimilationist educational practices on Aboriginal groups in Canada, arguing it was an attempt to extinguish 'Aboriginal conceptions of society'.[19] Similarly, Langton contends that in Australia 'Aboriginal peoples have been the subject of an extraordinary history of political experimentation, much of it predicated on the belief that the first Australians would disappear'.[20]

The dogged perseverance of Aboriginal communities and nations in Australia and Canada is one manifestation of the lack of effectiveness of the assimilationist approach to education. As Granatstein points out this approach was no more effective at breaking down other Canadians' sense of identification with their diverse cultural communities. 'Public school education, while compulsory, did little to crack such ethnic exclusiveness. The singing of *God save the King, Rule Britannia*, and *The Maple Leaf Forever*, and the reciting of patriotic poetry, could do little in and of themselves to teach the values of the wider Canadian community'.[21] Similarly, there is evidence that both national minority groups (i.e. Scots and Welsh) and immigrants continue to maintain a strong sense of dual identity in Great Britain despite the assumption they would discard those in favour of a common British identity.[22]

19   M. Battiste and H. Semaganis, 'First Thoughts on First Nations Citizenship: Issues in Education', in Y. Hébert, ed., *Citizenship in Transformation in Canada* (Toronto: University of Toronto Press, 2002), 93.

20   M. Langton, 'The Nations of Australia' in P. Boyer, L. Cardinal and D. Headon, eds, *From Subjects to Citizens: A Hundred Years of Citizenship in Australia and Canada* (Ottawa: University of Ottawa Press, 2004), 192.

21   J. L. Granatstein, 'The "Hard" Obligations of Citizenship: The Second World War in Canada' in W. Kaplan, ed., *Belonging*, 40.

22   Heath and Roberts, 'British Identity'.

While a number of Canadian scholars point out that initially these moves were seen as temporary, with assimilation remaining the long-term goal of education and other government programs, today multiculturalism is presented 'as the true and only basis of Canadian identity' and fostering respect for diversity, at least at some level, is a significant focus of public education across all three countries.[23] The revised National Curriculum in England, for example, mandates an explicit focus on 'identities and diversity' including a commitment to 'exploring the diverse national, regional, ethnic and religious cultures, groups and communities in the UK and the connections between them'.[24] Similarly, the Adelaide Declaration on National Goals for Schooling in the Twenty-First Century in Australia calls for all students to 'understand and acknowledge the value of cultural and linguistic diversity, and possess the knowledge, skills and understanding to contribute to, and benefit from, such diversity in the Australian community and internationally'.[25]

Nothingness: Inclusion, But in What?

A key focus for education generally and civic education in particular in more recent times has been inclusion. As Sears, Clark and Hughes point out, the idea of education as a doorway for individuals and groups to feel included in the mainstream civic life of the country in Canada has extended to at least an attempt to incorporate the voices of 'Aboriginal Peoples, women, diverse ethnic groups, disabled people, gays and lesbians'. This has resulted

23   H. Troper, 'The Historical Context for Citizenship Education in Urban Canada' in Hébert, *Citizenship*, 159.

24   Qualifications and Curriculum Authority (QCA), *Citizenship: Programme of Study for Key Stage 3 and Attainment Target* (London: QCA, 2007).

25   Australian Government Department of Education Science and Training, *The Adelaide Declaration on National Goals for Schooling in the Twenty-first Century – Preamble and Goals* (Canberra: Government of Australia, 1999).

in a widespread educational policy framework that promotes what they call 'the pluralist ideal'.[26] Central to this is an activist conception of citizenship in which every citizen, or group of citizens, will have the knowledge, skills and dispositions needed to participate in the civic life of the country and feel welcome to do so. It is important to note, that what citizens are being included in is not citizenship in the ethnic or sociological sense of belonging to a community but, rather, they are being included in the community of those who participate, who join in a process.

A broad international consensus exists around this activist/participatory conception of citizenship as the focus for civic education in democratic states. In McLaughlin's terms, for example, initiatives in England call for a 'maximal' rather than 'minimal' approach to citizenship; that is, citizens are expected to go far beyond minimal requirements of voting and obeying the law and to be actively engaged in both the formal mechanisms of the political system and the grassroots community involvement of civil society.[27]

A key feature of this approach to citizenship education is its almost blatant denial of identity as a key aspect of citizenship. Citizens' backgrounds and senses of self and others do not matter as long as they engage in liberal democratic practice. Kiwan found this when she interviewed key policy makers and practitioners in civic education in England who universally 'underplayed' identity-based conceptions of citizenship in favour of other models including the participatory ones.[28] When asked about this, Professor Bernard Crick, arguably the most influential single individual in the development of England's national curriculum in citizenship, said, 'We're not dealing with nationality, we're dealing with a skill, a knowledge, an attitude for citizenship'.[29] This is an almost perfect description of what we mean by a generic approach to citizenship.

26   A. Sears, M. Clarke and A. S. Hughes, 'Canadian Citizenship Education: The Pluralist Ideal and Citizenship Education for a Post-Modern State', in Torney-Purta et al, *Civic Education*, 113.

27   T. H. McLaughlin, 'Citizenship Education in England: The Crick Report and Beyond', *Journal of Philosophy of Education* 34 (2000), 550.

28   D. Kiwan, 'Citizenship Education in England at the Crossroads? Four Models of Citizenship and their Implications for Ethnic and Religious Diversity', *Oxford Review of Education* 34:1 (2008), 50.

29   Ibid., 46.

The move to a generic, participation focused approach has been driven by both ethical and pragmatic concerns. Policy makers and educators were and are genuinely concerned that a focus on identity, particularly any sense of national or collective identity, marginalizes and excludes some people and groups. A recent report on diversity in English schools noted the dangers of teaching 'Britishness': 'The term "British" means different things to different people. In addition, identities are typically constructed as multiple and plural. Throughout our consultations, concerns were expressed, however, about defining "Britishness", about the term's divisiveness and how it can be used to exclude others'.[30]

Identity often gets subverted because it is complex, difficult to deal with and has the potential to generate conflict. In studies of policy and practice in several Canadian provinces Bickmore found that schools and teachers generally avoided difficult issues with high potential for conflict including those involving ethnicity and identity. Instead, they focused on what she calls 'harmony building' and 'individual skill building' approaches rooted in conflict avoidance.[31] The first includes attention to the 'appreciation of diverse cultural heritages' but does not explore the real difference between and among those heritages. Similarly, Kiwan found that in England 'identity and diversity are being presented as something that pupils learn about, as opposed to actively engage with'. She calls this a 'pedagogy of acceptance', which entails 'being passive rather than active, engaging or challenging'.[32]

30   DfES, *Curriculum Review on Diversity and Citizenship (The Ajegbo Report)* (London: DfES, 2007), 8.
31   K. Bickmore, 'Foundations for Peacebuilding and Discursive Peacekeeping: Infusion and Exclusion of Conflict in Canadian Public School Curricula', *Journal of Peace Education* 2 (2005), 165.
32   Kiwan, 'Citizenship Education', 49.

The End of Nothingness: The Failure of Generic Approaches

Over the past 15 to 20 years a pervasive sense of crisis, or more accurately overlapping crises, have driven a flurry of reform in citizenship education around the world. Sears and Hyslop-Margison argue there is broad consensus about three crises which underlie the impetus to contemporary activity in citizenship education across the democratic world: ignorance – a lack of basic knowledge of democracy and democratic processes; alienation – from participating in key aspects of formal politics and civil society; and, agnosticism about (or hostility to) the values that underpin democratic societies.[33]

Recently, lack of cohesion has been identified as a key element of these crises. The authors of the *Diversity and Citizenship Curriculum Review* in England sum it up well: 'Major international events, such as 11 September 2001 and the London bombings in July 2005, have contributed to the debate on community cohesion and shared values. In the wake of these events, community cohesion is a key focus for the Government.'[34] Social cohesion is a ubiquitous concern for Canadian governments (federal and provincial) as well, and in Australia *The Values Education Study* and the resulting *National Framework for Values Education in Australian Schools* are indicative of similar concerns.[35] Kiwan points out, these all reflect 'a central tension in balancing unity and diversity, evident not only in discourses in England, but indeed internationally in a number of different nation-state contexts.'[36] As the Chief Inspector of Education, Children's Services and Skills for England wrote recently, 'schools have new responsibility to promote community cohesion.'[37]

---

33   A. Sears and E. J. Hyslop-Margison, 'Crisis as a Vehicle for Educational Reform: The
       Case of Citizenship Education', *Journal of Educational Thought* 41 (2007), 43–62.
34   *The Ajegbo Report* 18.
35   Department for Education Science and Training, *National Framework for Values
       Education in Australian Schools* (Canberra 2005).
36   Kiwan, 'Citizenship Education', 42.
37   Ofsted, *The Annual Report of Her Majesty's Chief Inspector of Children's Services and
       Skills* (2006–7), 8.

There is a widespread sense developing, even in Australia and England both of which have implemented substantial national programmess in the field, that citizenship education is not living up to its promise in a range of ways including the development of a deep sense of belonging and social cohesion among diverse citizens.[38] This has resulted in calls to give the subject more substantial focus and priority in the curriculum and to explicitly address issues related to identity, diversity and cohesion. Perhaps the most overt examples of the latter have come from England through the *Diversity and Citizenship Curriculum Review*, the so-called Ajegbo report, which concluded that 'the changing nature of the UK and potential for tension to arise now makes it ever more pressing for us to work towards community cohesion, fostering mutual understanding within schools so that valuing difference and understanding what binds us together become part of the way pupils think and behave.'[39] This report fostered many of the calls for teaching 'Britishness' in English schools and led directly to reforms of the National Curriculum including much more explicit attention to issues of identity and diversity.[40]

There are real issues to be faced regarding identity and cohesion in democratic societies and those generic approaches to citizenship education that largely ignore national context are not adequate to the task. However, the sense of crisis is often used as a convenient tool to push for public policy reform generally and education reform in particular but is a poor vehicle for fostering substantive and thoughtful change. Claims of crisis are often overblown and inaccurate and solutions proposed simplistic and ill-conceived. Sears and Hyslop-Margison, for example, call into question the empirical basis for the claims of the three crises of citizenship discussed above and we wonder if contemporary concerns about social fracture and the lack of sense of belonging are not being exaggerated as well.[41]

---

38 K. Faulks, 'Education for Citizenship in England's Secondary Schools: A Critique of Current Principle and Practice', *British Journal of Educational Studies* 55 (2007), 325–45.
39 *The Ajegbo Report*, 18.
40 QCA, *Citizenship*.
41 Sears and Hyslop-Margison, 'Crisis'.

A recent comprehensive meta-analysis of polling data in Great Britain over a number of years concluded that 'in all three territories [England, Scotland, Wales] a majority of residents have dual identities and there does not appear from these data to be a continuing decline in British identity or a continuing rise in exclusive national identities'.[42] This led Lord Goldsmith to conclude in his report to the Prime Minister, 'I do not assume that there is a crisis about our shared sense of citizenship'.[43]

Back to Britishness: Paying Attention to National Context in Citizenship Education

In discarding the overweening focus on nation – or empire as the case may be – because it was impractical and assimilationist, citizenship educators may have thrown the baby out with the bathwater. We concur with Barton and Levstik who write, 'some form of identification is necessary for democratic life, because without attachment to community individuals would be unlikely to take part in the hard work of seeking the common good'.[44] A substantial part of that identification should be with the nation state for two reasons.

First, paying attention to specific state contexts is important in citizenship education because while there are common or generic aspects to democratic citizenship that exist across jurisdictions, it is most often lived out on the ground in specific contexts that give it both form and function. We are not claiming there is no such thing as democratic theory apart from states but are arguing that democratic citizenship is operationalized differently across jurisdictions and those differences are important to

42   Heath and Roberts, *British Citizenship*, 8.
43   Goldsmith, *Citizenship*.
44   K. C. Barton and L. S. Levstik, *Teaching History for the Common Good* (Mahwah, New Jersey: Lawrence Erlbaum Associates, 2004), 46.

understand. Second, while we acknowledge profound shifts in geopolitics that are causing fundamental changes to the status and role of nation states, we do believe that for the foreseeable future they will remain key sites for the formation of identity and the exercise of citizenship.

In terms of the first argument, there is a set of underlying ideas or concepts inherent in democracy where ever it is found. De Tocqueville observed about the USA: 'from their origin, the sovereignty of the people was the fundamental principle of most of the British colonies in America. ... The people reign in the American political world as the Deity reigns in the universe'.[45] The concept of popular sovereignty still lies at the heart of democracy but it is not the only one. Kymlicka points out that a number of related ideas 'underlie the operation of Western liberal democracies,' including 'the rule of law, freedom of the press, freedom of conscience, habeas corpus, free elections, universal adult suffrage, etc'.[46] These principles provide a universal framework for judging whether or not a jurisdiction is democratic.

But democracy is understood differently and takes different forms across jurisdictions. Ideas and concepts do not have inherent meanings apart from those created and negotiated by people in particular contexts. Take the idea of popular sovereignty or democracy as government by the 'the consent of the governed,' for example. Rule by 'the people' is a necessary condition for democracy but there is wide disagreement about what precisely that means. In Ancient Athens, widely acknowledged as the first democracy, those included as citizens represented a minority of the total population: women, foreigners and slaves, although certainly governed, were not asked for their consent.

Contemporary Australia, Canada and England all allow a much larger percentage of the population to play a role in selecting those who govern

45 A. De Tocqueville, *Democracy in America*, ed. R. D. Heffner (New York: Mentor, 1956), 56–7.
46 W. Kymlicka, 'Western Political Theory and Ethnic Relations in Eastern Europe', in W. Kymlicka and M. Opalski, eds, *Can Liberalism be Exported? Western Political Theory and Ethnic Relations in Eastern Europe* (Oxford: Oxford University Press, 2001), 13.

but all restrict participation in particular ways and have developed their own mechanisms for obtaining the consent of the governed. Australian law, for example, compels eligible citizens to vote or face fines. Edwards draws on Rousseau to argue that it is sometimes appropriate to override the natural rights of citizens in order to force them to take up their democratic responsibilities and young Australians generally agree.[47] Neither Canada nor England (operating under electoral law that applies across the United Kingdom) requires citizens to vote and while Lord Goldsmith considered this option for the latter he concluded it would 'attract very significant resistance' and so chose not to recommend it.[48]

There are other institutional differences in the three democracies. Australia and Canada have been federal states since their independence from Britain and both have complex constitutional arrangements for power sharing between the provinces/states and the federal government. Although there has long been a significant element of Scottish and Welsh control over areas of social policy (most critically in this context education) the establishment of devolved institutions in Scotland and Wales in 1998 has strengthened sub-state decision-making and areas of relative legislative responsibility are still being worked out. Perhaps one of the most significant differences from the point of view of democratic theory is that both Britain and Canada have a legislative body as part of their national parliaments to which members are appointed rather than elected. That would be unthinkable in the Australian context where it is widely considered non-, or anti-democratic.

Democracy is also different across national contexts in spirit. The United States, for example, is by almost any measure the most religious of contemporary Western states and religion plays a significant role in civic life.[49] The 2004 book, *From Subjects to Citizens: A Hundred Years of Citizenship in Australia and Canada* focuses on institutional and legal differences but some focus on differences in style. Paquet argues that Australian civic

47   K. Edwards, 'Force Us To Be Free! Motivations of Australian School Students for Enrolling and Voting', in L. J. Saha, M. Print and K. Edwards, eds, *Youth and Political Participation* (Rotterdam: Sense, 2007).

48   Goldsmith, *Citizenship*, 107.

49   G. Wills, *Head and Heart: American Christianities* (New York: Penguin, 2007).

life includes 'a capacity for robust national debates… while in Canada there is a "sociality of consensus" and a taste for obfuscation, irony and bricolage in the public sphere'. He concludes: 'Australian and Canadian citizenships are emergent idiosyncratic realities'.[50] To effectively participate citizens have to be aware of these sensibilities.

Secondly, the nation state remains the primary location for the exercise of democratic citizenship. Barton writes, 'if citizens are to work together as members of a democratic society, they must share a sense of identity, and that identity must be parallel to the political system within which citizen action takes place – and in today's world, nations enjoy a privileged position in that regard'.[51]

We are not arguing that citizenship is only exercised in the political realm or that the nation state is the only political context in which citizens engage. Citizens, particularly young ones are finding myriad ways of participating and shaping their societies that stretch our understandings of democratic participation. We concur with Castles who points out, 'The principle of each individual being a citizen of just one nation-state no longer corresponds with reality for millions of people who move across borders and who belong in various ways in multiple places'.[52] But even Castles recognizes that the nation state remains the primary site for the exercise of democratic citizenship.

While there are essential and common attributes that constitute any democracy, democratic practice takes on particular features depending upon the context in which it exists and the primary context is the nation state. Citizens are not generic. They are British, Canadian, Australia or whatever and to understand and participate effectively as citizens they have to understand and participate in shaping what characterizes citizenship in their particular context.

50 G. Paquet, 'Governance and Emergent Transversal Citizenship: Towards a New Nexus of Moral Contracts in Boyer, Cardinal and Headon, eds, *From Subjects to Citizens*, 247 and 256.

51 K. Barton, 'History and Identity in Pluralist Democracies: Reflections on Research in the US and Northern Ireland', *Canadian Social Studies* (2005), 4.

52 S. Castles, 'Migration, Citizenship and Education' in J. A. Banks, ed., *Diversity and Citizenship Education: Global Perspectives* (San Francisco: Jossey-Bass, 2004), 18.

Ideas for a Way Forward

In England the Diversity and Citizenship Review Committee expressed concern that 'teaching Citizenship with History could mean a return to the old curriculum of British constitutional history and civics'.[53] Of course, if students are going to pay attention to the British context of being British Citizens in England they must learn about British constitutional history and civics. What the committee was really concerned about was not subject matter but pedagogical approach. They worried about a traditional approach that presented constitutional and legal structures as fixed, final and forever and students as sponges whose main function was to absorb that material and release it again when squeezed at exam time. Gardner calls this 'the correct answer compromise' where knowing is reduced to 'a ritualistic memorization of meaningless facts and disembodied procedures'.[54] This approach to history teaching has been all too common across the three countries examined here.[55]

In arguing for substantive attention to national context in civics we concur with Kiwan in calling for an end to this 'pedagogy of acceptance' and a move to a 'pedagogy of process'.[56] Specifically, we advocate involving students in the process of constructing the meaning of democratic ideas for their own time and place. In other words not telling them what it means to be Australian, Canadian or English but introducing them, in an informed way, to the discussion of what those identities have been, are, and should be in the future. This can best be done by engaging students with both the internal complexity of national identity in their particular context as well as with alternative constructions of national identity across the world.

53   *The Ajegbo Report*, 9.
54   H. Gardner, *The Development and Education of the Mind: The Selected Works of Howard Gardner* (London and New York: Routledge, 2006), 146–7.
55   A. B. Hodgetts, *What Culture? What Heritage? A Study of Civic Education in Canada* (Toronto: OISE, 1968); Clark, *History's Children*.
56   Kiwan, 'Citizenship Education', 54.

In reflecting on the struggle for democracy to take hold in the states of the former Soviet Union and Soviet Block, Tsilevich contends that one of the major difficulties is the importation of democratic ideas developed over many years in the West. He writes, 'Post-Communist countries [are] consumers, rather than co-authors, of this modern and generally accepted liberal democratic political philosophy'.[57] The same has been true with traditional approaches to civics: students have been treated as consumers of ideas rather than co-authors and consequently develop neither deep understanding of the ideas nor commitment to them. Democratic citizenship is fostered in co-authoring democratic ideas and practices through wrestling with what they have meant and mean and how they are and should be manifest in particular times and contexts. The assimilationist nature of national content can be mitigated by attention to the fluid and contested nature of democratic ideas both within the nation and outside of it.

Hughes and Sears have drawn on Vygotsky's social learning theory to develop an approach to teaching the fluctuating and contested nature of democratic ideas using Situated Learning and Anchored Instruction. The process requires an encounter between the learner and others (*inter-personal* learning). Then, possibilities are weighed, accepted, altered, discarded within the learner him or herself (*intra-personal* learning).[58]

Vygotsky pointed out that inter-personal communication can be more than conversation with one's peers and contemporaries. It can (and should) also be an interaction with the ideas contained in the artifacts of our collective historical, social and cultural development – books, articles, films, works of art, and in virtual environments. Pupils need to know not just what their peers and immediate teachers think: they also need contact with the ideas of knowledgeable others, indeed the world's best thinkers, from different eras and places. In an assimilationist model of civic education, students consider

57   B. Tsilevich, 'New Democracies in the Old World: Remarks on Kymlicka's Approach to Nation-Building in Post-Communist Europe' in Kymlicka and Opalski, *Can Liberalism be Exported?*, 156.

58   A. S. Hughes and A. Sears, 'Teaching the Contested and Controversial Nature of Democratic Ideas: Taking the Crisis out of Controversy' in H. Claire and C. Holden, eds, *The Challenge of Teaching Controversial Issues* (Stoke-on-Trent: Trentham Books, 2007), 83–93.

one consensus version of their nation's story past and present which they are expected to adopt as their own. We are proposing students will engage in inter-personal dialogue with a range of others over time and across contexts; others who have viewed and do view the nation differently.

This for example could include study of the evolution of the concept and practice of democracy as government by the consent of the governed: suffragettes struggling for the rights of women; Aboriginal peoples in Canada and Australia who were excluded from full political rights; African immigrants to Canada who, while having legal rights to participate, feel excluded by subtle social realities; and sixteen year-olds who have organized campaigns to lower the voting age in a range of democratic countries.

Students should discover that democratic ideas and structures in Australia, Canada, England and elsewhere have been and are both fluid and contested. They learn how democracy has been and is understood in their own national context as well as how it is contested within that context and understood and applied differently elsewhere. Knowing that there are alternative views of what democratic ideas mean both within their particular nation state as well as across states invites discussion about how those ideas should be understood and worked out now and in the future.

We have made a strong argument for the continued importance of nation states as sites for civic practice and we concur with others who argue that contemporary features of globalization including mass migration, individuals holding multiple and overlapping citizenships, and the rise of multinational institutions of governance such as the European Union and the system of international judicial tribunals challenge the often overly parochial nature of citizenship and citizenship education. Citizens must be prepared to engage both within and beyond the borders of their nation states.

We should pay serious attention to history in citizenship education and citizenship in history education. Democratic ideas have evolved (largely as the result of struggle) across time and context from Ancient Greece to the present and students have to know something about this. Contemporary generic approaches to civics and citizenship education are inappropriately disconnected from this historical context and, unfortunately, history education often takes the traditional didactic form that was identified as worrisome in the Ajegbo Report.

Unfortunately, history and citizenship education have often been described as being at war. Some such as Barton and Levstik argue that teaching history can make a contribution to building democracies that are 'participatory, pluralist, and deliberative'.[59] History can and should be taught in such as way as to 'promote reasoned judgment', 'promote an expanded view of humanity', and 'involve deliberation over the common good'.[60] They have shown how this might be done in ways that are consistent with Situated Learning and Anchored Instruction discussed above.

Barton and Levstik argue it is possible to teach history in a way that both develops a sense of national identity and explores the contested and complex nature of that identity; that opens up the discussions of difference, exclusion and inclusion. National history should focus in part on the struggle by various groups over time to be included in the national community both in the formal legal and political sense and also in more sociological ways as well. Australia, Canada and Britain, for example, are all recognized as multi-national states. Traditional and conservative approaches to history teaching regard this as a problem that can be fixed through the presentation of compelling and heroic versions of the nation's past. Barton and Levstik propose opening up this multinationalism investigation asking questions like: What groups or nations have been included in the state? How did they come to be included? Are all members of those nations happy about that inclusion? What, if any, legal and administrative structures are in place to recognize the various nations and provide them with some autonomy?

Kymlicka and Norman point out that national minorities are only one of a range of minority groups that exist in most modern nation states.[61] It is important in citizenship education to explore the range of experiences of exclusion, inclusion and social justice. Nuanced history programmes 'can help to establish a new narrative of the nation, including a new portrayal

---

59   Barston and Levstik, *Teaching*, 34–5.
60   Ibid. 36–8.
61   W. Kymlicka and W. Norman, eds, *Citizenship in Diverse Societies* (New York: Oxford University Press, 2000).

of the self and those previously designated as Other'.[62] It is also possible
for young children to begin to develop fairly complex understandings of
diversity and principled approaches to accommodation when there is specific attention to it by skilled teachers.

Conclusion

Australia, Canada and England have experienced citizenship education
differently. Both Australia and England conducted national consultations
and developed national programs in the field. In England there is a so-called
'light touch' national curriculum allowing schools some flexibility. In Australia the Federal Government and the States cooperated in developing the
Discovering Democracy Programme that included substantive materials for
a range of grade levels distributed to all schools and a nation-wide system
of professional development. The programme was not mandated, however,
and it was left to schools and teachers to decide how and where to use the
materials. Canada has had no national initiatives in citizenship education
and individual provinces have developed various approaches.

There are also very substantial similarities. There is a history of assimilationist approaches to citizenship education focused on creating a 'British'
citizenry; more generic, participation focused approaches to citizenship
education; and perceived lack of social cohesion with citizenship education
seen as the solution. There has been substantive criticism in all three about
the lack of a clear and specific place for citizenship education within the curriculum. Faulks in England and Print in Australia both present compelling
evidence that the flexible approach taken in both countries has led to very

---

62   E. A. Cole, 'Introduction: Reconciliation and History Education' in E. A. Cole, ed.,
      Teaching the Violent Past: History Education and Reconciliation (Lanham: Rowman
      and Littlefield, 2007), 20.

mixed results.[63] Similarly, Hughes and Sears present Canada as a dabbler in the field with the same mandate as the other states but extraordinarily weak capacity with which to carry it out.[64] Citizenship education can make a contribution to fostering citizens committed to pluralism, deliberation and the wider national community. This requires substantial commitment including substantive materials, opportunities for teacher education at the pre and in-service levels and dedicated space within the curriculum. It requires sustained attention to the national context. It is possible to develop a sense of being Australian, Canadian or British without being simplistic, narrow or final about what those labels mean.

63   Faulks, 'Education for Citizenship'; M. Print, M. 'Learning Political Engagement in Schools' in L. J. Saha, M. Print & K. Edwards, eds, *Youth and Political Participation* (Rotterdam: Sense Publishers, 2007), 95–112.

64   A. S. Hughes and A. Sears, 'The Struggle for Citizenship Education in Canada: The Centre Cannot Hold' in J. Arthur, I. Davies & C. Hahn, eds, *The Sage Handbook of Education for Citizenship and Democracy* (London: Sage, 2008), 124–38.

ANDREW MYCOCK, CATHERINE MCGLYNN AND RHYS ANDREWS

16 Understanding the 'History Wars' in Australia and the UK

The 'history wars' have proven to be a prominent feature of political discourse in Australia and the UK, reflecting concerns about a perceived dilution in popular ascription to a common national identity. Recent attempts to articulate a twenty first century Australianness or Britishness have highlighted the extent to which history teaching in schools continues to exert a powerful hold over the imagination of politicians, policy-makers and other commentators in inculcating a common national identity as this chapter will show.[1] Commentators have often drawn attention to a professed dilution in the standing of history in curricula and the need to teach 'proper' history. Such debates would appear cyclical, often somewhat predictably provoked by media representations of survey data that indicate a decline in young people's historical knowledge or reaction to government-led modification of the school history curriculum.[2]

---

1 See, for example, P. Keating, 'Keating's history wars', *Sydney Morning Herald*, 5 September 2003; G. Brown, *The Future of Britishness*, Speech to the Fabian Society New Year Conference, 14 January 2006; J. Howard, *Address to the National Press Club, Great Hall, Parliament House*, Canberra, 4 January 2006; D. Cameron, 'Proud to be British', ConservativeHome, 10 July 2009 http://conservativehome.blogs.com/platform/2009/07/david-cameron-proud-to-be-british.html, accessed 6 August 2010.

2 S. Wineburg, 'Making historical sense', In P. N. Stearns, P. Seixas and S. Wineburg, eds, *Knowing, Teaching and Learning History: National and International Perspectives* (New York: New York University Press, 2000), 306–25; H. Brocklehurst and R. Phillips, 'You're History! Media Representation, Nationhood and the National Past' in H. Brocklehurst and R. Roberts, eds, *History, Nationhood and the Question of Britain* (Basingstoke: Palgrave, 2004), 386–98.

For example, former Prime Minister, John Howard, suggested in 2006 that 'young people are at risk of being disinherited from their community if that community lacks the courage and confidence to teach its history'. In the UK, during their period in opposition, the Conservative party consistently accused the New Labour government of failing 'to give our children a connected sense of the narrative of our islands'. Attention was drawn to declining numbers taking History GCSE, with now Secretary of State for Education, Michael Gove, suggesting that 'we are looking at a whole generation that knows almost nothing about the history of their (or anyone else's) country'.[3]

Concern over the perceived decline in the quality and content of history education, and its deleterious impact on Australian or British national allegiance, has been a persistent feature of commentary of the importance of history education. Critics often suggest that current approaches to history education provide in Melanie Phillips' words 'no overarching national story to bind inhabitants together', which she believes means that future generations 'will be citizens of the republic of meaninglessness'.[4] Tensions have emerged about how the national past is understood and taught, particularly the importance of historical figures and events and how (or if) they should be depicted within the respective history curricula. Current approaches are often portrayed as a premeditated attack by 'politically correct' liberals who have ensured the teaching of history has become divorced from 'historical facts', suggesting the Australian and British states have deliberately estranged themselves from their own historical legacy.[5]

Such discussion of school history makes strong assumptions about the ability of history lessons to act as a conduit, whereby a mission of 'cultural

---

3   Howard, *Address to the National Press Club*; A. Lipsett, 'Less than one in three pupils taking history GCSE', *The Guardian* (26 May 2009); M. Gove, 'What is Education For?' Speech to the Royal Society for Arts (30 June 2009).

4   M. Phillips, 'The threat to national identity' *Daily Mail* (26 April 2006).

5   See, for example, F. Furedi, 'Britain: An island without a story', *Spiked*, 20 February 2008, www.spiked-online.com, accessed 16 September 2009; K. Windschuttle, 'The Nation and the Intellectual Left', *New Criterion*, 26, January 2007, 15–22.

transmission' can be enacted.[6] Commentators assume that school children can absorb and understand wholesale the key facts and messages of a national history, which will help them to take their place in a community with other similarly educated citizens. However, a growing body of empirical research challenges the notion that young people are innately receptive to any nation-building aims built into educational policy and curriculum design.[7] Our own data, which will be explored here and elsewhere,[8] shows that those in education are subject to a range of influences and hold a variety of opinions on their own sense of national identity and its relation to their experiences of history education. The chapter will explore the extent to which political and media debates about history teaching are reproduced amongst higher education students in Australia and the UK. It will specifically focus on how and in what ways the two distinct constructions of the national past which inform the 'history wars' in each country – positive/one-nation and interpretative/plural – influence how students understand the national past and identity.

Understanding the 'History Wars'

The battle over the role of history teaching and the desired content of lessons resonates with what have become known as the 'culture' or 'history wars' in many Western states. Focus on school history should be understood as the latest manifestation of a recurrent conflict about levels of historical knowledge and concerns over decline in ascription to a common national identity fought in universities, museums, newspapers and increasingly

---

6   T. Hadyn, 'History'. In White, J., ed., *Rethinking the School Curriculum: Values, Aims and Purposes* (Abingdon: Routledge Falmer, 2004), 89.

7   S. Fenton, 'Indifference towards National Identity: What Young Adults Think About Being English and British', *Nations and Nationalism* 13 (2) (2007), 321–9.

8   R. Andrews, C. McGlynn, and A. Mycock, 'Students' Attitudes Towards History: Does Self-Identity Matter?', *Educational Research* 51 (3) (2009), 365–77.

amongst the political classes.[9] Concerns over the teaching of history in schools are linked to broader questions about historiography of the nation, citizenship and national community. Debates about the content, quality and purpose of education in general and history teaching in particular are often representative of broader political narratives which conflate anxieties about future generations of young people and the state of the nation itself.

The modern 'history wars' can be traced back to at least the 1960s, being, in part, a reaction to the pedagogical development of 'new' history that put emphasis on the subject as a means of developing critical and interpretive skills rather than as the presentation of a monochrome national canon.[10] The superseding of 'traditional' or orthodox history in schools, and its perceived implications for the inculcation of a coherent national identity is seen as central to an emergent politics of history teaching.[11] 'New' history often drew on more critical historiographies which were prepared not only to question established nation-building historical narratives but also offered alternative interpretations prioritising class, gender and race/ethnicity. The 'history wars' are founded on therefore a binary approach in which either established (traditional) national narratives or revisionist constructions of the national past shape contemporary history lessons and textbooks.

For many professional historians and educators, teaching school history centres on balancing core national knowledge and what has been termed 'historical literacy'.[12] The teaching of revisionist historiography in schools therefore indicates a greater sensitivity for those pupils who have been consistently omitted or portrayed negatively within orthodox school

9   S. Macintyre and A. Clark, *The History Wars* (Carlton: Melbourne University Press, 2003).

10   R. Phillips, 'History Teaching, Nationhood and Politics in England and Wales in the Late Twentieth Century: A Historical Comparison', *History of Education* 28 (3) (1999), 351–63.

11   A. Waldman, 'The Politics of History Teaching in England and France during the 1980s', *History Journal Workshop*, 68 (1) (2009), 199–221.

12   A. Clark, '"Coalition of the Uncertain": Classroom Responses to Debates about History Teaching', *History Australia*, 4 (1) (2007), 12.1–12.12.

narratives.[13] However, others see this critical or negative ('Black Armband') history as undermining national cohesion through the deliberate dilution and liberalisation of organic historical narratives.[14] Proponents of a return to a 'golden age' where positive and largely uncritical traditional – 'three cheers' – forms of school history teaching dominated argue that young people need a positive understanding of the national past that is neither too critical nor chronologically fractured. Some such as Paul Gilroy dispute these charges and argue that a post-imperial melancholia persists whereby the national history of states such the UK and Australia have not yet come to terms with the plural nature of their contemporary societies.[15]

Such narratives accept that modern nation and state-building continues to be strongly informed by the role of national history, suggesting history teaching and national identities are viewed as interdependent. The intensity of current debates highlights a belief held by many in the enduring power of national historical narratives to shape identity. The political debate around history teaching then focuses on the content and purpose of the national story to be transmitted: should the primary aim be the inculcation of collective patriotism founded on a homogenous national history or the recognition of a plurality of national and other discourses.[16]

But those who seek to promote history education as a vehicle for teaching the nation tend to ignore the resonance of competing sub-national, national and transnational frameworks of historical interpretation and articulation. The UK is a multi-national union state with a tradition of decentralised education policy-making. Those politicians, academics and others who argue for the teaching of a traditional British history curriculum typically overlook resistance that devolution has engendered across the sub-state units of the UK. The British 'history wars' are in their infancy but there are indications that nationalists in Scotland and Wales are alive

13   J. Arthur, I. Davies, A. Wrenn, T. Haydn and D. Kerr, *Citizenship Through Secondary History* (London: Routledge-Falmer, 2001).

14   G. Blainey, 'Drawing up a Balance Sheet of Our History', *Quadrant* 37 (July/August 1993): 10–15.

15   P. Gilroy, *After Empire: Melancholia or Convivial Culture* (London: Routledge, 2004).

16   S. Lévesque, 'In Search of a Purpose for School History', *Journal of Curriculum Studies* 37 (3) (2006), 349–58.

to the potential for school history and citizenship education as vehicles to further secessionist aims.[17] In Australia, tensions between federal and state governments over content and delivery of school history have limited the development of a national history curriculum.[18] The place of transnational history in the various history curricula in the UK and Australia is also often overlooked, particularly that of newer migrant communities who often lack direct historical links within national or imperial contexts.

Notwithstanding such practical problems, it is unclear whether history teaching is effective in inculcating national belonging and there is little conclusive evidence to suggest that a prescriptive form of history teaching successfully embeds a sense of national identity. Some recent studies suggest that, although young people think it is important to have knowledge of history, many are, at best, indifferent to state-conceived school history programmes which seek to inculcate a common national identity.[19] It is this issue with which we now wish to engage.

The Australian 'History Wars'

Debates concerning Australian history and national identity have proved a fertile battleground for politicians, academics and the media, particularly during the past quarter of a century or so. Crucial to the Australian 'History

17   R. Phillips, P. Goalen, A. McNully, A. and S. Wood, 'Four Histories, One Nation? History teaching, nationhood and a British identity' *Compare: A Journal of Comparative and International Education* 29 (2) (1999), 153–69; R. Andrews and A. Mycock, 'Dilemmas of Devolution: The "Politics of Britishness" and Citizenship Education', *British Politics* 3 (2008), 139–55.

18   A. Clark (2008) *History's Children: History Wars in the Classroom* (University of New South Wales Press; Sydney); C. Harris-Hart, 'National Curriculum and Federalism: The Australian Experience', *Journal of Educational Administration and History*, 42 (3) (2010), 295–313.

19   M. Grever, T. Hadyn, and K. Ribbens, 'Identity and School History: The Perspective of Young People from the Netherlands and England', *British Journal of Educational Studies*, 55 (1) (2008), 1–19.

Wars' has been how Australia's colonial past and relations with its indigenous peoples are understood but other aspects of Australian social and political history have also stimulated emotive and controversial debate.[20] Until recently, Britishness figured prominently in the history of Australia, informing a distinctive British-Australian composite nationalism that drew on complementary ethnic and civic components.[21] But, as Ward argues, Australia's loosening of ties with the UK after the latter's accession to the European Economic Community (EEC) in 1973 encouraged wholesale re-evaluation of the national past and its constitutional present.[22]

Such debate has raised critical questions of national and imperial history and historiography concerning Australia's colonial past and multicultural present. The forging of a post-British Australian national identity increasingly drew on emergent historiographies that emphasised a distinctive national past, culture and territory. Central to this was a shift in historiographical focus as a new wave of Australian historians sought to narrate alternative histories that explored the pre- and post-federation periods. These explored issues such as class, gender, race and indigeneity through a critical lens that also sought to re-evaluate Australia's ties with the 'Mother Country'. As Meaney notes, revisionist national historiography sought the dissolution of Britishness in Australia whilst also exploring the darker aspects of Australian nation-building.[23]

This was not however a solely academic turn, and politicians and other commentators invested considerable time and effort in the re-articulation of the Australian national story. For many, the culmination of this was Australia's Bicentennial celebrations in 1988 and the election of Labor

---

20　A. Bonnell and M. Crotty, 'Australia's history under Howard, 1996–2007', *The ANNALS of the American Academy of Political and Social Science* 617 (2008), 149–65.

21　R. McGregor, 'The Necessity of Britishness: Ethno-Cultural roots of Australian Nationalism', *Nations and Nationalism* 12 (3) (2006), 493–511.

22　S. Ward, *Australia and the British Embrace: The Demise of the Imperial Ideal* (Melbourne: Melbourne University Press, 2001).

23　N. Meaney, 'Britishness and Australian Identity: the Problem of Nationalism in Australian History and Historiography', *Australian Historical Studies*, 32 (116) (2001), 76–90.

Prime Minister Paul Keating in 1991. Keating's speech in December 1992 at Redfern Park sought reconciliation with Australia's indigenous peoples by apologising for the crimes of European settlers. Though welcomed by many in Australia and elsewhere, it proved a defining point in debates about national identity and the 'history wars', provoking a number of historians and politicians to respond to what was seen as an overly-negative Australian history of apology. As Clark notes, historian Geoffrey Blainey's coining of the term 'Black Armband' history provided the largely historiographic debate with a persuasive term and new political impetus.[24] At the fore of this highly-politicised debate was John Howard whose interest in school history was part of a broader revolt against the liberalisation of Australian society. He drew attention repeatedly to the growth and impact of political correctness and social engineering, particularly in his campaign to defeat Paul Keating.

Howard saw the distortion of Australian history, particularly its overly-critical focus in rewriting British and Aboriginal history, as a manifestation of the politicising of national identity. In response, he undertook a sustained campaign to reassert Australian national values and identity through a series of controversial speeches and policy initiatives.[25] Howard used debates about Australian national identity to privilege Anglo-British, Judeo-Christian values and emphasise the need to teach school history founded on a single narrative that emphasised content and chronology over critical engagement. Arguing for a 'root and branch renewal of the teaching of Australian history in our schools', Howard proposed that the content should reflect 'the verdict of history is that Australia has been a remarkable success and we have built in this country a great nation'.[26]

In 2006, the Howard government held a national summit of politicians, historians and teachers and selected panel was commissioned to redraft a national history syllabus teaching under the leadership of

24   Macintyre and Clark, *The History Wars*, 537.
25   C. Johnson, 'John Howard's "Values" and Australian Identity', *Australian Journal of Political Science* 42 (2) (2007), 195–209.
26   J. Howard, Speech at Australia Day Citizenship Ceremony, Commonwealth Park, Canberra (26 January 2007).

historian Tony Taylor.[27] However its recommendations were sidelined and the draft was rewritten under the tutelage of conservative historian Geoffrey Blainey.[28] The election of Kevin Rudd meant this revised draft, considered 'barely unteachable' by Taylor, was not introduced into schools and the new Labor government undertook their own further review of the curriculum.[29] A new draft curriculum was published in March 2010 which, after a further period of consultation, the new Coalition federal government intends to introduce universally.[30]

The 'History Wars' in Australia are far from over. There remain strong reservations about the development of a federal government defined 'national' history curriculum, with particular resistance from some states. Some suggest the 'history wars' have polarised Australian society and paralysed some debates about Australia's national past.[31] History continues to play an important role in shaping identity in Australia, with historical figures and myths that shape national sentiments often mobilised by politicians.[32] Young people would appear to be sensitive to such divisions, expressing both traditional and more critical understandings of national

27   A report was prepared for this summit authored by Professor Greg Melleuish, see
      Australian Government, *The teaching of Australian history in Australian schools:
      a normative view* (Canberra: Dept. of Education, Science and Training, 2007).
      For an excellent overview of this review process, see B. Haynes, 'History Teaching
      for Patriotic Citizenship in Australia', *Educational Philosophy and Theory* 41 (4)
      (2009), 424–40.

28   Australian Government, *Guide to the teaching of Australian history in years 9 and 10*
      (Canberra: Dept. of Education, Science and Training, 2007).

29   Australian Curriculum, Assessment and Reporting Authority (2010) *National History
      Curriculum: Draft Consultation 1.10*, http://www.australiancurriculum.edu.au/
      Documents/History%20curriculum.pdf, accessed 6 October 2010.

30   A. Patty, 'History wars set to break out again', *Sydney Morning Herald* (31 August
      2010).

31   A. Dirk Moses, 'Moving the Genocide Debate Beyond the History Wars', *Australian
      Journal of Politics and History*, 54 (2) (2008), 248–70.

32   B. Tranter and J. Donoghue, 'Colonial and Post-Colonial aspects of Australian
      Identity', *The British Journal of Sociology* 58 (2) (2007), 165–83.

identity.[33] Divergence regarding issues such as immigration, multiculturalism, and the place of indigenous peoples in Australian society would appear to also shape young peoples' attitudes to nation and identity.

History Teaching and Britishness

The British 'history wars' have not – as yet – proven as visceral as in Australia, with little debate about the role of universities or museums in shaping and reshaping national identity. Debates about the content and delivery of school history have however proven increasingly divisive and politicised. This can in part be attributed to the introduction of the National Curriculum in England in 1990 which was somewhat informed by Conservative party concerns over the teaching of bespoke 'multicultural' history during the 1970s and 1980s.[34] Its introduction signalled the end of the informal consensus whereby schools were allowed freedom to teach the history curriculum as they saw fit, thus explicitly politicizing the role of the state in the process of identity formation.

On coming to power in 1997, the Labour government sought promote an 'enlightened patriotism' drawing predominantly on Gordon Brown's conception of Britishness which emphasised 'long-standing British values' such as decency, tolerance, liberty, fair-play, and duty as a 'golden thread' running through British history. These were linked to the modernisation of British institutions, such as parliament, the NHS and the BBC, to provide a common and distinct 'patriotic purpose as a nation and a sense of

---

33   Nola Purdie and Lynn Wilss, 'Australian National Identity: Young Peoples' Conceptions of What It Means to be Australian', *National Identities* 9 (1) (2007), 67–82.

34   K. Crawford, 'A History of the Right: The Battle for Control of National Curriculum History: 1989–1994', *British Journal of Educational Studies*, 43 (4) (1995), 433–56; R. Samuel, 'A Case for National History', *International Journal of Historical Teaching, Learning and Research*, 3 (1) (2003), 85–92.

direction and destiny' and inclusive British identity.[35] Labour saw history and citizenship education as a means of inculcating a sense of community amongst British citizens in the face of challenges posed not just by increasing diversity but also division and separation between different groups. The synonymous promotion of UK citizenship and Britishness prioritised 'a shared identity based on membership of a political community, rather than forced assimilation into a monoculture, or an unbridled multiculturalism which privileges difference over community cohesion'.[36]

The initial focus was on the introduction of statutory citizenship education in English schools from 2002. However, British history was presented as a vital component of this agenda because of the belief that a traditional programme telling the national story could still be progressive and resistant to racially exclusive definitions of belonging. Brown urged Britons to not 'recoil' from their national history, proposing that 'British history should be given much more prominence in the curriculum'.[37] He emphasised the need for the teaching of narrative history, alluding to professed shortcomings in current approaches, particularly after a number of reports raised concerns about the quality and coherence of school history in England. A government-sponsored *Curriculum Review on Diversity and Citizenship* (commonly known as the *Ajegbo Report*) reviewed the teaching of ethnic, religious and cultural diversity, considering shared British values and their influence on the development of UK history. The final report published in 2007 argued that UK citizenship should be viewed through 'the lens of history'.[38] Osler points out that the accompanying press release

---

35   Examples of the former Labour leadership's position on Britishness can be found in Tony Blair's *Speech to the Lord Mayor's Banquet* (13 November 2000) and Gordon Brown's article 'The Golden Thread that runs through our history', *The Guardian* (8 July 2004).

36   D. Blunkett, 'What does citizenship mean today?' *The Observer*, 15 September 2002.

37   Brown, *The Future of Britishness*.

38   Ofsted, *Ofsted Subject Reports 2002/3: History in secondary schools, HMI 1982* (London: HMSO 2004); QCA, *History: 2004/5 annual report on curriculum and assessment, QCA/05/2169* (London: QCA, 2005); DfES, *Curriculum Review on Diversity and Citizenship (The Ajegbo Report)*, (London: DfES, 2007).

for the report explicitly presented it as a response to growing division and extremism, with the events of 9/11 and 7/7 as the backdrop to Labour's discourse of history teaching and belonging.[39]

In opposition, the Conservative party argued vociferously that any decline in an ascription to a British national identity was linked to Labour's constitutional reform programme and their failure to ensure schools promoted a positive construction of the national past based on an established chronological narrative. Criticism of Labour's approach to school history was a persistent feature of the Conservatives period in opposition. Leading party figures such as Theresa May accused Labour of threatening the survival of the British nation as they were 'deliberately unravelling old national myths' and 'focusing on what divides us' to the point that 'under Labour, even history is history'.[40] Such criticisms were not confined to politicians and some sought to remedy shortcomings in the teaching of history by publishing old or new history books and even encouraging non-state private schools to counter the 'politically correct' history syllabus provided within the state sector.[41]

As party leader, David Cameron asserted 'it's vitally important that we bring back proper teaching of British history in our schools'. He argued that school history which focused on critical skills encouraged a 'tapas' approach that lacked chronology and connected focus. Michael Gove, then shadow Education secretary, suggested young people were 'generally unable to relate a longer narrative of the story of Britain'.[42] The Conservatives sought to make political capital out of Labour's uncertainties regarding the

39 A. Osler, 'Patriotism, multiculturalism and belonging: political discourse and the teaching of history' *Educational Review*, 61 (1) (2009), 85–100.

40 T. May, 'Under Labour, even history is history', *Daily Telegraph*, 5 August 1998; Collins, T. (2005) *Today*, BBC Radio 4 (27 January 2005); M. Howard, 'Talk about the British dream', *The Guardian* (17 August 2005).

41 In 2005, the Daily Telegraph and right-wing think-tank *Civitas* campaigned to provide a free copy of H. E. Marshall's book, *Our Island Story*, first published in 1905, to 'correct the imbalance' of 'trendy social history' (*Daily Telegraph*, 22 June 2005). In 2004, amateur historian, George Courtauld, published *The Pocket Book of Patriotism* to provide a patriotic overview of British history he believed was his was not taught at school. It has to date sold over 200,000 copies. An independent primary school in Islington, the 'New Model School', was opened in September 2004 to counter the 'gross ignorance of our history and tradition' (*The Guardian*, 31st August 2004).

42 Cameron, 'Proud to be British'; Gove, 'What is Education for?'

content and function of school history. In 2006, they convened a seminar on school history which led to the formation on an 'independent' History Practitioners Advisory Team of sympathetic academic and teachers who reported back in 2007. It was recommended that history become a compulsory subject, citizenship education be abolished and British history, taught chronologically, should be prioritised. Their concerns mirror others who, fearing school history faces 'extinction', seek to return to an unspecified 'golden age' of history teaching which centred on a strong core of narrative British history which is 'fundamental to our identity as a nation'.[43]

Since coming into office, the Conservative-led Coalition has continued to draw attention to the perceived failings of school history. Gove has suggested that 'guilt about Britain's past is misplaced' and immediately outlined plans for a review of the history curriculum to ensure all young people will be able to learn 'our island story'.[44] A number of leading British historians such as Niall Ferguson and Simon Schama have been recruited to rid the curriculum of 'junk history'.[45] Gove believes such reform will stop 'this trashing of our past' but some commentators have concerns that those recruited to revise the curriculum seek to promote an overly-triumphalist view of the national and imperial past.[46]

---

43 Historical Association, 'History Faces Extinction in English Schools' (13 September 2009), http://www.history.org.uk/news/news_415.html, accessed 15 August 2010; BBC News 'Tories want more history lessons' (15 June 2006), http://news.bbc. co.uk/1/hi/education/5080746.stm, accessed 9 May 2009. See also C. McGovern, 'The New History Boys' in R. Whelan (ed.), *The Corruption of the Curriculum* (London: Civitas, 2007), 58–85; D. Matthews, *The strange death of history teaching*, 2009, http://www.cardiff.ac.uk/carbs/faculty/matthewsdr/history4.pdf, accessed 16 September 2009.

44 A. Thomson, 'Gove unveils Tory plan for return to 'traditional' school lessons', *The Times* (6 March 2010). M. Gove, 'All pupils will learn our island story', speech to the Conservative conference, Birmingham, 5 October 2010, http://www.conservatives. com/News/Speeches/2010/10/Michael_Gove_All_pupils_will_learn_our_island_ story.aspx, accessed 6 October 2010.

45 A. Anushka, 'Niall Ferguson: "Rid our schools of junk history"', *The Observer* (21 March 2010).

46 See for example, L. Penny, 'Michael Gove and the Imperialists', *New Statesman* (1 June 2010).

Such concerns about history teaching are multiplied in the case of an avowedly multi-national post-devolution UK state. Education policy provides a clear example of the contentious nature of the British national past, particularly in Scotland where the SNP minority government have sought to 'embed Scottish history, culture and heritage in the curriculum' by introducing reforms to the History curriculum in Scottish schools. Former Education Minister Fiona Hyslop has argued that 'Scotland is one of the few countries in Europe which does not have teaching of its own culture and heritage as a core element of the curriculum'. Therefore 'Scotland's young people must reclaim the past and understand this nation's history'.[47] This has raised concerns that the 'Bruceification' of history teaching in Scottish school, with the greater emphasis on pre-Union Scottish history, will replace 'civic nationalism with the blood-and-soil variety' whilst also encouraging Anglophobia.[48] The British 'history wars' may be in their infancy but there are signs that they could prove as complex and divisive as those in Australia.

Young People and the 'History Wars'

Hadyn argues that one of the flaws inherent in policy-makers' attitudes towards the history curriculum has been the assumption that a message can be imposed upon pupils.[49] Evidence also suggests significant scepticism amongst history teachers about their ability and desire of schools to

---

47   F. Hyslop, 'Don't Make Our Scottish History History', *SNP news* (30 November 2005) http://www.snp.org/press-releases/2005/snp_press_release.2005–11-30.1325860718/, accessed 16 September 2009 and 'Learning about the past to shape the future', *The Scotsman* (21 January 2008).

48   R. Brown, 'Salmond accused of tapping dark side of nationalism', *The Scotsman* (25 October 2009).

49   Hadyn, 'History'.

teach patriotism.[50] Debates about the 'history wars' suggest that pupils do not enter the classroom as empty vessels and these findings accord with our research. An anonymous, voluntary and non-incentivised survey of four-hundred and sixty-two humanities and social science undergraduates was conducted in six universities in the North-West of England and Sydney, Australia in autumn 2006 and spring of 2007 and produced an informant response rate of 89.4 per cent. Quantitative and qualitative data produced evidence about citizenship, national identity and the impact of history teaching.

Within the survey respondents were asked this question, 'Do you have any comments regarding issues relating to your national identity, history or history teaching in schools?' The responses to this question provided insight into students' views on the desirability and possibility of using history to shape citizens' attitudes towards national identity. What emerged was a pattern of responses that suggested students' views on the purpose and impact of history teaching correlated strongly with the binaries identified previously. Therefore some students believed history education should draw on orthodox or traditional national narratives to stimulate loyalty to one nation. Other students supported the idea of skills-based interpretative history education that drew on revisionist narratives to encourage recognition of plural identities of which national identity is but one.

Given that the sample of students surveyed were currently studying degrees in the humanities and social sciences, it is perhaps unsurprising that there was a lack of negative attitudes towards the worth of history as a subject. Indeed, some respondents went out of their way to mark history out as an important and valuable element of education with straight-forward praise such as 'History is such an important subject. I love it!'

The views of students were consistent with broader themes shaping the Australian and British 'history wars' but *why* history was deemed important was usually not explained. There were complaints about the quality of history teaching that also drew on similar themes raised by politicians

---

50   M. Hands and J. Pearce, *Should Patriotism be Promoted, Tolerated or Discouraged in British Schools?* (London: Institute of Education, University of London, 2008).

and others relating to the content of the curriculum or to the poor quality of the methods chosen. One British student complained that 'History was taught really badly at my school. ... Watched videos called *Roots* for the whole of one year', whilst an Australian respondent felt that 'I finished school without a real understanding of our country's history, identity or relations with other countries'.

Some students were hostile to any attempts to 'edit' history either to promote a certain view of history or to avoid offence to a particular group. Students expressed concerns about the promotion by the state or political parties to develop history education to inculcate a sense of national identity. An Australian respondent, for example, expressed the view that there was 'too much political polarisation about Australian history – black armband versus the unapologetic view – especially in relation to Aboriginal reconciliation'. Our survey suggested though that students were sensitive to the need for balance in understanding the national past with another Australian student arguing 'I do think that both sides of the "settlement" debate needs to be taught, but one should not prevail over the other as the "right" interpretation'.

British students were more prepared to openly argue that censoring of some aspects of history should be avoided, with comments such as 'History should just be taught as it is with no cover-ups to protect people's religion or identity History is what it is' and 'I think straying away from some subjects rather than cause offence to a minority or religion is wrong. History is the past'. These comments suggest students believe that history can be taught in an apolitical context, that one can learn facts and debate ideas without becoming entangled in subjectivity or agendas. Hadyn argues that 'we have to accept that history teaching is inextricably political in nature, and make a virtue out of this'.[51] However, many who have experienced history teaching within the UK do not seem ready to accept this, preferring to downplay the idea that the curriculum is inescapably political. This insistence on thinking of history as being politically neutral was not however consistent. Some students were suspicious that their history lessons had been manipulated for certain purposes, but many still seemed to believe that there was a way to remedy this so that history could be rendered apolitical.

51   Hadyn, 'History', 98.

Such comments engage directly with a key dynamic of debates about history teaching: the extent to which revisionism has undermined the homogeneity and morality of the national narrative. What is clear from the responses is that, whilst politicians and commentators supporting an orthodox/one-nation position express concerns about the 'politicisation' of the history curriculum through 'new history', students who supported both positions were suspicious of state manipulation. References in the UK to religion and offence and the role of Aboriginal history in Australia straddled the conceptual divide in our survey and are issues that will need to be teased out in future research.

National History and National Identity

Some students reserved particular ire for the historical content of the curriculum, arguing for a more interpretative history curriculum. This raised questions about uncritical bias. Some British students berated their history lessons for problems such as leaning 'towards a particular "world view" in terms of the third world (white man's burden) [which] is not a critical assessment of good and bad of British history'. At the same time, some Australians felt that what was offered made it 'hard to balance your background and national pride with the country you live in'.

It was clear that some students shared the concerns of those who have argued for a broader, critically-informed and plural history curriculum. Some students commented that the teaching of Australian and British history was too insular (for example, 'Australian history is too narrow' or 'more on Asian and Africa, Brits are sometimes narrow-minded'). They often presented themselves as looking for an alternative story they felt was not being told in the classroom, an attitude which again corresponds with calls for more diversity and plurality with a number of responses from both countries offering suggestions for a broader curriculum, such as one British student's plea for 'education about rebellious figures – punk movement, feminist movement, anti-racist movement'.:

However, some students supported a return to more orthodox or traditional approaches to learning about 'national' history. An Australian student argued, for example, 'most things I have learnt about our country's history have been while studying at university and I feel these issues should be addressed at a much younger age to make us proud of Australia'. British students were more likely to make comments suggestive of a strong degree of pride in 'national' history and/or respect for institutions or traditions, including one British nineteen year-old male respondent who used the space for extra comments to simply draw a picture of the Union Flag. What united the comments made by these students was a sense of threat, where such institutions and traditions and the acceptance of the importance of teaching them was undervalued as this British student suggests:

> Learning about different cultures is very eye-opening but everything taught in history should apply to the students in that class. I'm proud of my country's history and feel despite religious criticisms it should be taught without fail as well as other cultures and countries. It feels as if there is a downplay on this country's history at the expense of others.

In the UK, what was particularly interesting in relation to this discussion of history and national pride was the uncertainty as to which nation, national identity and historical narrative some respondents were alluding. Those students who spoke of Englishness rather Britishness were particularly strident in their sense of defending their position with one respondent going so far as to state 'England was bad ass and should be portrayed as such. If you do not want to know about this country, then fuck off' whist another simply asserted 'teach more English history'.

This would suggest some awareness of the multi-national dimension of the British 'history wars'. But in both countries, some students indicated an awareness of other pathways that might be an appropriate vehicle for propagating a national identity. A British student echoed this sentiment with the assertion that 'studying history does make it easier to develop a national identity but a better way is to be aware of the issues around at present'.

However those arguing for a more pluralist approach tended to rebut the importance of national identity, either because it was not relevant to the modern Australian or UK state or because it did not fit with how they defined themselves. One Australian student's experience is instructive: 'School taught me I will never be "Australian" like other Anglo-Australians. Living in this country, despite the many wonderful things for which I am truly grateful, has neither made me want to be like a "real Australian" nor adopt their mentalities'.

One British student went into considerable depth, acknowledging their multi-layered understanding of identity and the contribution of history:

> I don't see nationality as an issue and see it as unnecessary means of dividing us. I am, however, proud of where I come from and believe it makes up an important part of who I am. I will always be Welsh, English and British but most importantly I am a citizen of the world. History teaching up to GCSE standard, however, can lead to over-simplification of British history, painting all too rosy a picture of our part in it.

Some students drew attention to what they saw was the potentially exclusive dimensions of ethnic nationalism and identity. One student commented 'I sometimes find it hard in Australia to be ethnic' whilst a British student noted 'cultural identity is not valuable to a peaceful society – if we accepted one another for who we are, not what we are there would be no problems.'

It was clear that, though students often did not directly engage with contemporary debates about the role of history education, they were divided on the binary identified earlier whereby some support a traditional 'teach the nation' approach and others seek a more revisionist and pluralist construction of the curriculum. Some even questioned the impact of school history itself in shaping attitudes to national identity. An Australian respondent felt that his national identity 'was developed and strengthened more by travelling to other countries and learning about their cultures through first hand experiences than through other means' whilst a British student stated 'I don't feel history teaching had a major impact on my national identity. I don't think national identity is important, particularly to me. I would rather be defined by my actions'. However, we feel that the last word should be left to a rather phlegmatic student who simply noted 'I have learnt lots about our national history. Some parts make you proud, and some make you ashamed. But that's just history'.

Conclusions

The teaching of history remains a contentious topic and one that garners a high volume of political and media coverage. Although the political, cultural and historical environments in which the Australian and British history wars are situated differ, there are strong commonalities in their structural development. In particular, it is evident that the key binary regarding the positive/one-nation and interpretative/plural versions of school history is shared. It is also clear that debates regarding the parameters of inclusion and exclusion with regards to the historical remit of 'national' history in plural societies produce many common tensions. There are however clear differences. The issue of indigeneity is salient in the Australian 'history wars', focusing on issues linked to colonisation and its aftermath. In the British case, it is post-imperialism and multi-nationality that drives much of this debate.

Our survey of undergraduates' attitudes to history teaching and national identity shows that students have also engaged with such debates. There is a strong resentment of perceived bias, manipulation and frustration with the history education experienced. Respondents were often hostile to what they saw as attempts to manipulate the curriculum to deliver idealised or de-sensitised versions of history. Comments on history teaching and national identity correlated strongly with conceptual and normative positions established in this article. Those on the interpretative/pluralist continuum were keen to present themselves as free of the ties of national identity allied to a more-celebratory view of the national past and were keen to treat history as a vehicle for uncovering buried pasts and undertaking of critical inquiry and analysis associated with 'new' history. Those on the orthodox/one-nation continuum were keener on the idea of history lessons as the correct space to teach 'national' history and respect for customs and tradition, although the presence of indigenous or religious groups as a potentially distorting and politicising force stretched across this pluralist/one-nation divide. Generally, it was noticeable that British students were more forceful and less-nuanced in their assertions about the 'history wars', this possibly due the less developed nature of such debates in the UK. This is an area for further research.

Students' reflections on their experiences of history, suggested that their time in school certainly informed their approach to identity and citizenship and also that they were more than capable of discerning agendas within history education. However, whilst students are aware of political currents within the curriculum, many of them hold fast to the belief that 'history is just the past'. This implies that a subject-based approach to history may have greater resonance with young people than the values-based approaches that currently characterise the 'history wars' and future studies of history teaching should pay close attention to the relevant influence of these approaches on students' attitudes towards national history and identity.

The exploratory nature of this study means it has some limitations. In particular, by drawing on the views of first-year undergraduates, we were aware they were only a sub-group who were not representative of young people in general. Moreover, we did not seek the views of secondary school students. The balance between the UK and Australian studies was also somewhat unequal, with the British study producing more responses than its Australian counterpart. However, we would argue that policy-makers should take from this research the understanding that students do not absorb educational messages in a state of pristine isolation. The contentious debate about the value and role of history education is often conducted in a way that suggests young people will be innately receptive to an approach and that what that approach should be can be resolved before the teacher enters the classroom. Instead, it should be accepted that anxieties about the politicisation of history percolate through a number of popular discourses as well as personal experience, meaning that students' attitudes develop in response to a range of influences and that they are wary of deliberate manipulation of their loyalties and identity. The idea that a national story can be imposed upon school children either as a traditional canon or as a pluralist celebration rests on flawed assumptions about the nature of transmission of ideas, values and interpretations of the past.

Select Bibliography

Abdel-Malek, A., 'Orientalism in Crisis', *Diogenes* 44 (1963), 103–40.

Abell, J. Condor, S., Lowe, R., Gibson, S. and Stevenson, R., 'Who Ate All the Pride? Patriotic sentiment and English national football support', *Nations and Nationalism* 13 (1) (2007), 97–116.

Achebe C., *Things fall apart* (London: Heinemann, 1958).

Achebe, C., *No longer at ease* (London: Heinemann, 1960).

Achebe, C., *Arrow of God* (London: Heinemann, 1964).

Achebe, C., *Girls at War & Other Stories* (London: Heinemann, 1986).

Adichie C., *Purple Hibiscus* (London: Fourth Estate, 2004).

Adichie, C., *Half of a yellow sun* (London: Fourth Estate, 2006).

Afigbo, A., *Ropes of Sand. Studies in Igbo History and Culture* (Ibadan & Oxford: Oxford University Press, 1981).

Alexander-Collier, A., *La Grande-Bretagne Eurosceptique? L'Europe dans le débat politique britannique* (Nantes: Editions du Temps, 2002).

Alexandre-Collier, A., D'Hellencourt, B. And Schnapper, P., eds, *Le Royaume-Uni et l'Europe depuis 1997* (Etudes Universitaires de Dijon, 2007).

Amit, V., ed., *Realizing Community: Concepts, Social Relationships, and Sentiments* (London and New York: Routledge, 2002).

Anderson, B., *Imagined Communities: Reflections on the Origin and Spread of Nationalism* (London: Verso, 1983).

Andrews, H., 'Feeling at Home: Embodying Britishness in a Spanish Charter Tourist Report', *Tourist Studies* 5 (3) (2005), 247–66.

Andrews, R. and Mycock, A., 'Dilemmas of Devolution: The "Politics of Britishness" and Citizenship Education', *British Politics*, 3 (2008), 139–55.

Andrews, R., McGlynn, C., and Mycock, A. 'Students' Attitudes Towards History: Does Self-Identity *Matter?*', *Educational Research*, 51 (3) (2009), 365–77.

Arthur, J., Davies, I., Wrenn, A., Haydn, T. and Kerr, D. *Citizenship Through Secondary History* (London: Routledge-Falmer, 2001).

Ballantine, S., 'English and Spanish in Gibraltar: Development and characteristics of two languages in a bilingual community', *Gibraltar Heritage Journal* 7 (2000), 115–24.

Barton, K., 'History and Identity in Pluralist Democracies: Reflections on Research in the U. S. and Northern Ireland', *Canadian Social Studies* (2005), online.

Barton, K. and Levstik, L. S., *Teaching History for the Common Good* (Mahwah, New Jersey: Lawrence Erlbaum Associates, 2004).

Basden, G., *Niger Ibos* (London: Frank Cass, 1966).

Bellot, L. J., *William Knox: The Life and Thought of an Eighteenth-Century Imperialist* (Austin & London: University of Texas Press, 1977).

Benwell, B., *Masculinity and Men's Lifestyle Magazines* (Oxford: Blackwell, 2003).

Benwell. B., 'Ironic Discourse: Evasive Masculinity in Men's Lifestyle Magazines', *Men and Masculinity* 73 (1) (2004).

Beynon, J., *Masculinities and Culture* (Buckingham: Open University Press, 2002).

Bickford-Smith, V., 'Revisiting Anglicisation in the Nineteenth Century Cape Colony', *Journal of Imperial and Commonwealth History* 31 (May 2003), 82–95.

Bickford-Smith, V., *Ethnic Pride and Racial Prejudice in Victorian Cape Town* (Cambridge: Cambridge University Press, 1995).

Bickmore, K., 'Foundations for Peacebuilding and Discursive Peacekeeping: Infusion and Exclusion of Conflict in Canadian Public School Curricula', *Journal of Peace Education*, 2 (2005), 161–81.

Blainey, G., 'Drawing up a balance sheet of our history', *Quadrant* 37 (July/August 1993): 10–15.

Boehmer, E., *Empire, the Nation and the Postcolonial: Resistance in Interaction* (Oxford: Oxford University Press, 2002).

Bonnell, A. and Crotty, M., 'Australia's history under Howard, 1996–2007', *The ANNALS of the American Academy of Political and Social Science*, 617 (2008), 149–65.

Boorstin, D., *The Image: Or, Whatever Happened to the American Dream* (London: Weidenfeld and Nicolson, 1961).

Born, G., *Uncertain Visions: Birt Dyke and the Reinvention of the BBC* (London: Vintage, 2005).

Bridge, C. and Fedorowich, K., eds, *The British World: Diaspora, Culture, and Identity* (New York: Routledge, 2003).

Briggs, A., *A History of Broadcasting in the United Kingdom, Volume II: The Golden Age of Wireless* (Oxford: Oxford University Press, 1995).

Brocklehurst, H. and Roberts, R., eds, *History, Nationhood and the Question of Britain* (Basingstoke: Palgrave, 2004).

Brown, G. W., Harman, E. and Jeanneret, M., *The Story of Canada* (Toronto: Copp Clark, 1950).

Brown, J. M., *Windows into the Past: Life Histories and the Historian of South Asia* (Notre Dame: Notre Dame Press, 2009).

Bryant, C., *The Nations of Britain* (Oxford: Oxford University Press 2005).

Buckner, P., ed., *Canada and the End of Empire* (Vancouver: University of British Columbia Press, 2005).

Buckner, P. and Douglas Francis, R., eds, *Rediscovering the British World* (Calgary: Calgary University Press, 2005).

Buckner, P. and Francis, R. D., eds., *Canada and the British World: Culture, Migration, and Identity* (Vancouver: University of British Columbia Press. 2006).

Bueltmann, T., '"Where the Measureless Ocean Between us will Roar": Scottish Emigration to New Zealand, Personal Correspondence and Epistolary Practices, c. 1850–1920' *Immigrants and Minorities*, 26 (3) (2008), 242–65.

Butterworth, S and Butterworth, G., *Chips off the Auld Rock: Shetlanders in New Zealand* (Wellington: Shetland Society of Wellington, 1997).

Cardus, N., *Cricket* (London: Longman, 1930).

Castles, S., 'Migration, Citizenship and Education', in J. A. Banks, ed., *Diversity and Citizenship Education: Global Perspectives* (San Francisco: Jossey-Bass, 2004), 17–48.

Cal Varela, M., *Algunos aspectos sociolingüísticos del inglés gibraltareño: Análisis cuantitativo de tres variables en el nivel fónico* (Santiago de Compostela: Universidad de Santiago de Compostela, 2001).

Cavilla, M., *Diccionario Yanito* 2nd edition (Gibraltar: MedSun 1990).

Chaudhuri, A., 'Poles of Recovery: From Dutt to Chaudhuri' *Interventions* 4:1 (2002), 89–105.

Chaudhuri, N., *A Passage to England* (London: Macmillan, 1959).

Chevrier, J., *Les Blancs vus par les Africains* (Lausanne: Favre, 1998).

Clark, A., '"Coalition of the Uncertain": Classroom Responses to Debates about History Teaching', *History Australia* 4 (1) (2007), 12.1–12.12.

Clark, A., *History's Children: History Wars in the Classroom* (Sydney: University of New South Wales Press, 2008).

Clifford, J., *Routes: Travel and Translation in the Late Twentieth Century* (Cambridge, MA and London: Harvard University Press, 1999).

Cohen, R., *Frontiers of Identity: the British and the Others* (London: Longman, 1994).

Cohen, R., 'Fuzzy Frontiers of Identity: The British Case.' *Social Identities* 1 (1) (1995), 35–62.

Cole, E. A., 'Introduction: Reconciliation and History Education' in E. A. Cole, ed., *Teaching the Violent Past: History Education and Reconciliation* (Lanham: Rowman & Littlefield, 2007), 1–28.

Colley, L., *Britons: Forging the Nation, 1707–1837* (New Haven and London: Yale University Press, 1992).

Colls, R. and Philip Dodd, eds. *Englishness: Politics and Culture 1880–1920* (London: Croom Helm, 1986).

Crouch, D., Aronsson, L. and Wahlstrom, L., 'Tourist Encounters' *Tourist Studies* 1 (3) (2001), 253–70.

Crawford, K., 'A History of the Right: The Battle for Control of National Curriculum History: 1989–1994', *British Journal of Educational Studies* 43 (4) (1995), 433–56.

Curtis, B., *Building the Educational State: Canada West, 1836–1871* (London, Ontario: The Althouse Press, 1988).

Davidson, A., *From Subject to Citizen: Australian Citizenship in the Twentieth Century* (Cambridge: Cambridge University Press, 1997).

Dennis, P., *Gibraltar and its People* (London: David & Charles, 1990).

Desai, A., *Bye Bye Blackbird* (Delhi: Hind Pocket Books, 1971).

Desani, G. V., *All About Mr. Hatterr: A Gesture* (London: Aldor, 1948).

De Tocqueville, A., *Democracy in America, edited and abridged by Richard D. Heffner* (New York; Mentor 1956).

Dirk Moses, A., 'Moving the Genocide Debate Beyond the History Wars', *Australian Journal of Politics and History*, 54 (2) (2008), 248–70.

Doerr, P. W., *British foreign policy 1919–1939. 'Hope for the best, prepare for the worst'* (Manchester and New York: Manchester University Press, 1998).

Donaldson, F., *The British Council: the First Fifty years* (London: Cape, 1984).

Dowd, G. E. *War under Heaven. Pontiac, the Indian Nations, & the British Empire* (Baltimore & London: Johns Hopkins University Press, 2002).

Eaton, D. and Newman, G., *Canada: A Nation Unfolding* (Toronto: McGraw-Hill Ryerson, 1994).

Edensor, T., 2002. 'Tourists at the Taj: walking and gazing' in S. Taylor, ed., *Ethnographic Research: a reader* (London: Sage, 2002).

Edensor, T., *Tourists at the Taj: performance and meaning at a symbolic site* (London: Routledge, 1998).

Edwards, K., 'Force Us To Be Free! Motivations of Australian School Students For Enrolling and Voting' in Saha, L. J., Print, M and Edwards, K., eds, *Youth and Political Participation* (Rotterdam: Sense, 2007), 79–94.

Ekwensi, C., *People of the City* (London: Heinemann, 1963).

Ellicot, D., *Our Gibraltar, a Short History of the Rock* (Gibraltar: Gibraltar Museum Committee, 1975).

Emecheta, B., *Head above water, an autobiography* (London: Heinemann 1986).

Entwistle, E., *History of the Gaelic Society of New Zealand, 1881–1981* (Dunedin, 1981).

Faulks, K., 'Education for Citizenship in England's Secondary Schools: A Critique of Current Principle and Practice' *Journal of Educational Policy*, 21 (2006), 59–74.

Fenton, S., 'Indifference towards national identity: what young adults think about being English and British' *Nations and Nationalism* 13 (2) (2007), 321–9.

Ferguson, N., *Empire: How Britain Made the Modern World* (London: Allen Lane and Penguin, 2003).

Fernández Martín, C., *An approach to language attitudes in Gibraltar* (Madrid: UMI-ProQuest Information and Learning, 2003).

Fernández Martín, C., 'Gibraltar and its Hinterland: Sociolinguistic Exchanges Between Two Neighbouring Communities' in R. Archer et al (eds), *Antes y Depués del Quijote* (Valencia: Biblioteca Valencia, 2005), 795–806.

Fierro Cubiella, E., *Gibraltar: aproximación a un estudio sociolingüístico y cultural de la Roca* (Cádiz: Universidad de Cádiz, 1997).

Finlay, R. J., 'Caledonia or North Britain? Scottish Identity in the Eighteenth Century' in Broun, D., Finlay, R. J. and Lynch, M. (eds), *Image and Identity: The Making and Re-making of Scotland Through the Ages* (Edinburgh: John Donald, 1998), 143–56.

Finlayson, T. J., *The Fortress Came First* (Gibraltar: Gibraltar Books, 1991).

Foucault, M., *The History of Sexuality: Volume 1: An Introduction* (Harmondsworth: Penguin, 1981).

Gandhi, L., *Affective Communities: Anticolonial Thought, Fin-de-Siecle Radicalism and the Politics of Friendship* (Durham and London: Duke UP, 2006).

García Martín, J. M., *Materiales para el estudio del español de Gibraltar. Aproximación sociolingüística al léxico español de los estudiantes de enseñanza secundaria* (Cádiz: Universidad de Cádiz, 1996).

García Martín, J. M., 'El español en Gibraltar. Panorama general' *Demófilo. Revista de cultura tradicional de Andalucía* 22 (1997), 141–54.

Gardner, H., *The Development and Education of the Mind: The Selected Works of Howard Gardner* (London and New York: Routledge 2006).

George, S., *An Awkward Partner: Britain in the European Community* (Oxford: Oxford University Press, 1998).

Gifford, C., 'The UK and the European Union: Dimensions of British Sovereignty and the Problem of Eurosceptic Britishness', *Parliamentary Affairs* 63 (2) (2010), 321–38.

Gilroy, M., 'The Partition of Nova Scotia' *Canadian Historical Review*, 14 (4) (December 1933), 375–91.

Gilroy, P., *Post Colonial Melancholia* (New York, Columbia University Press, 2004).

Gilroy, P., *After Empire: Melancholia or Convivial Culture* (London: Routledge, 2004).

Görög-Karady, V., *Noirs et Blancs. Leur image dans la littérature orale africaine* (Paris: SELAF, 1976).

Ghosh, S. K., *My English Journey* (Calcutta: Writers Workshop, 1961).

Granatstein, J. L., 'The "Hard" Obligations of Citizenship: The Second World War in Canada' in W. Kaplan, ed., *Belonging: The Meaning and Future of Canadian Citizenship* (Montreal & Kingston: McGill-Queens University Press, 1993), 36–49.

Grever, M., Hadyn, T. and Ribbens, K., 'Identity and School History: The Perspective of Young People from the Netherlands and England', *British Journal of Educational Studies* 55 (1) (2008), 1–19.

Grundy, D., *Secular Compulsory and Free: the education Act of 1872* (Carlton: Melbourne University Press, 2002).

Guha, R. A., *Corner of a Foreign Field: The Indian History of an English Game* (London: Picador, 2002).

Hadyn, T., 'History' In White, J., ed., *Rethinking the School Curriculum: Values, Aims and Purposes* (Abingdon: Routledge Falmer, 2004), 87–103.

Haldar, R. D., *The English Diary of an Indian Student, 1861–62: Being the Scribbling Diary of the Late Rakhal Das Haldar* (Dacca: Ashutosh Library, 1903).

Hall, C., *Civilising Subjects: Metropole and Colony in the English Imagination 1830–1867* (Cambridge: Polity, 2002).

Hammerton, A. J. and Thomson, A., *Ten Pound Poms: Australia's Invisible Migrants*(Manchester, Manchester University Press, 2005).

Handelman, D., 'The Organization of Ethnicity' *Ethnic Groups*, 1 (1977), 187–200.

Hands, M. and Pearce, J., *Should Patriotism be promoted, tolerated, or discouraged in British Schools?* (London: Institute of Education, University of London, 2008).

Harper, M., 'Enticing the Emigrant: Canadian Agents in Ireland and Scotland, c. 1870–c.1920', *Scottish Historical Review* 83 (1) (2004), 41–58.

Harris-Hart, H., 'National curriculum and federalism: the Australian experience', *Journal of Educational Administration and History*, 42 (3) (2010), 295–313.

Haynes, B., 'History Teaching for Patriotic Citizenship in Australia', *Educational Philosophy and Theory* 41 (4) (2009), 424–40.

Hébert, Y., ed., *Citizenship in Transformation in Canada* (Toronto: University of Toronto Press, 2002).

Hodgetts, A. B., *What Culture? What Heritage? A Study of Civic Education in Canada* (Toronto: OISE 1968).

Howes, H. G., *The Gibraltarian, the Origin and Development of the Population of Gibraltar from 1704* (Gibraltar: MedSun, 1982).

Hughes, A. S. and Sears, A., 'Teaching the Contested and Controversial Nature of Democratic Ideas: Taking the Crisis out of Controversy' in Claire, H. and

Holden, C., eds., *The Challenge of Teaching Controversial Issues* (Stoke on Kent, UK: Trentham Books, 2007), 83–93.

Hutchinson, J., Reynolds, S., Smith, A., Colls, R. and Kumar, K., 'Debate on Krishan Kumar's *The Making of English National Identity*', *Nations and Nationalism*, 13 (2) (2007), 179–204.

Ike, C., *Naked Gods* (London: Collins, 1970).

Irigaray, L., *Sexes et Parentes* (Paris: Minuit, 1987).

Jack, G. and Phipps, A. M., *Tourism and Intercultural Exchange: Why Tourism Matters* (Clevedon: Channel View, 2005).

James, C. L. R., *Beyond a Boundary* (London, Stanley Paul, 1963).

Johnson, C., 'John Howard's "Values" and Australian Identity', *Australian Journal of Political Science*, 42 (2) (2007), 195–209.

Jones, D. V., *License for Empire. Colonialism by Treaty in Early America* (Chicago and London: University of Chicago Press, 1982).

Jupp, J., *The English in Australia* (Melbourne, Cambridge University Press, 2004).

Kennedy, P. and Roudometof, V., 'Transnationalism in a Global Age' in Kennedy, P. and Roudometof, V. (eds), *Communities Across Borders: New Immigrants and Transnational Cultures* (London and New York: Routledge, 2002), 1–26.

Kerr, D., 'Re-examining Citizenship Education in England', in Torney-Purta, J., Schwille, J. and Amadeo, J., eds, *Civic Education Across Countries: Twenty-four National Case Studies from the IEA Civic Education Project* (Amsterdam: IEA, 1999), 203–28.

Kiwan, D., 'Citizenship Education in England at the Crossroads? Four Models of Citizenship and their Implications for Ethnic and Religious Diversity'. *Oxford Review of Education*, 34 (1) (2008), 39–58.

Knorr, K., *British Colonial Theories 1570–1850* (Toronto: University of Toronto Press, 1944).

Koebner, R., *Empire* (Cambridge: Cambridge University Press, 1961).

Kymlicka, W. and Opalski, M., eds, *Can Liberalism be Exported? Western Political Theory and Ethnic Relations in Eastern Europe* (Oxford: Oxford University Press, 2001).

Kymlicka, W. and Norman, W., eds., *Citizenship and Diverse Societies* (New York: Oxford University Press, 2000).

Kumar, K., *The Making of English National Identity* (Cambridge: Cambridge University Press, 2003).

Lambert, R. S., *The Great Heritage: A History of Britain for Canadians* (Toronto: The House of Grant, 1958).

Langlands, R., 'Britishness or Englishness: The Historical Problem of National Identity in Britain'. *Nations and Nationalism* 51 (1999): 53–69.

Langton, M., 'The Nations of Australia', in Boyer, P., Cardinal, L., and Headon, D., eds, *From Subjects to Citizens: A Hundred Years of Citizenship in Australia and Canada* (Ottawa: University of Ottawa Press, 2004), 191–209.

Lévesque, S., 'In search of a purpose for school history', *Journal of Curriculum Studies*, 37 (3) (2006), 349–58.

Lindfors, B., ed., *Conversations with Chinua Achebe* (Jackson: University Press of Mississippi, 1997).

MacCannell, D., *The Tourist: A New Theory of the Leisure Class* (New York: Shocken Books, 1976).

MacKenzie, J. M., 'Empire and National Identities: The Case of Scotland' *Transactions of the Royal Historical Society*, 6th series, vol. 8 (1998), 215–32.

MacKenzie, J. M. with Dalziel, N. R., *The Scots in South Africa: Ethnicity, Identity, Gender and Race, 1772–1914* (Manchester: Manchester University Press, 2007).

Macintyre, S. and Clark, A., *The History Wars* (Carlton: Melbourne University Press, 2003).

Malam, L., 'Performing Masculinity on the Thai Beach Scene' *Tourism Geographies* 6 (4) (2004), 455–71.

Mandler, P., *The English National Character: The History of an Idea from Edmund Burke to Tony Blair* (London & New Haven: Yale University Press, 2006).

Markanadaya, K., *Nowhere Man* (London: Allen Lane, 1972).

Matless, D., *Landscape and Englishness* (London: Reaktion, 1998).

McCarthy, A., '"For Spirit and Adventure": Personal Accounts of Scottish Migration to New Zealand, 1921–1961' in Brooking, T. and Coleman, J., eds, *The Heather and the Fern: Scottish Migration and New Zealand Settlement* (Dunedin: University of Otago Press, 2003), 117–32.

McCarthy, A., 'Personal Letters, Oral Testimony, and Scottish Migration to New Zealand in the 1950s: The Case of Lorna Carter' *Immigrants and Minorities* 23 (1) (2005), 59–79.

McCarthy, A., ed., *A Global Clan: Scottish Migrant Networks and Identities Since the Eighteenth Century* (London: Tauris Academic Studies, 2006).

McDougall, W. D., *The Commonwealth of Nations* (Toronto: The Ryerson Press, 1952).

McGovern, C., 'The New History Boys' In R. Whelan, ed., *The Corruption of the Curriculum* (London: Civitas, 2007), 58–85.

McGregor, R., 'The necessity of Britishness: ethno-cultural roots of Australian Nationalism', *Nations and Nationalism*, 12 (3) (2006), 493–511.

McKenna, M., *The Captive Republic. A History of Australian Republicanism, 1788–1996* (Cambridge: Cambridge University Press, 1996).

McLean, M., *The People of Glengarry: Highlanders in Transition, 1745–1820* (Montreal and Kingston: McGill-Queen's University Press, 1991).

McLaughlin, T. H., 'Citizenship Education in England: The Crick Report and Beyond' *Journal of Philosophy of Education*, 34 (2000), 541–70.

McNeill, D., *New Europe: Imagined Spaces* (London: Arnold, 2004).

Meaney, N., 'Britishness and Australian identity: the problem of nationalism in Australian history and historiography', *Australian Historical Studies*, 32 (116) (2001), 76–90.

Mehta, V., *Delinquent Chacha* (London: Collins, 1967).

Meyers, J., *Fiction and the Colonial Experience* (Ipswich: Boydell Press, 1973).

Miller, P., *Long Division: State Schooling in South Australian Society* (Adelaide: Wakefield Press, 1986).

Mohanti, P., *Through Brown Eyes* (Oxford: Oxford UP, 1985).

Molloy, M., *Those Who Speak to the Heart: The Nova Scotian Scots of Waipu, 1854–1920* (Palmerston North: Dunmore Press, 1991).

Mordue, T., 'Tourism, Performance and Social Exclusion in "Olde York"' *Annals of Tourism Research* 32 (1) (2005), 179–98.

Morton, D., 'Divided Loyalties? Divided Country?' in Kaplan, W., ed., *Belonging: The Meaning and Future of Canadian Citizenship* (Montreal & Kingston: McGill-Queens University Press, 1993), 50–63.

Moya, J. C., 'Immigrants and Associations: A Global and Historical Perspective' *Journal of Ethnic and Migration Studies* 31 (5) (2005), 833–64.

Mukherjee, S., *Nationalism, Education and Migrant Identities: The England-Returned* (London: Routledge, 2010).

Mycock, A., 'British Citizenship and the Legacy of Empires', *Parliamentary Affairs* 63 (2) (2010), 339–55.

Nandy, A., *The Intimate Enemy: Loss and Recovery of Self under Colonialism* (Delhi: Oxford University Press, 1983).

Nasson, B., *Abraham Esau's War: A Black South African War on the Cape, 1899–1902* (Cambridge: Cambridge University Press, 1991).

Nasson, B., 'Why They Fought: Black Cape Colonists and Imperial Wars, 1899–1918' *International Journal of African Historical Studies* 37 (Winter 2004): 55–70.

Obaro I., ed., *Groundwork of Nigerian History* (Ibadan: Heinemann, 1999).

Okret-Manville, C., 'La Politique Etrangère Culturelle, Outil de la Démocratie, du Fascisme et du Communisme. L'exemple du British Council, 1934–1953' *Relations Internationales* 115 (2003) 399–410.

O'Reilly, K., *The British on the Costa del Sol: Transnational Identities and Local Communities* (London: Routldege, 2000).

Osaghae, E., *Crippled Giant: Nigeria since Independence* (London, Hurst 1998).

Osler, A., 'Patriotism, multiculturalism and belonging: political discourse and the teaching of history' *Educational Review*, 61 (1) (2009), 85–100.

Paquet, G., 'Governance and Emergent Transversal Citizenship: Toward a New Nexus of Moral Contracts' in Boyer, P., Cardinal, L. and Headon, D., eds, *From Subjects to Citizens: A Hundred Years of Citizenship in Australia and Canada* (Ottawa: University of Ottawa Press, 2004), 231–61.

Paterson, G., *The Story of Our People* (Toronto: The Ryerson Press, 1933).

Phillips, P., 'History teaching, nationhood and politics in England and Wales in the late twentieth century: a historical comparison', *History of Education* 28 (3) (1999), 351–63.

Phillips, R., Goalen, P., McNully, A. and Wood, S., 'Four Histories, One Nation? History teaching, nationhood and a British identity' *Compare: A Journal of Comparative and International Education* 29 (2) (1999), 153–69.

Pittock, M. G. H., *Celtic Identity and the British Image* (Manchester and New York: Manchester University Press, 1999).

Pratt, M. L., 'Arts of the Contact Zone' *Profession* 91 (1991), 33–40.

Prentis, M., 'Haggis on the High Seas: Shipboard Experiences of Scottish Emigrants to Australia, 1821–1897' *Australian Historical Studies* 36 (124) (2004), 294–311.

Preston, P. W., *Relocating England* (Manchester: Manchester University Press, 2004).

Preston-Whyte, R., 'Constructed Leisure Space: The Seaside at Durban' *Annals of Tourism Research* 28 (3) (2001), 581–96.

Print, M., 'Citizenship education and youth participation in democracy' *British Journal of Educational Studies*, 55 (2007), 325–45.

Purdie, N. and Wilss, L., 'Australian National Identity: Young Peoples' Conceptions of What It Means to be Australian', *National Identities*, 9 (1) (2007), 67–82.

Rose, S. O., *Which People's War? National Identity and Citizenship in Britain 1939–1945* (Oxford & New York: Oxford University Press, 2003).

Ross, R., *Status and Respectability in the Cape Colony, 1750–1870: A Tragedy of Manners* (New York: Cambridge University Press, 1999).

Samuel, R., 'A Case for National History', *International Journal of Historical Teaching, Learning and Research* 3 (1) (2003), 85–92.

Scannell, P. and Cardiff, D., *A Social History of British Broadcasting, 1922–1938* (Oxford, Basil Blackwell, 1991).

Schech, S. and Haggis, J., 'Terrains of Migrancy and Whiteness: How British Migrants Locate Themselves in Australia', in Moreton-Robinson, A., (ed.) *Whitening Race* (Canberra, Aboriginal Studies Press, 2004), 176–91.

Schipper de Leeuw, M., *Le Blanc et l'Occident au miroir du roman africain de langue française* (Assen, Van Gorcum and Yaoundé: éditions CLE, 1973).

Schipper de Leeuw, M., 'Le Blanc dans la littérature africaine', *Afrikanische Literatur. Perspective und Probleme, Serie: Materialiën zum Internationalen Kulturaustauch*, 29 (3) (1979) 271–9.

Schnapper, P., *La Grande-Bretagne et l'Europe: le grand malentendu* (Paris, Presses de Sciences-Po, 2000).

Schneer, J., *London 1900: The Imperial Metropolis* (London: Yale University Press, 1999).

Schuerkens, U., *La colonisation dans la littérature africaine* (Paris: L'Harmattan, 1994).

Sears, A., Clarke, M. and Hughes, A. S., 'Canadian Citizenship Education: The Pluralist Ideal and Citizenship Education for a Post-Modern State' in Torney-Purta, J., Schwille, J. and Amadeo, J., eds, *Civic education across countries: Twenty-four national case studies from the IEA education project* (Amsterdam: IEA 1999), 111–36.

Selänniemi, T., 'On Holiday in the Liminoid Playground: Place, Time and Self in Tourism' in T. G. Bauer and B. McKercher, eds, *Sex And Tourism: Journeys of Romance, Love, and Lust* (Binghamton, NY: Haworth, 2003).

Sharma, M., *Postcolonial Indian Writing in English: Between Co-option and Resistance* (Jaipur: Rawat, 2003).

Shields, R., *Places on the Margin: alternative geographies of modernity* (London: Routledge, 1991).

Smith, A. D., *National Identity* (London: Penguin, 1991).

Smith, V. L., *Hosts and Guests: The Anthropology of Tourism* (Oxford: Blackwell, 1978).

Smout, T. C., 'Perspectives on the Scottish Identity' *Scottish Affairs* 6 (1994), 101–13.

Sosin, J. M., *Agents and Merchants: British Colonial Policy and the Origins of the American Revolution, 1763–1775* (Lincoln: University of Nebraska Press, 1965).

Spector, M. M., *The American Department of the British Government 1768–1782* (New York: Columbia University Press, 1940).

Sriskandarajah, D. and Drew, C., *Brits Abroad: Mapping the Scale and Nature of British Emigration*, London, Institute for Public Policy Research, 2006.

Stearns, P. N., Seixas, P., and Wineburg, S., eds, *Knowing, Teaching and Learning History: National and International Perspectives* (New York: New York University Press, 2000).

Symonds, R., *Oxford and Empire: The Last Lost Cause?* (New York: St Martin's Press, 1986).

Taylor, Philip M., *The Projection of Britain, British Overseas Publicity and Propaganda 1919–1939* (Cambridge: Cambridge University Press, 1981).

Thompson, A., 'The Languages of Loyalism in Southern Africa, c. 1870–1939' *British Historical Review* (June 2003), 617–50.

Tolz, V., *Russia: Inventing the Nation* (London: Arnold, 2001).

Tournier-Sol, K., ed., *Le Royaume-Uni dans le Monde depuis 2001* (Toulon: Revue Babel, n°21, 2010).

Tranter, B. and Donoghue, J., 'Colonial and post-colonial aspects of Australian identity', *The British Journal of Sociology*, 58 (2) (2007), 165–83.

Turner, L. and Ash, J., *The Golden Hordes: international tourism and the pleasure periphery* (London: Constable, 1975).

Ulasi, A., *Many Thing You no Understand* (London: Michael Joseph 1970).

Urry, J., *The Tourist Gaze: Leisure and Travel in Contemporary Socities* (London: Sage, 1990).

Urry, J., *Consuming Places* (London: Routledge, 2005).

Van Heyingen, E. and Merrett, P., '"The Healing Touch": The Guild of Loyal Women of South Africa 1900–1912' *South African Historical Journal* 47 (November 2003), 24–50.

Viswanathan, G., 'Currying Favor: The Politics of British Educational and Cultural Policy in India, 1813–1854.' *Social Text* 19/20 (1988): 85–104.

Waldman, A., 'The Politics of History Teaching in England and France during the 1980s', *History Journal Workshop* 68 (1) (2009), 199–221.

Wallace, W. S., *A New History of Great Britain and Canada* (Toronto: The Macmillan Company of Canada, 1934).

Ward, S., *Australia and the British Embrace: The Demise of the Imperial Ideal* (Melbourne: Melbourne University Press, 2001).

Webster, W., *Englishness and Empire 1939–1965* (Oxford & New York: Oxford University Press, 2005; paperback edition 2007).

Wellings, B., 'Empire-nation: national and imperial discourse in England', *Nations and Nationalism*, 8 (1) (2002), 95–109.

Wellings, B., 'Rump Britain: Englishness and Britishness, 1992–2001', *National Identities*, 9 (4) (2007), 395–412.

Whelehan, I., *Overloaded: Popular culture and the future of feminism* (London: Women's Press, 2000).

White, A. J. S., *The British Council: the First Twenty-Five Years, 1934–1959* (London: The British Council, 1965).

Wills, G., *Head and Heart: American Christianities* (New York: Penguin, 2007).

Woodward, K., *Boxing and Masculinity: the 'I' of the Tiger* (London: Routledge, 2007).

Woodward, K., *Embodied Sporting Practices, regulating and regulatory bodies* (Basingstoke, Palgrave MacMillan, 2009).

Young, H., *This Blessed Plot: Britain and Europe from Churchill to Blair* (London: Papermac, 1999).

Young, R., *White Mythologies: Writing History and the West* (London: Routledge, 1990).

Žižek, S., Multiculturalism, or, the Cultural Logic of Multinational capitalism' *New Left Review* 225 (September/October 1997), 28–51.

Notes on Contributors

RHYS ANDREWS is a senior research fellow at Cardiff Business School in the UK. His research interests focus on organizational environments, social capital and public service performance. He has published in several refereed journals including: *Human Relations, Journal of Public Administration Research and Theory, Public Administration Review, Regional Studies and Urban Studies*.

ELLEKE BOEHMER is the author of *Colonial and Postcolonial Literature* (1995, 2005), *Empire, the National and the Postcolonial, 1890–1920* (2002) and *Stories of Women* (2005), and the biography *Nelson Mandela* (2008). She has published four novels including *Screens against the Sky* (1990) and *Nile Baby* (2008). She edited Robert Baden-Powell's *Scouting for Boys* (2004) and the anthology *Empire Writing* (1998), and co-edited *JM Coetzee in Writing and Theory* (2009), *Terror and the Postcolonial* (2009), and *The Indian Postcolonial* (2010). *Sharmilla and Other Portraits* (2010) is her first short story collection. Elleke Boehmer is the Professor of World Literature in English at the University of Oxford.

IAN DAVIES is based at the University of York, in the UK, where he is Professor of Education and Director of the Centre for Research on Education and Social Justice. He has published extensively on citizenship education and has completed many international projects. He is editor of the journal *Citizenship Teaching and Learning*.

DAVID GOLDBLATT is a sports writer, broadcaster, and journalist; the author of *The Ball is Round: A Global History of Football* (2006), and the *World Football Yearbook* (2002). He has taught the sociology of sport at the University of Bristol in the UK and has run literacy programmes at football clubs. He has written for most of the quality broadsheets, and magazines such as the *New Statesman* and is currently the sports' columnist for *Prospect* magazine. He has made several *Crossing Continents* programmes and regularly contributes to BBC Radio 4 and the BBC World Service.

A. JAMES HAMMERTON is Emeritus Scholar in History at La Trobe University, Melbourne, Australia. He has published on nineteenth and twentieth century British migration and on gender, family and marriage in Britain and the British World. Currently he is writing an oral history of the late twentieth century British Diaspora.

DAVID LEVEY lectures in Phonetics and Linguistics at the University of Cadiz, in Spain. He has published on sociolinguistics, identity and language change in Gibraltar as well as language acquisition in Spain. Currently he is carrying out research into language transfer and changes in English language competence in Europe.

JAMES W. MCAULEY is Professor of Irish Studies and an associate dean at the University of Huddersfield. He has written extensively on Northern Irish politics and society, and especially on aspects of Ulster unionism and loyalism. His latest books include *Ulster's Last Stand* (2010) and the co-edited volume (with Graham Spencer) *Ulster Loyalism after the Good Friday Agreement* (2011). He researches on conflict transformation and broader aspects of British identity.

ANGELA MCCARTHY is Professor of Scottish and Irish History at the University of Otago, New Zealand, and Associate Director of its Centre for Irish and Scottish Studies. She is the author and editor of several books on Irish and Scottish migration, and is currently researching issues of migration, ethnicity, and madness.

CATHERINE MCGLYNN is a Senior Lecturer in Politics at the University of Huddersfield. Her research focuses on issues of national identity and citizenship, with special reference to ethnic differentiation and conflict resolution. She is co-author of *Abandoning Historical Conflict? Former Political Prisoners and Reconciliation in Northern Ireland* (2010) and is a founder member of the Political Studies Association's Specialist Group on Britishness.

ANTOINE MIOCHE is Chief Inspector of Schools in the French Ministry of Education. He was until 2009 Professor of British Studies at the Université de Paris III – Sorbonne nouvelle, of whose Centre for Research on the English-speaking World (CREW) he remains an associate member. He has published on British colonial and imperial matters, mostly from a political and legal-constitutional angle, with a special interest in Ireland, the Thirteen Colonies, Canada, India and China. He is now researching aspects of British exploration of Africa, in addition to work on colonial and imperial lives.

SUMITA MUKHERJEE has published widely on modern South Asian and British imperial history. She is the author of *Nationalism, Education and Migrant Identities: The England-Returned* (2009) and editor, with Rehana Ahmed, of *South Asian Resistances in Britain 1858–1947* (2011).

ANDREW MYCOCK is a Senior Lecturer in Politics at the University of Huddersfield. His key research and teaching interests focus on post-empire citizenship and national identity, particularly in the UK and the Russian Federation, and the impact of citizenship and history education programmes. He has published widely on the 'Politics of Britishness', education policy, citizenship, and democratic youth engagement. He was a Youth Citizenship Commissioner as part of the Governance of Britain reviews in 2008–9 and is co-convenor of the Academy for the Study of Britishness.

CHARLES V. REED is an Assistant Professor of History at Elizabeth City State University in North Carolina, USA. He is currently revising his dissertation, titled *Royal Subjects, Imperial Citizens: The Making of British Imperial Culture, 1860–1901* (University of Maryland, 2010), for publication. The project examines how nineteenth-century royal tours to the British Empire were imagined and used by different historical actors in Britain, the Cape Colony, New Zealand, and South Asia.

ALAN REID is Professor Emeritus of Education at the University of South Australia. His research and writing include educational policy, curriculum theory, citizenship education and the history and politics of public education. He has been a key figure in curriculum development at the state and national levels in Australia.

ALAN SEARS is a Professor in the Faculty of Education at the University of New Brunswick, Canada. He has written extensively on citizenship education and educational policy in Canada and internationally. He is co-editor of the book, *Globalization, The Nation-State, and the Citizen: Dilemmas and Directions for Civics and Citizenship Education* (2010).

MEENAKSHI SHARMA is an Associate Professor of Communications at the Indian Institute of Management Ahmedabad. She has published on corporate communications and postcolonial theory and literatures. Her current areas of interest are communication and organisational change, Women in tertiary education, and Indian writing in English.

KARINE TOURNIER-SOL is a senior lecturer in British politics at the University of Toulon, France. She has published on the UK and European integration; the British Conservative Party; the United Kingdom Independence Party (UKIP) and the 'special relationship' between the UK and the USA. She has recently published a book on British foreign policy since 2001.

THOMAS THURNELL-READ holds a teaching post at the Department of International Studies and Social Science at Coventry University, UK. His work explores gender and masculinities in relation to tourism, leisure and consumption. His research interests also include national identity, the sociology of the body and qualitative research methods. Currently he is developing research on embodied work and leisure practice.

FRANÇOISE UGOCHUKWU, a former Professor from the University of Nigeria, Nsukka and French Professor of comparative literature, has been lecturing in Higher Education in Nigeria, France and the UK. An Africanist, she is affiliated to the Open University UK and a collaborator to the Paris CNRS-LLACAN. Her main area of research is African Studies, focusing on Nigeria (Igbo) and intercultural encounters.

TAMARA VAN KESSEL is Assistant Professor of Culture Management at the University of Amsterdam. For her recently completed PhD dissertation she researched how the British Council and the Dante Alighieri Society promoted Britishness and 'italianità' respectively in the Mediterranean area during the 1930s. Her main interests are foreign cultural policy, cultural nationalism, identity politics and the culture industry.

AMY VON HEYKING is a Professor of Education at the University of Lethbridge in Alberta, Canada. She has published on the history of the Canadian school curriculum, particularly as it embodied images and ideals of identity and citizenship. Currently she is investigating the impact of progressive pedagogical innovations on Canadian classrooms.

BEN WELLINGS is Convenor of European Studies in the School of Politics and International Relations at the Australian National University in Canberra. He has published on the politics of contemporary English nationalism. He is currently completing (2011) a book with Peter Lang on Euroscepticism and English nationalism and is also researching the politics of the past in relation to Australian commemorative sites in Europe.

KATH WOODWARD is Professor of Sociology and Head of Department at the Open University. She worked on the AHRC Tuning In at the BBC World service project and is also a member of the ESRC centre CReSC working on gendered diasporic identifications and sporting embodied practices. She has contributed to BBC Radio 4, Canadian radio and Sky TV and to the boxing film *A Bloody Canvas*. Her most recent books are: *Boxing, Masculinity and Identity* (2007), *Embodied Sporting Practices* (2009) and, with Sophie Woodward, *Why Feminism Matters* (Palgrave 2009) and *Sex Power and the Games* (Palgrave 2011).

JAMES WYLLIE has worked as a screenwriter for film and TV, after graduating with a BA in Social and Political Science in 1988. In 1992, he was the winner of the Carl Foreman/BAFTA Screenwriting Award. His non-fiction book, *The Warlord and the Renegade: The Story of Hermann and Albert Goering* was published in 2006. He has written and co-hosted eight editions of *Jazz Legends* for Radio 3. He also works for the AHRC Black British Jazz project. He has worked for four years teaching drama at a specialist school for teenagers with autism.

Index

BRITISH IDENTITIES SINCE 1707

The historiography of British identities has flourished since the mid-1970s, spurred on by increasing national consciousness in England, Scotland, Wales and Northern Ireland, and since 1997 by devolution. Historians and other academics have become increasingly aware that identities in the British Isles have been fluid and that interactions between the different parts of the British Isles have been central to historical developments since, and indeed before, the Act of Union between England and Scotland in 1707.

This series seeks to encourage exploration of identities of place in the British Isles since the early eighteenth century, including intersections between competing and complementary identities such as region and nation. The series also advances discussion of other identities such as class, gender, religion, politics, ethnicity and culture when these are geographically located and positioned. While the series is historical, it welcomes cross- and interdisciplinary approaches to the study of British identities.

'British Identities since 1707' examines the unity and diversity of the British Isles, developing consideration of the multiplicity of negotiations that have taken place in such a multinational and multi-ethnic group of islands. It will include discussions of nationalism(s), of Britishness, Englishness, Scottishness, Welshness and Irishness, as well as 'regional' identities including, for example, those associated with Cornwall, the Gàidhealtachd region in Scotland and Gaeltacht areas in Ireland. The series will encompass discussions of relations with continental Europe and the United States, with ethnic and immigrant identities and with other forms of identity associated with the British Isles as place. The editors are interested in publishing books relating to the wider British world, including current and former parts of the British Empire and the Commonwealth, and places such as Gibraltar and the Falkland Islands and the smaller islands of the British archipelago. 'British Identities since 1707' reinforces the consideration of history, culture and politics as richly diverse across and within the borders of the British Isles.

Proposals are invited for monographs and edited collections, including those that arise from relevant conferences.